Introduction to Transnational Legal Transactions

Sponsored by
The American Association of Law Libraries

Edited by

Marylin J. Raisch
Roberta I. Shaffer

OCEANA PUBLICATIONS, INC.
New York * London * Rome

Library of Congress Cataloging-in-Publication Data

Introduction to transnational legal transactions / sponsored by the American Association of Law Libraries; edited by Marylin J. Raisch and Roberta I. Shaffer.

p. 26 cm.

Includes bibliographical references.

ISBN 0-379-21352-4 (hardcover)

1. Judicial assistance. 2. Criminal jurisdiction. 3. Criminal jurisdiction—Bibliography. 4. Conflict of laws. 5. Law—International unification. 6. Intellectual property—Bibliography. 7. Environmental law, International—Bibliography. I. Raisch, Marylin J. II. Shaffer, Roberta I. III. American Association of Law Libraries.

K7615.4.I58 1995

341.7'7—dc20

95-31699

CIP

ISBN: 0-379-21353-2

Published by Oceana Publications, Inc.

Manufactured in the United States of America on acid-free paper.

Introduction to Transnational Legal Transactions

edited by

Marylin J. Raisch
and Roberta I. Shaffer

Table Of Contents

International Criminal Litigation

Substantive Law Issues in Private International Law

Transnational Issues in Specific Public and Commercial Law Areas

International Commercial Arbitration

ACKNOWLEDGEMENTS

Many of the speakers at the American Association of Law Libraries' Institute on Transnational Legal Transactions have contributed chapters to this book. We wish to thank them for the substantial part they have played in making both the institute and the book possible.

At the conclusion of the Institute, the co-directors faced the challenge of editing and producing this volume. Several people assisted in that process and we take this opportunity to thank them in print.

We specifically wish to acknowledge the work of Michael Wasser, Ph.D., who displayed an uncanny ability to decipher and verify citations, and then put them into a standard format.

Marylin expresses her gratitude to James Hoover and her colleagues on the Columbia Law Library staff who supported her efforts to edit this book. In addition, she thanks her family for their cooperation and patience.

Roberta greatly appreciates the encouragement of Charles A. Miller and Stuart C. Stock, partners at Covington and Burling. Charlotte White, Jean Yablon, Rhea Wilson, and the entire Covington library staff must be recognized for the innumerable things that they did to smooth the way.

Last, we thank Michael Pollak for his significant assistance in formatting the manuscripts for publication.

Marylin J. Raisch
New York

Roberta I. Shaffer
Washington, DC

February, 1995

INTRODUCTION

Transnational Legal Transactions is the third in a series of institutes, sponsored by the American Association of Law Libraries, for the training of information professionals and for the use of any legal researcher in need of an introduction to other legal systems and international law.[1] These institutes cover topics in foreign, comparative, and international law which were chosen with care as part of an overall plan to increase the general expertise of law librarians in these subjects as well as to train new specialists.[2] The contributors to this textbook participated in the institute held at the University of Washington School of Law in Seattle July 5-8, 1994 entitled "Transnational Legal Transactions."[3] The subject-matter of this institute incorporates some elements of the study of the laws of foreign jurisdictions and also some aspects of the study of international organizations, which was the topic of the second institute in the series, held at Harvard in July, 1993. Our contributors address various aspects of legal issues that arise in transactions across jurisdictional boundaries, and our use of the term "transnational legal transactions" requires some explanation and a brief review of attempts at definition.

Claire Germain[4], in her treatise on transnational law,[5] summarizes very helpfully the various sub-topics that have been gathered under the rubric of transnational law. Both she and one of our

---

1 *See generally* Richard A. Danner, "Introduction: Researching Foreign Legal Systems" in *Introduction to Foreign Legal Systems* xxiii-xxvi (Richard A. Danner & Marie-Louise H. Bernal eds.) (1994) (provides a concise history of the Association's consistent support for the continuing education of its members and others in foreign law research; it also summarizes the development of the current series of training institutes).

2 *See* American Association of Law Libraries, National Legal Resources Committee, "Training Foreign and International Law Librarians: the Next Generation" (May 1992).

3 The editors wish to take this opportunity publicly to acknowledge, with thanks, the generous and professional job done by Penny Hazelton, Professor of Law and Law Librarian, University of Washington School of Law, Gallagher Law Library, and her staff, in providing local arrangements and for distributing written materials to participants and panelists.

4 Edward Cornell Law Librarian and Professor of Law, Cornell Law School.

5 *Germain's Transnational Law Research: A Guide for Attorneys* (1992). It should be noted here that Professor Germain was a proponent of the strategic training

contributors, Patrick L. Borchers,[6] begin with Joseph Story and his introduction of the term "private international law"[7] in 1834 to describe rules which determine what national state's law will apply or which will settle jurisdictional conflicts.[8] " Private international law" can be extended to include laws applied to non-nationals and even nationality law itself,[9] but "transnational law" is broader and can include an international procedural system, such as that for commercial arbitration, and even those rules of private municipal law which are "common to civilized nations."[10] This language is strikingly similar to that used in Article 38 of the Statute of the International Court of Justice to describe one of the sources of *public* international law available to the court.[11]

Wolfgang Friedmann,[12] in his 1964 treatise *The Changing Structure of International Law*, seems prescient in his assessment of where modern global trade and communications might take the rules governing transactions between private individuals or entities. Indeed, he seems to suggest that the need to harmonize and unify potentially conflicting laws and jurisdictional rules, both in matters where a state is involved and those concerning private parties only, may lead to a transforming of private international and transnational law into a type of public international law, by treaty and by recognition of uniform or universal laws:

> The neat distinction of the categories of public and private law has long ceased to be expressive of the realities of

---

plan and its chief architect.

6 Associate Professor and Associate Dean for Student Affairs, Albany Law School of Union University. See *infra* Chapter Six.

7 Germain, *supra* note 5 at 1-3 (sec.1.01.2); Borchers, *infra* Chapter Six at [2].

8 Joseph Story, *Commentaries on the Conflict of Laws* (1834); Germain, *supra* note 5 at 1-3 (sec. 1.01.2).

9 Germain, *supra* at 1-4 (sec. 1.01.2).

10 Albert Ehrenzweig, "Specific Principles of Private Transnational Law," 124 *Recueil des Cours* 167, 255 (1968-II).

11 United Nations, *Charter of the United Nations and Statute of the International Court of Justice*, U.N. Sales No. DPI/511 (year).

12 Professor of Law and Director of International Legal Studies at Columbia University School of Law from 1955 until his death in 1972.

> contemporary municipal, as well as international, law, even though the distinction still dominates the teaching curricula of law schools. There is today hardly any field of private law which could be adequately understood without a strong and often decisive admixture of public law.[13]

In another part of his work he also speaks of "the gradual extension of international criminal offenses outside the sphere of direct or indirect political state action"[14] because of severe deprivations of freedom, drug trafficking, and the like, and he concludes that "ultimately an international criminal court will have to be created to administer the expanding international criminal law."[15] To some extent "the formal limits of jurisdiction" are transcended when issues such as international welfare and "conservation of vital resources" [16] are concerned.

These observations of Professor Friedmann's serve to introduce and justify our including in this institute both substantive and bibliographic essays on international civil and commercial litigation (including arbitration), international criminal litigation, commercial law, unification of private law, intellectual property and the impact of environmental regulation on certain transactions in the business and trade arenas. (As an example of the latter one contributor focuses on the European Union and its regulatory system).

In a sense, this institute sits at the center of our series of five programs, Janus-faced, as it were, looking back at municipal regimes and intergovernmental cooperation and ahead to two more programs. One will undertake a more detailed exploration of business, trade and taxation regimes and the fifth and last will cover the traditional subject of public international law, the *ius gentium* that brings the modern international lawyer in touch with the legal descendants of the *commercium*, the Roman attempt to overcome boundaries to trade and to limits on the rights and duties of the global citizen of the then-known world.[17]

---

13 Wolfgang Friedmann, *The Changing Structure of International Law* 190 (1964).

14 *Id*. at 168.

15 *Id*. at 168.

16 *Id*. at 191.

17 *See generally* H.F. Jolowicz and Barry Nichols, *Historical Introduction to Roman Law* 58-59 and 102 (3d ed. 1972) (describing early treaties with Carthage and

This volume has been organized into larger headings and chapters to facilitate the researcher's access to the information that the book contains. This method of presentation should enable the researcher to read the book through completely and gain the sense of building a base of knowledge. In addition, this volume should be useful when discreet bits of information are needed.

The articles will provide an understanding of terminology and the legal principles governing the topic. The bibliographies and research guides will direct the researcher to the leading primary and secondary authorities.

The book begins with two essays and a bibliography. These three pieces serve to introduce the very large topic of international civil and commercial litigation. The first essay is a rather comprehensive review of enforcement and litigation issues. It is followed by a more geographically targeted discussion of U.S./European legal relations.

The next area of coverage is international criminal litigation. There is an indepth review of the sources and events that have influenced the development of the law. The bibliography provides a general coverage of the topic, and also provides a separate section on white collar transnational crimes.

The next part addresses substantive issues in private international law. This begins with a "choice of law" discussion and its history. It is then followed by a review of efforts regarding international harmonization and unification of laws. The narrative coverage is supplemented by a bibliography which focuses on the key organizations involved in the unification of private law. The final bibliography in this section sheds light upon the complex issues of estate planning and family law in a transnational context.

The next section moves the discussion from the general to the specific. It covers two topics--intellectual property and environmental law--that are of relatively new interest in the transnational arena. In the environmental area, waste disposal is

---

the Latin League which extended some benefits of Roman law to non-citizens and mutual protection of legal rights arising out of commerce and for the sake of advancing trade).

used as the example to explore the topic. This is followed by a comprehensive research guide. The Intellectual Property Research Guide examines the various aspects of the topic which runs the gamut from copyright to industrial property.

The book concludes with an entire part dedicated to International Commercial Arbitration. Arbitration has shown a growing prominence and presence in transnational transactions at all stages of the business relationship.

These articles and bibliographies give essential background to anyone researching transnational transactions in today's legal environment.

EDITORS

Marylin Johnson Raisch is the Librarian for International and Foreign Law at the Columbia University School of Law Library. She received her J.D. from Tulane University School of Law and holds degrees in English literature from Smith College and St. Hugh's College, University of Oxford, England. She received her M.L.S. from the Columbia University School of Library Service.

Roberta I. Shaffer is the Director of Library Services at the Washington, D.C.-based law firm of Covington & Burling. In addition to overseeing the firm's United States operations, she also has responsibility for the libraries in the foreign offices. Previously, she has held positions at George Washington University Law Center, the University of Houston Law Center and the Law Library of Congress. She was a Fulbright Scholar in Israel and Portugal in 1987-88. Roberta is an officer in the International Association of Law Libraries. She has her law degree from Tulane.

CONTRIBUTORS

Margaret A. Aycock is Foreign and International Law Librarian at the O'Quinn Law Library, the University of Houston. She is the former Assistant Editor of the *Marine Affairs Bibliography*.

Hugh F. Bangasser is a partner in the Seattle law firm of Preston, Thorgrimson, Shidler, Gates & Ellis. He is a graduate of Georgetown University Law Center. From 1973 to 1978, he was a trial attorney with the Bureau of Competition at the Federal Trade Commission.

Patrick Joseph Borchers is an Assistant Professor at Albany Law School, Union University (New York). He was a law clerk to Anthony Kennedy on the U.S. Court of Appeals for the Ninth Circuit, and practiced law in Sacramento, California for three years before he began his teaching career. He is the author of *Conflict of Laws* (Scoles & Hay, 1992).

Rodney L. Brown, Jr. is a partner in the Seattle office of Morrison & Foerster, where he practices environmental law. He is an honors graduate of the University of Texas Law School, where he served as Articles Editor for the Texas Law Review. After law school, he clerked for Judge Homer Thornberry of the U.S. Court of Appeals for the Fifth Circuit. He has represented numerous clients in the environmental aspects of international business transactions. He has also worked with several governments around the world, including the United States, the State of Washington, the Province of British Columbia, and the Russian Republic, to prepare environmental legislation and regulations.

George W. Coombe, Jr. is a partner in the San Francisco office of Graham & James. He has had a distinguished career serving as Assistant General Counsel at General Motors Corporation and as the General Counsel of the Bank of America Corporation. He has held various posts in the American and International Bar Associations, and since 1986 has been the Chairman of the Asia/Pacific Center for Resolution of International Business Disputes.

Donald C. Dowling, Jr. is a partner in the Cincinnati law firm of Graydon, Head & Ritchey. He is a graduate of the University of Florida Law School where he served as the Associate Editor of the law review. As a practitioner, he has published numerous articles dealing with international law and employment law.

Joan M. Fitzpatrick is a Professor of Law at the University of Washington (Seattle). She has her law degree from Harvard and received a Diploma in Law from Oxford. She is a recognized scholar on international human rights, and served on the executive council of the American Society of International Law from 1987 - 1990.

Jonathan Pratter is the International and Foreign Law Librarian and a Lecturer in Law at the Tarlton Law Library of the University of Texas. He is a member of the editorial advisory board of the *Texas International Law Journal*, and is a regular contributor to the *Texas Transnational Law Quarterly*.

Barbara Cantrell Rainwater is an international law reference librarian at the E.B. Williams Library at Georgetown University Law Center. She holds an M.L.S. from Indiana University, and has worked at the law libraries of Indiana University, the University of Denver, and the El Paso County Court (Colorado).

Edgardo Rotman is the Foreign and International Law Librarian at the University of Miami. He is a member of the bar in Argentina and Massachusetts. He is a qualified court expert in both Italian and Spanish law.

Kenneth Rudolf is a reference librarian at the Yale Law School Library where he divides his time between the Anglo-American and the Foreign/International libraries. He is editor of the *FCIL Newsletter*, a publication of the Foreign, Comparative and International Law Section of the American Association of Law Libraries.

Amber Lee Smith is Foreign and International Law Librarian at the Los Angeles County Law Library. She holds degrees in law from Washington and Lee School of Law and George Washington University. She is the 1994-95 Chair of the Index to Foreign Legal Periodicals Committee and a former chair of the Foreign, Comparative and International Law Special Interest Section of the American Association of Law Libraries.

Randall J. Snyder is Law Librarian in the Office of the Legal Adviser at the U.S. Department of State. He holds a J.D. and a

Diploma in Advanced International Legal Studies from the University of the Pacific, McGeorge School of Law, and a M.Libr. from the University of Washington.

Peter Winship is the James Cleo Thompson Sr. Trustee Professor at the Southern Methodist University School of Law. His LL.B. is from Harvard and he holds an LL.M. from the University of London. He has been a legal advisor to the Ethiopian Ministry of Commerce and Industry, and has served on the Advisory Committee on Private International Law, U.S. Secretary of State since 1990.

PROCEDURAL ASPECTS OF INTERNATIONAL CIVIL LITIGATION: SELECTED ISSUES RELATING TO SERVICE OF PROCESS, FOREIGN DISCOVERY FOR U.S. LITIGATION & ENFORCEMENT OF JUDGMENTS

Hugh Bangasser and Toussaint Myricks
Preston Gates & Ellis

I. Service of Process in International Litigation

On December 1, 1993, Congress enacted significant changes to the Federal Rules of Civil Procedure relating to personal jurisdiction and international service of process. These changes mark a divergence from prior practice and make it easier for U.S. plaintiffs to obtain personal jurisdiction over foreign defendants as well as to effect service of process over them.[1]

A. Adoption of "National Contact" Test for Personal Jurisdiction in Amendments to Federal Rules of Civil Procedure.

New Fed. R. Civ. P. 4(k)(2) appropriately has been characterized as a federal "longarm" statute.[2] Contrary to prior conflicting interpretations of the "minimum contacts" necessary to establish personal jurisdiction in international litigation,[3] the 1993 revision to

---

1 Amended Fed. R. Civ. P. Rule 4 authorizes U.S. courts to assess the *national* contacts of a foreign defendant rather than contacts with the specific jurisdiction. Formerly, absent a federal statute that permitted assessment of national contacts, a federal court had to examine the defendant's contacts within a particular jurisdiction.

2 David D. Siegel, "The New (Dec. 1, 1993) Rule 4 of the Federal Rules of Civil Procedure: Changes in Summons Service and Personal Jurisdiction", 151 F.R.D. 441, 442 (1994).

3 See, e.g., Omni Capital Int'l, Ltd. v. Rudolf Wolff & Co. Ltd., 484 U.S. 97 (1987). *Omni Capital* has been interpreted as providing that when federal courts premise personal jurisdiction on a state long-arm statute, the court will not find personal jurisdiction over a party when that party's conduct does not satisfy the state long-arm statute although the defendant's actions indicated that it had sufficient contacts with the entire nation. See Gary B. Born & Andrew N. Vollmer, "The Effect of the Revised Rules of Civil Procedure on Personal Jurisdiction, Service and Discovery in International Cases", 150

Rule 4 of the Fed. R. Civ. P. provides that defendants who lack "minimum contacts" with any state yet have sufficient contacts with the nation as a whole ("national contacts") may be subject to the personal jurisdiction of federal courts when federal claims arise from such contacts. Fed. R. Civ. P. 4(k)(2). Until these changes, it was widely interpreted that although a foreign defendant might have constitutionally sufficient minimum contacts through national contacts, absent *local* contacts, no jurisdiction could be established. As set forth in the Advisory Committee Notes, the test is whether a defendant has "contacts with the United States sufficient to justify the exercise of personal jurisdiction over that party." 146 F.R.D. 1571. Such minimum contacts must meet the requirements of the Due Process Clause of the Fifth Amendment.[4]

Jurisdiction under Fed. R. Civ. P. 4(k)(2) is limited to situations in which it is established that the defendant "is not subject to the jurisdiction of the courts of general jurisdiction of any state". Further, this provision does not apply when the claim is premised on state or foreign law; however, the doctrine of supplemental jurisdiction (28 U.S.C. §1367) may sanction consideration of such a claim in the event there is also a federal claim.

The Advisory Committee Notes caution that Rule 4(k)(2) should not be applied when:

- a defendant is subject to personal jurisdiction in a state;
- a plaintiff's forum might be so inconvenient to a defendant that it would be a denial of "fair play and substantial justice"; or
- an alien defendant would be subject to a forum selection "so onerous that injustice would result".

Essentially, this rule change in combination with new Fed. R. Civ. P. Rule 4(f) relating to service of process creates a form of global

---

F.R.D. 221, 224 (1994).

[4] The Judicial Conference's Committee on Rules of Practice and Procedure cautioned that Rule 4(k)(2) might run afoul of the Rules Enabling Act [28 U.S.C. § 2072] and suggested that this grant of jurisdiction might exceed the rule-making powers of the U.S. Supreme Court. 146 F.R.D. 557.

service of process and a national contacts test for determining jurisdiction for all federal question cases.[5]

B. Foreign Service of Process under Federal Rules of Civil Procedure

New Rule 4 permits foreign service of process in a broader range of cases, revamps the methods for obtaining foreign service of process, and adopts international conventions for service of process. Under some interpretations of former Rule 4(i), it was suggested that foreign service of process was not permitted absent express authorization in a statute. Under new Rule 4(f), there is no longer any requirement for an independent source of authority (e.g., the Clayton Act in the case of an antitrust act) to serve process outside the United States. Absent an express prohibition by federal law, service "may be effected in a place not within any judicial district of the United States..." Fed. R. Civ. P. Rule 4(f).

Rule 4(f) provides that service in a foreign country may be by:

(1) an internationally agreed means reasonably calculated to give notice such as those means authorized by the [Hague Service Convention]; or

(2) if there is no internationally agreed means of service or the applicable international agreement allows other means of service, the provision of such service must be reasonably calculated to give notice:

(A) in the manner prescribed by the law of the foreign country for service in that country in an action in any of its courts of general jurisdiction; or

(B) as directed by the foreign authority in response to a letter rogatory or letter of request; or

(C) unless prohibited by the law of the foreign country, by

---

5 Rule 4(k)(2) may also be interpreted to permit "tag" jurisdiction by which service is made on a person temporarily in the jurisdiction. The European Union, among other jurisdictions, has condemned such "tag" jurisdiction. *See* Restatement (Third) of the Foreign Relations Law of the United States § 421(2), comment e, & reporters' note 5 (1987).

(i) delivery to the individual personally of a copy of the summons and the complaint; or

(ii) any form of mail requiring a signed receipt to be addressed and dispatched by the clerk of the court to the party to be served;

(3) by other means not prohibited by international agreement as may be directed by the court.[6]

If a plaintiff is attempting to effect service in a country that is not a signatory to the Hague Service Convention (see below), it may use any of the alternative methods of service set forth in Rule 4(f)(2). For example, the Inter-American Convention on Letters Rogatory provides a non-exclusive, optional method of obtaining service of process which is often utilized to obtain service of process in several North and South American countries.[7]

These amendments also create an incentive for a defendant to avoid a fight over the legality of service. A plaintiff may send the defendant a summons and a complaint and request that the defendant "waive" formal service of process. For domestic litigation, a failure to waive service of process or to agree to waive service of process subjects a defendant to an award of fees and costs. Due to protest from foreign governments about the proposed cost-shifting provisions, the initial proposals for these provisions applicable in the context of foreign service of process were deleted from the adopted rule.[8]

---

[6] Although Rule 4(f) applies only to individuals, Rule 4(h)(2) essentially adopts the same rules of service for corporations and other business entities.

[7] See Inter-American Convention on Letters Rogatory, 43 O.A.S. T.S., reprinted in 14 I.L.M. 339 (1975) and Additional Protocol to the Inter-American Convention on Letters Rogatory, 56 O.A.S. T.S., reprinted in 18 I.L.M. 1238 (1979). Signatories to the Letters Rogatory Convention include Uruguay, Guatemala, Mexico, United States, Peru, Argentina, and Paraguay. The appropriate form adopted by the U.S. Government for use of this form of Letters Rogatory is USM-272.

[8] G. Born & A. Vollmer, *supra* note 3, at 229-34.

The Hague Service Convention

New Rule 4(f) expressly favors use of the Hague Convention on Service Abroad of Judicial and Extrajudicial Documents in Civil or Commercial Matters ("Hague Service Convention") where applicable.[9] This is the first multilateral treaty on international judicial assistance that the United States has joined. The Convention which came into force in the United States in February 1969 sets forth procedures and alternative methods to inform foreign defendants of the pendency of civil actions and to provide adequate time for response to those actions.[10]

The Hague Service Convention has been adopted by most of the United States' major trading partners and many other countries. The Convention requires that a plaintiff satisfy the requirements and adhere to the restrictions imposed by a signatory country on service within its territory. Some signatory countries have placed various conditions on executing the Convention, and before a party initiates service under its provisions, a careful review of those conditions should be undertaken.[11]

If the Hague Service Convention is available and service is made abroad, the U.S. plaintiff must comply with the Convention and failure to comply with it voids the service. *Volkswagenwerk A.G. v. Schlunk*, 486 U.S. 694, 699 (1988). The Convention, however, does not apply when service is achieved on a foreign defendant within the United States,[12] when the destination country is not a signatory

---

9 Hague Convention on Service Abroad of Judicial and Extrajudicial Documents in Civil or Commercial Matters (hereinafter "Hague Service Convention"). 658 U.N.T.S. 163, 20 U.S.T. 361, 4 I.L.M. 341. Although Rule 4(f) refers only to service abroad on foreign individuals, the rules governing service outside the country on corporations and associations incorporates the methods of Rule 4(f). See new Rule 4(h)(2).

10 The text of the Hague Service Convention is reprinted following Fed. R. Civ. P. 4 in the United States Code Annotated.

11 The U.S. Code Annotated section following Fed. R. Civ. P. 4 sets forth a list of all the signatory countries and indicates the varying restrictions placed on application of the Convention by the various signatory countries. Fed. R. Civ. P. 4, 28 U.S.C.A. at 218-229.

12 For example, service under the Hague Service Convention is unnecessary if the foreign defendant is doing business within the United States and has a local agent for service of process or a local presence. Volkswagenwerk A.G. v.

to the convention, or when the nature of the dispute, for example, a criminal matter, does not relate to "civil or commercial matters." It is unclear whether the Convention applies to family law, tax, administrative or public law issues.[13]

Mechanics of Service of Process

The Convention provides alternative means for achieving service of process:

> it requires each signatory country to establish a Central Authority and directs the Central Authority to receive requests for service from other countries and to proceed with service in conformity with the remaining provisions of the Convention;[14] or
>
> if the country of destination has not objected, the plaintiff may serve the defendant in the other country by mail, through the

---

Schlunk, 486 U.S. 694, 108 S.Ct. 2104, 100 L.Ed.2d 722 (1988). This decision has been criticized by commentators and foreign governments as creating a judicial exception to the exclusivity of the Hague Service Convention. *See* Brenda L. White, "Recent Developments - Service of Process: Application of the Hague Service Convention in the United States--*Volkswagen Altiengessellschaft v. Schlunk*, 108 S.Ct. 2108", 30 Harv. Int'l L.J. 277, 284-85 (1989). The governments of Germany, Japan, France and Great Britain submitted diplomatic notes to the U.S. Government protesting the decision of the Illinois Appellate Court permitting avoidance of the Hague Service Convention requirements. Brief for the United States as Amicus Curiae Supporting Respondent at 8 n.11, addenda A-D, Volkswagenwerk A.G. v. Schlunk, 108 S.Ct. at 2104 (1988). For a general discussion, see Kenneth B. Reisenfeld, "Service of United States Process Abroad: A Practical Guide to Service under the Hague Service Convention and the Federal Rules of Civil Procedure", 24 Int'l Lawyer 55, 62-66.

[13] *See* Gary B. Born, *International Civil Litigation in United States Courts: Commentary and Materials* (2d ed.), pp. 186-188 for a discussion of the scope of the Hague Service Convention. *See also* Committee on Federal Courts, N.Y. State Bar Ass'n, "Service of Process Abroad: A Nuts and Bolts Guide", 122 F.R.D. 63 (1989); Comment, "Service of Process Abroad Under the Hague Convention", 71 Marq. L.Rev. 649 (1988).

[14] Hague Service Convention, Art. 2. The Central Authority established by the U.S. is the Foreign Litigation Section of the Civil Division within the U.S. Department of Justice. The Central Authorities for other signatory countries are identified in the ratifications or accessions of those countries to the Convention.

judicial officers of that country, or through consular or diplomatic channels;[15] or

any method of service of process permitted by the internal laws of the country of destination.[16]

There is conflicting case law as to whether a plaintiff must use a Central Authority procedure to obtain service in a signatory country or if the plaintiff can rely on other means of service permitted in the country of destination. Some reported decisions have held that Central Authority procedures must be used even when foreign law permits or authorizes alternative means of perfecting service. See, e.g., *Teknekron Mgt v. Quante Fernmeldtechnik*, 115 F.R.D. 175, 176 (D.Nev.1987). Other courts have adopted a more liberal interpretation permitting alternative forms of service if such forms of service either are not prohibited or are expressly authorized by the country of destination. *DeJames v. Magnificence Carriers, Inc.*, 654 F.2d 280, 288 (3d Cr.), *cert. denied*, 454 U.S. 1085 (1981).[17]

The methodology for utilizing the Central Authority procedures and the form of the letter of request are not unduly complex.[18] The packet of documents to be provided to the Central Authority of the country of destination includes:

- a list of the documents identifying the person to be served and the documents to be served on the individual;

---

15 Hague Service Convention, *supra* note 9, Art. 10.

16 Hague Service Convention, *supra* note 9 at Art. 19.

17 Reversing former practice under old Rule 4(i), new Rule 4(f)(2) bars use of alternative methods of service that violate foreign law.

18 In the U.S., customary practice is for the plaintiff's counsel to prepare and execute the letters of request which it sends to the Central Authority of the country of destination. The U.S. Marshal's Service will not normally send such letters for plaintiff's counsel. There has been some dispute with certain signatory countries (e.g., United Kingdom) as to whether they will accept letters of request prepared by plaintiff's counsel. See Reisenfeld, *supra* note 12, at 62 n.33. To avoid delay, it has been suggested that the applicable forms (USM-94 forms) should include a notation that the counsel for the plaintiff "is duly authorized under applicable U.S. law [citing the local rule of federal district court or a state rule or statute] to request service pursuant to the Hague Service Convention." See Born, *supra* note 13, at 192-93.

- a summary which briefly describes the enclosed documents and the litigation for which service of process is sought;
- a draft certificate to be completed by the Central Authority and returned to the applicant. The certificate describes the manner in which service was accomplished.

For the letter of request, U.S. plaintiffs should utilize USM-94 forms which can be obtained from the U.S. Marshal's Office. These forms should be completed in English and the official language of the country of destination and should be submitted in duplicate by the plaintiff's counsel. It is a good precaution to provide translations of the summons, complaint and any attachments to the complaint. It is likely that 4-6 weeks will expire before counsel receives the Certificate of Service from the Central Authority of the country of destination.

Alternative service under Article 10 of the Convention is subject to important limitations. Each member state may object to the proposed alternative form of service. Thus, before such service is commenced, a careful review of the service laws of the country of destination should be initiated.[19] The starting point for such a review is the accessions of the member states to the Convention. Several countries have objected to various forms of service:

- service by direct mail. Most countries have not objected to direct mail service; however, some countries such as Germany bar this form of service of process.
- service by process server. The Convention appears to permit service by someone other than a judicial officer. Japan, Germany, and the United Kingdom, among others, have objected to this form of service.

Regardless of procedural defects in service under the Hague Service Convention, if the defendant does not assert that procedural infirmity in its first responsive paper, it waives its right

---

[19] The Office of Consular Affairs of the U.S. Department of State is a source of information regarding the interpretation of such accessions by signatory countries.

to the protections of the Convention. *Photolab Corp. v. Simplex Specially Co.*, 6 Fed.R.Serv.3d 965 (8th Cir. 1986).

II. Foreign Discovery In United States Courts

Civil litigants in U.S. courts increasingly seek discovery in foreign countries. Such efforts in U.S. litigation frequently result in protracted wrangling over appropriate use of the discovery tools of the Federal Rules of Civil Procedure and the application of the Convention on the Taking of Evidence Abroad in Civil or Commercial Matters (the "Hague Evidence Convention").[20] The Hague Evidence Convention provides an alternative to the Federal Rules of Civil Procedure for procuring discovery in foreign countries. The U.S. Supreme Court in a 1987 5-4 decision held that the Hague Evidence Convention does not provide the exclusive or mandatory procedure for discovery documents and information located abroad. As the majority noted, it is just an "optional procedure" to obtain such materials and information.[21]

Rule 28 of the Fed. R. Civ. P. was amended in 1993, in part, to make effective use of the Hague Evidence Convention. The Advisory Note to Rule 28 states that: "[t]he party taking the deposition is *ordinarily obliged* to conform to [the treaty] if an effective deposition can be taken...even though a verbatim transcript is not available or testimony cannot be taken under oath." (Emphasis added.) (Note may be found at Fed. R. Civ. P. 28, 28 U.S.C.A. (West Supp. 1994 at 33).

---

20 Hague Convention on the Taking of Evidence Abroad in Civil or Commercial Matters, (hereinafter, the "Hague Evidence Convention") 847 U.N.T.S. 231, 23 U.S.T. 2555.

21 Societe Nationale Industrielle Aerospatiale v. United States District Court for the Southern District of Iowa, 482 U.S. 522, 541 (1987). In that decision, a sharply divided U.S. Supreme Court held that the Hague Evidence Convention was merely one available option to the discovery provisions of the Federal Rules of Civil Procedure. The majority noted that international comity necessitated a case-specific balancing of various national interests that could in certain circumstances require first resort to the procedures in the Convention. 482 U.S. 543-44. When the new amendments to the Federal Rules of Civil Procedure were first proposed, the initial proposal attempted to reverse the *Societe Nationale* decision and to require first resort to Hague Evidence Convention. Ultimately, this proposal was rejected. See, Born & Vollmer, *supra* note 3, at 241-45.

A. General U.S. and Foreign Discovery Practices

1. U.S. Discovery Practice

- No distinction is made between U.S. and foreign discovery for most purposes. All discovery tools provided in the Federal Rules of Civil Procedure are available for foreign as well as domestic discovery – depositions on oral examination, requests and subpoenas for production of documents, interrogatories, requests for admission, etc.
- Scope of discovery is quite broad -- "discovery regarding any matter, not privileged, which is relevant to the subject matter involved in the pending action." Fed. R. Civ. P. Rule 26(b)(1).
- Discovery is initiated by the parties rather than the courts, and most discovery does not require judicial intervention. In the context of international litigation, however, courts have been more pro-active in supervising discovery practice.[22]
- Courts often rely on the unilateral provisions of the Federal Rules of Civil Procedure, rather than on multi-lateral treaties providing for judicial assistance, to procure requested discovery.[23]
- Failure to comply with court orders requiring compliance with discovery orders has subjected numerous foreign parties to sanctions under Fed. R. Civ. P. Rule 37.

2. Foreign Discovery Practice

- In civil law countries, "discovery" is tightly controlled by the judiciary. Discovery in the sense used by U.S. litigators is substantially constrained. The judiciary directs the discovery and actively participates in, if not dominates, the actual conduct of it.

---

[22] Id. at 546. See also *Restatement (Third) of Foreign Relations Law of the United States* 442 (1987).

[23] The Supreme Court in *Societe Nationale* held that international comity did not mandate initial resort to the Hague Evidence Convention rather than the Federal Rules of Civil Procedure. Comity required "prior scrutiny in each case of the particular facts, sovereign interests, and likelihood that resort [to the Hague Evidence Convention] will prove effective." 482 U.S. at 544.

- The scope of discovery in most foreign countries is more restrictive than under comparable U.S. rules.
- U.S. discovery orders have been greeted with hostility by numerous foreign states and resulted in the enactment of legislation restricting unilateral U.S. discovery ("blocking statutes") (see discussion below).

B. Hague Evidence Convention

In contrast to the broad range of civil discovery permitted by the Federal Rules of Civil Procedure, the Hague Evidence Convention has a limited scope. The signatory countries to the Hague Evidence Convention have excluded or limited certain forms of discovery practice. The Convention addresses only requests of "judicial" authorities for assistance in conducting foreign discovery[24] and not all judicial acts are covered. Rather, powers under the Convention are limited to requests to obtain evidence in pending litigation. Accordingly, requests for orders compelling arbitration or the appointment of a receiver may be outside the scope of the Convention. Further, like the Hague Service Convention, it only applies to disputes of a "civil or commercial" nature. In civil disputes that may have criminal implications, e.g., antitrust litigation, countries from whom assistance has been sought have sometimes refused cooperation. [25]

The chief device for procuring evidence under the Convention is through a "letter of request." A Central Authority is created in each signatory country and all letters of request from foreign courts are directed to that repository.[26] The Central Authority is also responsible for the transmittal of the request for execution by the appropriate government authorities. It can obtain the requested information or documents by "appropriate measures of

---

24 Hague Evidence Convention, Art. 16.

25 *See* Rio Tinto Zinc Corp. v. Westinghouse Electric Corp., 1978 App. Cas. 547 (appeal taken from C.A.).

26 Some signatory countries have taken advantage of Convention provisions to designate additional authorities and multiple Central Authorities for receipt of letters of request. Hague Evidence Convention, *supra* note 20 at Art. 2 and Art. 24.

compulsion", if necessary, and the requests must be executed "expeditiously."[27]

The Convention includes several exceptions to the general rule of cooperating with the requesting authorities. For example, Central Authorities can refuse to execute a letter of request that does not comply with the provisions of the Convention.[28] Such defects include the failure to comply with the language and information requirements of the Convention. A critical exception is Article 23 that permits the signatory countries to refuse to execute a Letters of Request when that request is "[i]ssued for purpose of obtaining pretrial discovery of documents as known in Common Law countries."[29] Note that this restriction only applies to *documents;* it has no application to requests for oral testimony. Although the restriction of Article 23 is limited to documents, however, courts in numerous signatory countries have applied their local laws to restrict U.S. requests for oral depositions. The chief complaint is that the American plaintiff is engaged in a "fishing expedition."[30]

1. Depositions and Document Requests under the Fed. R. Civ. P. Rules 28 and 30

Methods for taking depositions in a foreign country --- Notice, Commission, Letter of Request (formerly known as a Letter Rogatory), Stipulation or Applicable Treaty or Convention.

- Notice procedure is almost identical to the procedure used in domestic depositions. No court intervention is required. By designating the person who is authorized to administer oaths under foreign law, false statements at the deposition might result in sanctions under the foreign jurisdiction's perjury laws.

---

27 Hague Evidence Convention, *supra* note 20 at Art. 10.

28 *Id.*, Art 5.

29 *Id.*, Art. 23. Some signatory countries bar any pretrial document discovery (e.g., Norway and France); other countries permit certain document discovery when the letter of request identifies specific documents or a specific group of documents (e.g., Sweden and United Kingdom).

30 See, *e.g.*, In re Asbestos Insurance, [1985] 1 W.L.R. 331 (House of Lords).

- Commission procedure requires application to the court for permission to conduct the deposition and for the court's appointment of the person before whom the deposition will be conducted.

- Letter of Request procedure involves a formal request from a U.S. court to a foreign court to perform some judicial act such as the taking of a deposition. This procedure is often used when a deposition is taken in a country that prohibits depositions by notice or commission. Issuance may be conditioned on various terms that are "just and appropriate." The deposition is governed by the procedures of the country in which the deposition will occur. For example, the judge may question the witness, and the lawyers merely submit questions to the court for inquiries but the asking of such questions is in the sole discretion of the judge.[31]

- Stipulation procedure merely permits depositions to be taken pursuant to the written agreement of the parties "before any person, at any time or place, upon any notice, and in any manner." Fed. R. Civ. P. Rule 29. A cautionary note: although the parties may agree to certain discovery procedures, in certain civil law countries (e.g., Switzerland) such procedures are within the sole purview of the court and private agreements are not only irrelevant but also unlawful absent consent by government authorities.

- Use of an evidence treaty such as the Hague Evidence Convention. (See discussion below.)

2. Depositions and Document Requests under the Hague Evidence Convention

There are three methods of obtaining oral deposition testimony or documents --- notice to appear before a consular officer,

---

[31] For details on the practical differences between methods used by courts in other countries to control the use of depositions and requests for documents, see Platto, Charles, ed. *Obtaining Evidence in Another Jurisdiction in Business Disputes*. International Bar Association Series, 1988; McClatchey, John F. et al., eds. *Obtaining Discovery Abroad.* (Antitrust Trial Practice Handbook Series, No. 1, 1990.)

designation of a private commissioner, or use of a letter of request. Hague Evidence Convention, Arts. 1-22. Notice and Commission procedures are used when the witness appears voluntarily. Generally, when compulsion is needed to obtain the evidence-taking, a letter of request is required.[32]

A consular officer can take evidence from its own nationals but normally this is only after the requesting party has obtained permission from the local authorities where the evidence is being taken in a proceeding that has already commenced in the consular officer's home country.[33] A consular officer may also take evidence from a national of the country where it is residing for currently pending proceedings in the consular's country and it has obtained prior approval in each instance for such a proceeding.[34] For use of a Commissioner, similar restrictions apply. In addition, the Commissioner must be appointed by the court in the requesting country and not by a private entity (e.g., the American Arbitration Association).[35]

Commissioners and Consular officers are authorized to administer oaths and take evidence in any form so long as it is not "incompatible with the law of the State where the evidence is taken or contrary to any permission granted" to the Consular officer or Commissioner. In addition, certain procedural requirements are defined in the Convention: the person/entity providing the evidence must be given the request in the language of the host country; the person/entity must be informed of the right to legal representation, of the absence of a legal obligation to provide the evidence, and of the right to invoke various privileges and immunities.[36] If reserved by a signatory country, a letter of request must be translated into the language of the receiving country.

---

32 See Born, *supra* note 13, at 419 for a discussion of situations in which compulsion can be required even though evidence-taking is before a consular officer or a private commissioner.

33 Hague Evidence Convention, *supra* note 20 at Art. 15.

34 *Id.*, Art. 16.

35 *Id.*, Art 17.

36 *Id.*, Art. 21.

Absent such a reservation, the letter of request may be submitted in English or French.

The Hague Evidence Convention does not include a specific form for letters of request. However, certain information should be provided:

- identity of the requesting and requested authority,
- identities and addresses of all parties and their respective counsel,
- a description of the nature of the proceeding for which the requested information is sought,
- a description of the evidence that the requesting party intends to take,
- identification of all witnesses including their addresses,
- the questions to be asked of the witnesses or the subject matters of inquiry,
- the documents to be examined,
- the requirements, if any, for an oath or affirmation, and
- identification of any special method or procedure that will be followed in the evidence taking proceeding.[37]

3. Foreign Blocking Statutes To Preclude Foreign Discovery in U.S. Litigation

In response to efforts by plaintiffs in U.S. antitrust actions to obtain substantial discovery from foreign companies located in Australia, Canada and the United Kingdom, these countries among others have enacted "blocking statutes." These statutes seek to preclude use of American discovery practices in their countries and to

[37] This provision (Hague Evidence Convention, supra note 20 at Art. 9) is very important to many U.S. lawyers because in several of the signatory countries, particularly civil law countries, a judge rather than a lawyer conducts oral depositions, and verbatim transcripts are not taken or witnesses are not sworn. This provision permits U.S. lawyers to request various procedures customary in U.S. litigation practice but not normally found in the host country's procedures.

prevent the disclosure of documents and information located in those countries. Accordingly, foreign governments penalize any national for compliance with the discovery requests of a U.S. court.[38] The leading U.S. case, Société Internationale v. Rogers,[39] upheld the possibility that good faith compliance with a foreign blocking statute would not subject a foreign party to sanctions under the discovery rules of the Federal Rules of Civil Procedure. Later courts have held that persons refusing discovery must make good-faith efforts to obtain permission from the foreign government for release of documents or the taking of a deposition.[40]

III. The Recognition and Enforcement of Foreign Judgments

A. General Principles

The judgment of a court normally has no effect outside that court's jurisdiction. As noted by the U.S. Supreme Court, absent another jurisdiction's commitment by treaty, statute or other agreement or for other reasons of the foreign sovereign, acts of governments including the judiciary are limited to the territory of the sovereign.[41] As aptly noted by a scholar of international litigation, the only accepted principle of international law in this area is that ".. no state recognizes or enforces the judgment of another state rendered without jurisdiction of the judgment debtor."[42] Thus, a judgment will have an effect in another jurisdiction only if the foreign jurisdiction agrees to recognize or enforce the judgment. Therefore, in order to effect recovery on a judgment outside the jurisdiction, nations have developed various procedures to give recognition and effect to foreign judgments.[43]

---

38 See In re Uranium Antitrust Litigation, 480 F.Supp. 1138, 1143 (N.D.Ill. 1979); In re. Anschuetz & Co., 754 F.2d 602, 614 n.29 (5th Cir. 1985).

39 357 U.S. 197 (1958).

40 For a detailed discussion of the conflicts between U.S. discovery rules and foreign blocking statutes, see Barry Hawk, *United States, Common Market and International Antitrust*, Vol. I, (3d ed. 1992).

41 Hilton v. Guyot, 159 U.S. 113, 163 (1895).

42 Andreas F. Lowenfeld, *International Litigation and Arbitration*, 368 (1993).

43 "Recognition" and "enforcement" while related concepts have different meanings. "Recognition" involves a decision by a foreign court that it will not

Issues of recognition and enforcement of foreign judgments in the United States are a matter of state -- not federal law, in most countries the effect of such laws is national in scope.[44] The result is that in the United States the recognition and enforcement of foreign judgments involves mostly a combination of judge-made law and state statutory law. In contrast, bilateral and multilateral treaties often are the principle basis for recognition and enforcement of judgments between sister countries (e.g., the European Union countries). Absent statutes, treaties and conventions, governing principles in this area have mostly developed from tradition.

B. Recognition and Enforcement of U.S. Judgments Abroad

The recognition and enforcement of U. S. judgments abroad is mostly a matter of pursuing separate claims in the countries where jurisdiction is possible. With two exceptions, the U.S. is not a party to any treaty concerning recognition and enforcement of judgments. One exception is the Berne Convention that protects copyright owners from infringement and provides the copyright owners with the ability to enforce judgments without cumbersome procedures that would be required absent the convention. [45]

All of this may change. In May 1992, the United States submitted a proposal to the Hague Conference on Private International Law for a new convention on the recognition and enforcement of judgments and indicated that the U.S. is prepared to be a signatory country to such a convention. The matter was not considered at the Seventeenth Session of the Hague Conference on Private International Law held in

---

permit litigation of a specific issue or factual dispute that was previously litigated in another court. "Enforcement" involves the jurisdiction's exercise of its judicial powers to compel compliance with a judgment rendered in another jurisdiction. *See Restatement (Third) Foreign Relations Law of the United States* 481, comments a & b (1987).

44 Charles Platto, *Enforcement of Foreign Judgments Worldwide (Int'l Bar Assn. Series*, 2d ed., 1993).

45 Lowenfeld, *supra* note 42, at 369. The U.S. is also a party to the Hague Convention on the Civil Aspects of International Child Abduction which does not depend on recognition of judgments but may have that effect since it gives priority to the rights of custody at the habitual residence of the child. *See* Hague Convention on the Civil Aspects of International Child Abductoin, T.I.A.S. 11670, Hague Conference on Private International Law. *Recueil des Conventions* 264.

1993 but a Working Group was created at the Hague to consider the proposal and a Special Commission has been created to make proposals as to creation of such a convention.[46] The Working Group concluded that a convention was both desirable and technically feasible. It is expected that the Special Commission will submit proposals to the Eighteenth Session in 1995-96.[47]

A foreign enforcement action is usually required when a plaintiff in a U.S. action is unable to obtain satisfaction of a judgment from assets located in the U.S. or foreign assets made available for satisfaction of the judgment. To satisfy the judgment, the plaintiff must file an action in jurisdictions in which the defendant's assets are located requesting the assistance of foreign courts to enforce the U.S. judgment and satisfy it from the foreign assets. Without any treaty for enforcement of judgments, the U.S. plaintiff must rely on the domestic law of the foreign country in which it seeks an order to obtain satisfaction.[48]

1. Representative Requirements For, Or Bars To, Recognition and Enforcement of Foreign Judgments

- proof of reciprocity required (Germany)[49]
- no proof of reciprocity required (France)[50]

---

[46] Hague Conference on Private International Law, Final Act of the Seventeenth Session, done May 29, 1993, 32 I.L.M. 1139, 1145.

[47] Peter Pfund, "The Hague Conference Celebrates Its 100th Anniversary", 28 Texas Int'l L.J. 531, 537-38 (1993); Ronald Brand, "Enforcement of Judgments in the United States and Europe", 13 J. Law & Commerce 193, 207-09 (1994).

[48] Information on the domestic laws relating to recognition and enforcement of foreign judgments is not an unduly high hurdle to a practitioner. *See, e.g., World Litigation Law & Practice* (Ronald E. Myrick ed., 1990); *Enforcement of Money Judgments Abroad* (Phillip R. Weems ed., New York, Matthew Bender 1991); David Westin, *U.S. Judgments Abroad* (New York, Matthew Bender 1991).

[49] Code of Civil Procedure (2 PO), § 328.

[50] Munzer v. Jacoby-Munzer, Cass. Civ. 1re Jan. 7, 1964, [1964] J.C.P. II, No. 13590.

- no review of the merits although some countries have a reservation of a right to review the merits of foreign judgments, which right is not customarily exercised (Belgium)[51]
- no enforcement of foreign judgments in the absence of a treaty (Netherlands)[52]
- similar treatment for default judgments and contested judgments (U.S.)
- enforcement of default judgments in only limited circumstances (Britain)[53]
- translation of the judgment to be enforcement by the foreign court
- no enforcement unless the U.S. judgment must be final and conclusive
- no enforcement when the judgment is void according to the laws of the court which entered the judgment
- no enforcement when the foreign judgment was against a person who is protected by immunity
- no enforcement if the rendering court did not have proper jurisdiction
- no enforcement if there was a failure of due and timely service of the documents which initiated the enforcement proceeding
- no enforcement if the foreign judgment conflicts with other proceedings or judgments
- no enforcement if enforcement of the foreign judgment would violate domestic public policy.

---

51 Judicial Code (Code Judicière), Art. 570 (as adopted in 1967).

52 Code of Civil Procedure, (Rv.) Art. 431.

53 Lowenfeld, supra note 42, 368 (1993).

2. European Recognition/Enforcement of Judgments

The Treaty of Rome of 1957 established the European Economic Community by providing that "[m]ember states shall, so far as is necessary, enter into negotiations with each other with a view to securing for the benefit of their nationals ... the simplification of formalities governing the reciprocal recognition and enforcement of judgments of courts or tribunals and of arbitration awards." Treaty of Rome, Art. 220 (1957).

In furtherance of the goal of simplifying the formalities among member states, the European Commission (EC) enacted the EEC Convention on Jurisdiction and Enforcement of Judgments in Civil and Commercial Matters. This agreement was drafted as part of the Brussels Convention.[54] Title 3 of the agreement covers the recognition and enforcement of judgments of member states. The agreement covers both monetary and equitable judgments. This agreement may be more relevant to subsidiaries of American companies operating in Europe who are either being sued or seek to sue parties in the other member states.

Enforcement proceedings will normally be commenced with a special proceeding called a "coming up to a judgment for enforcement." The Brussels Convention and the Lugano Convention provide a somewhat simplified procedure for enforcement of judgments between the signatory countries.

The requirements established under this agreement for the recognition of a judgment by a state which is a member of the

---

[54] Convention on Jurisdiction and the Enforcement of Judgments in Civil and Commercial Matters, (hereinafter, the "Brussels Convention"), Sept 27, 1968, 262 U.N.T.S. 153 (including 1971 protocol), *text as amended by* the 1978 Accession Convention (Denmark, Ireland, United Kingdom), the 1982 Accession Convention (Greece) and the 1989 Accession Convention (Spain, Portugal), 1990 O.J. (C 189) 2 *reprinted in* 29 I.L.M. 1413 (1990); Convention on Jurisdiction and the Enforcement of Judgments in Civil and Commercial Matters, (hereinafter the "Lugano Convention") Sept. 16, 1988, 1988 O.J. (L 319) 9, *reprinted in* 28 I.L.M. 620 (1989). The Brussels Convention is a multilateral convention comprising the 12 members of the European Commission plus 6 members of the European Free Trade Area. The European Free Trade Area (EFTA) is a regional convention consisting of mostly west European countries. The Lugano Convention established the membership of the EFTA members in the Brussels Convention.

European Economic Community or the European Free Trade Area (i.e., a "Contracting State") are that:

(i) the judgment not be contrary to public policy in the State in which recognition is sought;

(ii) the defendant be given adequate service of process with sufficient time to arrange for a defense;

(iii) the judgment not be one which is irreconcilable with a judgment given in a dispute between the same parties in the State in which recognition is sought;

(iv) the judgment of the State of origin must not have involved the determination of a preliminary question which conflicts with a rule of private international law of the State in which recognition is sought;

(v) the judgment must not be irreconcilable with an earlier judgment given in a non-contracting State involving the same cause of action and between the same parties.

GERMANY

Key requirements from the German Code of Civil Procedure that must be considered include:

- the judgment of a foreign court will not be enforced except by virtue of a judgment for enforcement
- jurisdiction to pronounce the judgment for enforcement shall be the court with general jurisdiction over the debtor
- the judgment of enforcement will be rendered without review of the merits of the case
- no judgment of enforcement will be entered until the judgment of the foreign court is final and conclusive
- no judgment will be recognized when:
  - the foreign court has no jurisdiction under German law
  - the documents instigating the proceedings were not properly served on the defendant and the defendant made no appearance and he pleads such facts

- when the judgment conflicts with a German judgment or with an earlier recognizable foreign judgment or where the proceedings underlying the foreign judgment conflict with a German proceeding that began before the foreign proceeding

- when recognition of the judgment would lead to a result that would clearly conflict with essential principles of German law, in particular where recognition would conflict with the German constitution

- when reciprocity is not guaranteed.[55]

Recent major decision in Germany addressed several issues relating to enforcement of U.S. judgments and the application of the German Code of Civil Procedure. In June 1992, the Federal Supreme Court interpreted the public policy exception to enforcement of foreign judgments in the context of enforcement of a California judgment.[56] In that action, a 14 year old plaintiff had been sexually molested by a U.S. defendant with German citizenship and no assets in the U.S. The plaintiff was awarded actual and punitive damages and a contingency fee award was given to the plaintiff's counsel. The Federal Supreme Court held, among others, that:

- evidence collected during pretrial discovery in U.S. proceedings could not constitute a basis for denying enforcement even though the method used might violate German views on fair trial practices

- although the award of damage for future medical expenses was not recognized in German law, it was permissible to enforce this aspect of the award

- even though contingency fee agreements are banned in Germany, that provision would be enforced

---

55 Code of Civil Procedure (ZPO), 722, 23, and 328.

56 Judgment of June 4, 1992, BGHZ, 1992 WM 1451 (F.R.G.), translated in 32 I.L.M. 1320 (1993).

- although the award for anxiety, pain and suffering was an amount in excess of amounts granted in German courts in similar circumstances, the public policy exception was not applicable
- while refusing to award punitive and exemplary damages which are contrary to fundamental German public policy, the court in the future will not bar such awards in certain circumstances.

3. Pacific Rim Recognition/Enforcement of Foreign Judgments

No multilateral or bilateral treaties exist which specifically address recognition and enforcement of U.S. judgments in Asia. Japan and Taiwan offer representative examples of enforcement schemes adopted in the Pacific Rim.

JAPAN

(a) Judgment Types[57]

(i) Civil Affairs

(ii) Criminal Affairs

(iii) Administrative Affairs

(b) Recognition of Foreign Judgments. Foreign judgments must satisfy (i) or (ii) below:

(i) Judgment must satisfy Article 200 of the Japanese Code of Civil Procedure

› The foreign judgment must be final and conclusive. (finality)

› Jurisdiction of the foreign court must not be denied in laws and ordinances or by treaty; (jurisdiction)

---

[57] Only civil affairs judgments are recognized and enforced. *See* Louis Garb and Julian Law, *Enforcement of Foreign Judgements*, 4-5 Japan (1994).

- The defeated Japanese defendant must have received service of summons or any other necessary orders to commence procedure otherwise by a public notice or has appeared without receiving notice thereof; (service of process)
- The judgment of the foreign court is not contrary to public order or good morals in Japan. (public policy)
- There is a mutual guarantee. (reciprocity)

(ii) Judgment must be certified as final and conclusive.

(c) Enforcement of Foreign Judgments

- Requires further application for a judgment of execution
- The judgment of execution must be rendered without inquiry into the correctness of the decision.[58]
- No specific recognition for default judgments
- No separate standards of recognition/ execution for money judgments and non-money judgments (e.g., foreign alimony or maintenance orders).

TAIWAN (REPUBLIC OF CHINA)

(a) Recognition of Foreign Judgments. The recognition and enforcement of foreign judgments are governed by Article 402 of the Taiwanese Code of Civil Procedure. ROC courts require the following for recognition and enforcement of foreign judgments: (i) jurisdiction, (ii)

---

[58] Foreign judgments deciding title to land in Japan will not be recognized. These matters are under the exclusive jurisdiction of Japanese courts. *See generally Id.*, "Japan."

proper service of process, (iii) public order/good moral requirement, and (iv) reciprocity. Section 4 of Article 402 of the CCP provides that judgments of foreign courts which do not recognize judgments by courts of the ROC will be deemed invalid. However, the Supreme Court of the Republic of China has held that judgments by U. S. courts meet the requirement of reciprocity and are enforceable.

(b) Procedure for Enforceability. Enforcement of a foreign judgment requires filing a lawsuit in a competent ROC court for permission to enforce the judgment.[59].

C. Recognition and Enforcement of Foreign Judgments in the United States

The general rule is that a foreign judgment will be recognized and enforced in the United States as a matter of comity pursuant to the rationale behind the full faith and credit clause of the United States Constitution (Article 4, 1). This clause states that "[f]ull faith and credit shall be given in each State to the public Acts, Records and judicial Proceedings of every other State." U.S. Const., Art IV, 1. Act of May 26, 1790, c. 11, 1 Stat. 122; Rev. Stat. 905.

1. Rationale for Law

(a) Act of State Doctrine (Comity): Inherent Expectation of Reciprocity [Analogy: Full Faith and Credit Clause of the U. S. Constitution.]

(b) Desirability for an end to litigation[60]

(c) Recognition that a judgment creates vested rights or imposes obligations that merit support[61]

---

[59] Law of Compulsory Execution, Article 43 [translated in *Major Laws of the Republic of China on Taiwan* (1991).

[60] Restatement (Second) Conflict of Laws, 98, comment b (1971 and 1988 Revisions).

[61] 1 Dicey and Morris on the Conflict of Laws 420-421 (11th ed. Collins 1987).

2. Key Factors Affecting Recognition and Enforcement of Foreign Judgments in the United States

(a) Central Concern: "The opportunity for a full and fair trial before a court of competent jurisdiction." Hilton v. Guyot, 159 U.S. 113 (1895).

(b) Recognition will not be accorded in these instances:

- the judgment is of an *ad hoc* tribunal
- the judgment is of a court that treats aliens differently from citizens.
- the foreign proceeding was unfair or biased
- the foreign court lacked subject matter jurisdiction over the dispute
- there is a showing of fraud or other irregularity in the foreign proceeding
- the foreign litigation or judgment violates U.S. public policy
- the foreign court would not grant reciprocal treatment to enforce U.S. judgments

3. Uniform Foreign Money-Judgments Recognition Act

The Uniform Foreign Money-Judgments Recognition Act[62] is a codification of the state rules that had been applied by the majority of courts in the United States.[63] It permits plaintiffs to sue in the

---

62 13 ULA 263 (1986).

63 This Act had been adopted in the following 21 states as of year-end 1991: Alaska, *Alaska Stat.* § 09.30.100 to 09.30.180 (1990); California, *Cal. Civ. Proc. Code* § 1713 to 1713.8 (West 1982); Colorado, *Colo. Rev. Stat. Ann.* §§ 13-62-101 to 13-62-109 (West 1989); Connecticut, *Conn. Gen. Stat. Ann.* §§ 50a-30 to 50a-38 (West 1994); Georgia, Official Code of Georgia, Annotated. §§ 9-12-110 to 9-12-117 (Michie, 1993); Idaho, *Idaho Code Ann.* § 10-1401 to 10-1409 (Michie, 1990); Illinois, *Ill. Rev. Stat.* ch. 5 para. 12-618 to 12-626; Iowa, *Iowa Code Ann.* § 626B.1 to 626B.8 (West Supp. 1994); Maryland, *Md. Courts and Judicial*

U.S. to enforce foreign judgments issued by foreign courts. A "foreign judgment" is defined as "any judgment of a foreign state granting or denying recovery of **a sum of money**, other than a judgment for support in matrimonial or family matters." 13 ULA 263, 1 (1986) (emphasis added). The Act is applicable only to foreign judgments which are final, conclusive and enforceable where rendered "even though an appeal therefrom is pending or it is subject to appeal." 13 ULA 263, 2 (1986). Section 3 addresses recognition and enforcement of foreign judgments. It states that "a foreign judgment...is conclusive between the parties to the extent that it grants or denies recovery of a sum of money. The foreign judgment is enforceable in the same manner as the judgment of a sister state which is entitled to full faith and credit."

The Act also lists the grounds for non-recognition in section 4 and the requirements for personal jurisdiction in section 5. A foreign money judgment will not be considered conclusive if:

> (a) the judgment was rendered under a system which does not provide impartial tribunals or procedures compatible with the requirements of due process of law;
>
> (b) the foreign court did not have personal jurisdiction over the defendant; or

---

Proceedings Code Ann., § 10-701 to 10-709619; Massachusetts, *Ann. Laws of Mass.* ch. 235, § 23A (West 1988); Missouri, *Mo. Ann. Stat.* § 511.770-511.787 (Vernon Supp. 1994); Montana, *Mont. Code Ann.* § 25-9-601 to 25-9-609 (Montana Leg. Council. 1993); New Mexico, *N.M. Stat. Ann.* § 39-4B-1 to 39-4B-9 (Michie 1991 (repl.)); New York, *N.Y. Civ. Prac. L. & R.* § 5301 to 5309 (McKinney 1978); North Carolina, *N.C. Gen. Stat.* § IC-1800 to IC-1808 (Michie 19); Ohio, *Ohio Rev. Code Ann.* § 2329.90 to 2329.94 (Baldwin, 1993); Oklahoma, *Okla. Stat. Ann.* tit [12] § 710 to 718 (West 1988); Oregon, *Or. Rev. Stat. Ann.* § 24.200 to 24.255 (Butterworth 1988); Pennsylvania (nothing in 1994 index); Texas, *Tex. Civil Practice and Remedies Code Ann.* § 36.001 to 36.008 (West 1986); Virgin Islands, *V.I. Code Ann.* § 5, (Butterworth Supp. 1994); Virginia, *Va. Code Ann.* § 8.01-465 to 8.01-465.13 (Michie 1992); Washington, *Wash. Rev. Code. Ann.* § 6.40-010 to 6.40-915 (West Supp. 1995). In New York, section 4 of the Act was amended to provide courts with discretionary power to refuse recognition of a foreign judgment if the foreign court lacked subject matter jurisdiction. This differs from the Uniform Act which mandates non-recognition of the foreign judgment if the foreign court lacked subject matter jurisdiction. See supra, note 62 at 263, 26 9 § 4.

(c) the foreign court did not have jurisdiction over the subject matter.

Further, a foreign money judgment need not be recognized if:

(a) the defendant in the proceedings in the foreign court did not receive notice of the proceedings in sufficient time to enable him to defend;

(b) the judgment was obtained by fraud;

(c) the cause of action or claim for relief on which the judgment is based is repugnant to the public policy of the state;

(d) the judgment conflicts with another final and conclusive judgment;

(e) the proceeding in the foreign court was contrary to an agreement between the parties under which the dispute in question was to be settled otherwise than by proceedings in that court; or

(f) in the case of jurisdiction based only on personal service, the foreign court was a seriously inconvenient forum for the trial of the action.

4. Enforcement of foreign non-money (i.e., equitable) judgments in the U. S.

The traditional rule has been that full faith and credit need not be given to foreign injunctions which affect land. However, they may be honored as a matter of comity. Generally, enforcement of equitable judgments may be pursued under the Uniform Enforcement of Foreign Judgments Act, 13 ULA 149 § 1 (1986). This Act recognizes a "foreign judgment" as "any judgment, decree, or order of a court of the United States or of any other court which is entitled to full faith and credit ..."

5. The Restatement (Third) of Foreign Relations Law

The *Restatement (Third) of Foreign Relations Law* is a persuasive source of authority which applies in states which have not adopted the Uniform Act. It is applicable to **both** money and non-money judgments and serves to document the "American rule" on the recognition and enforcement of foreign judgments. The portion of this "American rule" which addresses money judgments is the same as the rule stated in the Uniform Act. The *Restatement* will generally be accepted by foreign courts for judgments in U. S. states which have not adopted the Uniform Act.[64] The requirements of the *Restatement* closely resemble the requirements of the Uniform Foreign Money-Judgments Recognition Act. However, the uniform act, unlike the Restatement, forbids enforcement in certain situations and merely permits but does not require courts to deny recognition in other situations.

IV. CONDENSED BIBLIOGRAPHY

Treaties & Conventions

Actes et Documents. *Conference de la Haye de Droit International Privé,* The Hague, Imprimerie Nationale, 1893-___.

The 10th Proceedings of the Hague Conference on Private International Law, vol. III. [Includes the preparatory documents (legislative history) for the Hague Service Convention]

11th Proceedings of the Hague Conference on Private International Law, vol. IV [includes the preparatory documents (legislative history) for the Hague Evidence Convention.]

Zamora, Stephen , and Ronald A. Brand, eds. *Basic Documents of International Economic Law.* Chicago: Commerce Clearing House, 1990. (Volume 2, pt. 7 includes certain international litigation treaties).

Convention on Jurisdiction and Enforcement of Judgments in Civil and Commercial Matters ("Brussels Convention"), concluded September 27, 1968, 1990 Official Journal of the European Communities [O.J.] (C 189) 1, reprinted in 29 I.L.M. 1413 (1990).

---

64 This is particularly important for countries which condition recognition and enforcement of U.S. judgments on reciprocal recognition of foreign judgments from their countries (e.g., Germany), *ZPO, supra* note 55, § 328.

Convention on Jurisdiction and Enforcement of Judgments in Civil and Commercial Matters (EC-EFTA)("Lugano Convention"), concluded September 16, 1988, 1988 [O.J.] (L 319) 9, reprinted in 28 I.L.M. 620 (1989).

Convention on Service Abroad of Judicial and Extrajudicial Documents in Civil or Commercial Matters, concluded Nov. 15, 1965 ("Hague Service Convention"), 658 U.N.T.S. 163, 20 U.S.T. 361, T.I.A.S. 6638, 4 I.L.M. 341.

Convention on the Taking of Evidence Abroad in Civil or Commercial Matters, concluded March 18, 1970 ("Hague Evidence Convention"), 847 U.N.T.S. 231, 23 U.S.T. 2555, T.I.A.S. 7444, 8 I.L.M. 37.

Inter-American Convention on Letters Rogatory, concluded Jan. 30, 1975, O.A.S. Treaty Series No., 43, reprinted in 14 I.L.M. 339 (1975).

Additional Protocol to the Inter-American Convention on Letters Rogatory, O.A.S. Treaty Series No. 56, reprinted in 18 I.L.M. 1238 (1979).

United Nations Convention on the Recognition and Enforcement of Foreign Arbitral Awards ("New York Convention"), concluded June 10, 1958, 21 U.S.T. 2517, 330 U.N.T.S. 38.

Statutes & Rules

28 U.S.C. § 1608 (1988) [service on foreign state or political subdivision of a foreign state.].

28 U.S.C. § 1696 (1988) [service in foreign and international litigation].

28 U.S.C. § 1781 (1988) [transmittal of letter rogatory or request].

28 U.S.C. § 1782 (1988) [assistance to foreign and international tribunals and to litigants before such tribunals].

28 U.S.C. § 1783 (1988) [Subpoena of person in foreign country].

Uniform Enforcement of Foreign Judgments Act, 13 U.L.A. 149 (1986).

Uniform Foreign-Money Claims Act, 13 U.L.A. 42 (Supp. 1994).

Uniform Foreign Money-Judgments Recognition Act, 13 U.L.A. 263 (1986).

Fed. R. Civ. P. 4(e) [Summons: Service upon individuals within a Judicial District of the United States]].

Fed. R. Civ. P. 4(f) [Alternative Provisions for Service in a Foreign Country].

Cases

Asahi Metal Industry Co., Ltd. v. Superior Court of California, 480 U.S. 102, 107 S.Ct. 1026, 94 L.Ed.2d 92 (1987).

Burnham v. Superior Court of California, 495 U.S. 604, 110 S.Ct. 2105, 109 L.Ed.2d 631 (1990).

Helicopteros Nacionales de Columbia, S.A. v. Hall, 466 U.S. 408, 104 S.Ct. 1868, 80 L.ed. 404 (1984).

Omni Capital International V. Rudolf Wolff & Co., Ltd., 484 U.S. 97, 108 S.Ct. 404, 98 L.Ed.2d 415 (1987).

Societe Internationale pour Participantions Industrielles et Commerciales, S.A. v. Rogers, 357 U.S. 197, 78 S.Ct. 1087, 2 L.Ed. 2d 1255 (1958).

Societe Nationale Industrielle Aerospatiale v. U.S. District Court for the Southern District of Iowa, 482 U.S. 522, 107 S.Ct. 2542, 96 L.Ed. 2d 461 (1987).

Books & Articles

Born, Gary B., and David Westin, *International Civil Litigation in United States Courts: Commentary and Materials*. 2d ed. Boston: Kluwer Law and Taxation Publishers, 1992.

Brand, Ronald Al., ed., *Enforcing Foreign Judgments in the United States and United States Judgments Abroad*. Chicago: Section of International Law and Practice, American Bar Association, 1992.

Cromie, Stephen. *International Commercial Litigation*. London: Butterworths, 1990.

Fernelius, Stephen M., and Rebecca J. Cole, *Practical Guide for Conducting Extra-Judicial Discovery for Use in U.S. Litigation*. Chicago: International Association of Defense Counsel, 1992.

International Judicial Assistance (Civil and Commercial) (Bruno A. Ristau, ed., Washington, D.C., International Law Institute (1984).

Lowenfeld, Andreas F. *International Litigation and Arbitration*. St. Paul, MN: West, 1992.

Robert E. Lutz, "Enforcement of Foreign Judgments, Part I: A Selected Bibliography on United States Enforcement of Judgments Rendered Abroad", 27 *Int'l Lawyer* 471 (Summer, 1993); "Enforcement of Foreign Judgments, Part II: A Selected Bibliography on Enforcement of U.S. Judgments on Foreign Countries", 27 *Int'l Lawyer* 1029 (Winter 1993).

McClatchey, John F. et al., eds. *Obtaining Discovery Abroad*. Chicago: Section of Antitrust Law, American Bar Association, 1990.

McClean, David. *International Judicial Assistance*. Oxford, Eng.:Oxford Univ. Press, 1992.

Platto, Charles, ed., *Enforcement of Foreign Judgments Worldwide*. London: Graham & Trotman, International Bar Association, 1989.

Platto, Charles, ed. *Obtaining Evidence in Another Jurisdiction in Business Disputes*. London: Graham & Trotman; International Bar Association, 1988.

Jonathan Pratter & Joseph R. Profaizer, "A Practitioner's Research Guide and Bibliography to International Civil Litigation", 28 *Texas International L. J.* 633 (1993).

Practical Handbook on the Operation of the Hague Convention of 15 November 1985 on the Service Abroad of Judicial and Extrajudicial Documents in Civil or Commercial Matters. Antwerp, Belgium: Kluwer Law & Taxation Publishers, 1983.

Kenneth B. Reisenfed, "Service of United States Process Abroad: A Practical Guide to Service Under the Hague Service Convention and the Federal Rules of Civil Procedure", 24 *Int'l Lawyer* 55 (1990).

Restatement of the Law, Third: The Foreign Relations Law of the United States. American Law Institute. St. Paul, MN: American Law Institute Publishers, 1987.

C. Wright & A.Miller, *Federal Practice and Procedure* § 2083 (1970).

TRANSNATIONAL LITIGATIONCONCEPTS -- SERVICE, EVIDENCE, & JUDGMENTS

Barbara Rainwater
E.B. Williams Library
Georgetown University Law Center

TEXTS AND TREATISES

1. Collins, Lawrence. *Essays in International Litigation and the Conflict of Laws.* Oxford: Clarendon, 1994. 466 p.

2. Dicey, Albert Venn. *Dicey and Morris on the Conflict of Laws.* 12th ed. London: Sweet & Maxwell, 1993. 2 vols. 1602 p.

3. *Law and Reality: Essays on National and International Procedural Law in Honour of Cornelis Carel Albert Voskuil.* Dordrecht: M. Nijhoff, 1992. 413 p.

4. Lowenfeld, Andreas F. *International Litigation and Arbitration, Selected Treaties, Statutes and Rules.* American casebook series. St. Paul, Minn.: West Pub. Co., 1993. 277 p.

5. McClean, David. *International Judicial Assistance.* Oxford: Clarendon Press, 1992. 372 p.

6. Scoles, Eugene F. *Conflict of Laws.* 2nd ed. St. Paul, Minn.: West Pub. Co., 1992. 1160 p.

GUIDES AND COMMENTARIES

7. Born, Gary. *International Civil Litigation in United States Courts: Commentary and Materials.* 2nd ed. Boston: Kluwer Law and Taxation Publishers, 1992. 928 p.

8. Epstein, David. *International Litigation: a Guide to Jurisdiction, Practice and Strategy.* Englewood Cliffs, N.J.: Prentice Hall Law & Business, 1993. loose-leaf for updating.

9. Germain, Claire M. *Germain's Transnational Law Research: a Guide for Attorneys.* Ardsley-on-Hudson, N.Y.: Transnational

Juris Publications, Inc., 1991. loose-leaf for updating. (has 1992 update).

10. Nanda, Ved P. *Litigation of International Disputes in U.S. Courts.* International business & law series, v. 4. New York, N.Y.: C. Boardman Co., 1986. loose-leaf for updating. (has 1994 update).

11. Pratter, Jonathan. "A Practitioner's Research Guide and Bibliography to International Civil Litigation," by Pratter and Joseph R. Profaizer. 28 *Texas International Law Journal* 633, Summer, 1993.

12. Ristau, Bruno A. *International Judicial Assistance (Civil and Commercial).* Washington, D.C., International Law Institute, 1984. 2 vol. loose-leaf for updating. (update expected summer, 1994).

JOURNALS OF PARTICULAR INTEREST

13. *American Journal of Comparative Law.* Vol. 1-; 1952-. Ann Arbor, MI: American Association for the Comparative Study of Law.

14. *American Journal of International Law.* Vol. 1-; Jan. 1907-. Washington, D.C.: American Society of International Law.

15. *International and Comparative Law Quarterly.* Vol. 1-; Jan. 1952-. London: British Institute of International and Comparative Law.

16. *International Business Lawyer.* Vol. 1-; 1973-. London: International Bar Association.

17. *International Lawyer.* Vol. 1-; 1966-. Chicago: American Bar Association, Section of International Law.

Almost any law journal with the word "international" or "transnational" in the title.

INFORMATION AND CASES OUTSIDE U.S.A.

18. *International Litigation Procedure.* London, Sweet & Maxwell, 1990-. Cases from 1987-.

19. *Yearbook of European Law.* Oxford, Clarendon Press, 1982-.

Country yearbooks of international law

SOURCES OF PRIMARY MATERIALS

20. *United States Treaties and Other International Agreements.* Washington, D.C.: United States Department of State, 1952-.

21. *United Nations Treaty Series.* New York: United Nations, 1947-.

22. *International Legal Materials.* Washington, D.C., American Society of International Law, 1962-.

23. Martindale-Hubbell International Law Digest in *Martindale-Hubbell Law Directory.* Vol.1-; 1931-. New Providence, N.J., Reed Pub. Co., Annual volume containing "Selected International Conventions."

24. *Code of Federal Regulations.* 1949-. Washington, D.C.: U.S. Govt. Print. Off. Annual. Title 22, Consular Regulations.

25. United States. Dept. of State. Office of the Legal Adviser. *Treaties in Force; a List of Treaties and Other International Agreements of the United States.* Washington, U.S. Govt. Print. Off., Annual.

U.S. MATERIALS

26. *Federal Rules of Civil Procedure,* Rule 4 in *United States Code.* washington, DC: U.S. Govt. Print. Off., 1926-. Can Shepardize these.

27. *Shepard's Federal Rules Citations: a Compilation of Citations to the Federal Rules of Civil Procedure.* Colorado Springs, CO, Shepard's/McGraw-Hill, 1987-.

28. *Restatement of the Law Third: the Foreign Relations Law of the United States.* 3rd ed. Philadelphia, PA, the American Law Institute, 1987. kept up to date with pocket supplements. Section 422.

29. *Restatement of the Law Second: Conflict of Laws* 2d. St. Paul, MN, American Law Institute, 1971. kept up to date with pocket supplements.

30. *Uniform Laws Annotated, master ed.* St. Paul, MN: West, 1968-.

Uniform Interstate and International Procedure Act. 13 ULA 382 (1986).

Uniform Foreign Money-Judgments Recognition Act. 13 ULA 261 (1962).

31. *Moore's Federal Practice.* 2d ed. New York, N.Y., M. Bender, 1948-. Loose-leaf for updating. (has 1994 update).

32. Wright, Charles Alan. *Federal Practice and Procedure.* 2d ed. St. Paul, MN, West Pub. Co., 1982-. Kept up to date with pocket supplements.

33. *Treaties and Other International Agreements: the Role of the United States Senate: a Study.* [Prepared by the Congressional Research Service for U.S. Senate, Committee on Foreign Relations.] Washington, D.C., U.S. Govt. Print. Off., 1993.

34. *Digest of International Law,* prepared by Marjorie Whiteman. Washington, D.C., U.S. Dept. of State, 1963-73.

35. *Digest of United States Practice in International Law.* Washington, D.C., Office of the Legal Adviser, Dept. of State, 1973-.

SERVICE OF PROCESS

36. *Hague Convention on the Service Abroad of Judicial And Extrajudicial Documents in Civil or Commercial Matters.* November 15, 1965. 20 UST 361, TIAS 6638, 658 U.N.T.S. 163, 4 I.L.M. 341. Reprinted in *Martindale-Hubbell.* Reprinted in 28 *USCA* following Federal Rule of Civil Procedure 4. Reprints include list of member states and texts of their declarations of ratifications.

37. *Practical handbook on the operation of the Hague Convention of 15 November 1965 on the Service Abroad of Judicial and Extrajudicial Documents in Civil or Commercial Matters.* 2d ed. Antwerpen, MAKLU Uitgevers, 1992. Loose-leaf.

38. "Service of process abroad: a nuts and bolts guide," The Committee on Federal Courts of the New York State Bar Association, 1989. 122 *Federal Rules Decisions* 63.

39. State "Long-arm statutes".

40. State Rules of Civil Procedure.

SERVICE OF PROCESS – CONTACTS

41. Office of Citizens Consular Services
U.S. Department of State
2120 C Street, NW
Washington, DC 20520
202/647-3666 (voice)
202/647-3000 (fax)
members and non-members of the HAGUE CONVENTION.

42. Office of International Judicial Assistance
U.S. Department of Justice, Civil Division
Todd Building, Room 8201
550 11th Street, NW
Washington, DC 20530
202/514-7455

43. ONE COMMERCIAL COMPANY PERFORMING SERVICE OF PROCESS
APS International (Attorneys Process Service)
APS International Plaza
7800 Glenroy Road
Minneapolis, MN 55439-3122
1-800/328-7171 (voice for information)612/831-8150 (fax)

TAKING OF EVIDENCE ABROAD

44. *Hague Convention on the Taking of Evidence Abroad in Civil or Commercial Matters*. March 18, 1970. 23 U.S.T. 2555, T.I.A.S. 7444, 847 U.N.T.S. 231, 8 I.L.M. 37. reprinted in *Martindale-Hubbell*. reprinted in 28 USCA following section 1781.

45. *Inter-American Convention on Letters Rogatory*, January 30, 1975. O.A.S. Treaty Series #43, 14 I.L.M. 339.

46. *Additional Protocol to the Inter-American Convention on Letters Rogatory*, May 8, 1979. O.A.S. Treaty Series #56, 18 *I.L.M.* 1238.

47. *Practical Handbook on the Operation of the Hague Convention of 18 March 1970 on the Taking of Evidence Abroad in Civil or Commercial Matters.* Antwerpen, Maarten Kinwer's Internationale Litgeversonderneming, 1984. Loose-leaf.

48. *Extraterritorial Discovery in International Litigation.* New York, N.Y., Practising Law Institute, 1984. 592 p.

49. *Obtaining Discovery Abroad.* Chicago, IL, Section of Antitrust Law, American Bar Association, 1990. 213p.

50. *Obtaining Evidence in Another Jurisdiction in Business Disputes.* International Bar Association series. London, Graham & Trotman, International Bar Association, 1993. 214 p.

EVIDENCE--FOREIGN LAWS

51. Blocking statutes in foreign jurisdictions.
Public Policy concerns.
Laws, Rules and Procedures in foreign jurisdictions.
Some may be found in materials listed herein.

52. Reynolds, Thomas H. *Foreign Law: Current Sources of Codes and Basic Legislation in Jurisdictions of the World*, by Reynolds and Arturo A. Flores. Littleton, CO, F.B. Rothman, 1989-. 3 vols. Loose-leaf for updating. (has 1993 update).

ENFORCEMENT OF JUDGMENTS

53. *Convention on Jurisdiction and Enforcement of Judgments in Civil and Commercial Matters. (Brussels Convention).* September 27, 1968. 1978 O.J. L 304/77, 29 ILM 1413. European Community/European Union members only.

54. *Convention on Jurisdiction and the Enforcement of Judgments in Civil and Commercial Matters. (Lugano Convention).* September 16, 1988. 1988 0.7. L319/9, 28 ILM620. EXtends Brussels Convention to EFTA countries.

55. *The Brussels Convention on Jurisdiction and the Enforcement of Foreign Judgements: papers and precedents from the joint conference with the Union des avocats europeens held in Cork, September 1989.* ICEL (Series), no. 8 Dublin, Irish Centre for European Law, 1989. 251 p.

56. *Enforcement of Foreign Judgments Worldwide.* Charles Platto, ed. 2d ed. International Bar Association Series, London, Graham & Trotman and International Bar Association, 1993.

57. *Enforcement of Money Judgments Abroad.* Philip Weems, ed. New York, N.Y., M. Bender, 1988-. 2 vols. loose-leaf for updating (has 1993 update).

58. *Enforcing Foreign Judgments in the United States and United States judgments Abroad.* Chicago, IL, Section of International Law and Practice, American Bar Association, 1992. 192 p.

59. *International Execution Against Judgment Debtors.* Dennis Campbell, ed., published under the auspices of the Center for International Legal Studies, Salzburg, Austria. London, Sweet & Maxwell, Clark Boardman Callaghan, 1993-. 2 vols. Loose-leaf for updating.

60. *Public Policy in Transnational Relationships.* Boston, Kluwer Law and Taxation Publishers, 1990- 1 vol. Loose-leaf for updating (has 1993 update).

61. Lutz, Robert E. "Enforcement of Judgments, Part I: A Selected Bibliography of U.S. Enforcement of Judgments Rendered Abroad," 27 *International Lawyer* 471 (1993).

62. ______________. "Enforcement of Foreign Judgments, Part II: A Selected Bibliography on Enforcement of U.S. Judgments in Foreign Countries," 27 *International Lawyer* 1029 (1993).

HEADINGS TO SEARCH BY

PUBLIC CATALOG

Civil Procedure (International Law
Comparative Law
Conflict of LawsConflict of Laws (Public Policy)
Convention on the....
Discovery (Law)
Executions (Law)
Foreign Law (Pleading and Proof)
Forum non conveniens
Hague Convention on the....
Judgments. Foreign
Judicial Assistance
Jurisdiction (International Law)
Letters Rogatory Process

LEGAL RESOURCES INDEX or CURRENT LAW INDEX

Civil procedure--International....
Discovery--Law
Federal Rules of Civil Procedure--
abbreviation and rule number
Hague Convention on the....
Judicial Assistance--International
Jurisdiction--International Law
Process--International....
Restatement of the....
Venue--International Aspects

INDEX TO LEGAL PERIODICALS

Enforcement of Judgments abroad
Extraterritoriality
International Judicial Assistance
Jurisdiction
Process

FORUM SHOPPING AND OTHER REFLECTIONS ON LITIGATION INVOLVING U.S. AND EUROPEAN BUSINESSES

Donald C. Dowling, Jr.
Graydon, Head and Ritchey

I. Introduction: International Litigation And International Business Transactions

When U.S. lawyers say they practice "international law," they usually mean "international transactional law." These lawyers help set up international deals. But just as domestic business deals give rise to disputes that wind up in litigation, international business deals which go sour often find their way into tribunals, like courts, and the arbitration process. A key part of international law practice is, therefore, resolving international disputes.

U.S. lawyers -- more so then their European counterparts -- draw a sharp distinction between transactional and litigation practice. However, an understanding of international business dispute resolution is essential for structuring successful international deals: You cannot set up a deal properly if you do not plan for what will happen if the deal goes bad.

In fact, sometimes dispute issues are central elements to an international deal. I recently worked with a U.S.-based company which had developed a cutting-edge technology unavailable outside the U.S. The client, which did not have a European presence, was talking with an Italian counterpart which enjoyed a major European market share. The Italian concern wanted to license the innovative U.S. technology and distribute the resulting products throughout Europe. The relationship had the makings of a classic "win-win" scenario: each party had something the other wanted. The sticking point was enforcement, how to avoid disputes over compliance. The U.S. company had a hard time proposing a workable royalty licensing arrangement, because all the sales information would be in the hands of the Italian company -- an arms-length competitor on the other side of the Atlantic. The Americans were reluctant to disclose valuable trade secrets to a foreign competitor which would be in a position to exploit the information for its own gain. While the deal at first appeared simple, it ended up being virtually unworkable because the specter of disputes loomed too large. The deal's weakness was the unavailability of a viable dispute resolution mechanism.

This illustrates why even transactional lawyers representing U.S. companies with international business interests need to be able to spot and address international dispute resolution issues. This paper will attempt to flush out those issues, raising them in their broadest possible context and illustrating them with examples from and reflections on my own experience. This is a practice-oriented discussion which has as its goal the examination of the link between dispute resolution procedures and U.S. businesses' transactions with Europe.[65]

II. Initial Considerations: Forum Selection, Arbitration Clauses, And The Differences Between U.S. And European Court Procedures

When businesses in two different countries have a dispute which leads to litigation, the first and probably most important issue is forum selection, or "forum shopping." ("Forum selection" and "forum shopping" address the same thing; the difference is who is speaking. The party choosing the forum is engaged in "forum selection," while the party dragged into a forum against its will accuses its adversary of "forum shopping.") Because international business disputes often center on contracts, the primary issue governing international forum selection is the text of the parties' contract. The secondary issue is the geographical location of the party which files the litigation, and the location of its law firm.

---

65 This paper offers a "hypothesis-forming," as opposed to "hypothesis-testing," treatment of international litigation issues. *See* Walter O. Weyrauch, *The Personality of Lawyers* 4-5 (1964); *see also* generally Donald C. Dowling, Jr., "General Propositions and Concrete Cases: The Search for a Standard in the Conflict Between Individual Property Rights and the Social Interest," 1 *J. Land Use & Environmental Law* 353, 357 n. 30 (1985). Only a book-length treatment could possibly flesh out the legal principles behind all the international litigation issues discussed here. Currently, the two leading treatises attempting to do this by addressing the law of international litigation in U.S. courts are Gary B. Born & David Westin, *International Civil Litigation in United States Courts, Commentary and Materials* (2d ed. 1992) and David Epstein & Jeffrey L. Snyder, *International Litigation: A Guide to Jurisdiction, Practice and Strategy* (2d ed. 1994).

A. Contractual Forum Selection Provisions

Structuring a forum selection clause in an international contract is perhaps the most important example of how international litigation issues fit into international transactional practice. The transaction lawyer who negotiated an original contract and its forum selection clause often has a greater impact on the outcome of an after-arising dispute than does the litigation attorney who ends up handling the case.[66]

The drafter of a forum selection clause must distinguish choice of *law* from choice of *forum location*, and must distinguish both of these from choice of forum *type*. Choice of law is simply the choice of which legal system will govern the contract. Usually this is the legal system of a country the parties designate,[67] but this can also be a legal system the parties designate which otherwise would not bind either of them. For example, parties from countries not signatory to the U.N. Convention on Contracts for the International Sale of Goods might nevertheless incorporate that Convention as a term in their contracts.[68]

Choice of forum location is an issue entirely separate from choice of law -- although it is surprising how often contract drafters inadvertently truncate these two issues and designate one without

---

66 *See*, e.g., Interamerican Trade Corp. v. Companhia Fabricadora de Pecas, 973 F.2d 487 (6th Cir. 1992) (enforcing contractual selection of Brazilian forum); Riley v. Kingsley Underwriting Agencies, LTD, 969 F.2d 953 (10th Cir. 1992) (enforcing contractual selection of British forum), *cert. den.* 113 S. Ct. 658 (1992). *See generally* Michael F. Solimine, "Forum Selection Clauses and the Privatization of Procedure," 25 *Cornell Int'l L.J.* 51 (1992). *See also generally* discussion *infra* at § V.

67 On occasion, resolving international disputes pursuant to an arbitration clause can involve applying the law of more than one legal system. *Cf.* Craig M. Gertz, Comment, "The Selection of Choice of Law Provisions in International Commercial Arbitration: A Case for Contractual *Depeçage*, 12 *Nw. J. Int'l L. & Bus.* 163 (1991).

68 U.N. Convention on Contracts for the International Sale of Goods, Apr. 11, 1980, U.N. Doc. A/Conf. 97/18, 19 I.L.M. 668, 671 (1980) (also available in *Martindale-Hubbell International Law Digest*, Part VII, 29). This Convention is a treaty which has 34 signatory countries (including the U.S. and European Union [EU] member states Denmark, France, Germany, Italy, the Netherlands, and Spain), but parties in non-signatory states can invoke the Convention by incorporation as a term in a contract.

mentioning the other. Often as a means of compromise parties which do distinguish these will stipulate that one party's national law apply to a contract while the other party's national courts will serve as the site for litigation arising out of the deal.[69]

The third issue related to choice of law and choice of forum location is choice of forum *type*. At its most basic, this is the question of "to arbitrate or to litigate?."[70] Deciding between arbitration and litigation depends on many factors, including a party's assessment at the transaction stage [71] of who is most likely to initiate proceedings in the event of a dispute, how trustworthy are the courts in the respective parties' jurisdictions, and how enforceable a court award would be against the other side.

One common justification for arbitration -- speed and cost-savings -- is in today's environment largely illusory. The reality of scheduling international arbitrations, especially those with panels of three arbitrators, can lead to delays similar to those inherent in court proceedings. Also, complex business arbitrations involving U.S. parties can be as expensive as court proceedings. I was recently involved in an international business arbitration in which the hearing ended up lasting more than a month, and in which the pre-hearing discovery proceedings had been more elaborate than those in most international-context court lawsuits. One of my

---

69 Courts around the world generally respect contracting parties' right to stipulate that the law of a non-forum country will apply to a dispute within the forum. *See, e.g.*, citations *supra* at note 2. Usually courts require only that the country chosen for its governing law have some rational connection to the deal. Thus, if a U.S. company and a Spanish company enter a joint venture to be performed in Germany, the parties' contract could safely designate the laws of the U.S., Spain, or Germany. If, however, the parties decided to invoke Nigerian law, their selection likely would not stand up if challenged later in a court with a more logical connection to the deal.

70 Actually this is an oversimplification, because alternative dispute resolution clauses often contain other options, including forms of mediation. Usually, however, the *final* dispute resolution step will be arbitration. *Cf.* Steven C. Nelson, "Alternatives to Litigation of International Disputes," 23 *Int'l Law.* 187 (1989) (article discussing international dispute resolution "alternatives" devotes 11 pages (193-203) to arbitration and less than 3 pages (204-06) to all other "alternatives").

71 Theoretically, after a dispute arises the parties can jointly opt for arbitration, even if no arbitration clause had been worked into the contract at the transaction stage. In practice, however, this almost never happens.

partners spent two weeks flying all over the Far East taking depositions in a trip that ended up covering more ground than Marco Polo's.

Yet international arbitration has two important advantages which keep it at the forefront of dispute resolution options in international deals. The first is neutrality. Arbitration is a natural middle ground: A foreign adversary's local courts usually appear biased, and your country's courts usually appear just as biased to your adversary. International arbitration associations, on the other hand, generally do not play favorites. Parties to a deal can also select both a site and a language for an arbitration proceeding which favors neither side.

Perhaps most important, arbitrations are -- believe it or not -- more readily enforceable abroad than court awards, at least among the 83 countries which have signed the New York Convention.[72] As a practical matter, a U.S. party which gets a judgment in a U.S. *court* against a European defendant which does not have sufficient assets in the U.S. will end up re-litigating in a European court, to get the Europeans to enforce the judgment against the defendants' European assets. Enforcing an arbitration award within a New York Convention country, on the other hand, is much simpler.[73]

B. Location of the Party Bringing the Dispute to the Forum, and Location of its Law Firm

If no underlying contract unequivocally designates the forum before which the international dispute must be brought, the most important factor governing choice of forum becomes the geographical location of the party filing the action, and the location

---

72 1958 New York Convention on the Recognition and Enforcement of Foreign Arbitral Awards, June 10, 1958, 21 U.S.T. 2517, T.I.A.S. No. 6999, 330 U.N.T.S. 38, 9 U.S.C. § 201 (the 83 signatory countries include the U.S. and all European Union [EU] states except Portugal); David Rivkin, "International Arbitration," in *Commercial Arbitration for the 1990's* 123, 124 (Richard J. Medalie, ed., 1991) ("international arbitration awards are easier to enforce than foreign court judgments"); cf. Ramona Martinez, "Recognition and Enforcement of International Arbitral Awards Under the U.N. Convention of 1958: The 'Refusal' Provisions," 24 *Int'l Law.* 487 (1990).

73 In fact, New York Convention arbitrations circumvent most of the problems discussed in the rest of this paper.

of its law firm. This issue can start a "race to the courthouse" in those disputes where each party can articulate some claim against the other.

When the claimant bringing the dispute is based in the U.S. and has U.S. counsel, that party almost always favors U.S. courts. The chief reason is the fabled "home court advantage." [74] Although statistics are hard to come by, experience -- both personal and by reading enough reported case decisions -- shows that judges in every country do indeed tend to favor local parties over foreigners. "Home court advantage" is, therefore, a legitimate factor to consider when selecting a forum.

However, this factor should not overwhelm the other issues in play -- especially when a U.S.-based company has a substantial presence in the adversary's forum, and is to that extent effectively local. There is a huge Toyota plant in the small Kentucky town of Georgetown, and Procter & Gamble has extensive operations near Brussels, Belgium. Neither Japan's Toyota nor U.S. Procter & Gamble would have to worry about getting "home-towned" in, respectively, Kentucky or Brussels courts. Additionally, a neutral court forum is available whenever parties from two countries are doing business in a third country.

A key choice of law factor is the applicable legal systems' substantive laws governing the actual dispute. Too often U.S. parties and their lawyers reflexively decide that U.S. law is inherently better for U.S. clients. But conceptually, every time U.S. law differs from a foreign doctrine, there is a 50% chance that the foreign rule will be better for the U.S. client (legal rules almost always exist in isolation from party nationality). An informed choice of law decision is therefore impossible before researching both legal systems's applicable rules. A knee-jerk preference for U.S. law can be a real disservice to clients. [75]

---

[74] Another important reason U.S. claimants favor U.S. courts is the higher amount of damages frequently available. However, this is not as significant a factor in breach of contract litigation (like so many business disputes), because U.S. courts more strictly limit breach of contract damages than damages under other legal theories.

[75] U.S. businesses' (and lawyers') knee-jerk-like preference for a U.S. forum can lead to illogical results. I once saw a draft of a form employment contract

Additionally, having the home court advantage and even winning a judgment are meaningless if the judgment will not be enforceable against the defendant's assets. Too often U.S. parties and their lawyers maneuver for a U.S. court forum even when a U.S. judgment will ultimately prove worthless. I know a U.S.-born and -trained lawyer acting as a legal consultant in Salzburg, Austria who limits his consulting practice to helping enforce U.S. judgments throughout Europe. This consultant laments that he has seen too many cases where U.S. clients' lawyers had treated cases in U.S. courts against solvent European defendants just like domestic cases -- they focused on proving liability and damages, but effectively ignored the international litigation issues of transnational service of process, personal jurisdiction, and enforcement of judgments abroad -- until it was too late. U.S. parties and their lawyers often expend substantial time and resources -- and sometimes even win multimillion dollar verdicts -- but end up recovering nothing, because the defendant's foreign assets prove unreachable. The lesson is that while having the "home court advantage" can indeed be important, a claimant's lawyer should not let it lure the client away from its real ultimate goal -- collecting a judgment.

---

between a U.S.-based company with a U.K. office and its U.K.-citizen employees working in the U.K. The draft, which contained non-compete provisions, called for U.S. law and courts to adjudicate all disputes. But U.K. employment law (like that of most countries, including the U.S.) cannot be opted out of; this contract was therefore unenforceable, because key terms of the parties' relationship -- such as minimum wage, workplace safety, collective bargaining, sick leave, maternity pay, and severance pay -- were necessarily governed by U.K. law. Further, designating a U.S. forum often makes little sense when the other party has no ties to, assets in, nor reason to travel to the U.S. The employer in this scenario might have rather easily convinced a U.S. court to award a default judgment after a litigated dispute arose, such as for breach of the non-competition clause, and the employee failed to show up in the stateside court. But getting a U.K. court to *enforce* the default judgment would be another matter entirely. And a non-competition or non-solicitation injunction from a U.S. court would be toothless if an ex-employee were competing overseas. Also, if a U.K. ex-employee sued on an employment theory in a U.K. tribunal, the British forum would almost certainly retain jurisdiction -- even notwithstanding the choice-of-U.S.-forum clause.

C. Discovery - a Critical Difference Between U.S. and Foreign Procedure

A vast gulf separates U.S. pretrial procedures from those of the rest of the world. Ironically, while U.S. business people often complain about the expense of domestic U.S. litigation, once an international dispute actually arises, these same executives often feel more comfortable in U.S. courts precisely because they offer more elaborate pre-trial discovery procedures. [76] Yet this same issue (the availability of broad U.S. discovery) gives rise to European businesses' healthy aversion to U.S. courts.

When facing a forum selection decision -- particularly one in which you feel tempted to undo a European claimant's choice of a European forum -- try the exercise of looking at the litigation process from the European viewpoint. According to one French-born- and -licensed lawyer who is also admitted to practice in the U.S.:

- U.S.-style procedural rules, the absence of which U.S. litigants tend to criticize in European courts, are precisely those considered to be the most outrageous by European litigants in U.S. courts; and

- Europeans are wary of U.S. jury trials because of the wide discrepancies in awards between [European] Community and U.S. jurisdictions. In civil law countries, juries do not participate in civil or commercial matters.[77]

---

[76] A vivid example of this thinking is the surprising 1993 ruling from highly-respected U.S. Seventh Circuit Court of Appeals judge Richard Posner in Allendale Mut. Ins. Co. v. Bull Data Systems, Inc. 10 F.3d 425, 430 (7th Cir. 1993), *later proc.* 32 F.3d 1175 (1994). This opinion allows litigation over a French warehouse fire to proceed in a U.S. court, notwithstanding the intrinsically French nature of the dispute, because "[it does not] appear that the Commercial Court of Lille [France] is equipped to resolve a massive document case."

[77] Patrick Thieffry, "European Integration in Transnational Litigation," 13 *B.C. Int'l & Comp. L. Rev.* 339, 356-57 (1990). The point here is that a U.S. defendant to European court litigation should think hard before urging to a European tribunal that U.S. courts are more appropriate. This is particularly true when the claimant's ties to the particular European forum at issue are not substantially stronger than the U.S. defendant's.

III. International Litigation In U.S. Courts, From Service Of Process Through Enforcement Of Judgment

Notwithstanding all the foregoing, quite often U.S. parties to international deals end up litigating international disputes in U.S. courts. While many aspects of these cases are identical to domestic business litigation, certain key procedural issues take on special importance in the international context – particularly service or process, personal jurisdiction, discovery, and enforcement of foreign judgments.

A. Service of Process

Domestically, service of process is usually a relatively simple issue which paralegals and court personnel can handle without the need for attention from lawyers. In international-context litigation, however, service of process is far more complex, because service of process on a foreign defendant involves sovereignty and international diplomacy. By effecting service abroad, the forum country is taking an act with legal effect inside the recipient country's national borders. Service of U.S. process on European parties, therefore, requires special attention.

I recently worked on a case in which our client was an English defendant sued in a Tennessee federal court. A solid argument existed that the service of process was technically improper, so we challenged it. But our Tennessee local counsel asked several times why we were expending so much legal time, effort, and expense on a service of process issue likely to be resolved against us. Indeed, because domestic service of process deficiencies are usually curable, domestic service technicalities often are not worth expensive collateral litigation. But the analysis is quite different in the foreign context: many U.S. judgments against foreign defendants have been rendered unenforceable due to service of process defects established in foreign courts at the enforcement stage. Defendants who neglect to preserve their service challenges at the outset can later be held to have waived these potentially-dispositive defenses.

The first question regarding how to perfect service of process abroad is whether the defendant's country is one of the 30 signatories to the Hague Service Convention [78] (the U.S. and all European Union

---

[78] The Convention on Service of Process of Judicial and Extrajudicial Documents

member states except Ireland are). Each Hague Service Convention country designates a "Central Authority" through which a party from abroad seeking service must transmit judicial documents. The country's Central Authority then itself takes care of service. This circumvents the diplomatic breach-of-sovereignty concern; under the Hague Service Convention, defendant countries' own officials serve process, after finding out what a foreign lawsuit is all about.[79]

However, while the Convention is theoretically "mandatory" in signatory countries,[80] there exist certain procedures which effectively streamline the Convention and allow a few simplified service routes entirely short-circuiting the Central Authority.[81]

---

in Civil and Commercial Matters, 1965, 20 U.S.T. 361, T.I.A.S. No. 6638, 658 U.N.T.S. 163. As to foreign service of U.S. process, see Fed. R. Civ. P. 4(f). *See generally Hague Conference on Private International Law, Practical Handbook on the Operation of the Hague Convention of 15 November 1965 on the Service Abroad of Judicial and Extrajudicial Documents in Civil or Commercial Matters* (1992); Kenneth B. Reisenfeld, "Service of U.S. Process Abroad: A Practical Guide to Service Under the Hague Service Convention and the Federal Rules of Civil Procedure," 24 *Int'l Law.* 55 (1990).

79 A country's authorities can and sometimes do reject service of a foreign complaint which violates internal public policy. In the context of Western Europe, this is especially a concern with Switzerland, which, due to differences between Swiss and U.S. policy, with some regularity rejects U.S. court complaints. *See, e.g.,* U.S. Department of State, "Judicial Assistance in Switzerland" (unpublished paper available from Department of State at (202) 647-6445).

80 Volkswagenwerk A.G. v. Schlunk, 486 U.S. 694, 699 (1988).

81 One such shortcut is international service of process by mail. Some Hague countries (for example Canada and Pakistan) expressly allow international mail service, via statements in their accessions to the convention itself. Others (for example Germany and the Czech Republic) expressly forbid it. An argument exists that the Convention's § 10(a) authorizes mail service in the rest of the signatory countries. Cf. Note, "International Service of Process by Mail Under the Hague Service Convention," 13 Mich. J. Int'l L. 698 (1992). Other such shortcuts exist due to various Hague signatories' pronouncements allowing service which does not conform to the letter of the Convention. For example, although the texts of the Convention and its accession statements do not say so, the United Kingdom allows "any person in another Contracting State [to effect] service 'directly' [in the U.K.] through a competent person other than a judicial officer or official, e.g. a solicitor." Letter from W. Jones (U.K. Nationality and Treaty Dep't) to J.H.A. van Loon (Permanent Bureau, Hague Conference on Private International Law) (Sept. 11, 1980).

Service of process in countries which have not ratified the Hague Service Convention requires research into these countries' specific national laws. The usual procedure is to serve "letters rogatory," which in this context means a formal request for service to the proper foreign official. This procedure (which, for example, must be followed in Switzerland) can take a lot of time and be quite frustrating, as when foreign functionaries reject requests due to technical or *de minimus* violations. The U.S. State Department is helpful in researching foreign service matters; it publishes detailed papers on specific topics like "Judicial Assistance in Switzerland."[82]

B. Personal Jurisdiction

Personal jurisdiction in international-context litigation, like service of process, usually requires more attention than it does in domestic lawsuits. Traditionally, under U.S. law the legal analysis was effectively the same in both types of case: In order for an American court to be able to exercise jurisdiction, the defendant had to have sufficient "minimum contacts" with the forum U.S. state consistent with the state's "long-arm" statute and with the "due process" clause of the U.S. Constitution. Because U.S. federal courts adopt the service of process law of the state in which they sit, even in U.S. federal court lawsuits the issue traditionally came down to assessing a foreign defendants' contacts with the particular U.S. forum state (except in actions under those few federal statutes which have national service of process provisions and therefore apply a "national minimum contacts" test to overseas defendants).

For example, if a U.S.-based plaintiff sued a French defendant in Oklahoma federal or state court, the personal jurisdiction analysis would focus on whether the French entity had sufficient "minimum contacts" with Oklahoma. The French defendants' contacts with all the other U.S. states and territories would, for the most part, have been irrelevant. Frustrations arose when a foreign defendant had substantial contacts with the U.S. as a whole, but when these contacts were sufficiently spread out so that no one state or territory had enough "minimum contacts" to assert personal

---

[82] The State Department will assist researchers over the telephone at (202) 647-3445, and will provide copies of these unpublished papers on request. On letters rogatory generally, see 28 U.S.C. § 1781 (1994).

jurisdiction under the Constitution or under any applicable "long arm" statute.

Some argued that a "U.S. national contacts" analysis should apply against foreign parties, at least in federal court proceedings. But the authoritative case law never went this far. In fact, the U.S. Supreme Court implied that when a defendant is foreign, U.S. plaintiffs should have to prove *greater* "minimum contacts" with the forum state than in a domestic proceeding.[83]

This "traditional" analysis still applies in state court cases and in federal court diversity lawsuits. But as of very recently -- effective since December 1, 1993 -- the Federal Rules of Civil Procedure have allowed that, as to "claims arising under federal law," personal jurisdiction exists over any foreign defendant who is properly served, as long as "the exercise of jurisdiction is consistent with the Constitution and laws of the United States..."[84] This effectively creates a "U.S. national contacts" test extending personal jurisdiction as far as the Constitution allows.

C. Discovery

Once a plaintiff establishes service of process and personal jurisdiction in a U.S. court, the focus turns to discovery, the process by which each side has to show its opponent most of the cards in its hand. The U.S. practice of broad pre-trial discovery including depositions, physical examinations, site inspections, document production, and interrogatories [85] is virtually unknown in the rest of the world. Even in common-law England (from which the U.S. derives its legal system) pre-trial discovery is extremely limited and depositions are rare. In fact, there are only a handful of court

---

[83] Asahi Metal Ind. v. Sup. Ct. Calif., 480 U.S. 102, 114 (1987) ("The unique burdens placed upon one who must defend oneself in a foreign legal system should have significant weight in assessing the reasonableness of stretching the long arm of [U.S.] personal jurisdiction over national borders."). *But cf.* S&S Screw Machine Co. v. Cosa Corp., 647 F. Supp. 600 (M.D. Tenn. 1986); McCombs v. Cerco Rentals, 622 S.W. 2d 822 (Tenn. Ct. App. 1981).

[84] *Fed. R. Civ. P.* 4(k)(2). Service must be consistent with the qualifications set out in *Fed. R. Civ. P.* 4(k)(1).

[85] *See Fed. R. Civ. P.* 27-36.

reporters in London, and these stenographers subsist chiefly on work for U.S. lawyers deposing British witnesses for U.S. lawsuits.

In civil law countries (including those of Continental Europe), discovery is far more limited than in the U.S. Rather than exchange documents and take each others' depositions, in Continental Europe parties submit briefs explaining their cases and attaching all of the key documents. In Europe, judges, not lawyers, are fact-finders, and documents are more important in trial than is oral testimony.

When a party to a U.S. lawsuit must take evidence abroad, an initial inquiry is whether the foreign country is a signatory to the Hague *Evidence* Convention.[86] More than 20 countries (including the U.S.) have signed on to the Hague Evidence Convention, but three European Union member states -- Belgium, Ireland, and Greece -- have not.

The Hague *Evidence* Convention, like the Hague *Service* Convention, funnels requests for judicial assistance through a national "Central Authority" which each signatory country has designated.[87] For obtaining discovery in non-Hague Evidence Convention Countries, research into local law is especially important.[88] In some countries, including Switzerland, taking a

---

86 Convention on Taking Evidence Abroad in Civil and Commercial Matters, Mar. 18, 1970, 23 U.S.T. 2555, T.I.A.S. No. 7444, 847 U.N.T.S. 231. For comment on this Convention, see, e.g., Darrell Prescott & Edwin Alley, "Effective Evidence-Taking Under the Hague Convention," 22 *Int'l Law.* 939 (1988).

87 However, the Hague Evidence Convention is not mandatory, so parties can take discovery through other routes. *See* Société Nationale Industrielle Aérospatiale v. U.S. Dist. Court, for the Southern Dist. of Iowa, 482 U.S. 522 (1987); Gary Born & Scott Hoing, "Comity and the Lower Courts: Post-*Aérospatiale* Applications of the Hague Evidence Convention, 24 *Int'l Law.* 393 (1990); Joseph Griffin & Mark Bravin, "Beyond *Aérospatile:* A Commentary on Foreign Discovery Provisions of the Restatement (Third) and the Proposed Amendments to the Federal Rules of Civil Procedure," 25 *Int'l Law.* 331 (1991). *See generally Fed. R. Civ. P.* 28(b) (depositions in foreign countries); 28 U.S.C. § 1781 (1994) (letters rogatory); 28 U.S.C. §1783 (1994) (subpoena of person in foreign country).

88 Here again the U.S. State Department can be an invaluable research source, via its series of relevant papers, including "Obtaining Evidence Abroad," "Hague Convention on the Taking of Evidence Abroad in Civil or Commercial Matters," and country-specific reports such as "Judicial Assistance in

deposition is a criminal act, because it threatens national sovereignty by forcing a domestic citizen to appear and testify on penalty of a foreign country's perjury laws. There are stories of lawyers who, ignorant of this, found themselves lead out of deposition conference rooms in handcuffs![89]

The reciprocal issue, getting discovery in the U.S. for European court proceedings, is seldom problematic. A U.S. statute offers broad assistance.[90] Since U.S. discovery is broader than discovery in Europe, U.S. courts usually find their foreign counterparts' information requests reasonable.

D. Recognition and Enforcement of Foreign Judgments

Before suing a party who resides abroad, a claimant must consider the location of the defendants' assets and craft an appropriate strategy. Many foreign-based corporations have sufficient assets in the U.S. to render collection abroad a non-issue. But when investigation reveals that a defendants' assets are or can be moved abroad, the plaintiffs' litigation strategy from the outset must account for the inevitability of having to enforce abroad any successful U.S. judgment.[91] When arbitration is not an option, often the enforcement factor will militate strongly toward suing abroad, on the *defendant's* home turf. The benefits of "home court advantage" and enhanced remedies available in U.S. litigation such as treble and punitive damages are illusory if the defendants' jurisdiction will not enforce U.S. judgments with these types of

---

Switzerland" -- and through its telephone assistance. *See supra* notes 79, 82.

89 *See supra* discussion at § III(A), p. 49. Note that because discovery is so radically different in foreign countries, even when a party to a U.S. lawsuit is entitled to take evidence abroad (through the Hague Evidence Convention or through letters rogatory), the foreign authorities may well impose conditions which are, by U.S. standards, bizarre. For example, a foreign magistrate, not a U.S. lawyer, may do the questioning, and the magistrate may summarize testimony in a report, rather than allow a verbatim transcript.

90 28 U.S.C. § 1782 (1994).

91 *See generally* Werner Ebke & Mary Parker, "Foreign Country Money-Judgments and Arbitral Awards and the Restatement (Third) of Foreign Relations Law of the U.S.: A Conventional Approach," 24 *Int'l Law*. 21 (1990).

damages -- as for example is the case in Switzerland and, often, Germany.[92]

A claimant who must enforce a judgment abroad has to win twice -- once in the U.S. court and once in collateral enforcement litigation on the defendant's home turf. On occasion a foreign defendant will even craft a strategy to U.S. litigation which relies on its winning at home at the enforcement level. In one U.S. federal court lawsuit a Swiss company which manufactures a consumer product well-known in the U.S. found itself sued stateside by its American distributor. The Swiss lawyers determined that their company would not be held subject to U.S. jurisdiction, at least under *Swiss law* principles. However, under U.S. law a U.S. court was very likely to (and ultimately did) exercise personal jurisdiction. Because its assets were all in Europe, the Swiss company decided to challenge jurisdiction and service of process in the U.S. federal court; after losing that challenge it planned simply to stop defending the case. The theory was that a U.S. default judgment would be worthless if the plaintiff could not get it enforced in Switzerland. The Swiss lawyers were that confident that a Swiss court would indeed re-open the jurisdiction issue (given that the company had preserved the point by challenging jurisdiction in the U.S. proceeding)[93] and would ultimately decide, under Swiss law, that no U.S. jurisdiction had existed.

The reciprocal enforcement-of-judgment issue is the question of how to enforce a European-rendered judgment in the U.S. against an American defendant whose assets are stateside.

---

92 *See* Martin Bernet & Nicholas Ulmer, "Recognition and Enforcement of Foreign Civil Judgments in Switzerland," 27 *Int'l Law*. 317, 326-29 (1993); Hartwin Bungert, "Enforcing U.S. Excessive and Punitive Damages Awards in Germany," 27 *Int'l Law*. 1075 (1993). For a collection of sources on the recognition and enforcement of U.S. judgments outside the U.S., see Robert Lutz, "Enforcement of Foreign Judgments, Part II: A Selected Bibliography on Enforcement of U.S. Judgments in Foreign Countries," 27 *Int'l Law*. 1029 (1993). *See also generally International Execution Against Judgment Debtors* (Dennis Campbell, ed., 1994); *International Recognition and Enforcement of Money Judgments* (Gregory Paley, ed., 1994).

93 A defendant who "objects to jurisdiction" in a proceeding outside of Switzerland "will not, under Swiss principles, be deemed to have submitted to foreign jurisdiction." Martin Bernet & Nicholas Ulmer, *supra* note 92, at 323.

When a European court has rendered such a judgment, the applicable law governing enforcement is the law of the U.S. state in which the defendant holds assets.[94] Many U.S. states have adopted the "Uniform Foreign Money-Judgments Recognition Act,"[95] a model act which seeks to bring all U.S. states' laws into conformity with prevailing internationally-accepted enforcement principles. The Uniform Act contains exceptions rendering judgments unenforceable when they violate a U.S. state's public policy, and when they were obtained by fraud. Also, a reciprocity provision in the Act requires that the country from which the judgment comes similarly respect U.S. judgments. Service of process is another key issue under the Uniform Act -- a U.S. defendant who was not properly served in the foreign action can escape enforcement in the U.S.[96]

IV. Forum Selection Within Europe

When a U.S. party finds itself in a dispute with a European, the initial forum selection issue is usually "U.S. versus Europe." When U.S. courts win out, the question turns to which U.S. court to select -- state or federal, and in which state. When the European forum wins out, forum analysis can turn to the issue of which European court and country to select.

Each European Union [EU] member state[97] has its own unique court system, over which exists the European Community Court of

---

94 For a collection of sources on the recognition and enforcement in the U.S. of foreign country judgments, see Robert E. Lutz, "Enforcement of Foreign Judgments, Part I: A Selected Bibliography on U.S. Enforcement of Judgments Rendered Abroad," 27 *Int'l Law.* 471 (1993).

95 13 U.L.A. 261 (1962), *codified at, for e.g.*, Ohio Revised Code §§ 2329.90-.94 (1994). See Alan Sorkowitz, "Enforcing Judgments Under the Uniform Foreign Money-Judgments Recognition Act," 37 Prac. Law. 57 (July 1991).

96 *See generally* Ronald Brand, "Enforcement of Foreign Money-Judgments in the U.S.: In Search of Uniformity and International Acceptance," 67 *Notre Dame L. Rev.* 253 (1991).

97 The European Union (which is for most practical purposes synonymous with the older terms "European Community" and "European Common Market") is a unique, often-amended treaty which superimposes a quasi-federalist governmental structure over the legal systems of its signatory "member states." For overviews of the EU structure, see, e.g., Lucie A. Carswell & Xavier De Sarrao, *Law & Business in the European Single Market*, chaps. 1-3 (1993); Desmond Dinan, *Ever Closer Union? An Introduction to the European*

Justice (based in Luxembourg) and the European Community Court of First Instance.[98] Certain other disputes also get heard by the European Community Commission, an administrative body. But these European tribunals only adjudicate some matters of EU law (much EU law gets adjudicated in the member state courts under the "direct effect" doctrine). The vast majority of disputes between U.S. and European business never make their way before these three EU tribunals.

A unique treaty called the Brussels Convention[99] controls questions of jurisdiction among the courts of the EU member states. If you win a lawsuit in Denmark against a Greek defendant, it is the Brussels Convention which will allow you to execute on your judgment in Greece. The *raison d'être* of the European Union is to encourage the free movement of goods, services, and capital among the member states. The idea behind the Brussels Convention is the

---

Community, chaps. 7-10 (1994); *European Community Law After 1992: A Practical Guide for Lawyers Outside the Common Market*, chaps. 1, 23 (Ralph Folsom, Ralph Lake, & Ved Nanda, eds., 1993); and Jean Thieffry, Philip Van Doorn & Simon Lowe, "The Single European Market: A Practitioner's Guide to 1992," 12 *B.C. Int'l Comp & L. Rev.* 357 (1989). This author has written about other aspects of EU law in Donald C. Dowling, Jr., "Employment Matters and the Social Charter," *chapter 19 in European Community Law After 1992* (Folsom, Lake & Nanda, eds., 1993); Nancy E. Honig & Donald C. Dowling, Jr., "How to Handle Employment Issues in European Deals," 13 *Preventive L. Rep.* 3 (Spring 1994); Donald C. Dowling, Jr., "EC Employment Law After Maastricht: Continental Social Europe?," 27 *Int'l Law.* 1 (1993) *reprinted as chapter 16.1 in European Economic Community Law* (W. Hancock, ed., 1994); Donald C. Dowling, Jr., "How Does Europe Regulate Power Within Its Corporations?," 12 *Nw. J. Int'l L. & Bus.* 601 (1992) (book review); Donald C. Dowling, Jr., "L'Europa Sociale: Il Punto di Vista delle Imprese Multinazionali USA," 25-26 *Industria e Sindacato* 16 (1991) (Rome); Donald C. Dowling, Jr., "Worker Rights in the Post-1992 EC: What 'Social Europe' Means to U.S.-Based Multinational Employers," 11 *Nw. J. Int'l L. & Bus.* 564 (1991), *reprinted as chapter 16 in European Economic Community Law* (W. Hancock, ed., 1992).

98 For a non-technical discussion of how the two European Union courts allocate jurisdiction between themselves and with the member states' courts, see, e.g., Desmond Dinan, *supra* note 33, at 295-310.

99 Convention on Jurisdiction and Enforcement of Judgments in Civil and Commercial Matters, [hereinafter Brussels Convention]. Sept 27, 1968, 1262 U.N.T.S. 153 (including 1971 protocol), *text as amended by* the 1978 Accession Convention (Denmark, Ireland, United Kingdom), the 1982 Accession Convention (Greece) and the 1989 Accession Convention (Spain, Portugal), 1990 O.J. (C189) 2, *reprinted in* 29 I.L.M. 1413 (1990).

concomitant goal of encouraging the free movement of *judgments*.[100]

Technically the Brussels Convention is not an EU instrument; it is an entirely separate international treaty which exists as a parallel universe to the EU treaties themselves. But all the EU member states ratified the Brussels Convention, and it is adjudicated by the EU's Court of Justice.[101]

The Brussels Convention's Article 26 says "a judgment given in a Contracting State shall be recognized in the other Contracting States without any special procedure being required."[102] However, even inter-EU judgments will not be respected if they are contrary to public policy in the enforcing state, if there was a service of process problem and a default judgment was entered, or if the judgment is irreconcilable with a prior judgment.[103]

V. Conclusion: Procedural Dispute Resolution Issues Often Have Critical Substantive Effect

In order effectively to represent a client in an international transaction, those who put deals together need to focus on all the dispute resolution issues which can come into play -- even though the team structuring the deal hopes for future cooperation, not dissention. The best international transactions are structured so

---

[100] Because the Brussels Convention effectively allows free enforcement of judgments among member states, some U.S. litigators have considered seeking enforcement of a U.S. judgment in the friendliest possible EU member state -- say England -- and then invoking the Brussels Convention to enforce that "English" judgment in a less-friendly member state where the defendant has assets -- say Germany, when there is a treble or punitive damage component to the original U.S. award (*see supra* note 92 and accompanying text). The European Court of Justice has not yet spoken on this issue.

[101] A proposed parallel treaty is the Lugano Convention on Jurisdiction and Enforcement of Judgments in Civil and Commercial Matters Between the Member States of the European Communities and of the European Free Trade Association, September 16, 1988, 1988 O.J. (L319) 9, *reprinted in* 28 I.L.M. 620 (1989). This proposal exists to address enforcement of judgments between EU and European Free Trade Agreement [EFTA] member states. However, the Lugano Convention has never been implemented. Now that most EFTA nations are being admitted into the EU, perhaps it never will be.

[102] Brussels Convention, *supra* note 99, at Art. 26.

[103] Brussels Convention, *supra* note 99 at Art 27.

that disputes which pop up later resolve themselves. From the point of view of a transactional lawyer, this resolution should of course be to the client's own advantage.

Not long ago my law firm had the good fortune to be involved in such a case. Our client was a Dutch machine manufacturer which had sold a large piece of equipment to a customer in Washington state. The sale documents had contained a boilerplate clause saying that all disputes would be resolved via arbitration at the Hague -- Holland, a home court advantage for our client. At the time of the transaction the Washington customer, focusing on getting the equipment and not on fighting over it later, said nothing about this forum selection provision. When a dispute did arise, the customer sued in Washington federal court. We immediately raised the boilerplate arbitration clause by motion, moving to dismiss on arbitrability. After a hearing, the court ruled it had to uphold the clause, so it dismissed the case. The U.S. plaintiff, no longer able to play on its home court, gave up -- never filing for a Hague arbitration! Careful attention to dispute resolution up front, at the transaction stage, actually won a litigated dispute which arose later.

International Criminal Law

Joan Fitzpatrick
Professor of Law
University of Washington, Seattle

I. Introduction

Rapid change and complexity characterize the subject of international criminal law. This chapter will first profile the causes of the volatility and growing importance of this area of law. The remainder of the chapter will focus upon methods of cooperation among law enforcement authorities to combat crime with a transnational dimension. The following topics will be addressed: the basic principles of extraterritorial criminal jurisdiction, the influence of crime-defining treaties, the mechanics of international cooperation at the police level, systems of international judicial cooperation, extradition norms and practices, and agreements for prisoner transfer. The norms and institutions for prosecution of war crimes and crimes against humanity will not be discussed.

Crime with a transnational dimension has been a growth industry for some decades, and legal standards and institutions have begun to adapt to this reality. The worldwide challenge posed by drug trafficking has been most influential in stimulating international cooperation in the fight against crime. Given the transnational nature of the drug traffic, states pursuing a "war on drugs" have discovered that enhanced international cooperation in law enforcement techniques is indispensable.

But other factors have also contributed to the rapid evolution of international criminal law. The drug trade generated a striking increase in transnational money laundering, tax evasion and other financial crimes, which are also fueled by growing worldwide economic interdependence and exchange. Criminal enterprises specializing in international traffic in persons, such as alien smuggling and prostitution, have also been recognized as growing social problems requiring international solutions.

A distinct influence attracting government interest in enhanced cooperation to combat transnational crime has been the concern of the past several decades with international terrorism, hijacking and attacks upon diplomats. State security interests have likewise contributed to improvements in techniques of law enforcement across borders to combat espionage and related offenses.

Crime with a transnational dimension is not a phenomenon unique to the late twentieth century, however. Common criminals have long sought to escape justice by fleeing the nation in which their crime was committed. Because of greater proximity and ease in crossing national boundaries, European states launched efforts for international cooperation in law enforcement earlier than the United States, which until recently enjoyed a relative geographic isolation. Developments in international transportation have now progressed to the point where the vast majority of states perceive themselves as having a significant stake in improving mechanisms for international cooperation in fighting crime. The revolution in electronic communications and an accompanying growth in crime committed by electronic means are expected to accelerate this trend.

Recent developments in international criminal law have also been fueled by frustration with the inadequacy of traditional methods of international evidence-gathering. Letters rogatory, a significant device for evidence-gathering in transnational civil litigation, have played a central role in the criminal context. But law enforcement experts regard letters rogatory as excessively slow, cumbersome and unreliable.

One alternative to the letter rogatory is police-level cooperation across borders. This cooperation has escalated dramatically in recent years, characterized by posting of greater numbers of law enforcement agents in foreign countries and the drafting of a number of mutual legal assistance treaties. Transnational police-level action is governed by important sovereignty-based principles, such as the prohibition on exercise of law enforcement authority by foreign police agents without the consent of the territorial state. In the United States this principle is reflected in 18 U.S.C. §951 (1988), which requires that foreign police agents be announced and sponsored and criminalizes the conduct of foreign police failing to receive advance approval.

Letters rogatory suffer from the further defect that they often do not produce evidence in a form admissible in criminal proceedings. For example, civil law courts may not provide a verbatim transcript of witness testimony taken by letter rogatory. In United States courts, this creates constitutional difficulties under the confrontation clause of the Sixth Amendment.

An important political factor stimulating rapid improvements in international cooperation in criminal matters has been the controversy surrounding the issuance of *subpoenas duces tecum* and the use of other coercive discovery methods in criminal investigations and civil suits by United States courts against transnational corporations. While some nations responded aggressively to these discovery measures with blocking statutes and secrecy laws, the tension created between otherwise friendly governments has induced states to seek alternate means to reconcile their differences, particularly mutual legal assistance treaties.

The volatility of international criminal law, created by a combination of the factors described above, poses a challenge for researchers. As summarized by Ethan Nadelmann in *Cops Across Borders* 314-315 (1993):[104]

> The pace of developments in the area of international evidence-gathering is such that any analysis rapidly becomes dated. New treaties and other international agreements are being negotiated by the Justice Department, the Treasury Department, the SEC [Securities and Exchange Commission], and the CFTC [Commodities Futures Trading Commission] each year. New legislation is being enacted by Congress in one session after another. Growing numbers of federal and even state prosecutors are looking and traveling abroad in search of evidence, and the more innovative among them are devising new and increasingly effective means of obtaining that evidence. Federal courts are deciding dozens of relevant cases annually, and generally validating the prosecutors' innovations. New offices charged with responsibility for international law enforcement are popping up throughout the federal law enforcement bureaucracy. Foreign states are similarly enacting new laws and regulations -- sometimes of their own initiative,

---

[104] *Cops Across Borders: The Internationalization of U.S. Criminal Law Enforcement* (University Park, PA.: Pennsylvania State Univerisity Press 1993), at 314-315.

sometimes in response to U.S. examples, actions and pressures -- with great import for U.S. evidence-gathering efforts. And international meetings, conventions, and organizations are introducing resolutions, promoting and adopting model legislation, and otherwise attempting to facilitate international cooperation in the transmission of evidence.

II. Basics of Extraterritorial Jurisdiction

States differ in the extent to which and the premise upon which they seek to criminalize conduct with a transnational dimension. Nevertheless, it is possible to identify five generally recognized bases for criminal jurisdiction: (1) territorial, (2) objective territorial or "effects," (3) nationality, (4) passive personality and (5) universal. Territorial jurisdiction, or jurisdiction exercised by the state in which the criminal conduct took place, is the most widely recognized basis for criminal prosecution. Increasingly important but also controversial is objective territorial or "effects" jurisdiction, exercised by a state that suffers the ill effects of criminal conduct committed in whole or in part within the territory of another state. This principle serves as the basis for prosecution in many high-profile United States criminal cases, such as the drug prosecution of Panamanian General Manuel Noriega. The nationality principle permits prosecution by the state of the criminal suspect's citizenship, regardless of the locale of the crime; this principle is widely recognized in civil law countries but not traditionally in common law jurisdictions. The passive personality principle permits prosecution of crimes committed against nationals of the prosecuting state, regardless of the locale of the crime. Universal jurisdiction permits prosecution by any state in which the offender can be located; traditionally applied to crimes such as piracy, it is of growing importance with respect to certain crimes against humanity.

The United States has been accused of exercising unduly expansive extraterritorial criminal jurisdiction, especially on the basis of the objective territorial or "effects" theory. There are no well-settled constitutional limits on Congress' ability to invoke extraterritorial prescriptive jurisdiction. Various enumerated Congressional powers such as the foreign commerce power, the foreign affairs power and the power to define and punish offenses against the law of nations can easily serve as a constitutional basis for criminalizing conduct with a transnational dimension. However, there are important constitutional limits on adjudicative jurisdiction, derived from the Due Process Clause and mandating proof of minimum contacts and reasonableness.

A key issue in determining whether extraterritorial criminal jurisdiction exists is the interpretation of Congressional intent in adopting the criminal statute in question. All statutes are subject to a presumed intent to conform to international law if at all possible. Whether public international law limits states' ability to define their prescriptive criminal jurisdiction by reliance upon the objective territorial or "effects" principle is a matter of some controversy. In any case, principles of international comity may influence a court to decline the exercise of jurisdiction over extraterritorial acts where the interests of the territorial state outweigh those of the forum state.

Initially, the United States Supreme Court applied a strong presumption against extraterritorial application of regulatory laws in areas such as antitrust. *American Banana Co. v. United Fruit Co,* 213 U.S. 347 (1909). This interpretive presumption began to erode with cases such as *United States v. Aluminum Co. of Am. (Alcoa),* 148 F.2d 416 (2d Cir. 1945). Even where statutes appear to permit jurisdiction under the objective territorial principle, some lower courts adopt an interest balancing approach to determine when international comity should cause the courts to decline that jurisdiction. *Timberlane Lumber Co. v. Bank of America,* 549 F.2d 597 (9th Cir. 1976); *Mannington Mills, Inc. v. Congoleum Corp.,* 595 F.2d 1287 (3d Cir. 1979). The Restatement (Third) Foreign Relations Law of the United States (1987), in its sections 402, 403, 415, and 416, adapts the *Timberlane* factors and supports the interest balancing approach. The Supreme Court's recent decision in *Hartford Fire Insurance Co. v. California, _____U.S._____,* 113 S. Ct. 2891 (1993), 2appears to limit concern with international comity to situations where it is impossible to comply with both the laws of the United States and the laws of the state in whose territory the acts occurred. But where a statute is silent as to its applicability outside the United States, the Supreme Court remains inclined to find that no extraterritorial application was intended by Congress. *Sale v. Haitian Centers Council,* _____U.S._____, 113 S. Ct. 3028 (1993).

An important issue of extraterritoriality in the criminal context is the extent to which constitutional protections for criminal defendants apply outside the United States. In *United States v.*

Verdugo-Urquidez, 494 U.S. 259 (1990), the Supreme Court held that the Fourth Amendment protects only "the People," and thus is inapplicable to foreign searches of aliens' homes by U.S. agents, even where the seized evidence is introduced at trial against the defendant in the United States. Lower courts have found that due process protections are available to aliens subjected abroad to outrageous abuse by U.S. law enforcement agents and may require dismissal of charges. *United States v. Toscanino*, 500 F.2d 267 (2d Cir. 1974). Many scholars have commented critically upon the extension of U.S. criminal jurisdiction to acts committed abroad without coterminous extension of constitutional protections.

III. Crime-Defining Treaties

With respect to the substance of "international criminal law" (leaving aside war crimes and crimes against humanity), the treaty-making process has played an important role in gaining broader recognition of and more effective action against certain types of crimes. In the area of terrorism, the Hague Convention for the Suppression of Unlawful Seizure of Aircraft, Dec. 16, 1970, 22 U.S.T. 1641; the Convention for the Suppression of Unlawful Acts Against the Safety of Civil Aviation, Sept. 23, 1971, 24 U.S.T. 567, 974 U.N.T.S. 177; the Convention on the Prevention and Punishment of Crimes Against Internationally Protected Persons, Including Diplomatic Agents, Dec. 14, 1973, T.I.A.S. No. 8532; and the International Convention Against the Taking of Hostages, Dec. 17, 1979, 18 I.L.M. 1456 (1979), have defined terrorism-related crimes, required states parties to prosecute or extradite and improved international cooperation to detect and punish these offenses. Under the United Nations Convention Against Illicit Traffic in Narcotic Drugs and Psychotropic Substances, Dec. 19, 1988, 28 I.L.M. 493 (1989), states parties must criminalize money laundering.

IV. International Cooperation at the Police Level

Despite sovereignty-based limits on non-consensual law enforcement activities within territory of another state, many opportunities exist for police-level cooperation to combat transnational crime. A central institution facilitating this cooperation is the International Criminal Police Organization (Interpol). Each state participating in Interpol establishes a National Central Bureau to coordinate requests for assistance.

Within the United States, the National Central Bureau is located in the Department of Justice pursuant to 22 U.S.C. §263a (1988).

The rapid recent growth in the degree of international cooperation and assistance among law enforcement agencies is reflected in statistics concerning the number of U.S. law enforcement agents posted abroad. The number of federal narcotics agency personnel located in foreign countries grew from 34 in 1969 to 416 in 1993; the number of FBI foreign liaison posts grew from 11 in 1965 to 20 in 1993.

Police-level international cooperation may take a variety of forms, including: (1) location of fugitives, suspects and witnesses; (2) questioning witnesses; (3) obtaining public records; (4) conducting searches and wiretaps; (5) serving documents upon defendants and witnesses; (6) conducting joint investigations; and (7) transporting witnesses to the requesting state.

V. International Judicial Cooperation

Cooperation between the judiciaries of the United States and foreign countries in criminal matters is affected by important constitutional norms, including the Sixth Amendment confrontation clause (especially in relation to admission of deposition testimony and authentication of documents); the Sixth Amendment compulsory process clause (with respect to defendants' ability to invoke the same mechanisms as the prosecution to secure the testimony of witnesses located in foreign countries); and the Fourth Amendment (especially in the context of serving search warrants in the United States to assist foreign investigations or prosecutions).

A number of important federal statutes provide various avenues for international judicial assistance in criminal matters. These include the provision for letters rogatory in 28 U.S.C. §1781 (1988); the provision for compelled testimony and document production by a U.S. national or resident located abroad pursuant to the Walsh Act, 28 U.S.C. §1783 (1988); rules on the admissibility of foreign official records set forth in 28 U.S.C. §1741 (1988) and Rule 27 (1988), Federal Rules of Criminal Procedure; the rules concerning admissibility of foreign business records, 18 U.S.C. §3505 (1988); provisions for holding depositions before U.S. consular officials, 22 U.S.C. §4221 (1988)and Rule 15(d) (1988), Federal Rules of Criminal

Procedure; the mechanism for appointment of a special master to take a deposition in a foreign country, 18 U.S.C. §3507 (1988); Congress' extension of the statute of limitations and the speedy trial period in cases requiring evidence located in foreign countries, 18 U.S.C. §§3292, 3161(h) (1988); provisions for the transfer to the United States of a witness in foreign custody, 18 U.S.C. §3508 (1988); definition of the role of the Office of International Affairs of the Department of Justice in the execution of foreign letters rogatory, 28 U.S.C. §1781 (1988); rules for service of foreign process, 28 U.S.C. §1696 (1988); and rules governing depositions and document production in aid of foreign proceedings, 28 U.S.C. §1782 (1988).

At the international level, a number of treaties have been adopted to promote international cooperation in criminal matters. These include the case-specific, bilateral "Lockheed Agreements" that the United States negotiated to secure evidence for specific prosecutions, often involving bribery of foreign officials. Several multilateral and bilateral narcotics treaties have included precedent-setting measures to enhance international judicial assistance in criminal matters, including the Single Convention on Narcotic Drugs, 1961 done Mar. 30 1961, entered into force Dec.13, 1961, 18 UST 1407, TIAS 6298,520 UNTS 204 ; the United Nations Convention Against Illicit Traffic in Narcotic Drugs and Psychotropic Substances, 1988 U.N. Doc E/con F. 82/15, opened for signature Dec. 19, 1988, 28 I.L.M. 493 (1989); and the Agreement on Cooperation in Combatting Narcotics Trafficking and Drug Dependency, 1989, United States - Mexico, done Feb. 23 1989, entered into force July 30, 1989, 29 I.L.M. 58 (1990).

In recent years much effort has been devoted to negotiation of mutual legal assistance treaties, obliging the states parties to render certain assistance to the law enforcement authorities of the other states parties in gathering evidence to prosecute transnational crimes. The purposes of mutual legal assistance treaties are to impose obligations to cooperate in criminal matters, to insure that evidence is provided in admissible form, to promote cooperation in undertaking search and seizure, to secure the testimony of witnesses and transfer of witnesses, and to facilitate the forfeiture of assets located abroad.

The United States has in recent years developed a strong interest in mutual legal assistance treaties for a variety of reasons. One influential factor has been an aim to overcome foreign blocking statutes and to provide a consensual alternative to coercive discovery methods. Another driving factor has been a desire to cooperate in the suppression of particular crimes, especially drug trafficking. The United States currently has in force eleven mutual legal assistance treaties (with Argentina, the Bahamas, Canada, Italy, Mexico, Netherlands, Spain, Switzerland, Thailand, Turkey, the United Kingdom).[105] Six more have been negotiated but are not yet in force (with Belgium, Colombia, Morocco, Nigeria, Panama, and Uruguay). Europe developed an interest in such treaties in advance of the United States, as reflected in the European Convention on Mutual Assistance in Criminal Matters, done Apr. 20, 1959, European Treaty Series No. 30. Bodies such as the United Nations have taken steps to draft model conventions on mutual legal assistance that can be adopted on a multilateral or bilateral basis.

States, especially the United States, may also resort to coercive discovery methods aimed at persons or entities located abroad where cooperative means are unavailable. Under the Walsh Act (currently codified at 28 U.S.C. §1783) (1988), testimony by U.S. nationals and residents located abroad may be compelled upon pain of contempt. A *subpoena duces tecum* may issue to the U.S. branch of a foreign entity (*e.g.*, a bank) for evidence located abroad.

---

105 Argentina, signed Dec. 4, 1990, entered into force Feb. 9, 1993, Treaty Doc. 102-18; the Bahamas, signed June 12, 1987, entered into force June 18, 1990, Treaty Doc. 100-17; Canada, signed Mar. 18, 1985, entered into force Jan 24, 1990, Treaty Doc. 100-14, 24 I.L.M. 1092 (1985); Italy, signed Nov. 9, 1982, entered into force Nov. 13, 1985, Sen. Ex. 98-25. Mexico signed Dec. 9, 1987, entered into force May 3, 1991, Treaty Doc. 100-13, 24 I.L.M. 447 (1985); the Netherlands signed June 12, 1981, entered into froce Sept. 15, 1983, TIAS 10734; Spain, signed Nov. 20, 1990, entered into force June 30, Treaty Doc. 102-21; Switerland, signed May 25, 1973, entered into force Jan. 23, 1977, TIAS 8302, 20 UST 2019; Thailand, signed Mar.19, 1986, entered into force, June 10,1993, Treaty Doc. 100-18; Turkey, signed June 7, 1979, entered into force Jan. 1, 1981, TIAS 9891, United Kingdom (Caymen Isl.); July 3, 1986, Mar. 19, 1990, Treaty Doc. 100-8, 26 I.L.M. 536. Belgium, signed Jan. 28, 1988, Treaty Doc. 100-16; Colombia, Aug. 20, 1980, Treaty Doc. 97-11; Jamaica, signed July 7, 1989, Treaty Doc. 102-16; Morocco, signed Oct. 17, 1983, Sen. Ex. 98-24; Nigeria, signed Sept. 13, 1989, Treaty Doc. 102-26; Panama, signed Apr. 11, 1991, Sept. 13, 1989, Treaty Doc. 102-15; Uruguary, signed May 6, 1991, Treaty Doc. 102-16.

Such subpoenas create a dilemma for the foreign target where the foreign state has enacted a blocking statute or a secrecy law that prohibits compliance with the request for documents. U.S. courts have nevertheless sometimes imposed contempt sanctions against U.S. subsidiaries refusing to comply with such subpoenas.

Other coercive discovery means used by U.S. prosecutors include "compelled consent" by U.S.-located depositors with foreign bank accounts in bank secrecy jurisdictions, whereby contempt sanctions are threatened unless the depositor in writing agrees to waive the protections provided by foreign bank secrecy laws. While these agreements have withstood Fifth Amendment challenges, some bank secrecy jurisdictions do not recognize compelled waivers as valid. Finally, the most coercive means of pursuing prosecution of foreign defendants include illegal conduct by U.S. police agents, such as kidnapping of suspects, non-consensual searches, and torture.

VI. Extradition to and from the United States

An important principle of extradition from the United States is that an order of extradition must be based upon a treaty. As of May 1, 1993, the United States had bilateral extradition treaties with 107 foreign states.[106] In addition, an increasing number of multilateral treaties contain an extradition component. Extradition is dominated by the federal government in the United States, particularly the State Department and the federal courts.

Typical provisions of extradition treaties include the following: (1) the obligation to extradite or prosecute the requested individual; (2) a definition of extraditable offenses (which may include felonies, only certain specifically listed offenses, or all but certain excluded offenses); (3) a provision requiring "dual criminality" (*i.e.*, the offense must be criminal under the laws both the requested and requesting states); (4) the rule of specialty (*i.e.*, the extradited individual may only be prosecuted for the offenses upon which he or she was extradited); (5) special rules of application to nationals of the requested country (many civil law countries prohibit the

---

[106] *See* Nadelmann, *Cops Across Borders*, *supra* at Appendix F.

extradition of their nationals but will promise to submit the defendant for prosecution under the nationality principle of criminal jurisdiction); (6) a political offense exception; (7) a prohibition of extradition for prosecution for military offenses; (8) a prohibition of extradition in cases where capital punishment is sought; (9) specification of what quantum of evidence of guilt is necessary at the stage of requesting extradition; and (10) provisions relating to the retroactive application of the treaty to crimes committed prior to its entry into force.

Extradition procedures generally follow a particular sequence. Upon receipt of an extradition request, the authorities of the requested state will seek to locate the requested person. Once the person has been located, a warrant of apprehension issues, and the person is taken into custody. Bail may be sought. A judicial extradition hearing will be held to determine if the person is subject to extradition under the terms of the relevant treaty. A determination by a federal extradition magistrate that a person is not subject to extradition is not appealable. If the person is found to be subject to extradition, a surrender warrant will be issued by the responsible executive official. A person ordered to be extradited from the United States may challenge that order by means of a petition for a writ of habeas corpus.

An informal, controversial but sometimes effective substitute for formal extradition is irregular rendition. This may take the form of deportation to or from United States. For example, in the case of *INS v. Doherty*, 502 U.S. 314 (1992), a person who was not extraditable because of the political offense exception of the relevant treaty was nevertheless deported to the country that had sought his extradition.

An even more controversial "alternative" to extradition is the kidnapping by U.S. agents of criminal suspects located abroad, especially where the kidnapping occurs in a state with which the United States has an extradition treaty. *Alvarez-Machain v. United States*, 504 U.S. 655 (1992). The *Alvarez-Machain* case has generated much critical commentary, but the actual decision is narrower than is frequently portrayed. The Supreme Court limited its opinion to a finding that the text of the U.S.-Mexico extradition treaty did not contain a specific prohibition on kidnapping. The Supreme Court did not reach the issue of whether a kidnapped defendant has "standing" to demand dismissal of criminal charges because of a violation of an extradition treaty, given its failure to find a breach of the treaty. And the Supreme Court definitely did not hold that the United States had a right to breach its treaty obligations with Mexico, though the decision is sometimes characterized in such terms. The United States has agreed to renegotiate the treaty with Mexico to include a specific anti-kidnapping clause, but the two nations have continuing disagreements concerning the extradition of their own nationals, with Mexico preferring to prosecute its nationals for acts that violate U.S. law, under either the territoriality principle or the nationality principle depending upon the locale of the crime.

Alvarez-Machain leaves many important issues undecided. These include whether other multilateral treaties or customary international law prohibit the kidnapping of suspects without the consent of the territorial state and the consequences of violations of such norms in a subsequent prosecution.

VII. Prisoner Transfer

The idea of one state agreeing to incarcerate individuals convicted of crimes under the laws and in the courts of another state would not have been acceptable under traditional principles of international law, by which no state would execute the penal laws of another. *The Antelope*, 23 U.S. (10 Wheat.) 66 (1825). But compelling social and political factors have moderated this attitude in recent decades and have led to the drafting of a number of prisoner transfer treaties. These factors include pressure by families and sympathetic policy-makers to permit convicts to serve their sentences in closer, more culturally compatible and more humane settings; the administrative problems encountered by prison authorities in dealing with foreign prisoners; the burden upon consular services in having to handle the affairs of large numbers of incarcerated nationals; and recognition that rehabilitation and reintegration of prisoners would be enhanced by incarceration in the state of nationality, and harsh or discriminatory treatment could be avoided.

The United States has bilateral prisoner transfer treaties with Bolivia, Canada, France, Mexico, Panama, Peru, Thailand, and Turkey. Europe has been a leader in this area, with the influential Council of Europe Convention on the Transfer of Sentenced

Persons. Relevant implementing statutes in the United States include 18 U.S.C. §§4100-4115, 3244 (1988).

Typical provisions of prisoner transfer treaties include: (1) application only to nationals of administering country; (2) a requirement of dual criminality; (3) a requirement that conviction be final; (4) limitation to convicts with a specified minimum sentence still to be served; (5) the exclusion of political offenses; (6) the exclusion of capital offenses; (7) requirement of the consent of the sentencing country, the administering country, and the offender (with provision for substituted consent in the case of incompetent offenders); (8) specification of the consequences of return by the offender to the sentencing country during the intended period of incarceration; and (9) provisions concerning the denial of transfer requests and reviewability of the judgment or sentence.

INTERNATIONAL CRIMINAL LAW: SELECTED SOURCES

Edgardo Rotman
Foreign and International Law Librarian
University of Miami

and

S. A. Patchett

I. Introduction

This paper has two aims. First, we hope to introduce some of the major treatises on international criminal law. Our second aim is to provide a highly selective guide to some of the more common white collar transnational crimes and United States laws which proscribe them. Of the vast literature these crimes and their control have spawned, we describe only those we think may serve as "jumping off points" into myraid treatises, looseleaf services, law review articles, and other writings. The magnitude of the field and the fuzziness of its borders explain, if they do not excuse, our numerous omissions. We have only touched upon some international crimes and have emphasized domestic crimes with transnational impact.

II. International Criminal Law

The very existence of international criminal law as an autonomous branch of law remained controversial until recently. Today, however, crime's increasing internationalization, the requirement for international crime control cooperation, treaty proliferation, attempts to codify international crime as well as create an international criminal court evidence this branch of the law's reality. This section introduces some international criminal law publications. For convenience we classify them as procedural or substantive, though for most purposes the distinction is artificial.

A conspicuous example of procedural and substantive unity is: *Principles and Procedures for a New Transnational Criminal Law* , edited by Albin Eser and Otto Lagodny (Freiburg im Breisgau: Max Planck Institute for Foreign and International Criminal Law,

1992). The editors have arranged this collection's 31 papers, originally presented at an international workshop in Freiburg sponsored in 1991 by the Society for the Reform of Criminal Law and the Max Planck Institute, under four headings: national criminal laws competing on the international level, international cooperation in criminal matters, supranational crimes and courts (regional and global) and international human rights as the "third dimension" in international criminal law.

Another example of procedure and substance combined is *The International Enforcement Law Reporter*, a monthly newsletter edited and published by the prominent specialist, Bruce Zagaris (818 Connecticut Ave., N.W., Suite 700, Washington, D.C.). Each issue presents a rich bag of current information as well as very useful bibliographies.

A. Procedural Aspects

Among international criminal law's procedural aspects are international judicial assistance, extraterritorial jurisdiction, protection of human rights, and extradition practices. We describe only a limited number of significant works on the first three topics while listing rather more extensively writings on United States extradition law.

1. International Judicial Assistance

Probably the most comprehensive treatment of United States judicial assistance in criminal matters are the last four volumes of Michael Abbell and Bruno A. Ristau's six volume *International Judicial Assistance* (Washington, D.C.: International Law Institute, 1990). Volume 3 covers obtaining evidence abroad for criminal investigations and prosecutions, volumes 4 and 5 deal with extradition, and volume 6 with offenders' transfers.

International Judicial Assistance, by David McClean (Oxford: Clarendon Press, 1992), provides a British perspective and offers a useful analysis of relevant international treaties, including the 1959 European Convention on Mutual Assistance in Criminal Matters, the 1972 European Convention on the Transfer of Proceedings in Criminal Matters, the Commonwealth Scheme for Mutual Assistance in Criminal Matters, and the United Nations Model Treaty on the Transfer of Proceedings in Criminal Matters. McClean also addresses international cooperation in controlling drug trafficking and money laundering, criminal proceeds forfeiture, United Kingdom mutual assistance treaties, and international efforts to defeat bank secrecy and insider trading. An appendix includes selected documents.

Ethan A. Nadelmann provides a fascinating historical account of United States law enforcement officials' attempts to extend Uncle Sam's long arm abroad in *Cops Across Borders: the Internationalization of U.S. Criminal Law Enforcement* (University Park, PA: Pennsylvania State University Press, 1993). The work's chapters on institutionalized Latin American corruption, international evidence gathering, and fugitive rendition are helpful guides. Multinational police cooperation is Michael Fooner's subject in *Interpol: Issues in World Crime and International Criminal Justice* (New York: Plenum Press, 1989). He gives the organization's history and describes its management and operations.

An invaluable article by Bruce Zagaris, "Developments in International Judicial Assistance and Related Matters," *Denver Journal of International Law and Policy* 18 (1990): 339-86, discusses judicial assistance in the fight against the narcotics trade. Zagaris gives particular attention to the United Nations Convention Against Illicit Traffic in Narcotic Drugs and Psychotropic Substances, various United States mutual assistance treaties, as well as the Comprehensive Crime Control Act of 1984, Anti-Drug Abuse Act of 1986, and Anti-Drug Abuse Act of 1988.

In an earlier essay, "Judicial Assistance Under U.S. Bilateral Treaties" in *Legal Responses to International Terrorism: U.S. Procedural Aspects* edited by Cherif Bassiouni (Boston: M. Nijhoff, 1988), p. 219-30, Zagaris and David Simonetti analyzed mutual assistance agreements. Two other useful treatments are:

Ellis, Allan and Robert L. Pisani. "The United States Treaties on Mutual Assistance in Criminal Matters: A Comparative Analysis." *International Lawyer* 19 (1985): 189-223.

Nadelmann, Ethan A. "Negotiations in Criminal Law Assistance Treaties." *American Journal of Comparative Law* 33 (1985): 467-504.

2. Extraterritorial Jurisdiction

Underscoring the necessity of prosecuting those who commit crimes beyond the United States' borders is Richard D. Gregorie's

"Extraterritorial Jurisdiction: Its Use, Its Roots and Its Viability," *Nova Law Review* 15 (1991): 625-60. The author, a former federal prosecutor in Miami, shows how this was done in a number of narcotics cases from the Southern District of Florida.

A recent monograph on extraterritoriality is *The Protective Principle of International Criminal Jurisdiction*, by Iain Cameron (Aldershot: Dartmouth, 1994). This principle permits a state to "grant extraterritorial effect to legislation criminalizing conduct damaging to national security other central state interests." (p.2). The work deals primarily with international aspects of domestic criminal law and not with internationally proscribed criminal conduct. It examines state claims to exercise extraterritorial jurisdiction of Sweden, Denmark, Norway, and the United States.

3. Human Rights and United States Criminal Procedure

Hurst Hannum's *Materials on International Human Rights and U.S. Criminal Law and Procedure* (Washington, D.C.: Procedural Aspects of International Law Institute, 1989) addresses international human rights' impact on United States courts, sources of human rights law, and international human rights bodies' jurisdiction and powers. As well as chapters on abuse of arrest and detention powers in the light of international conventions, habeas corpus, Eighth Amendment concerns, fair trial and other prisoners' rights, the work has appendices of documentary sources and selected excerpts.

4. Extradition

Extradition to and from foreign countries in United States law is a mix of statutes, treaties, and case law. The statutes are *U.S. Code.*, Title 18, secs. 3181-3196 (1988 & Supp. V 1993). Section 3181 mandates that all the subsequent sections' provisions regarding surrender of fugitives from foreign countries shall remain in force only while an extradition treaty with each such country exists. Section 3184 establishes the procedure for apprehending a foreign fugitive in the United States, hearing the evidence of criminality against him by a justice or judge of the United States, a magistrate authorized for the purpose by a United States court, or a judge of any state court of record of general jurisdiction, and if the hearing judge deems the evidence sufficient under the relevant treaty, for his certification of this fact to the Secretary of State, who may issue a warrant for the fugitive's surrender. Section 3196 authorizes the Secretary of State to order an American citizen's surrender at a foreign state's request if the extradition treaty with that country does not require the United States to extradite its citizens but all the other requirements of the treaty are satisfied.

Two useful sources of the United States' extradition treaties with foreign states are *Extradition Laws and Treaties: United States,* edited by I.I. Kavass and A. Sprudzs (Buffalo, N.Y.: Hein, 1980-), a loose-leaf service in two volumes reprinting the texts of all treaties to which the United States is party, with historical notes for dates of entry into force and termination, and Vol. 5, " Criminal: Extradition (Appendices)" of Michael Abbell & Bruno A. Ristau, *International Judicial Assistance* (Washington, D.C.: International Law Institute, 1990). Abbell & Ristau provide the full texts of bi-lateral treaties and the extradition provisions of multilateral treaties to which the United States is party.

The *Restatement (Third) of Foreign Relations Law of the United States Purt IV,* chap. 7, subchap. B (St. Paul, Minn.: American Law Institute Publishers, 1987) summarizes United States case law on extradition. Section 475 provides the basic rule that states parties to extradition treaties must deliver a fugitive sought by another state party if it shows that it seeks the person for trial or punishment after conviction and flight. Section 478 states United States extradition procedure.

A number of treatises on extradition are helpful. As an introduction and "how-to-do it" guide Michael Abbell & Bruno A. Ristau, *International Judicial Assistance* is probably the best. Its fourth volume includes the *U.S. Attorney's Manual* sections on preparing extradition requests. The authors give a clear explication of the content of typical United States extradition treaties. Useful also is M. Cherif Bassiouni, *International Extradition: United States Law and Practice* 2d ed. (Dobbs Ferry, N.Y.: Oceana, 1987). Its chapters on the legal bases for extradition in the United States, the use of immigration laws as disguised extradition, irregular methods of rendition (abduction & kidnapping), the rules of double criminality, specialty doctrine, and reciprocity complement the author's treatment of United States extradition practice. In an earlier work *International Extradition and World Public Order* (Dobbs Ferry, N.Y.: Oceana, 1974), Bassiouni places extradition in international legal theoretical context. Geoff Gilbert, *Aspects of*

Extradition Law (Boston: M. Nijhoff, 1991), is a clearly written introduction. Though the chapters on war crimes, the political offence exception, and refugees, are not germane to ordinary white collar international crimes, his treatment of options open to fugitives seeking to challenge their extradition merits close reading, and the volume's bibliography charts a good path through extradition's literature. An older work, still often cited, is I.A. Shearer, *Extradition in International Law* (Dobbs Ferry, N.Y.: Oceana, 1971).

Two brief guides warrant special mention. The first, Christopher L. Blakesley, "International Extradition for Business Crimes," chap. 17 in *International Trade: Avoiding Criminal Risks*, edited by William M. Hannay (Salem, N.H.: Butterworth, 1991-), warns that the tremendous growth in criminalization of fraud and drug-related financial transfers poses serious risks for international business persons and entitities. He notes the decreasing availability of the double criminality and specialty defenses to extradition., and clearly outlines the United States extradition process. John G. Kester, "Some Myths of United States Extradition Law," *Georgetown Law Journal* 76 (1988): 1441-93, explodes seventeen "myths" of extradition law. His last myth, happily enough, is that the government always wins in extradition proceedings.

5. U.S. Extradition Law: A Checklist

a. Extradition in General

i. Treaties

Abbell, Michael and Bruno A Ristau. *International Judicial Assistance*. Vol. 5 Washington, D.C.: International Law Institute, 1990. Contains a list of U.S. extradition treaties in force as of July 1, 1988- giving date of signature, date of entry into force, and official citation for each (Appendix H); the full texts of these treaties (Appendix I); the text of the Pan-American Convention on Extradition (Appendix J); and extradition provisions of multilateral treaties to which the U.S. is a party (Appendix K).

Extradition Laws and Treaties: United States. Edited by I.I. Kavass and A. Sprudzs. Buffalo, N.Y.: Hein, 1980-. This two volume looseleaf service reprints, in alphabetic order of countries' names, the texts of all U.S. extradition treaties with other countries. It includes historical notes on dates of termination or entry into force.

ii. Statutes

U.S. Code. Title 18, secs. 3181-96 (1988 & Supp. V 1993).

iii. Restatements

Restatement (Third) of Foreign Relations Law. Chap. 7, Subchap. B St. Paul, Minn.: American Law Institute Press, 1987. Sec. 475 states the basic rule that states parties to extradition treaties must arrest and deliver a person sought by another state party if it shows the person is sought for trial or punishment after conviction and flight. Sec. 476 states the three grounds for non-extradition. Sec. 477 contains the specialty doctrine, and Sec. 478 describes United States extradition procedure.

iv. Treatises

Abbell, Michael and Bruno A Ristau. *International Judicial Assistance.* Vol. 4 Washington, D.C.: International Law Institute, 1990. How-to-do-it, nuts and bolts treatment of extradition from, and to, the United States. Statutes, treaties, procedure- this tells all. Includes a very clear explication of the components of a typical U.S. extradition treaty. Among its useful appendices are the text of U.S. statutes regulating extradition, the U.S. Attorney's Manual sections on extradition request procedures, the Dept. of State's Form Surrender Warrant, and that Department's form authorizing a U.S. agent to receive an extraditee. Also the text of the European Convention on Extradition. All this plus a usable index.

Bassiouni, M. Cherif. *International Extradition and World Public Order.* Dobbs Ferry, N.Y.: Oceana, 1974. Try to find a major law review article on extradition that fails to cite this work!

__________. *International Extradition: United States Law and Practice.* 2d ed. Dobbs Ferry, N.Y.: Oceana, 1987. The major work. Chapters II, "Legal Bases for Extradition in the United States," IV, "Disguised Extradition: the Use of Immigration Laws as Alternatives to Extradition," V, "Abduction and Unlawful Seizure as Alternatives to Extradition," VII, on reciprocity, double criminality, specialty, and IX, "Extradition Procedure in the United States," are of the most useful. The Table of Authorities is a helpful bibliography through 1986.

Bedi, Satya Deva. *Extradition in International Law and Practice.* Buffalo, N.Y.: Hein, 1968.

Biron, Chartres and Kenneth E. Chalmers. *Law and Practice of Extradition.* Littleton, CO.: F.B. Rothman, 1903.

Gilbert, Geoff. *Aspects of Extradition Law.* Boston: M. Nijhoff, 1991. A clearly written introduction to the sources of extradition law, legal options open to fugitives attempting to challenge their extradition, and the lawfulness of "other means of rendition." The chapters on extradition mechanisms (chap.2), extradition procedure (chap.3), restrictions on return (chap.5), and irregular rendition (chap.7) (including a pre-*Alvarez-Machain* glance at the Ker-Frisbie Doctrine) repay close reading. There are also chapters on war crimes, the political offence exception, and refugees. Has a helpful, selective bibliography and a case table arranged by jurisdictions.

Shearer, I. A. *Extradition in International Law.* Dobbs Ferry, N.Y.: Oceana, 1971. Cited almost as often as Bassiouni, this views extradition with a non-American eye.

Yarnold, Barbara M. *International Fugitives: A New Role for the International Court of Justice.* New York: Praeger, 1991. Offers a critique of contemporary extradition practice and proposes a solution- wake up the ICJ and add zest to its justices' dry pursuits by placing the Court in charge of all international extradition (and subsequent trials of extraditees/relators). Chapter Two is a case study of extradition proceedings in U.S. district courts as reported in the *Federal Supplement* from 1932 to 1990 showing that the case outcomes were related to political factors- particularly ethnicity. It demonstrates that judges in extradition proceedings have, and use, great discretion.

v. Articles and Essays

Blakesley, Christopher L. "International Extradition for Business Crimes." In *International Trade: Avoiding Criminal Risks.* Edited by William M. Hannay. Salem, N.H.: Butterworth, 1991. Chap.17, a brief, clearly written guide to extradition. Emphasizes the increasing number of extraditable offences- particularly RICO and fraud- applicable to business people. Warns of the decreasing availability of the double criminality and specialty defenses to extradition.

Kester, John G. "Some Myths of United States Extradition Law." *Georgetown Law Journal* 76 (1988): 1441-93. Must reading, this examines with critical eye and caustic pen 17 common misconceptions about extradition. The first is that extradition is not a criminal proceeding. Kester shows that extradition procedure lacks many of ordinary criminal proceedings' safeguards for defendants, but it results in the eventual imposition of criminal penalties. Unfortunately, the Supreme Court, in *Alvarez-Machain*, paid no heed to the author's trenchant critique of the myth (as he believed) that official kidnapping was a perfectly legal alternative to extradition. He explodes swiftly the myth that extradition treaties grant no rights to individuals. Kester shows that the U.S. State and Justice Departments have blurred the distinctions between U.S. crimes of mail and wire fraud and foreign concepts of fraud. He is no more complimentary about State Department pains taken in examining foreign extradition requests. The examiners are the very country desk officers whose main job is to keep relations with the requesting countries harmonious.

Semmelman, Jacques "Federal Courts, the Constitution, and the Rule of Non-Inquiry in International Extradition Proceedings." *Cornell Law Review* 76 (1991): 1198-1241. An analysis of the rule that precludes a U.S. court from examining the criminal justice process of a country requesting a U.S. citizen's or resident's extradition. Argues that the rule should remain unchanged, despite a great deal of criticism, because courts' examination of other countries' judicial systems would provoke international discord, invade the executive branch's powers, and infringe other nation's treaty rights. Should be read as an antidote to Kester's comments on the rule of non-enquiry.

b. Double Criminality

i. Cases

Factor v. Laubenheimer, 290 U.S. 276 (1933).

United States. v. Levy, 905 F.2d 326 (10th Cir. 1990), *cert. denied*, 498 U.S. 1049 (1991).

United States. v. Sensi, 879 F.2d 888 (D.C. Cir. 1989).

Peters v. Egnor, 888 F.2d 713 (10th Cir. 1989).

Hu Yau-Leung v. Soscia, 649 F.2d 914 (2d Cir. 1981), *cert. denied*, 454 U.S. 971 (1981).

Brauch v. Raiche, 618 F.2d 843 (1st Cir. 1980).

ii. Restatement

Restatement (Third) of Foreign Relations Law. Sec. 476 (1)(c), cmt. d & rep. n.1. St. Paul, Minn.: American Law Institute Press, 1987.

iii. Articles and Essays

Herman, G. Nicholas, Steven A. Bernholz, and Martin J. Bernholz. "Double Criminality and Complex Crimes," in *International Criminal Law; A Guide to U.S. Practice and Procedure*, ch. 12, pp. 365-391, ed. Ved P. Nanda and M. Cherif Bassiouni. New York: Practising Law Institute, 1987. Explains the principle of double criminality as an extradition requirement and applies it to RICO related extradition requests.

Williams, Sharon A. "The Double Criminality Rule and Extradition: a Comparative Analysis." *Nova Law Review* 15 (1991): 581-623. A comparison of the rule's use in the U.S., U.K., and Canada. Gives greatest attention to Canadian extradition law- important for Americans because Canada is this country's greatest extradition trading partner.

c. Specialty Doctrine

i. Cases

United States. v. Rauscher, 119 U.S. 407 (1886).

United States v. Abello-Silva, 948 F.2d 1168 (10th Cir. 1991), *cert. denied*, 113 S.Ct. 107 (1992), *rehearing denied*, 113 S.Ct. 1068 (1993). Government may prosecute extraditee (here a Colombian drug dealer) on the basis of facts different from those it included in its extradition request, if the offense for which it prosecutes him remains that stated in the extradition request.

Koskotas v. Roche, 931 F.2d 169 (1st Cir. 1991).

United States v. Riviere, 924 F.2d 1289 (3d Cir. 1991).

United States v. Sensi, 879 F.2d 888 (D.C. Cir. 1989).

United States v. Kaufman, 858 F.2d 994 (5th Cir. 1988), *rehearing denied*, 874 F.2d 242 (5th Cir. 1989).

United States v. Cuevas, 847 F.2d 1417 (9th Cir. 1988), *cert. denied*, 489 U.S. 1012 (1989). Individual had right to raise claims that might have been raised by asylum state. Here the extraditee was convicted of conspiracy to possess and distribute cocaine and violating federal currency reporting laws. He has a Miami connection because Cuevas's co-conspirator shipped him in Switzerland seven bags of cash from Miami in a month before customs agents opened one bag to discover $240,000 and began a process leading to Cuevas's 1985 arrest in Zurich. He argued on appeal that his conviction for currency related offenses must be reversed because they were "fiscal acts" which the Swiss extradition order appeared to enjoin. Applying the specialty test "whether the extraditing country would consider the acts for which the defendant was prosecuted as independent from those for which he was extradited," the court upheld the conviction because it was sure the Swiss court had seen the narcotics and currency offenses as "integrally related" and its reference to "fiscal acts" was merely to any tax penalties Cuevas might have incurred.

United States v. Thirion, 813 F.2d 146 (8th Cir. 1987).

United States v. Najohn, 785 F.2d 1420 (9th Cir. 1986), *cert. denied*, 479 U.S. 1009 (1986).

United States v. Flores, 538 F.2d 939 (2d Cir. 1976).

Shapiro v. Fernandina, 478 F.2d 894 (2d Cir. 1973), *cert. dismissed*, 414 U.S. 884 (1973).

Fiocconi v. Attorney General of the United States, 462 F.2d 475 (2d Cir. 1972), *cert. denied*, 409 U.S. 1059 (1972).

United States v. Paroutian, 299 F.2d 486 (2d Cir. 1962).

ii. Restatement

Restatement (Third) of Foreign Relations Law. Sec. 477. St. Paul, Minn.: American Law Institute Press, 1987.

iii. Articles

George, Jonathan. "Towards a More Principled Approach to the Principle of Specialty." *Cornell International Law Journal*. 12 (1979): 309-27. Examines the question whether the specialty doctrine confers rights on the extraditee as well as his nation. Suggests U.S. courts should grant right to invoke the doctrine to individuals as well as to surrendering states. Several circuits have adopted this view since 1979.

Morvillo, Christopher J. "Individual Rights and the Doctrine of Speciality: The Deterioration of *United States v. Rauscher*." *Fordham International Law Journal* 14 (1990-91): 987-1026. Also argues that the specialty doctrine confers rights on individuals which they may invoke in U.S. extradition proceedings. Reviews court decisions to the contrary and more recent cases affirming the individual rights concept.

Runtz, David. "The Principle of Specialty: A Bifurcated Analysis of the Rights of the Accused." *Columbia Journal of Transnational Law* 29 (1991): 407-37.

Weinstein, Mark S. "A License to Mislead: *United States v. Abello-Silva*." *University of Miami Inter-American Law Review* 24 (1992): 161-90. A vehement critique of the 10th Circuit Court of Appeal's decision, this explains the specialty doctrine's development and the importance of facts as well as offenses in extradition requests. Claims the Abello-Silva decision opens the door for unscrupulous prosecutors to obtain surrender of fugitives under false pretences.

d. Short Cuts: Abductions and Kidnappings

i. Cases

United States v. Alvarez-Machain, 112 S.Ct. 2188 (1992). No express term in the U.S.-Mexican extradition treaty prohibited the abduction of a Mexican doctor in his own country for trial in the U.S. on charges of assisting in the murder and torture of a DEA agent. The Court refused to find any implied term in the treaty prohibiting such an abduction, leaving it free to apply the Ker-Frisbie doctrine that the manner of a defendant's arrival before a U.S. court does not affect its jurisdiction.

Frisbie v. Collins, 342 U.S. 519 (1952).

Ker v. Illinois, 119 U.S. 436 (1886). Held that a private abduction of a fugitive in Peru and enforced return for trial before Illinois state courts did not deprive the abductee of due process of law or a right to asylum in Peru. In dictum, the Court said that such an abduction would not otherwise, under common law or international law, deprive the state courts of personal jurisdiction.

United States v. Toscanino, 500 F.2d 267 (2d Cir. 1974). Toscanino, abducted in Uruguay by U.S. agents, claimed he was tortured and detained for seventeen days in Brazil prior to enforced return to the U.S. for trial. The court relied on Supreme Court domestic decisions which had greatly expanded law enforcement misconduct as violation of due process since *Frisbie v. Collins* in sending the case back to the trial court for an evidentiary hearing on the torture claims. Honored by legal writers but not used as precedent by U.S. courts.

ii. Articles and Essays

Abramovsky, Abraham. "Extraterritorial Abductions: America's "Catch and Snatch" Policy Run Amok." *Virginia Journal of International Law* 31 (1990): 151-210.

Bassiouni, M. Cherif. "Unlawful Seizures and Irregular Rendition Devices as Alternatives to Extradition." *Vanderbilt Journal of Transnational Law* 7 (1973): 25-70.

Bush, Jonathan A. ""How Did We Get Here? Foreign Abductions after *Alvarez-Machain*." *Stanford Law Review* 45 (1993): 939-83.

Carlisle, Jeffrey J. "Extradition of Government Agents as a Municipal Law Remedy for State-sponsored Kidnapping." *California Law Review* 81 (1993): 1541-86.

Lowenfeld, Andreas F. "Still More on Kidnapping." *American Journal of International Law* 85 (1991): 655-61.

_______. "U.S. Law Enforcement Abroad: The Constitution and International Law, Continued." *American Journal of International Law* 84 (1990): 444-93.

Mann, F. A. "Reflections on the Prosecution of Persons Abducted in Breach of International Law." In *International Law at a Time of Perplexity* . Edited by Yoram Dinstein. Boston: M. Nijhoff, 1989. p.407-21.

Schwabach, Aaron and S. A. Patchett. "Doctrine or Dictum: the Ker-Frisbie Doctrine and Official Abductions Which Breach International Law." *University of Miami Inter-American Law Review* 25 (1993): 19-56.

Semmelman, Jacques. "Due Process, International Law, and Jurisdiction over Criminal Defendants Abducted Extrateritorially: the Ker-Frisbie Doctrine Reexamined." Columbia Journal of Transnational Law 30 (1992): 513-76.

B. International Crimes: A Selection

1. General Works

A comprehensive treatise which illustrates the sweeping variety of what the world once called delicta juris gentium is Farhad Malekian's *International Criminal Law: The Legal and Critical Analysis of International Crimes* (Uppsala: F. Malekian, 1991). This work's first volume covers the general idea of international criminal law, aggression and war crimes, slavery, genocide, racial discrimination, torture, human experimentation, piracy, and hijacking. The second deals with hostage taking, crimes against internationally protected persons, terrorism, drug offenses, theft or destruction of cultural property, environmental crimes, counterfeiting, maritime offenses other than piracy, and pornography.

Dated but still useful is Bart de Schutter, *Bibliography on International Criminal Law* (Leiden: A. W. Sijthoff, 1972). This lists 2201 works in a variety of languages.

United Nations efforts to codify international criminal law and establish an international criminal court are M. Cherif Bassiouni's tale in *Draft International Criminal Code and Draft Statute on International Criminal Tribunal* 2d ed. (Boston: M. Nijhoff, 1987). Here Bassiouni analyzes the nature of international crimes and presents his draft international code and its enforcing tribunal's statute. The work's extensive bibliography is a valuable guide to pre-1987 literature and international documents. Another guide to international materials by the same author, *International Crimes: Digest/Index of International Instruments 1815-1985* (New York: Oceana, 1986), indexes 312 instruments and gives appropriate references, alternative sources, plus data on these instruments' applicability to different crimes.

The United Nations International Law Commission has been working on an international criminal code and a court for some time. Its Working Group on a Draft Statute for an International Criminal Court's 1994 *Report*, which includes the "Draft Statute for an International Criminal Tribunal," appears in *International Legal Materials* 32 (1994): 253-96. Professor James Crawford, a member of the International Law Commission, provides a useful gloss on the Draft Statute in his article, "The ILC's Draft Statute for an International Criminal Tribunal," *American Journal of International Law* 88 (1994): 140-52.

2. Crimes Against Humanity

A comprehensive examination is M. Cherif Bassiouni, *Crimes Against Humanity in International Criminal Law* (Boston: M. Nijhoff, 1992). This gives the legislative history of the 1945 London Agreement's Art. 6(c), defining crimes against humanity for purposes of the Nuremburg Tribunal, discusses individual criminal responsibility and international prosecutions, elements of crimes, defenses and exonerations, and a host of related topics. It includes a 256 page section reprinting most relevant documents. In his *Individual Responsibility in International Law for Serious Human Rights Violations* (Boston: M. Nijhoff, 1992), Lyal S. Sunga argues that a new international legal norm imposing such responsibility is forming.

Yugoslavia's collapse and subsequent horrors there occasioned the United Nations Security Council's *Report on Aspects of Establishing an International Tribunal for the Prosecution of Persons Responsible for Serious Violations of International Humanitarian Law Committed in the Territory of the Former Yugoslavia*, S/25704, 1993, reprinted in *International Legal Materials* 32 (1993): 1159-1202 (ILM). Hard on this document's heels in the same issue of *ILM* at pp. 1203-5 appears the Security Council's May 25, 1993 Resolution 827 establishing the Tribunal. A constructive critique of the Tribunal is the American Bar Association Section of International Law and Practice's *Report on the International Tribunal to Adjudicate War Crimes Committed in the Former Yugoslavia* (Washington, D.C. Section of International Law and Practice, American Bar Association, 1993). James C. O'Brien, an attorney-advisor in the State Department's Office of the Legal Advisor, recounts the background of the Tribunal's establishment and describes its organization and operation in "The International Tribunal for

Violations of International Humanitarian Law in the Former Yugoslavia," *American Journal of International Law* 87 (1993): 639-59.

Far from disappearing, that archtypical crime against humanity, genocide, appears to be undergoing a renaissance. Leo Kuper's *Prevention of Genocide* (New Haven: Yale University Press, 1985) examines "domestic" genocide, campaigns of extermination arising from nations' internal strife. *Genocide: A People's Will to Live* (Buffalo: Hein, 1992) by W. Freedman provides an historical perspective, discusses the judiciary's role in punishing the crime, and examines the 1948 United Nations Convention prohibiting it. Papers by a number of experts convened at a 1991 Yale Law School Conference appear in *Genocide: Conceptual and Historical Dimensions*, edited by George J. Andreopoulos (Philadelphia: University of Pennsylvania Press, 1994). In Part One several writers offer definitions of the crime, while Part Two contains case studies from Armenia, Kurdistan, East Timor, and Cambodia. Third in a series on genocide, *The Widening Circle of Genocide*, edited by Israel W. Charny (New Brunswick, N.J.: Transaction Publishers, 1994), contains an up to date bibliography.

3. Terrorism

Terrorism is another international criminal growth industry. A comprehensive compilation of international treaties aimed at its deterrence is *International Terrorism: Political and Legal Documents*, edited by Yonah Alexander (Boston: M. Nijhoff, 1992). Joseph A. Lambert's *Terrorism and Hostages in International Law- A Commentary on the Hostages Convention 1979* (Cambridge: Grotius, 1990) analyzes one of these. *Legal Responses to International Terrorism: U.S. Procedural Aspects*, edited by M. Cherif Bassiouni Boston: M. Nijhoff, 1988), has contributions on judicial assistance, the Immigration and Nationalization Service's response to terrorism, the political offense exception in extradition law, and use of the alien tort statute by victims. A useful bibliography (Chapter VII of which devotes itself to legal aspects) is Amos Lakos, *International Terrorism: A Bibliography* (Boulder, Colorado: Westview, 1986).

III. Selected Transnational White Collar Crimes in United States Law

A. General Works

Not limited to transnational crimes but certainly encompassing them in its sweeping embrace is F. Lee Bailey and Henry B. Rothblatt, *Defending Business and White Collar Crimes: Federal and State*, 2d ed. (Rochester, N.Y.: Lawyers Co-operative Publishing Co., 1984). The first volume guides practitioners through procedure from initial interview to sentencing. It also addresses tax crimes and bank fraud. The second volume includes, among others, mail and wire fraud, RICO, insurance fraud, forgery, and securities offenses. Another omnibus is the looseleaf *White Collar Crime: Business and Regulatory Offenses,* edited by Otto G. Obermaier and Robert G. Morvillo (New York: Law Journal Seminars Press, 1990-). Its chapters on banking crimes, defending conspiracy charges, forfeitures, Rico, securities fraud and the splendidly titled "Federalization of Fraud: Mail and Wire Fraud Statutes" are particularly germane.

Kathleen F. Brickey covers organizations as perpetrators in her triple decker, *Corporate Criminal Liability: a Treatise on the Criminal Liability of Corporations, Their Officers and Agents* 2d ed. (Deerfield, Ill.: Clark Boardman Callaghan, 1991). After general analysis of corporate criminal conduct and intent and attribution of conduct to officers and managers in volume 1, Brickey devotes her second and third volumes to conduct criminalized by major federal statutes. Included are conspiracy, securities and mail/wire fraud, foreign corrupt practices, tax crimes, and money laundering. The final chapters deal with obstruction of justice and false statements.

Foreign commerce and its dangers were the themes of 1988 and 1989 American Bar Association Convention programs. Papers originally presented there are the contents of *International Trade: Avoiding Criminal Risks,* edited by William M. Hannay (Salem, N.H.: Butterworth, 1991). This volume's first part offers essays on other countries' criminal laws which pose hazards for American exporters and importers. The second part addresses United States laws that may snare those trading abroad: money laundering, securities transactions, "greasing" overseas wheels, and export controls are among the perils proffered by the expert authors.

A looseleaf service, *White Collar Crime Reporter: Information and Analyses Converning White Collar Practice* (Westown, PA.: Andrews Publications, 1987- .), treats one topic in depth in each issue as well as providing news and interviews. *The American Criminal Law Review*, published by the Georgetown University Law Center, Washington, D.C., produces useful, annual, white collar crime surveys.

B. Transborder Frauds and Deceits: Of RICO and Its Predicates

Of RICO writings there is no end! Though a forest fancier contemplating the paper consumed by explications and commentaries on the Racketeer Influenced and Corrupt Organizations Act might accuse Congress of causing a massive environmental crime, the Act's authors actually intended to expunge organized crime from America's commerce. To accomplish this, Congress made, in title 18, U.S.C. § 1962 (1988), 1962. the acquisition or establishment of an enterprise through a pattern of racketeering activity a crime itself. Congress defined "racketeering activity" in Section. 1961 as acts of or involving murder, gambling, bribery, extortion, narcotics dealing, and kidnapping contrary to any state law and a plethora of acts indictable under various federal statutes.

Commitment of any two or more of these acts, whether or not they have resulted in an indictment, in an activity such that they are continuous and related, constitutes a "pattern of racketeeering." RICO provides heftier penalties for this pattern than state and federal statutes do for the underlying acts themselves, and it also provides for forfeitures of the criminals' interests in enterprises and their profits which have been acquired through a pattern of racketeering or from such a pattern's proceeds.

RICO itself is codified at .18 lh U.S.C,. § 1961-68 (1988 and Supp. V 1993). Section 1961 contains the list of predicate acts which constitute racketeering. Section 1962 prohibits any person from receiving income from a pattern of racketeering activity, from investing this income or using it to acquire or establish any enterprise engaged in or affecting interstate or foreign commerce, from carrying out any such enterprise's affairs through a pattern of racketeering activity or by collecting unlawful debts, and from conspiring to do any of these nefarious things. Section 1963 states the criminal penalties for violating the Act, while Section 1964 allows persons injured by racketeering to seek civil and punitive (treble) damages from the racketeers.

The most common predicate federal white collar crimes associated with RICO have been mail and wire fraud, which are prohibited by 18, U.S.C. § 1341 and 1343 respectively. Often also associated with fraud crimes are those of transporting money or property stolen or taken by fraud in interstate or foreign trade (18 U.S.C. § 2314), making false statements in applications to federally insured banks or savings and loan associations (18 U.S.C. § 1014), and making false statements or concealing knowingly a material fact in matters within the jurisdiction of a U.S. department or agency (18 U.S.C. § 1001).

Two RICO cases have particular relevance to transnational white collar criminal activity. In the first, *United States v. Parness*, 503 F.2d 430 (2d Cir. 1974), *cert denied*, 419 U.S. 1105 (1975), a defendant argued on appeal against a RICO conviction that his Netherland Antilles corporation could not be an enterprise within the Act's meaning because it was not in the United States. The court held, however, that enterprises could be non-U.S. corporations. Sixteen years later a much higher profile, khaki collared (but for our purposes we assume he wore his dress white uniform) defendant, apprehended in his own country by a particularly large and heavily armed posse and returned to Miami to face RICO charges, argued that RICO did not apply to conduct outside the United States. In *United States v. Noriega*, 746 F. Supp. 1506 (S.D. Fla. 1990), the court held that if the conduct produced or was intended to produce effects in the United States RICO applied to it.

For an introduction to RICO citing all the most relevant cases, *RICO Civil and Criminal Law and Strategy*, edited by Jed Rakoff and Howard W. Goldstein (New York: Law Journal Seminars Press, 1989) in one looseleaf volume is excellent. Also helpful is Paul Vizcarrondo, Jr., "Racketeer Influenced and Corrupt Organizations (RICO), chapter 11 in *White Collar Crime: Business and Regulatory Offenses*, edited by Otto G. Obermaier and Robert G. Morvillo (New York:Law Journal Seminars Press, 1990). Another chapter, the ninth, in the same work, John C. Coffee, Jr. & Charles K. Whitehead, "The Federalization of Fraud: Mail and Wire Fraud Statutes, " describes the most often encountered RICO predicates.

Law review articles on RICO are rife. Still useful despite its antiquity is G. Robert Blakey & Brian Gettings, "Racketeer Influenced and Corrupt Organizations (RICO): Basic Concepts-Criminal and Civil Remedies," *Temple Law Quarterly*. 53 (1980): 1009-48. Author of RICO, proud and protective of his progeny, Professor Blakey suggests its detractors are, well, deluded, in G. Robert Blakey & Thomas A. Perry, "An Analysis of the Myths That Bolster Efforts to Rewrite RICO and the Various Proposals for Reform: 'Mother of God- Is This the End of RICO?'" *Vanderbilt Law Review* 43 (1990): 851-1101. A supremely Panglossian piece (RICO works just fine and only minor alterations in Justice Dept. policies, which we certainly are making, etc.) by the man then in charge of RICO at the Department of Justice, is Edward S. G. Dennis, Jr.," Current RICO Policies of the Department of Justice," *Vanderbilt Law Review* 43 (1990): 651-72. An oft-cited, quite critical duo are Gerard E. Lynch, "RICO: The Crime of Being a Criminal (Parts I & II)," *Columbia Law Review* 87 (1987): 661-764 and Gerard E. Lynch, "RICO: The Crime of Being a Criminal (Parts III & IV)," *Columbia Law Review*. 87 (1988): 920-84. A vision of the future, which General Noriega perhaps might have read with profit, was John C. Fricano, "RICO Extraterritoriality- Just a Matter of Time?" *International Business Lawyer*. 13 (1985) 201-8 Equally prophetic, rather more scholarly, very much longer, and *not* limited to civil aspects of RICO, is Michael Goldsmith & Vicki Rinne," Civil RICO, Foreign Defendants, and 'ET'," *Minnesota Law Review* 73 (1989): 1023 -80.

Those who enjoy their explicatory pills encased in a flavorsome, witty, capsule will find Jed. S. Rakoff, "The Federal Mail Fraud Statute (Part I)," *Duquesne Law Review* 18 (1980): 771-822, easy to swallow. Harder to get down (and digest) but well worth the effort is Ellen S. Podgor, "Mail Fraud: Opening Letters," *South Carolina Law Review* 43 (1992): 223-71.

1. Rico: A Checklist

a. Statutes

Racketeer Influenced and Corrupt Organizations Act (RICO), 18 U.S.C. § 1961-68 (1988 & Supp. V 1993).

Sec. 1961 - Definitions

Sec. 1962 - Prohibited Racketeering Activities.

§ 1962 (a) prohibits any person receiving income derived from a pattern of racketeering activity, as defined in Sec. 1961, from investing this income or using it to acquire, establish, or operate any enterprise engaged in or effecting interstate or foreign commerce.

§ 1962(b) makes it a crime for any person through a pattern of racketeering activity to acquire or maintain an interest in any enterprise engaged in or affecting interstate and foreign trade.

§ 1962(c) prohibits any person employed by or associated with an establishment engaged in or affecting interstate or foreign commerce to carry out the enterprise's affairs through a pattern of racketeering activity or collection of unlawful debt.

§1962(d) makes it unlawful for any person to conspire to violate any of the previous subsections.

Sec. 1963 - Criminal Penalties. Provides for fines, imprisonment. Combined or alternating with these are mandatory asset forfeitures. The section also allows pre-indictment restraining orders and attachment of funds paid to third parties, including attorneys.

Sec. 1964 - Civil Remedies. Allows any person injured by violation of §1962 to bring a civil action for damages. Such a plaintiff may seek treble damages, costs and attorney fees.

Sec. 1965 - Venue & Process.

Sec. 1966 - Expedition of Actions

Sec. 1967 - Evidence

Sec. 1968 - Civil Investigative Demand

b. Cases

H.J. Inc. v. Northwestern Bell Telephone Co., 492 U.S. 229 (1989). An attempt to clarify the meaning of the continuity plus relationship test for a pattern of racketeering established in *Sedima, infra.* Justice Scalia's concuring opinion suggests disquiet in the Court over the question of RICO vagueness.

United States v. Monsanto, 491 U.S. 600 (1989). No exemption in RICO for forfeiture of attorneys' fees. Such forfeiture not contra the Fifth or Sixth Amendments.

Sedima S.P.R.L. v. Imrex Co., 473 U.S. 479 (1985). Held pattern of racketeering of predicate crimes must include continuity plus relationship.

Rusello v. United States, 464 U.S. 16 (1983). Held that racketeering activity profits are subject to forfeiture under §1963 (a)(1).

United States v. Turkette, 452 U.S. 576 (1981). "Enterprise" is a separate element which prosecution in RICO action must prove, but it includes both legitimate and illegitimate bodies.

United States v. Parness, 503 F.2d 430 (2d Cir. 1974), *cert. denied,* 419 U.S. 1105 (1975). An enterprise may include a non-U.S. corporation.

United States v. Noriega, 746 F. Supp. 1506 (S.D. Fla. 1990). Held RICO applicable to conduct outside U.S. if it produced or was intended to produce effects in the U.S.

c. Official Materials

U.S. Department of Justice. Criminal Division. *Racketeer Influenced and Corrupt Organizations (RICO): A Manual for Federal Prosecutors.* 2d rev. ed. Washington, D.C.: U.S. Government Printing Office, 1988.

U.S. Department of Justice. Criminal Division. *United States Attorneys' Manual.* Washington, D.C.: U.S. Government Printing Office, 1988. Secs. 9-110.

d. Bibliography

Dickinson, Peter Somers. *Civil Rico: A Research Guide to Civil Liability for Business Crimes.* Buffalo, N.Y.: Hein, 1989. Although limited to civil RICO litigation, much of this guide's content is equally useful for criminal RICO research. The sections on treatises, legislative materials, books, ALR annotations, and law review articles are helpful starting points.

e. Treatises

Brickey, Kathleen F. *Corporate Criminal Liability.* 2d ed. Deerfield, Ill.: Clark Boardman Callaghan, 1993. Chap. 7. In addition to describing the Act, outlining elements of the RICO offenses, discussing the awful prospect of forfeitures and other penalties, this includes a helpful table of federal statutes, arranged by section numbers and providing captions for each section, for each RICO predicate crime.

Cafone, Joan P., "'RICO' Racketeer - Influenced and Corrupt Organizations Act," (Chap. 24) in *Business Crime: Criminal Liability of the Business Community*. New York: M. Bender, 1981.

Guide to RICO: A Practical Guide for the Corporate Counselor. Edited by J. C. Fricano. Washington, D.C.: Bureau of National Affairs, 1986.

McCormack, David. *RICO- Racketeer Influenced Corrupt Organization*. Fort Worth: Knowles, 1986-. 2 looseleaf vols.

Mathews, Arthur F. et al. *Civil Rico Litigation*. 2d ed. Englewood Cliffs, N.J.: Prentice-Hall, 1992- . 3 looseleaf vols. Be not deceived by the title- most of this treatise applies equally to criminal RICO. In vol. 1, the legislative history and chapters on predicate acts, pattern of racketeering activity and criminal enterprise are good summaries, citing the major (& most minor) cases. Vol. 2's chapters 6 & 7 on the nexus between pattern and enterprise are also useful. Vol. 3 includes the text of the RICO sections of the 1983 and 1989 *U.S. Attorneys' Manuals*.

RICO Civil and Criminal Law and Strategy. Edited by Jed S. Rakoff and Howard W. Goldstein. New York: Law Journal Seminars Press, 1989- . 1 v. looseleaf. Chapter 1 on RICO fundamentals is a first-rate introduction. Chapters 5 & 6 deal with criminal RICO and forfeitures. The ninth chapter outlines considerations for prosecutors while the tenth suggests defense stategy. Chapter 11 tells what may happen in parallel civil/criminal RICO proceedings.

Roddy, Kevin P. *RICO in Business and Commercial Litigation*. New York: McGraw-Hill, 1991-. 2 looseleaf vols. Chapter 2, describing the various types of racketeering activities, 3, on the RICO enterprise, 4, on patterns of racketeering activity, and 5, on the conduct prohibited by§ 1962 are very useful. Appendix H in Vol. 2 reprints the RICO section from the U.S. Attorney's manual while Appendix I reproduces the first edition of *Racketeer Influenced and Corrupt Organizations: a Manual for Federal Prosecutors*.

Vizcarrondo, Paul, Jr. "Racketeer Influenced and Corrupt Organizations (RICO)." In White Collar Crime: Business and

Regulatory Offenses. Edited by Otto G. Obermaier and Robert G. Morvillo. New York: Law Journal Seminars Press, 1990. Chap. 11.

f. Articles

Blakey, G. Robert and Thomas A. Perry. "An Analysis of the Myths That Bolster Efforts to Rewrite RICO and the Various Proposals for Reform: 'Mother of God- Is This the End of RICO?'" Vanderbilt Law Review 43 (1990): 851-1101.

________. and Brian Gettings. "Racketeer Influenced and Corrupt Organizations (RICO): Basic Concepts- Criminal and Civil Remedies." *Temple Law Quarterly*. 53(1980):1009-48. A short history of RICO and description of its structure by two of its progenitors. Excellent guide to the appellate cases through 1979.

________ et al. "What's Next? The Future of RICO." *Notre Dame Law Review*. 65 (1990): 1073-1105.

Breshnahan, Arthur Patrick et al. "Eighth Survey of White Collar Crime: Racketeer Influenced and Corrupt Organizations." *American Criminal Law Review* 30 (1993): 847-907.

Brown, Stephen D. and Alan M. Lieberman. "RICO Basics: a Primer." *Villanova Law Review* 35 (1990): 865-81. This concise guide clearly explains the prohibitions in § 1962.

Coble, Jessica et al. "Seventh Survey of White Collar Crime: Racketeer Influenced and Corrupt Organizations." *American Criminal Law Review* 29 (1992): 495-556.

Dennis, Edward S. G., Jr. "Current RICO Policies of the Department of Justice." *Vanderbilt Law Review* 43 (1990): 651-72.

Fricano, John C. "RICO Extraterritoriality- Just a Matter of Time?" *International Business Lawyer* 13 (1985): 201-8.

Goldsmith, Michael and Vicki Rinne. "Civil RICO, Foreign Defendants, and 'ET'." *Minnesota Law Review* 73 (1989): 1023-80. Most of this article's content applies to criminal RICO.

________ "RICO and Enterprise Criminality: A Response to Gerald E. Lynch." *Columbia Law Review* 88 (1988)774-801.

Lynch, Gerald E. "RICO: The Crime of Being a Criminal (Parts I & II)," *Columbia Law Review* 87 (1987): 661-764

__________. "RICO: The Crime of Being a Criminal (Parts III & IV)," *Columbia Law Review* 87 (1988): 920-84.

Tarlow, Barry "RICO Revisited." *Georgia Law Review* 17 (1983): 291-424.

__________. "RICO: The New Darling of the Prosecutor's Nursery." *Fordham Law Review* 49 (1980): 165-306.

2. Mail and Wire Fraud with Related Crimes: A Checklist

a. Statutes

18 U.S.C. § 371 (1988). This statute makes it a crime for two or more persons to conspire to commit an offense against or defraud the U.S. or its agencies in any manner, if one or more of those persons does an act to "effect the object of the conspiracy."

18 U.S.C. § 1001 (1988). This statute criminalizes making in any matter within the jurisdiction of a U.S. department or agency any false or fraudulent statement or knowingly concealng, falsifying or covering up a material fact.

18 U.S.C. § 014 (1988 & Supp. V 1993). Makes criminal any knowingly false statement or report made to federal financial institutions and FSLIC or FDIC insured banks for the purpose of influencing those bodies' actions on applications, loans, commitments and their extensions or renewals.

18 U.S.C. § 1341-1346 (1988 & Supp. V 1993).

Sec. 1341 - The Mail Fraud Statute. Makes it a crime to devise or intend to devise a scheme to defraud or obtain by false pretences money or property and to further knowingly these ends by placing in or causing to be placed in the U.S. Post Office or receiving from it any matter or thing

Sec. 1342 - Fictitious Name or Address. Makes criminal the use of a false name or address in pursuit of mail fraud as defined in § 1341 or in pursuit of "any other unlawful business"

Sec. 1343 - Fraud by Wire, Radio or Television Fraud Statute.

Sec. 1344 - Bank Fraud Statute

Sec. 1345 - Injunctions Against Fraud. Authorises Attorney General to seek injunctions & restraining orders against persons violating or about to violate any of the above sections,18 U.S.C. § 287, § 371(if involving a conspiracy to defraud the U.S. or its agencies), 1001, and any banking law violation (as defined in 3322(d).

Sec.1346 - Definition of "Scheme or Artifice to Defraud." States that "scheme or artifice to defraud" within the preceding sections includes deprival of a person's intangible right of honest services.

18 U.S.C. § 2314 (1988 & Supp. V 1993). This section makes criminal the transportation, transfer, or transmission in interstate or foreign trade of goods, securities or money valued in excess of $5,000 when the transferor knows they have been stolen converted or taken by fraud. It also makes criminal transportation or inducing or causing the transportation or travel of a person in interstate or foreign commerce in execution of a scheme to defraud that person of money or property valued at $5,000 or more.

49 U.S.C. § 121 (1988). This section of the Bill of Lading Act states that any person who knowingly with intent to defraud "falsely makes, alters, forges, counterfeits, prints, or photographs any bill of lading purporting to represent goods received for shipment among the several States or with foreign nations" or who with fraudulent intent knowingly publishes or utters such a bill of lading or issues oraids in issuing such a bill of lading will be guilty of a midemeanor punishable for each offense by imprisonment of five years or less and a fine of $5.000 or less- or both.

b. Cases

Schmuck v. United States, 489 U.S. 705 (1989). Defendant, who had altered odometers on used cars he sold to retail dealers at inflated prices based on low mileage, attacked his mail fraud conviction, maintaining that the retail dealers' mailings of title application forms bearing the false odometer information to state transportation department for issuance of title to new buyers were not in furtherance of his fraudulent scheme. The Court held that if the mailing was part of the perpetrator's perception of his scheme at the time he devised it- as here it must have been- then it comprised the mailing element of the mail fraud offense.

Carpenter v. United States, 484 U.S. 19 (1987). Upheld a *Wall St. Journal* reporter's mail and wire fraud convictions for giving financial information he had acquired on the job about companies to investors before the Journal published it. Important for recognition of business information as intangible property protected by the fraud statutes and for holding that mere deprivation of the owner's use of his private information without demonstration of actual financial loss thereby violates the statutes. The case also made clear that intangible property- as well as money and physical property is within the scope of the statutes a point not clear after *McNally v. United States, infra,* decided earlier in 1987.

McNally v. United States, 483 U.S. 350 (1987). Held mail (and by implication wire) fraud statute protects money or property but not intangible rights to "good government," thus severely restricting the fraud statutes' increasingly broad application during the 1970's and 1980's. Congress reversed this holding by enacting in 1988 *U.S.Code.,* vol. 18, sec. 1346, *supra.*

United States v. Woodward, 469 U.S. 105 (1985).

18 U.S.C. § 1001 is available to prosecutors even when, as in this case involving a defendant's lie in response to Customs questions at the border whether he was carrying more than $5,000, more specific statutes exist, whether or not the prosecutors use them.

United States v. Rodgers, 466 U.S. 475 (1984). The false statement statute (Sec. 1001) applies to statement made in FBI and Secret Service investigations.

United States v. Maze, 414 U.S. 395 (1974). User of a stolen credit card to buy lodging and meals in several states not guilty of mail fraud because merchants' mailing of charge slips to issuing bank was not a mailing in furtherance of scheme to defraud. The mailing took place after the scheme came to fruition with defendant's stays in the motels and his repasts. Also the mailings were counterproductive to the success of his scheme because they brought it to light- his success would have lasted much longer had the slips never been mailed. These two defenses to the mailing in furtherance of the scheme to defraud element of the mail fraud offense have since been narrowed by *Schmuck, supra.*

Yates v. United States, 354 U.S. 298 (1957). The overt act of a conspirator need not be a crime itself if it furthers a conspiracy against the U.S.

Pereira v. United States, 347 U.S. 1 (1954). Clearly states the elements prosecution must prove for mail fraud: existence of scheme to defraud, intent to defraud through the scheme, and use of the mail to further the scheme.

Blumenthal v. United States, 332 U.S. 539 (1947). Because secrecy and concealment essential to a conspiracy, government need not for conviction show defendant knew all the details or other participants- only that he knew the plan's essential nature.

Pinkerton v. United States, 328 U.S. 640 (1946). Substantive offenses charged with conspiracy are separate offenses and contrary to common law do not "merge". Government need prove only a co-conspirator's participation in the conspiracy to obtain his conviction for any substantive offenses committed by other conspirators in effecting the conspiracy's ends.

United States v. Hutto, 256 U.S. 524 (1921). The overt act done to effect a conspiracy's object need not itself be a criminal offense.

Durland v. United States, 161 U.S. 306 (1896). Held that government need not prove that mailings were successful in carrying out a scheme to defraud.

NOTE: We include the following cases primarily as illustrations of the use of the fraud and related statutes to combat transnational white collar crime.

United States v. Merritt, 988 F.2d 1298 (2d Cir.1993), *cert. denied*, 113 S.Ct. 2933 (1993). Here is fraud perpetrated upon the U.S. (18 U.S.C. § 1031), conspiracy (18 U.S.C. § 371), and wire fraud (18 U.S.C. § 1343), for all of which Merritt was convicted after supplying animal feed unfit for human consumption instead of the milk powder he had contracted to provide and ship to the Sudan under a U.S.A.I.D. contract. With the aid of a false bill of lading he procured payment from Citibank of $936, 870 in A.I.D. funds. After making a plea agreement with the U.S. Attorney's Office, this humanitarian forged a document showing he had paid the feed supplier all but $75,000 of his ill-gotten gains when he had in fact paid the supplier naught. He appealed the trial court's upward departure, for his post-plea conduct, from the Sentencing Guidelines!

United States v. LaSpesa, 956 F.2d 1027 (11th Cir. 1992). Illustrates a combination of charges of mail fraud, conspiracy to commit mail fraud, and illegal transportation of money taken by fraud all arising from defendants' loan arrangement scam in which they collected huge advance fees from entrepreneurs seeking investment loans in return for promises to arrange large credits from an Anguillan bank owned by one of the conspirators.

United States v. Gardner, 894 F.2d 708 (5th Cir. 1990). An importer of used Mercedes Benz cars sought to avoid the expense of converting his imports to comply with Clean Air Act requirements by paying individuals $50 each to use their names on EPA forms applying for personal use exemptions and submitting the forms to U.S. Customs. The court rejected Gardner's appeal that Sec.1001 did not apply because the customs laws do not require "importers" to have an ownership interest in the imported items by holding that the individuals' lack of ownership was a material fact for Customs and EPA purposes and thus within their jurisdiction.

United States v. Gafyczk, 847 F.2d 685 (11th Cir. 1988). To avoid a hefty duty imposed by Italy on imported cigarettes, the defendants shipped large quantities of cigarettes from Miami concealed in containers full of other materials and mislabeled. Only the disguising materials were listed on the shippers' export declarations and bills of lading prepared for these containers and submitted to U.S. Customs as part of the normal export procedure. After the discovery of their enterprise, a U.S. district court convicted them of making false statements in matters within the jurisdiction of a U.S. agency (18 U.S.C. § 1001), making false bills of lading (49 U.S.C. app.§ 121), and conspiracy to commit an offense against the U.S. (18 U.S.C. § 371). The court of appeals reversed the false bill of lading conviction because there was no evidence that defendants had intended to defraud (as opposed to merely misleading) U.S. Customs. Here the court relied on McNally, supra, in finding that fraud must include deprivations of its victim's property - U.S. Customs lost no property : defendants had intended to defraud Italy instead. The indictment, however, made no mention of Italy as the object of the defendants' fraud. The court rejected defendants' claim that the shippers' export declarations were not within the jurisdiction of U.S. Customs, as asserted in the

1001 counts of their indictments because they were Dept. of Commerce forms- the government had proven that U.S. Customs work. used the forms for its purposes and falsified forms could impair its

United States v. Goldberg, 830 F.2d 459 (3d Cir. 1987). Upheld a wire fraud conviction when one of the relevant wire transmissions was a wire transfer of funds from Montreal to Nassau. The court rejected Goldberg's claim that the trial court lacked jurisdiction over this offense because it took place outside the U.S. by finding that the relevant count in the indictment also included Goldberg's telephone call from the U.S. to Montreal instructing his bank to make the wire transfer.

United States v. Fermin Castillo, 829 F.2d 1194 (1st Cir. 1987). This wire fraud case involved a sale of chicken feed from Puerto Rico to a chicken farm in the Dominican Republic. The defendant seller presented faulty documents required by a letter of credit issued by the buyer's Dominican bank, and the Puerto Rico corresponding bank to which he presented the non-conforming documents sought the issuing banks approval by telex before paying the fraudster- who never shipped any chicken feed. The court demolished his contention that his conviction of wire fraud should be reversed because the telexes between the banks were not in furtherance of his scheme to defraud by holding that he must have forseen that such telexes would be sent and that they were essential to the execution of his fraudulent scheme.

United States v. Castro, 829 F.2d 1038 (11th Cir. 1987), *rehearing denied*, 837 F.2d 441 (11th Cir. 1988). A bitter brew for Colombian coffee oligarch Alberto Duque, this opinion rejected his appeal against conviction for creating false bills of lading for coffee supposedly shipped from Colombia to the U.S. He maintained that 49 U.S.C. app.§ 121 applied only to bills of lading issued in the U.S. and not to those issued in foreign countries. The court rejected this reading of the Bill of Lading Act and held 121 applied to bills of lading issued in foreign countries for goods shipped to the U.S.

United States v. Mueller, 786 F.2d 293 (7th Cir. 1986). Illustrative of the wire fraud statute's use in combination with the statute criminalizing false statements to federally insured banks (18 U.S.C. § 1014), this is the sad saga of a German aircraft broker who branched out to the U.S., with unhappy results. Buying four light planes with funds borrowed from German banks, Mueller deposited with the banks the planes' bills of sale, had the planes de-registered in Germany, transported to and re-registered with the FAA in the U.S, and sold them to Americans. In this process he communicated with the German lenders by wire and transferred the purchase price of a buyer from a Jackson, Miss. bank to one in Niagara, Wisconsin by wire. Sending only partial payment to the German lenders and retaining the balance from his American sales, Mueller also applied for a loan from the Wisconsin bank, using one of the planes as collateral and representing in his application that the plane was free of all liens, encumbrances, and security interests. The appeals court rejected his claims of good faith and refusal by the trial court to decide that under American commercial law the German lenders lacked a security interest in the plane he used as collateral.

United States v. Tucker, 773 F.2d 136 (7th Cir. 1985), *cert. denied*, 478 U.S. 1022, *rehearing denied*, 478 U.S. 1035 (1986). Held for the first time, in a fascinating case involving the failure to ship and deliver 6,000 tons of beans to a Guatemalan importer and the defendants' presentation of false documents to a Chicago correspondent bank to obtain payment on a letter of credit issued by the buyer's Guatemalan bank, that a letter of credit is within the scope of 18 U.S.C. § 1014. The defendants' false documents supported their application which they intended would induce the Chicago bank to honor its commitment to pay on the letter of credit.

United States v. Beck, 615 F.2d 441 (7th Cir. 1980). A South African gun importer here appealed his conviction for aiding and abetting the illegal export of arms and filing of false customs declarations required for export in violation of 18 U.S.C. § 1001. Although Beck did not himself prepare the false export declaration forms, the court held, he particpated in the plan to export arms which necessarily involved forseeability on his part that false information would be prsented to Customs, and he thus aided and abetted the violation of § 1001.

United States v. Parness, 503 F.2d 430 (2nd Cir.1974), *cert. denied*, 419 U.S. 1105 (1975). An early example of RICO use and illustrative of § 2314, supra, as RICO predicate crime. An organizer of gambling junkets to a St. Maarten hotel casino withheld gamblers' debts he had collected on behalf of the hotel's owner, making that owner unable to repay a large loan secured by the hotel's stock. Having bought the loan from the original lender with money he had withheld from the hotel owner and transferred it to a Netherlands Antilles paper corporation, the defendant himself made a new loan to the owner to enable him to repay the first and ultimately foreclosed, acquiring the hotel. In the process he caused the original owner to travel to New Jersey from New York to sign papers and he arranged for purchase of cashiers checks at a New Jersey bank and brought them to New York. Convicted on several counts for violating 18 U.S.C. § 2314, the defendant also had a conviction under RICO (18 U.S.C. § 1962 (b)). The appellate court dismissed his claims that RICO was unconstitutionally vague and did not encompass the acquisition of foreign businesses with criminal proceeds.

c. Official Materials

U.S. Department of Justice. Criminal Division. *United States Attorneys' Manual.* Washington, D.C.: U.S. Government Printing Office, 1988. Secs. 9-42, 9-43, 9-44. Sec. 9-42 is the prosecutor's guide to the false statements statute (Sec. 1001). Sec. 9-43 deals with the mail fraud statute while 9-44 covers wire fraud. All clearly outline the offenses' elements, venue, indictment drafting, and required evidence. Each section cites those cases the Justice Dept. considers most significant. Sec. 9-43 also has a section on conspiracy to violate the mail fraud statute.

d. Treatises

Brickey, Kathleen F. *Corporate Criminal Liability.* 2d ed. Deerfield, Ill.: Clark Boardman Callaghan, 1993. Chap. 8.II.

Coffee, John C., Jr. and Charles K. Whitehead. "The Federalization of Fraud: Mail and Wire Fraud Statutes." In *White Collar Crime: Business and Regulatory Offenses*. Edited by Otto E. Obermaier and Robert G. Morvillo. New York: Law Journal Seminars Press, 1990. Chap. 9.

Marcus, Paul. *Prosecution and Defense of Criminal Conspiracy Cases.* New York: M. Bender, 1978. 1 looseleaf vol.

e. Articles

Burgman, Dierdre A. "Unilateral Conspiracy: Three Critical Perspectives." *De Paul Law Review* 29 (1979): 75-113.

Dolan, John F. "Letter of Credit Practice: Torts, Crimes, and Some Other Don'ts." *Banking Law Journal* 104, (1987): 36-41. Points out a new peril posed by *United States v. Tucker, supra*- criminal charges under 18 U.S.C. § 1014.

Gagliardi, John E. "Back to the Future: Federal Mail and Wire Fraud under 18 U.S.C. § 1346." Washington Law Review 68 (1993):901-21. Addresses the question: what are "honest services" as used in Sec.1346 and argues that the fraud statutes should extend only to fiduciary duty breaches involving reasonable forseeability by the breacher of pecuniary harm to persons owed the fiduciary duty.

Gambale, Jo Ann and Jeffrey E. Richardson. "Eighth Survey of White Collar Crime: False Statements." *American Criminal Law Review* 30. (1993): 659-83.

Goldstein, Abraham S. "Conspiracy to Defraud the United States." *Yale Law Journal* 68 (1959): 405-63.

Kane, Tracy Anne, Comment, "Foreign Commerce: Federal Bill of Lading Act, *United States v. Castro*," 829 F.2d 1038 (11th Cir. 1987) *Suffolk Transnational Law Journal* 12 (1989): 647-58. Useful for its history of the Bill of Lading Act's criminal section, as well as its comment on this case.

Lynch, Thomas and William A. McConagha. "Seventh Survey of White Collar Crime: Mail and Wire Fraud." *American Criminal Law Review* 29 (1992):.465-94. A clear explication of the elements of mail and wire fraud, the impact of *McNally v. United States* and subsequent enactment of 18 U.S.C. § 1346 by Congress, this also indicates the most common defenses in fraud cases. Handily arranges citations to major appellate cases on each topic by circuits, making this not only explication but case locator.

Marcus, Paul. "Conspiracy: The Criminal Agreement in Theory and Practice." *Georgetown Law Journal* 65 (1977): 925-69.

________. "Criminal Conspiracy Law: Time to Turn Back from an Ever Expanding, Ever More Troubling Area" *William & Mary Bill of Rights Law Journal* 1 (1992): 1-45.

Miller, Kenneth M. "Materiality: an Element of 18 U.S.C. 1001 and a Question for the Jury" *Loyola of Los Angeles Law Review* 23 (1990): 989-1022.

Orkin, Marilyn E. "Corporate Counsel's Guide to the Mail and Wire Fraud Statutes." *Corp. Couns. Quarterly* 5:2 (April, 1989): 1-41.

Podgor, Ellen S. "Mail Fraud: Opening Letters." *South Carolina Law Review* 43 (1992):.223-71. A small scale treatise on mail fraud, this explains its two required elements- existence of a scheme to defraud and mailing[s] in furtherance of the scheme. Covers all major Supreme Court and circuit cases. Argues the centrality of *Schmuck, supra,* and says post-*Schmuck* prosecutors need really only demonstrate existence of a scheme to defraud and a mail which the defendant saw as part of his scheme's execution. Whether the defendant did see this will be a matter for the jury. Also usefully analyzes mail fraud as RICO predicate. Concludes that the statute is dangerously open-ended and requires rewriting.

Rakoff, Jed S. "The Federal Mail Fraud Statute (Part I)." *Duquesne Law Review* 18 (1980). 771-822. Witty and acute, this is still one of the best introductions to the mail fraud statute and its history.

Schleicher, Lisa M. and Derek M. Stoldt. "Eighth Survey of White Collar Crime: Federal Criminal Conspiracy." *American Criminal Law Review* 30 (1993): 685-716.

Smith, Michael Clay. "Recklessness and Good Faith under the Mail Fraud Statute: Mens Rea by Accident?" *Criminal Law Bulletin* 27 (1991): 315-33.

Tosi, L. T. "Seventh Survey of White Collar Crime: False Statements." *American Criminal Law Review* 29 (1992): 369-88. Clearly explains the elements of an offense under 18 U.S.C. § 1001, the prosecutors' "catch-all" statute, often used in conjunction with the fraud statutes. Gives a useful summary of the "exculpatory no" exception and its relation to the Fifth Amendment.

Whitzman, Stephen. "Proof of Conspiracy: The Co-conspirator's Exception to the Hearsay Rule." *Criminal Law Quarterly* 28 (1986): 203-25.

C. Bribery of Foreign Officials

One of President Richard Nixon's inadvertent legacies to his country, the Foreign Corrupt Practices Act, *U.S.Code*, Title. 15, secs. 78b, 78m, 78dd-1, 78dd-2, 78ff, criminalising the payment of bribes to foreign officials, sprang out of the Watergate scandal revelations. Sections 78dd-1 and 78dd-2 contain the Act's anti-bribery provisions. Section 78m(b) requires companies to keep adequate accounting records, thus ensuring that payments to foreign officials meet their auditors' and regulators' eyes.

Anyone first approaching this area should consult Steven C. Perkins, " Bibliography on the Foreign Corrupt Practices Act of 1977," *Western State University Law Review.* 14 (1987): 491-521. Too early to catch the Act's 1988 Amendments, this is still useful for its lists of legislative materials, looseleaf manuals, theses, monographs, and numerous articles. An index to cases, as well as a compendium of the cases themselves and a wealth of other material, is the *Foreign Corrupt Practices Reporter* (Bus. Laws Inc. 1979-).

The standard text on the Act is George C. Greanias and Duane Windsor, *The Foreign Corrupt Practices Act: Anatomy of a Statute* (Lexington, Mass.: Lexington Books,1982). Covering the 1988 Amendments and predicting the possibility of a RICO icing on the cake of charges which a briber may find on his prosecutor's platter, is Hurd Baruch, "International Transactions Which Violate the Foreign Corrupt Practices Act or Other Criminal Statutes," in *Law and Practice of United States Regulation of International Trade*, edited by Charles R. Johnston, Jr.(New York: Oceana, 1987-.). Also helpful is Robert James Gareis and William Joseph Linklater's "The Foreign Corrupt Practices Act: a Pragmatic Analysis," chap. 13 in *International Trade: Avoiding Criminal Risks* , edited by William M. Hannay (Salem, N.H.: Butterworth, 1991).

Woe and damnation are the cries of Bartley A. Brennan in "The Foreign Corrupt Practices Act Amendments of 1988: 'Death' of a Law," *North Carolina Journal of International Law and Commercial Regulation.* 15 (1990): 229-47. These amendments, he maintains, effectively gutted the Act. Eschewing opinion on the amendments' effects but offering excellent explication of the amended Act's requirements, elements of offenses under it, possible defenses- all citing most of the major appellate cases dealing with such matters-is Katherine M. Albright and Grace Won, "Eighth Survey of White Collar Crime- Foreign Corrupt Practices Act," *American Criminal Law Review* 30 (1993): 773-88. John E. Impert proffers some excellent advice on compliance in his article, " A Program for Compliance with the Foreign Corrupt Practices Act and Foreign Law Restrictions on the Use of Sales Agents," *International Lawyer*. 24 (1990): 1009-28.

A different take on bribery abroad, not strictly within our scope because concerned with foreign corporate bribers unburdened by any FCPA equivalent in their countries' laws, is Franklin A. Gevurtz, "Using the Antitrust Laws to Combat Overseas Bribery by Foreign Countries: a Step to Even the Odds in International Trade," *Virginia Journal of International Law*. 27 (1987): 211-72. He examines the possibility of walloping these foreigners with the Sherman Act, Federal Trade Commission Act or the Robinson-Patman Act so as to even the playing field for our clean-playing corporations. Damn extraterritoriality- full speed ahead! An antidote to this overdose of the screaming eagle is the sympathetic and insightful examination of gifts' social and cultural role in developing countries' business offered by Jeffrey A. Fadiman in his "A Traveler's Guide to Gifts and Bribes," *Harvard Business Review* 86:4 (July-Aug., 1986): 122-36.

Bribery of Officials Abroad: U.S. Criminal Law.
A Checklist

a. Statutes

Foreign Corrupt Practices Act. *U.S.Code*. Title 15, secs. 78b,78m, 78dd-1, 78dd-2., 78ff (1988 & Supp. V 1993).

Sec.78m(b) requires adequate accounting record keeping. Sec. 78m(b)(5) prohibits any person from knowingly failing to "implement a system of internal accounting controls" and forbids him to "falsify any book, record, or account . . . ."

Secs.78dd-1 and 78dd-2 are the Act's antibribery provisions

Sec. 78ff prescribes penalties for violations.

b. Regulations

Code of Federal Regulations.Title 22, pt. 709 (1993). These regulations make individuals and companies, under Sec. 237(1) of the Foreign Assistance Act of 1961 as amended, ineligible for Overseas Private

Investment Corporation services if convicted of an FCPA offense "related to an OPIC-supported project."

Internal Revenue Service Regulations. Code of Federal Regulations. Title 26, Sec. 1.952-1(a)(4) (1993).

Foreign Corrupt Practices Act Opinion Procedure. Code of Federal Regulations. Title 28, pt.80 (1993). Issued by the Department of Justice in September, 1992, this procedure makes it possible for issuers and domestic concerns to obtain the Attorney-General's opinion on whether specified prospective conduct complies with the Department's enforcement policies for the Act's antibribery provisions in 15 U.S.C. § 78dd-1 & 78dd-2. Pt. 80.10 establishes a rebuttable presumption in any action under 15 U.S.C. 78dd-1 & 78dd-2 that conduct, which an Attorney-General's opinion has indicated conforms, complies with sections 78dd-1 & 78dd-2. Pt. 80.14 prohibits disclosure to the public of any document or other material provided to the Department of Justice in connection with a request for an opinion.

c. Cases

W.S. Kirkpatrick & Co. v. Environmental Tectonics Corp., Int., 493 U.S. 400 (1990). In a civil RICO action, brought by an unsuccessful bidder for a Nigerian military construction contract against the successful bidder, which had earlier pleaded guilty to violations of the FCPA in bribing Nigerian officials to obtain the contract, the Supreme Court held that the act of state doctrine did not bar pursuit of the action. The case required no judgement by the court as to the legality of Nigeria's actions in Nigeria. Mere embarassment at their disclosure would not implicate the act of state doctrine.

United States v. O'Hara, 960 F.2d 11 (2d Cir. 1992). Affirmed a trial court's denial of a defendant's motion to withdraw his guilty plea to a single count of aiding and abetting false record-keeping by the Harris Corporation contrary to 15 U.S.C. 78m(b)(2)(A) (1988) & 18 U.S.C. 2 (1988) after a federal court in California directed a verdict of acquittal for his alleged co-conspirators in a trial where the defendant appeared as a prosecution witness concerning bribes to Colombian government officials involved in awarding telecommunications contracts.

United States v. Castle, 925 F.2d 831 (5th Cir. 1991) (*per curiam*). The United States cannot prosecute foreign officials under 18 U.S.C. 371 for conspiracy to violate the FCPA. Two Americans were indicted for violating the Act by paying $50,000 to two Canadian officials to ensure acceptance of their company's bid to sell buses to a provincial government. The United States also indicted all four defendants for conspiracy to violate the Act. The Court of Appeals affirmed and appended the trial court's opinion dismissing the charges against the Canadians on the grounds that the FCPA does not make acceptance by a foreign official a crime and Congress did not intend that they should be prosecuted for conspiring to violate the Act. The trial court opinion originally appeared as *United States v. Blondak*, 741 F. Supp. 116 (N.D. Tex. 1990).

United States v. Liebo, 923 F.2d 1308 (8th Cir.1991). Suggests that an employee's gift or gratuity to a foreign official will not be given "corruptly" within the meaning of the FCPA if the employee's supervisor instructed him to make it. Here a military parts supply company's employee paid for a Niger official's honeymoon trip to Paris, Stockholm and London. After the employee's conviction, the trial court denied his motion for a new trial based on newly discovered evidence that his supervisor, the company's president, approved use of the company's Diner's Club card to purchase the tickets. The Court of Appeals reversed, finding this information was strong evidence from which the jury might find the employee acted under his supervisor's instructions rather than voluntarily- and thus did not act "corruptly" within the Act's meaning.

Lamb v. Phillip Morris, Inc., 915 F.2d 1024 (6th Cir. 1990), *cert. denied*, 498 U.S. 1086 (1991). Held that the FCPA included no implied private right of enforcement.

McLean v. International Harvester Co., 902 F.2d 372 (5th Cir. 1990).

McLean v. International Harvester Co., 817 F.2d 1214 (5th Cir. 1987). Here Mr. McLean appealed unsuccessfully against a trial court's dismissal of his civil action against his former employer for conspiracy to violate his civil rights and for casting him in a false light when it negotiated its own guilty plea in an FCPA prosecution.

United States v. McLean, 738 F.2d 655 (5th Cir. 1984), *cert. denied*, 470 U.S. 1050 (1985). Although this was an appeal by the government from a trial court's dismissal of charges against George S. McLean, a former Vice-President of International Harvester Corp., for violation of the FCPA on the ground that the Eckhardt Amendment, 15 U.S.C. 78ff(c)(3) (1982), required conviction of McLean's employer for violating the Act before the employee could be convicted, and the 1988 Amendments to the FCPA removed the Eckhardt Amendment, making the case's holding no longer valid, the opinion is of interest for the light it throws on International Harvester's bribery of PEMEX officials to obtain the Mexican national oil company's orders for turbine compressors in the 1970's.

United States v. International Harvester Co., 720 F.2d 418 (5th Cir. 1983), *cert. denied*, 466 U.S. 939 (1984). Denied Mr. George S. McLean's appeal against a trial court's refusal to expunge his name from an information which named him as a co-conspirator in a 1982 prosecution of his employer undr the FCPA for bribing PEMEX officials. When International Harvester pleaded guilty, the government filed an offer of proof naming McLean. McLean's attempt to expunge his name failed because he had already been charged separately for the same offense and thus could defend his good name in his own trial.

d. Bibliography

Perkins, Steven C. "Bibliography on the Foreign Corrupt Practices Act of 1977." *Western State University Law Review* 14 (1987): 491-521. Lists legislative materials, looseleaf services, 18 monographs, 12 theses, and numerous newspaper, law review, and accounting/business journal articles. No annotations.

e. Looseleaf Services

Foreign Corrupt Practices Act Reporter. Chesterland, Ohio: Business Laws Inc., 1979-.

Kugel, Yerachmiel and Neal P. Cohen. *Government Regulation of Business Ethics* Dobbs Ferry, N.Y.: Oceana, 1977-.

f. Treatises

Baruch Hurd. "International Transactions Which Violate the Foreign Corrupt Practices Act or Other Criminal Statutes." in *Law and Practice of United States Regulation of International Trade*. Edited by Charles R. Johnston, Jr. New York: Oceana, 1987-. Chap. 11. Covers the 1988 Amendments to the Act. In addition to ample explication of the elements of offences under the Act, its enforcement, and penalties, this also examines possible violations of the mail and wire fraud statutes, RICO, and 18 U.S.C. 1001, which criminalises the making of "false official statements."

Gareis, Robert J. and Paul McCarthy. "Foreign Corrupt Practices Act and Related Statutes." In *International Criminal Law: A Guide to U.S. Practice and Procedure*. Edited by Ved P. Nanda and M. Cherif Bassiouni. New York: Practising Law Institute, 1987. p.193-229 Antedates the 1988 Amendments. Chapter 7.

_______. and William Joseph Linklater. "The Foreign Corrupt Practices Act: a Pragmatic Analysis." In *International Trade: Avoiding Criminal Risks*. Edited by William M. Hannay. Salem, N.H.: Butterworth, 1991. Chap. 13.

Gevurtz, Franklin A. "The United States Approach to Combating International Bribery in the Sale of Goods." In *Survey of the International Sale of Goods*. Edited by Louis Lafili et al. Boston: Kluwer, 1986. p.333-45. Chap 14.

Greanias, George C. and Duane Windsor. *The Foreign Corrupt Practices Act: Anatomy of a Statute*. Lexington, Mass.: Lexington Books, 1982.

Jones, Glower W. et al. "The Foreign Corrupt Practices Act." In *Doing Business in Kuwait and Saudi Arabia*. Atlanta: Smith, Currie & Hancock, 1991. p.84-98. Here in 15 pages is a useful summary description of the FCPA- and how to comply with it.

Mitchell, Roy S. and Markham Ball. "The Foreign Corrupt Practices Act." In *A Guide to Contracting in the Middle East*. Washington, D.C.: Federal Publications, 1991. Chap. VI. Chapter VI clearly outlines the record keeping and anti-bribery provisions of the Act and its enforcement by the SEC and Department of Justice.

g. Articles

NOTE: We have limited the list below to articles published after 1988. Perkins, *supra*, offers a comprehensive list of articles on the Act through 1987

Albright, Katherine M. and Grace Won. "Eighth Survey of White Collar Crime- Foreign Corrupt Practices Act." *American Criminal*

Law Review 30 (1993): 773-88. Discusses the elements of offenses under the Act, the two affirmative defenses it provides, penalties for violations, and enforcement.

Bliss, Julia Christine and Gregory J. Spak. "The Foreign Corrupt Practices Act of 1988: Clarification or Evisceration?" *Law and Policy in International Business* 20 (1989): 441-69.

Brennan, Bartley A. "The Foreign Corrupt Practices Act Amendments of 1988: 'Death' of a Law." *North Carolina Journal of International Law and Commercial Regulation* 15 (1990): 229-47. A critical analysis of changes made by the amendments. Argues that they effectively "gutted" the original Act.

Earle, Beverley H. "Foreign Corrupt Practices Act Amendments: The Omnibus Trade and Competitiveness Act's Focus on Improving Investment Opportunities." *Cleveland State Law Review* 37 (1989): 549-56. Useful solely for its summary description of the amendments. Contains no actual analysis of their contribution to improved investment opportunities.

Fadiman, Jeffrey A. "A Traveler's Guide to Gifts and Bribes." *Harvard Business Review* 64:4 (July-Aug., 1986): 122-36. Examines sympathetically the cultural motivations behind many requests for gifts in developing countries and suggests legal alternatives to bribes that may meet these motivations. Combines empathy with readability- obviously a non-attorney author!

Fremantle, Adam and Sherman Katz. "The Foreign Corrupt Practices Act Amendments of 1988." *International Lawyer* 23 (1989): 755-67. Describes clearly and succinctly the original provisions of the 1977 Act, problems it posed for business, and the changes wrought by the 1988 amendments in the Omnibus Trade and Competitiveness Act. Examines the alterations to the antibribery provisions more extensively than those to the act's accounting sections.

Gevurtz, Franklin A. "Using the Antitrust Laws to Combat Overseas Bribery by Foreign Countries: A Step to Even the Odds in International Trade." *Virginia Journal of International Law* 27 (1987): 211-72. Examines the potential of the Sherman Act, Federal Trade Commission Act, and the Robinson-Patman Act for prosecution of foreign corporate bribers whose success in overseas markets has deleterious effects on American exporters.

Joy, S. Gregory "Application of Selected American Laws to United States Companies Transacting Business in Kuwait: Foreign Corrupt Practices Act and Antiboycott Legislation." *Mercer Law Review* 43 (1992): 691-723. A clear exposition of the Act's accounting and antibribery provisions, its enforcement, and penalties for its violation.

Impert, John E. "A Program for Compliance with the Foreign Corrupt Practices Act and Foreign Law Restrictions on the Use of Sales Agents." *International Lawyer* 24 (1990): 1009-28.

Mazzarantani, George H. "White Collar Crime: Fifth Survey of Law- Foreign Corrupt Practices Act." *American Criminal Law Review* 26 (1989): 855-73.

Shaw, Bill. "Foreign Corrupt Practices Act: Amendments of 1988." *Maryland Journal of International Law and Trade* 14 (1990): 161-74. Gives the background of the amendments and comments favorably on three changes: adoption of the prudent official standard for the "reasonable detail" and "reasonable assurance" record keeping requirements in the Act's accounting section; substitution of actual knowledge for "reason to know" as the basis for criminal liability for providing funds or other things of value to third parties who may in turn use these to bribe officials; and the exception for payments to procure "routine governmental action."

D. Money Laundering

The United States' "war on drugs" has created a web of statutes intended to extirpate the money trade fathered by, and essential to, international narcotics trading. An excellent guide to this web is Fletcher N. Baldwin, Jr. and Robert J. Munro's magisterial *Money Laundering, Asset Forfeiture and International Crimes* (Dobbs Ferry, N.Y.: Oceana, 1993- .). This three volume looseleaf work also has a useful chapter on RICO and money laundering as well as summary descriptions of eighty-six other nations' money laundering law. Useful for its treatment of British Commonwealth jurisdictions (several of which are or have been popular bank secrecy havens) is *International Efforts to Combat Money Laundering,* edited by W. C. Gilmore (Cambridge: Grotius Publications, 1992). A worldwide guide to bank secrecy laws, *International Bank Secrecy,* edited by Dennis Campbell (London: Sweet & Maxwell, 1992) has in its chapter 36 a clear and succinct treatment of United States laws.

Devoted exclusively to money laundering and its Siamese twin, bank secrecy, is Miami-published *Money Laundering Alert*, a monthly newsletter.

A Checklist of U.S. Law

a. Statutes

12 U.S.C. § 3403 (c) (1988 & Supp. V 1993). This section of the Right to Financial Privacy Act allows financial institutions and their officers, employes, or agents to notify government authorities that they have information relevant to possible law violation by a customer. It allows disclosure to such authorities of customer name or other identifying information, nature of suspected illegality. Relieves the institution and its employees from liability to the customer for such disclosure and failure to inform the customer of it.

18 U.S.C. § 981-82 (1988 & Supp. V 1993).

Sec. 981 provides for civil forfeiture of real or personal property involved in attempted or actual transactions violating 31 U.S.C. § 5313(a) or 5324 and 18 U.S.C. 1956-57.

Sec. 982 requires court in imposing sentence for violation of 31 U.S.C. 5313(a) & 5324 or 18 U.S.C. 1956-57 to order the forfeiture to the U.S. of any real or personal property involved in the offense or traceable to it. Has exception for property of financial institutions & their employees who violate 31 U.S.C. 5313(a).

18 U.S.C. § 1956-57 (1988 & Supp. V 1993).

Sec. 1956 makes it a crime to carry out or attempt to carry out a transaction with guilty intent knowing that the property involved is proceeds of unlawful activity (specified in 1956(c)(7)- includes all RICO predicate offenses & most other white collar crimes; to transport, transfer, or transmit a monetary instrument out of or into the U.S. with guilty intent; and to conduct or attempt to conduct a financial transaction involving property which a law enforcement officer says is unlawful proceeds (e.g., a sting).

Sec. 1957 makes it a crime to knowingly engage in a monetary transaction in criminally derived property valued greater than $10,000.

18 U.S.C. § 1960 (Supp. V 1993).

This section, added by the Annunzio-Wylie Anti-Money Laundering Act, Pub. L. No. 102-550, § 1512(a) of 1992, makes it a federal crime to control, own, manage, or direct all or part of a business knowing it to be a money transmitting business affecting interstate or foreign commerce that operates in a State without an appropriate state money transmitting license or where state law makes its operation a misdemeanor or felony.

26 U.S.C. § 6050I (1988 & Supp. V1993).

Requires anyone receiving $10,000 in cash in the course of trade or business to report it to the I.R.S. Failure so to report is a crime, as is structuring to avoid the necessity of reporting.

31 U.S.C. § 5311-28 (1988 & Supp. V 1993).

These are the reporting and record keeping of monetary transactions sections of the Bank Secrecy Act of 1970.

Sec. 5312 - Definitions and Application

"Financial institution" in 5312(a)(2) includes FDIC insured banks, commercial banks, private banks, thrifts, SEC-registered brokers, currency exchanges, travellers check issuers & cashers, credit card operators, pawnbrokers, travel agents, the U.S. Postal Service, and, just in case, any other business the Secretary of the Treasury may designate by regulation.

Sec. 5313. Reports on domestic coin & currency transactions.

Sec. 5314. Records and reports on foreign financial agency transactions.

Sec. 5315. Reports on foreign currency transactions. Requires the Secretary of the Treasury to prescribe by regulation required reports on foreign currency transactions by United States persons and foreign persons controlled by a United States person as these are defined by the Securities & Exchange Act § 7(f)(2)(A) & (C).

Sec. 5318. Compliance, exemptions and summons authority. Includes, since 1992, new subsec. (g) enabling Sec. of Treasury to require reporting by financial institutions of "suspicious" transactions relevant to possible violations of laws or regulations.

Sec. 5319. Availability of reports Requires Sec. of Treasury to make available at request of head of an agency of the U.S. information in reports filed under 5313, 5314, or 5316.

Sec. 5321. Civil penalties.

Sec. 5322. Criminal penalties

Sec. 5323. Rewards for informants

Sec. 5324. Structuring transactions to evade reporting requirements. Prohibits any person from structuring or assisting/attempting to structure any transaction with one or more domestic financial institutions or cause such institutions to fail to file or file with a material ommission or misstatement of fact a report required by 5313(a).

Sec. 5325. Identification required to purchase certain monetary instruments.

Sec. 5327. Identification of financial institutions requirements.

Sec. 5328. Whistleblower protections.

b. Regulations

Code of Federal Regulations. Title 26,. sec. 1.6050I (1994). Makes "cash" in 26 U.S.C. § 6050I include checks, money orders, travellers checks, and cashiers checks- and requires filing of the report required by 6050I on I.R.S. Form 8300.

Financial Recordkeeoing and Reporting of Currency and Foreign Transactions Regulations. *Code of Federal Regulations*. Title 31, secs. 103.11-77 & app. (1994).

c. Cases

California Bankers Association v. Shultz, Secretary of the Treasury, 416 U.S. 21 (1974). Upheld constitutionality of the Bank Secrecy Act.

United States v. Campbell, 977 F.2d 854 (4th Cir. 1992), *cert. denied*, 113 S.Ct. 1331 (1993). For conviction on § 1956 charges, government must show defendant had knowledge that a real estate sale she brokered was designed to conceal illegal proceeds. Also contains clear statement of the 1957 offense elements, stressing centrality of defendant's knowledge that propery involved in transaction is criminally derived.

United States v. Elgersma, 971 F.2d 690 (11th Cir. 1992) (en banc). Because criminal forfeiture is not an element of a narcotics violation, the government's standard of proof need not be proof beyond a reasonable doubt but merely preponderance of the evidence.

United States v. Montoya, 945 F.2d 1068 (9th Cir. 1991). Affirmed the conviction of a California state legislator under § 1956(a)(1)(A)(i) for depositing a check for $3,000, paid him as a bribe by FBI agents, in his bank account. The deposit, the court held, was "promotion" of the unlawful activity of bribery.

United States v. Lee, 937 F.2d 1388 (9th Cir. 1991), *cert. denied*, 112 S.Ct. 977 (1992). Appealing their convictions for violating the Lacey Act by importing tons of salmon contrary to Taiwanese law and violating 18 U.S.C. § 1956 by transferring monetary instruments from Taiwan to the U.S. with intent to promote a specified illegal activity, Taiwanese fishermen claimed that while 18 U.S.C. 545 violation was a specified unlawful activity, violation of the Lacey Act itself was not, therefore prosecutors could § not base their 1956 charge on violation of 545, which merely prohibits importation of merchandise "contrary to law." The court rejected this argument, holding 1956 permitted the pyramiding of offenses involved because a violation of 545 always requires reference to another statute- such as the Lacey Act- in order for importation to be contrary to law.

United States v. Sanders, 929 F.2d 1466 (10th Cir. 1991), *cert. denied*, 112 S.Ct. 143 (1991). In an appeal against conviction under § 1956(a)(1)(B)(i), the court reversed defendant's conviction based on purchase of two new cars with illegally derived funds, because the purchase was open and without attempt to conceal or disguise the purchase funds' source and nature.

United States v. Bank of New England, 821 F.2d 844, (1st Cir. 1987), *cert. denied,* 484 U.S. 943 (1987). Upheld conviction of bank for willful failure to report multiple cash transactions over $10,000 as violations of Currency Transaction Reporting Act when jury had acquitted all the bank's employees of intentionally failing to report the transactions but found the bank itself had displayed "flagrant organizational indifference" to the statute and its requirements. The bank had collective knowledge greater than that possessed by any individual staff member.

United States v. All Monies ($477,048.62) in Account No. 90-3617-3, 754 F. Supp. 1467 (D. Haw. 1991). In a § 981 forfeiture action the prosecution showed probable cause that more than half the money in a foreign exchange bank account was property involved in illegal money laundering. Regarding the owner's claim for the balance, the court held that 981(a)(1)(A) applied to all property which facilitates violations of 18 U.S.C. 1956-57. It also noted that 981-82 forfeitures were, unlike similar forfeitures in RICO, in rem actions.

d. Official Materials

U.S. Department of Justice. Criminal Division. *United States Attorneys' Manual.* Washington, D.C.: U.S. Government Printing Office, 1988. Sec. 9-105 .

President's Commission on Organized Crime. *Interim Report. The Cash Connection: Organized Crime, Financial Institutions, and Money Laundering.* Washington, D.C. Government Printing Office, 1984.

United States Sentencing Commission. *Federal Sentencing Guidelines Manual.* St. Paul, Minn. West Publishing Co., 1993. Chap. 8.

e. Bibliography

McCarl, Henry N. and Chiang-Hsing Yang. *Economic Impact of the Underground Economy; a Bibliography on Money Laundering and Other Aspects of Off-the-Record Economic Transactions.* Monticello, Ill.: Vance Bibliographies, 1989.

f. Treatises

Adams, James R. and Douglas Frantz. *A Full Service Bank: How BCCI Stole Millions Around the World* . New York: Pocket Books, 1992. The BCCI saga makes fascinating reading and illustrates how a tremendous transnational enterprise became entangled in the U.S. white collar crime legal net.

Baldwin, Fletcher N. Jr. and Robert J. Munro. *Money Laundering, Asset Forfeiture and International Crimes.* Dobbs Ferry, N.Y.: Oceana, 1993. 3 looseleaf vols.

Beaty, Jonathan and S. C. Gwynne. *The Outlaw Bank: a Wild Ride into the Secret Heart of BCCI.* New York: Random House, 1993.

Carberry, Charles M. *Money Laundering: Reporting & Regulatory Requirements* New York: Law Journal Seminars Press, 1992.

Cohen, Melanie Rovner et al. "United States." In *International Bank Secrecy.* Edited by Dennis Campbell. London: Sweet & Maxwell, 1992. Chap. 36. Clarity and brevity make this outline of the Bank Secrecy Act, Money Laundering Control Act, and the wonderfully named Right to Financial Privacy Act a helpful introduction. Covers enforcement and penalties as well as elements of offenses.

Duffy, Joseph J. and John A. Hedges. "United States Money Laundering Statutes: the Business Executive's Conundrum." In *International Trade: Avoiding Criminal Risks.* Edited by William M.Hannay. Salem, N.H.: Butterworth, 1991. Chap. 14. Analyzes the Money Laundering Control Act of 1986, elements of the offenses it creates, advises on record keeping and reporting requirements, and suggests compliance techniques. Also tells how to deal with investigations for non-compliance.

Fischer, L. Richard. *The Law of Financial Privacy: a Compliance Guide.* 2d ed. Boston: Warren, Gorham & Lamont, 1991.

*International Efforts to Combat Money Laundering.*Edited by W.C. Gilmore. Cambridge: Grotius Pub., 1992.

*Money Laundering and Forfeiture*Edited by Charles Carberry and Gary P. Naftalis. New York: Law Journal Seminars Press, 1992.

The Money Trail: Confiscation of Proceeds of Crime, Money Laundering and Cash Transaction Reporting. Edited by Brent Fisse et al. New York: Law Book Co.,1992.

Truell, Peter and Larry Gurwin. *False Profits: The Inside Story of BCCI, the World's Most Corrupt Financial Empire.* Boston: Houghton Mifflin,1992.

Villa, John K. *Banking Crimes: Fraud, Money Laundering, and Embezzlement*. Deerfield, Ill.: Clark Boardman Callaghan, 1987. 1 looseleaf vol.

g. Newsletters

Money Laundering Alert. Miami: ALERT Publication Partners, 1989-. (Monthly.). Not exactly "how to do it," but offers an awful lot of how it is done and the latest attempts to stamp it out. New cases, regulations, enforcement actions, and international activities on laundering and forfeiture.

h. Articles

Adams, Whitney. "Effective Strategies for Banks in Avoiding Criminal, Civil, and Forfeiture Liability in Money Laundering Cases." *Alabama Law Review* 44 (1993): 669-701. A clear explication of the Bank Secrecy Act's reporting requirements and of the Money Laundering Control Act's provisions. Shows how forfeiture provisions can endanger bank security interests in real estate, deposits, and inventories as well as the banks' own property. Provides advice on compliance.

Carpenter, Kelly Neal. "Eighth Survey of White Collar Crime: Money Laundering." *American Criminal Law Review* 30 (1993): 813-45. Read in conjunction with Catania's piece in the same issue on the Bank Secrecy Act, this will serve as an excellent source of appellate cases nicely cited under discussion of the elements of offenses and common defenses.

Catania, David A. et al. *"Eighth Survey of White Collar Crime: Financial Institutions Fraud." American Criminal Law Review* 30 (1993): 735-72. Has description of Bank Secrecy Act's recording requirements and the crime of structuring to avoid them. Cites all the major appellate cases on elements of offenses and defenses.

Chaikin, David A. "Money Laundering: an Investigatory Prespective." *Criminal Law Forum* 2 (1991): 467-510. An Australian barrister, and former Senior Commonwealth Fraud Officer in the Commonwealth Secretariat's Commercial Crime Unit, here describes money laundering and international efforts to curb it. Particularly helpful in outlining the actual steps involved in laundering money, but also deals with cash transaction report requirements in U.S., Australia, & U.K., forefeitures, use of informants, mutual assistance treaties, and, briefly, Interpol.

DeFeo, Michael A. "Depriving International Narcotics Traffickers and Other Organized Criminals of Illegal Proceeds and Combatting Money Laundering." *Denver Journal of International Law and Policy* 18 (1990): 405-15. The Deputy Chief of the Organized Crime & Racketeering Section of the U.S. Justice Dept.'s Criminal Division, here gives a brief history of U.S. laws to control money laundering and compell forfeiture of criminal proceeds or property purchased with such proceeds. He notes happily that Congress in the War on Drugs has given law enforcement organizations a wealth of new tools for gathering information- and forfeitures, and that these tools can be most useful in controlling all crime, not just drug dealing, but law enforcers should expand their use carefully so as not to provoke public resentment (and possible revocation).

Eberhardt, Michael C. and Keven J. Darken. "Defending against Allegations of Corporate Criminal Liability under *Bank of New England*." *Corporate. Couns. Quarterly*. 9 (July, 1993): 55-71. Attacks the "collective knowledge" concept upheld by *United States v. Bank of New England*, (see cases *supra*). Authors maintain corporations cannot have intent, but they concede that regulatory statutes placing corporations on notice that particular acts must be done, such as currency reporting requirements, may give rise to collective knowledge charges. They suggest ways to avoid and counter these.

Fine, Allen S. "Of Forfeiture, Facilitation and Foreign Innocent Owners: Is a Bank Account Containing Parallel Market Funds Fair Game?" *Nova Law Review*. 16 (1992): 1125-60.

Gilmore, William C. "International Efforts to Combat Money Laundering." *Commonwealth Law Bulletin* 18 (1992): 1129-42.

Harmon, James D. Jr. "United States Money Laundering Laws: International Implications." *New York Law School Journal of International and Comparative Law* 9 (1988):1-45. The former Executive Director of the President's Commission on Organized Crime describes in detail the Money Laundering Control Act that grew partly out of the Commission's recommendations. He analyzes the Act's extraterritorial application and prophesises yet another contribution to international comity by Uncle Sam: grand jury subpoenas served on foreign corporations without any U.S.

contacts, for money laundering offenses committed entirely outside the U.S.

Johnson, D. Randall. "The Criminally Derived Property Satute: Constitutional and Interpretive Issues Raised by 18 U.S.C. § 1957." *William and Mary Law Review 34 (1993):1291-1366*. Gives § 1957's history, discusses elements of the offense it creates, and argues that the statute is not unconstitutionally vague. Insists that jury instructions in prosecutions for its violation must emphasise the necessity of the jury's finding that the prosecution has established the defendant's knowledge that the transaction giving rise to the charge actually involved criminally derived property.

Kriz, George J. "International Co-operation to Combat Money Laundering: the Nature and Role of Mutual Legal Assistance Treaties." Commonwealth Law Bulletin 18 (1992): 723-34.

Plombeck, Charles T. "Confidentiality and Disclosure: the Money Laundering Control Act of 1986 and Banking Secrecy." *International Lawyer* 22 (1988): 69 98.

Popham, John and Matthew Probus. "Structured Transactions in Money Laundering: Dealing with Tax Evaders, Smurfs, and Other Enemies of the People." *American Journal of Criminal Law* 15 (1987):83-114.

Rusch, Jonathan. "Hue and Cry in the Counting House: Some Observations on the Bank Secrecy Act." *Catholic University Law Review* 37 (1988): 465-88.

Strafer, G. Richard. "Money Laundering: the Crime of the '90's." *American Criminal Law Review* 27 (1989): 149-207.

Thompson, Larry D. and Elizabeth Barry Johnson. "Money Laundering: Business Beware." *Alabama Law Review* 44 (1993): 703-23. Noting that the anti-money laundering statutes are becoming federal proscutors' new RICO for attacking business crimes, the authors argue that these statutes are too vague and broad to be constitutional.

Villa, John K. "A Critical View of Bank Secrecy Act Enforcement and the Money Laundering Statutes." *Catholic University Law Review* 37 (1988): 489-509.

Welling, Sarah N. "Smurfs, Money Laundering, and the Federal Criminal Law: the Crime of Structuring Transactions." *Florida Law Review* 41 (1989): 287-343. Very extensive analysis of 31 U.S.C. § 5324, the anti-smurfing statute. Author a strong law and order proponent, unworried at "minor" loss of citizens' privacy in cause of fighting the drug war.

Wyrsch, Gerard. "Treasury Regulation of International Wire Transfer and Money Laundering: a Case for a Permanent Moratorium." *Denver Journal of International Law and Policy* 20 (1992): 515-35.

Zagaris, Bruce and Elizabeth Kingma. "Asset Forfeiture International and Foreign Law: an Emerging Regime." *Emory International Law Review* 5 (1991): 445-513.

_______ and Sheila M. Castilla. "Constructing an International Financial Enforcement Subregime: the Implementation of Anti-Money-Laundering Policy." *Brooklyn Journal of International Law* 19 (1993): 871-965.

______. and Scott B. MacDonald. "Money Laundering, Financial Fraud, and Technology: the Perils of an Instantaneous Economy." *George Washington Journal of International Law and Economics* 26 (1992): 61-107.

E. Securities Fraud[107]

The internationalization of securities markets has made possible new transnational frauds and deceptive behaviors. The Securities and Exchange Commission (SEC) is the agency most involved in attempting to prevent these. Here we examine its statutory armory, methods of obtaining judicial assistance abroad, and we list a selection of useful law review articles.

1. Statutes

The SEC has primary responsibility for administration and enforcement of the following seven statutes:

[107] We happily acknowledge the substantial contribution of Betty Blanco, Research Assistant, University of Miami School of Law, to this section's completion.

Securities Act of 1933, U.S. Code, Title 15, secs. 77a-77aa (1988);

Securities Exchange Act of 1934, U.S. Code, Title 15, secs. 78a-78ll (1988).

Investment Company Act of 1940, U.S. Code, Title 15, secs. 80a-1 et seq. (1988);

Investment Advisors Act of 1940, U.S. Code, Title 15, secs. 80b-1-21 (1988);

Trust Indenture Act of 1939, U.S. Code, Title 15, secs. 77aaa-bbbb (1988);

Public Utility Holding Company Act of 1935, U.S. Code, Title 15, secs. 79-79z-6 (1988);

Securities Investor Protection Act of 1970, U.S. Code, Title 15, secs. 78aaa-lll (1988).

All these statutes, save the Securities Investor Protection Act of 1970, have general provisions under "Penalties" making a crime of any willful violation of substantive provisions contained in the statutes themselves or administrative rules and regulations promulgated under them. In addition, the Insider Trading Sanctions Act (ITSA), Pub. L. No. 100-704, 102 Stat. 4677 (1988), amending Section 21(d) of the 1934 Act and codified at 15 U.S.C. 78u-1, contains severe civil sanctions for unlawful purchase or sale of securities by insider traders. Other applicable statutes are the federal mail and wire fraud statutes, the federal conspiracy law, the Federal Fraud Act (see III B 2 *supra*), and the Criminal Victims Rights Statute, 18, U.S.C § 3663 ff.

Among the more common activities made criminal by the Securities Act of 1933 and prosecuted under *U.S. Code,* Title 15, sec. 77 are:

fraudulent offer or sale of securities using interstate commerce - Sec. 77q(a);

failure to register the sale of securities - Sec. 77e;

filing false registration statements or false amendments - Sec.77x;

fraudulent use of the mail and interstate commerce in connection with sale of stocks - Sec. 77q;

affixing a signature to a registration statement without the purported signer's authority - Sec. 77f(a); and

false representations to prospective securities purchasors that the SEC has approved the veracity, correctness, or adequacy of a registration statement or has stated its position on the worth of a security being marketed - Sec. 77w.

Types of activity made illegal and prosecuted under the Securities and Exchange Act of 1934, *U.S. Code*, Title 15, sec. 78 include:

fraud in securities' sale or purchase - Sec. 78j(b);

manipulation of listed securities - Sec. 78(i);

manipulation of unlisted securities - Sec. 78j(b);

violation of credit provisions - Sec. 78g(c);

violation of short selling provisions - Sec. 78j(a);

failure to file, impeding, blocking, or delaying filing of required reports, filing false reports, or manipulation of false reports in dealings with shareholders or prospective shareholders - Secs. 78m-78q; and

fraudulent broker/dealer practices- Secs. 78o(c)(1) and 78j(b).

Violation of civil court injunctions issued to prevent securities law infringements can result in criminal prosecutions under Secs. 78u(C) and 78v.

The International Securities Enforcement Cooperation Act of 1990, Pub. Law No. 101-550, 104 Stat. 2714, strengthened international cooperation in securities law enforcement. Its provisions are scattered in sections of *U.S. Code*, Titles 7 and 15 (Supp. V 1993)

2. Judicial Assistance

For information and evidence on transnational securities frauds the SEC has used a number of mutual assistance treaties with other countries. Particularly fruitful have been the following:

U.S. Department of State. "Treaty on Mutual Assistance in Criminal Matters, U.S.-Switzerland," 25 May 1973, *United States Treaties and Other International Agreements*, vol. 27, p.2019.

___________."Treaty on Mutual Assistance in Criminal Matters, U.S.- Bahamas," 12 June and 18 August 1987, S. Treaty Doc. 100-17.

___________."Treaty on Mutual Legal Assistance in Criminal Matters, U.S.- Canada," 18 March 1985, S. Treaty Doc. 100-14, reprinted in *International Legal Materials* 24 (1985): 1092-1099.

___________."Treaty Concerning the Cayman Islands Relating to Mutual Assistance in Criminal Matters with Protocol, U.S.- U.K.," 3 July 1986, S. Treaty Doc. 100-8, reprinted in *International Legal Materials* 26 (1987): 537-49.

___________."Treaty on Mutual Assistance in Criminal Matters, U.S.- Italy," 9 November 1982, S. Treaty Doc. 98-25.

___________."Treaty on Mutual Assistance in Criminal Matters, U.S.- Netherlands," 15 September 1983, TIAS No. 10734, *United States Treaties and Other International Acts Series.*

Not requiring the Senate's consent, memoranda of understanding ("MOUs") have been useful to the SEC. It has negotiated several directly with the securities regulators of other countries. These provide for mutual assistance in investigations and evidence procurement for prosecutions. Typical of such MOUs are the following:

"Memorandum of Understanding to Establish Mutually Acceptable Means for Improving International Law Enforcement Cooperation in the Field of Insider Trading, U.S. - Switzerland," 31 August 1982, reprinted in *International Legal Materials* 22 (1983): 1-12.

"Memorandum of Understanding on Exchange of Information in Matters Relating to Securities and Futures, U.S.- U.K.," 23 September 1986, reprinted in *International Legal Materials* 25 (1986): 1431-37.

"Memorandum of Understanding on Administration and Enforcement of Securities Laws, U.S.- Canada," 7 January 1988, reprinted in *International Legal Materials* 27 (1988): 410-21.

3. Selected Articles

Du Puy, F. Russell, III. "International Cooperation in Securities Enforcement." *Washington and Lee Law Review* 46 (1989): 713-39.

Hermann, Donald H. J. "Extraterritorial Criminal Jurisdiction in Securities Laws Regulation." *Cumberland Law Review* 16 (1986): 207-28.

Moessle, Klaus P. "The Basic Structure of United States Securities Law Enforcement in International Cases." *California Western International Law Journal* 16 (1986): 1-51.

Phillips, Richard M. et al. "The Internationalization of Securities Fraud Enforcement in the 1990's." *Annual Institute on Securities Regulation* 23 (1991): 381-459.

F. Export Controls

Four statutes and a host of subsidiary regulations control United States exports. Particularly significant are the Arms Export Control Act, 22 U.S.C. § 2751-99, and the Export Administration Act, 50 U.S.C. § App. 2401-20. Section 2778(c) of the Arms Control Act makes it a crime to violate secs. 2778-79 or to make a willful misstatement or omission in any registration, license application or report required by the Act or its regulations. Secs. 2780(j) and 2780(d) provide for fines and or imprisonment for exporting arms to countries which the Secretary of State has determined "repeatedly provided support for acts of international terrorism." 22 U.S.C. § 401 authorizes the Secretary of the Treasury to seize and detain arms and munitions illegally exported as well as any aircraft, vessels, or vehicles used in their carriage and provides for forfeiture of anything so seized. The International Traffic in Arms Regulations, *Code of Federal Regulations*, Title 22, sec. 127, implement this Act's provisions.

Section 2410 of the Export Administration Act, contains its criminal penalties and provides for forefeiture of any interest or claim to property involved in export contrary to the Act owned by a person convicted for its violation. The Export Administration Regulations, *Code of Federal Regulations*, title15, secs. 768-99, implement this Act. Section 787 repeats the penalties provided in 50 U.S.C. § 2410 and itemises acts forbidden by the statute.

Other statutes regulating exports and providing criminal penalties for their violation are the Trading with the Enemy Act, 50, U.S.C. § 1-44, and the International Emergency Economic Powers Act, 50 U.S.C. § 1701-06. The Foreign Assets Control and Transaction Control Regulations, *Code of Federal Regulations*, Title 31, secs.

500-585, detail prohibitions of exports to particular countries. Sec. 580, for example, governs exports (among a number of other sanctions) to Haiti.

A first rate guide through the export controls maze is *Coping with U.S. Export Controls*, Practising Law Institute, 1993 (PLI Com. Law & Practice Course Handbook Series No. A-675). John K. Koontz's "Select Bibliography on Export Controls," in *Export Controls in Transition: Perspectives, Problems and Prospects*, edited by Gary K. Bertsch and Steven Elliott-Gower (Durham: Duke University Press, 1992), lists 32 books, 25 law review articles and a number of official publications published through1991. An older bibliography is Stephen M. Boyd & Linda A. Whisman, "The U.S. Law of Export Controls: a Bibliography," *International Lawyer*.18 (1984): 483-90.

William A. Root and John R. Liebman's *United States Export Controls* 3rd ed. (Englewood Cliffs, N.J., Prentice-Hall,1991), a looseleaf manual, covers the various statute's criminal provisions and discusses the major cases. *International Law of Export Control: Jurisdictional Issues*, edited by Karl M. Meessen (Boston: Graham & Trotman,1992) contains a number of country reports prepared for the International Law Association's Committee on Legal Aspects of Extraterritorial Jurisdiction. The report on the United States, by W. Michael Reisman and William D. Araiza, is at p. 163.

Non exporters, too, may find themselves enmeshed in U.S. export controls. Robert C. Sexton, "Liability of Nonexporters under the United States Export Laws," *International Lawyer* 24 (1990): 1029-42, recounts some perils posed to manufacturers whose products get incorporated as parts of items the export of which is illegal.

A thoroughly down to earth, "how to do it" or "how to make darned sure nobody in your company *is* doing it" guide for exporters is Laura Carlson Chen's article, "Compliance with U.S. Export Control Laws," *Corporate Couns. Quarterly* 9 (July, 1993): 26-43. She advises companies to establish a comprehensive compliance program and tells how. We particularly admire her advice to be sure not to allow enforcement types on initial investigatory visits to "wander around" the plant!

Export Controls: A Checklist

a. Statutes

Arms Export Control Act. 22 U.S.C. § 2751-99 (1988 & Supp.V 1993).

Sec. 2778(c) - Provides for fines not exceeding $1,000,000 or imprisonment of up to 10 years or both for each violation of § 2278-79 or regulations issued under each section or for willful statement or omission of a material fact in a registration, license application, or required report.

Sec. 2780(j) - Provides for fines not exceeding $1,000,000 and/or imprisonment of up to 10 years for each violation of § 2780 - prohibiting export of arms to countries which the Secretary of State has determined "repeatedly provided support for acts of international terrorism" §2780(d).

22 U.S.C.§ 401 (1988). Authorizes the Secretary of the Treasury or "any person duly authorized for the purpose by the President" to seize and detain arms and munitions illegally exported and any vessel, vehicle, or aircraft used in their export and provides for forfeiture of any items so seized. Exec. Order No. 10,863, 3 C.F.R. 397 (1959-1963) authorized the Attorney-General to seize and detain under §401.

Export Administration Act of 1979. 50 U.S.C. § 2401-20 (1988)

Sec. 2410(a) - Provides for fines of not more than five times the valua of exports involved or $50,000, whichever is greater, or up to five years imprisonment for "whoever knowingly violates or conspires or attempts to violate" the Act or regulations, orders, licenses issued under it.

Sec. 2410(b)(1) - Provides for individual fines up to $250,000 and/or imprisonment of up to ten years and for all other persons fines up to five times the value of exports involved or $1,000,000, whichever is greater, for willful violations, conspiracies to violate, or attempts to violate any of the Act's provisions or those of regulations, orders, and licenses issued under it when the persons have knowledge that the exports involved will be used for the benefit of, or that the destination or intended destination of the goods or technology involved is any controlled country or any country to which exports are controlled.

Sec.2410(b)(2) - Provides for individuals fines up to $250,000 or up to five years imprisonment, or both, and for other persons fines up to five times the value of exports involved or $1,000,000, whichever is greater, for failure to report to the Secretary of Defense the person's knowledge that goods or technology exported under a license issued under the Act are being used for military or intelligence purposes contrary to the license's conditions.

Sec. 2410(g) - Provides for the forefeiture by any person convicted of a violation of § 2404 under § 2410(a) or (b) of that person's interest, claim, security of or other property or contractual rights to the goods or tangible items that were the subject of the violation, tangible property used in the export or attempt to export, and property constituting or derived from any direct or indirect proceeds resulting from the violation.

Trading with the Enemy Act of 1917. 50 U.S.C. § 1-44 (1988)

Sec.16-Provides for fines up to $50,000 and/or, for natural persons, imprisonment up to ten years for willful violation of § 1-6, 7-39, and 41-44 of the Act or of a license, regulation, or rule issued under it, or for willful violation, neglect, or refusal to comply with any order of the President issued in compliance with the Act.

International Emergency Economic Powers Act. 50 U.S.C. § 1701-06 (1988)

Sec.1705(b)-Provides for fines of up to $50,000 and/or, for natural persons, imprisonment up to ten years for willful violation of any license, order, or regulation issued under the Act and imposes the same penalties on any corporation's officer, director, or agent who knowingly particpates in such a violation.

b. Regulations

International Traffic in Arms Regulations. Code of Federal Regulations. Title 22, sec. 127 (1994).

Secs. 127.1-2 - Define violations of the Arms Export Control Act.

Sec. 127.3 - Provides penalties for violations as prescribed in 22 U.S.C. 2778(c).

Sec. 127.5 - Provides for seizure and forfeiture of defense articles exported in violation of law as well as any vessel, vehicle, or aircraft involved in the violation.

Export Administration Regulations. 15 C.F.R. §768-799 (1994).

Sec. 787 - Repeats the penalties provided in 50 U.S.C. § 2410 and itemizes actions forbidden under the Act.

Foreign Assets Control and Transaction Control Regulations. 31 C.F.R. § 500-585 (1994) The following sections contain export prohibitions:

Sec. 505 - Regulations Prohibiting Transactions Involving the Shipment of Certain Merchandise Between Foreign Countries

Sec. 515 - Cuban Assets Control Regulations

Sec. 550 - Libyan Sanctions Regulations

Sec. 575 - Iraqi Sanctions Regulations

Sec. 580 - Haitian Transactions Regulations

Sec. 585 - Federal Republic of Yugoslavia (Serbia & Montenegro) Sanctions Regulations

c. Cases

United States v. Murphy, 852 F.2d 1 (1st Cir. 1988), *cert. denied* 489 U.S. 1022 (1989). To convict under the Arms Export Control Act, the government, to show he willfully violated the Act, must prove that the defendant "knew he had a legal duty" not to export weapons but it need not prove that the defendant knew that the weapons he conspired to export to Ireland were on the U.S. Munitions List or that he had to register with the U.S. government before exporting the arms.

United States v. Spawr Optical Research, 864 F.2d 1467 (9th Cir. 1988), *cert. denied* 493 U.S. 809 (1989). An item's inclusion on the Commodity Control List under the Export Administration Act is at the Commerce Department's absolute discretion, and that it ought not to be on the list cannot be argued as a defense to a prosection for violation of the Act for its export.

United States v. Durrani, 835 F.2d 410 (2d Cir. 1987)(22 U.S.C. §2778).

United States v. Gregg, 829 F.2d 1430 (8th Cir. 1987). Export Administration Act

United States v. Mechanic, 809 F.2d 1111 (5th Cir. 1987).

United States v. Golitschek, 808 F.2d 195 (2d Cir. 1986)

United States v. Beck, 615 F.2d 441 (7th Cir. 1980). For conviction under 22 U.S.C. § 2278(a) & (c) & 22 C.F.R. § 127.01 the government must prove first, that the defendant exported or attempted to export, second, goods which were on the U.S. Munitions List, third, without having obtained first a license to export them, and, fourth, that he did so willfully. Willfully means only that the defendant knew of a legal duty not to export the articles when he exported or attempted to export them.

United States v. Edler Industries, Inc., 579 F.2d 516 (9th Cir. 1978)

Samora v. United States, 406 F.2d 1095 (5th Cir. 1969)

United States v. Adames, 683 F. Supp. 255 (S.D. Fla. 1988), *aff'd*. 878 F.2d 1374 (11th Cir. 1989). A notice printed on a gun sales receipt that "certain products" may not be exported without government approval was not adequate notice to the defendant buyer that export was illegal, hence he lacked specific intent necessary for willfulness under Arms Export Control Act.

United States v. Moller-Butcher, 560 F. Supp. 550 (D. Mass. 1983.), *appeal dismissed* , 723 F.2d 189 (1st Cir. 1983)

d. Bibliographies

Koontz, John K. "A Select Bibliography on Export Controls ." In *Export Controls in Transition: Perspectives, Problems and Prospects*. Edited by Gary K. Bertsch and Steven Elliott-Gower. Durham: Duke University Press, 1992. Lists 32 books, 25 law review and other scholarly journal articles, and 14 government publications. Current through 1991. Works listed treat export controls generally. Hence primarily for background information.

Boyd, Stephen M. and Linda A. Whisman. "The U.S. Law of Export Controls: a Selected Bibliography." *International Lawyer*. 18 (1984): 483-90. Although dated, this is still a useful, unannotated list of statutes, their legislative history, related legislative materials, regulations, other government documents, and law review articles.

e. Treatises and Collected Works

Berlack, Evan R. and Cecil Hunt. "Overview of U.S. Export Controls." In *Coping with U.S. Export Controls.* New York: Practising Law Institute,1993 (PLI Commercial. Law and Practice Course Handbook Series No. A-675). p.11ff. A brief, clear guide for the novice to agencies, procedures, and policies.

Dubelier, Eric A. "Extraterritorial Application of the Arms Export Control Act and the International Traffic in Arms Regulations, the Prosecution Japan Aviation Electronics Industry Ltd., et al " In *Coping with U.S. Export Controls.* New York: Practising Law Institute, 1993 (PLI Commercial. Law and Practice Course Handbook Series No. A-675). p.601ff. A fascinating account of the prosecution of a Miami company's foreign subsidiaries and a Japanese corporation for violating the Arms Export Control Act by selling items to Iran in Japan which had been manufactured in Japan under license from an American company.

Hunt, Cecil and Pamela Breed. "Export Administration Act: Penalties and Enforcement Process." In *Coping with U.S. Export Controls.* New York: Practising Law Institute, 1993 (PLI Commercial. Law and Practice Course Handbook Series No. A-675). p.647ff.

Kathrein, Reed R. "Criminal Enforcement of the Export Administration Act." In *International Criminal Law: A Guide to U.S. Practice and Procedure.* Edited by Ved P. Nanda and M. Cherif Bassiouni. New York: Practising Law Institute, 1987. p. 141-68. Chap. 5.

Morehead, Jere W. "Enforcing Export Controls: Improving the Effectiveness of U.S. and Multilateral Export Controls," in *Export Controls in Transition: Perspectives, Problems and Prospects.* Edited by Gary K. Bertsch & Steven Elliott-Gower. Durham: Duke University Press, 1992. p.128-47. A former Assistant U.S. Attorney in the Justice Department describes U.S. export control legislation and enforcement difficulties caused by over-lapping authority of the Commerce Cepartment, U.S. Customs, and other agencies.

Newcomb, R. Richard. "Foreign Assets Control," in *Coping with U.S. Export Controls.* New York: Practising Law Institute,1993 (PLI Commercial. Law and Practice Course Handbook Series No. A-675). p. 435ff. Outlines the powers and functions of the Office of Foreign Assets Control in the Department of the Treasury under the Trading with the Enemy Act, International Emergency Economic Powers Act, International Security and Development Cooperation Act, 22 U.S.C.§ 2349aa-849, and United Nations Participation Act, 22 U.S.C. 287c. Among the economic sanctions enforced by this Office are export embargoes. Summarizes the penalties for violation of (as well as other provisions of) the Cuban Asset Control Regulations, Foreign Asset Control Regulations, Iraqi Sanctions Regulations, Libyan Sanctions Regulations, and the Transaction Control Regulations.

Reisman, W. Michael and William D. Araiza. "United States of America." In *International Law of Export Control: Jurisdictional Issues.* Edited by Karl M. Meessen . Boston: Graham & Trotman, 1992. p.163-73. One of a series of country reports prepared for the International Law Association's Committee on Legal Aspects of Extraterritorial Jurisdiction, this discusses the extraterritorial application of the Export Administration Act, the International Emergency Economic Powers Act, and the Anti-Boycott Statute. Useful only as background information.

Root, William A. and John R. Liebman. *United States Export Controls.* 3d ed. Englewood Cliffs, N.J.: Prentice-Hall,1991-. (Loose-leaf). Section 2.8 summarizes the enforcement provisions of the Arms Export Control Act and its International Traffic in Arms Regulations. Section 3.8 describes enforcement of the Trading with the Enemy Act and International Emergency Economic Powers Act. Chapter 9 outlines enforcement provisions of the Export Administration Act.

Smith, Donald W. "Defense of Export Control Enforcement Actions" in *Coping with U.S. Export Controls.* New York: Practising Law Institute,1993 (PLI Commercial. Law and Practice Course Handbook Series No. A-675). p. 677ff. A "how to do it" guide.

Spanner, Robert Alan. "The Application of United States Criminal Statutes to International Industrial and Technology Transfers " in *International Trade: Avoiding Criminal Risks.* Edited by William H. Hannah. Salem, N.H.: Butterworth, 1991-, Chap. 15. Treats the application of the Export Administration Act and Arms Export Control Act to the export of information. Discusses the most common defenses to prosecutions brought for violation of each and penalties each prescribes.

f. Articles

Bialos, Jeffrey P. "The Detection and Disclosure of Violations of U.S. Export Controls: Management Choices and Their National Security Implications." *Virginia Journal of International Law* 29 (1989): 567-620. Advice on what to consider before making a clean breast of one's sins to Uncle Sam- and into which of Sam's many ears to confess.

Chen, Laura Carlson. "Compliance with U.S. Export Control Laws." *Corp. Couns. Quarterly* 9 (July, 1993): 26-43. Offers practical advice on establishing an internal company compliance program, including an export policy statement, customer investigation procedure, training, adequate documentation. Gives a "red flag" checklist for dicey customers and their orders. The final section provides guidance on coping with investigations and enforcement.

McNamara, Stephen P. Comment, "Criminal and Administrative Sanctions under United States Export Laws." *Connecticut Journal of International Law* 2 (1986): 157-80. Limited to the Export Administration Act and the Arms Export Control Act.

Sexton, Robert C. "Liability of Nonexporters under the United States Export Laws." *International Lawyer* 24 (1990): 1029-42. Charts the perils posed to domestic manufacturers whose products may be incorporated in exports prohibited by the Export Administration Act and its regulations or the Arms Export Control Act and the International Traffic in Arms Regulations.

THE TRIUMPH OF SUBSTANCE OVER RULES OF CHOICE IN INTERNATIONAL COMMERCIAL TRANSACTIONS: FROM THE LEX MERCATORIA TO MODERN STANDARDS

Patrick J. Borchers
Professor and Associate Dean for Student Affairs
Albany Law School of Union University

I. Introduction

As a discipline, conflict of laws usually is divided into three parts -- choice of law, jurisdiction, and judgment recognition.[108] In commercial transactions, particularly international[109] ones, the first of these three is crucial because of the important planning function of substantive rules. Unlike torts and less significant transactions -- which are generally unplanned -- international commercial transactions can carry with them expectation interests in the billions ot dollars.[110] Parties must be able to predict with confidence the substantive rules that will govern the transaction in order to assess intelligently the transaction's risks. Uncertainty, for instance, as to whether dramatic variations in the price of a crucial commodity will excuse performance of a transnational contract makes the already risky business of international trade akin to economic suicide.[111]

---

[108] David D. Siegel, *A Retrospective on Babcock v. Jackson, A Personal View*, 56 Alb. L. Rev. 693 (1993).

[109] For purpose of this paper I will use the terms "international commerce," "transnational commerce," "cross-border commerce" and derivatives thereof, interchangeably. Some commentators use the first to refer to commerce that involves sovereign nations and the latter two to refer to private trade between traders of different nations. But since nothing I will say here depends on these distinctions, I attach no linguistic significance to them.

[110] *See* Bernardo M. Cremades & Steven L. Plehn, *The New Lex Mercatoria and the Harmonization of the Laws of International Commercial Transactions*, 2 B.U. Int'l L.J. 317, 338-46 (1984)(discussing several large arbitration cases).

[111] *See, e.g.*, Sabine Corp. v. Ong Western, Inc., 725 F. Supp. 1157 (W.D. Okla. 1989). *See also* Cremades, *supra* note 3, at 338-43 (discussing impossibility and unforeseeable circumstances defenses in arbitration); Dietrich Maskow, *Hardship and Force Majeure*, 40 Am. J. Comp. L. 657 (1992).

It comes as no surprise that conflicts doctrine is perceived as having great importance in this context. In fact, the term that Joseph Story coined for our discipline -- "private international law"[112] -- is itself suggestive of the crucial role that it plays here. Orthodox conflicts doctrine is, in some ways, worse equipped to respond to the need for certainty in international commercial transactions than it was a century ago. Modern "policy," "interest" and other non-rule approaches have rewritten the subject. This is particularly true for tort matters, but the effect of the "conflicts revolution"[113] has been significant in contracts as well.[114] Many commentators -- myself included[115] -- have applauded the ability of these trends to ferret out justice in the individual case.[116] But there is no denying that where predictability is at a premium, this helter-skelter approach advocated by American courts and some of their foreign counterparts just will not do.[117]

This situation is not unprecedented. Ever since the invention of conflict of laws as a discipline -- in a modern sense in the twelfth century by the Italian glossators[118] -- conflicts writers have evinced an "astonishing lack of consensus on the discipline's goals and methods."[119] This has led to wide vacillations both in theory and practice throughout the centuries, and both in continental Europe and the common law countries. But the need of international traders to protect expectation interests has not varied. And the method for protecting expectation interests has been every bit as uniform as conflicts doctrine has been disuniform. That method is the application of specialized substantive rules to transnational

---

[112] Joseph Story, *Commentaries on the Conflict of Laws* 9 (1834)("This branch of public law may be fitly denominated private international law ....").

[113] Albert Ehrenzweig coined the term. Albert Ehrenzweig, *A Counter-Revolution in Conflicts Law? From Beale to Cavers*, 80 Harv. L. Rev. 377 (1966).

[114] Eugene Scoles & Peter Hay, *Conflict of Laws* 678 (2d ed. 1992).

[115] Patrick J. Borchers, *Conflicts Pragmatism*, 56 Alb. L. Rev. 883, 899 (1993).

[116] Patrick J. Borchers, *The Choice-of-Law Revolution: An Empirical Study*, 49 Wash. & Lee L. Rev. 357, 380-82 (1992).

[117] Scoles & Hay, *supra* note 113, at 657.

[118] Friedrich K. Juenger, *Choice of Law and Multistate Justice* 11 (1993).

[119] *Id.* at 11.

transactions and the consequent obliteration of the need for rules of choice. In this essay, I argue that the success of this approach is both descriptive of the past and prescriptive for the future.

I will proceed in three parts. First, I will give a brief overview of the development of conflicts doctrine both on the continent of Europe and in the common law countries. Second, I will argue that the dominant approach to resolving choice-of-law issues for transnational commerce has not been and continues not to be rules of choice, but instead the application of specialized substantive rules. This tendency finds its expression both in the ancient *lex mercatoria*, and in the modern trend of drafting international standards of universal or near-universal purport, which some have termed the "new *lex mercatoria*."[120] Third, I argue that the dominance of the substantive law approach is not an historical accident, but is rather reflective of the truth that the substantive law approach is superior to rules of choice in protecting party expectations and producing satisfactory outcomes to transnational commercial disputes.

II. A Bit of Conflicts History

One of the topics that I was asked to address is the civil law tradition in conflicts. This is both a difficult and an easy task. It is difficult because the continent of Europe -- Bologna to be exact[121] -- was the birthplace of the conflict of laws as a discipline. The civil law tradition, as one might therefore expect, has produced a tradition of astonishing richness and depth. The task's difficulty is mitigated, however, by the fact that the American tradition owes perhaps more to the civilians here than in any other area of the law. Indeed, it is true -- as one of the major American casebooks on the subject says -- that "our debt to England is here not as large as in other fields."[122] As I shall discuss below, accidents both of history and geography account for this state of affairs. But at the outset it should be clear that the history of the civilian and common law

---

[120] *See generally Lex Mercatoria and Arbitration: A discussion of the New Law Merchant* (Thomas E. Carbonneau, ed., 1990).

[121] Juenger, *supra* note 118, at 11.

[122] Willis Reese, Maurice Rosenberg & Peter Hay, *Cases and Materials on Conflict of Laws* 4 (9th ed. 1990).

traditions cannot be told in isolation. Instead, it makes more sense to see conflicts development in the western world as one organism.

History reveals only three general categories of solutions to choice-of-law problems. The first is the multilateral approach. It solves choice-of-law problems by the interposition of choice-of-law rules, often tied to the substantive law category to which the dispute is assigned.[123] The traditional rule that the validity of a contract is determined by the law of the place of its acceptance is an example of a multilateral rule.[124] It categorizes the substantive nature of the dispute (contract law), interposes a choice-of-law rule (the place of the acceptance) and solves the legal problem by the standards of the referenced local law.

The second is the unilateral approach. Instead of interposing choice-of-law rules, the unilateral approach aims to ascertain the spatial reach of the substantive laws in question. The Italian glossators in the twelfth century A.D. distinguished between what they termed "real" and "personal" statutes.[125] "Real" statutes were confined in operation to the territorial reach of the government enacting them; "personal" laws, however, followed a government's subjects wherever they travelled.[126]

The third is the substantive law approach. Unlike either the unilateral or multilateral approach -- which are united fundamentally in that they both attempt to make a "choice" of laws -- the substantive law approach posits the need for, and existence of, specialized substantive laws applicable to interstate transactions. As we will see below, the *lex mercatoria* is an example of the substantive law tradition in conflicts.

Concern for the special problems of international trade between merchants from different legal systems extends at least as far back as the Greeks and the Romans. The Greeks did not solve these problems by reference to choice-of-law rules. Instead, as far back as

---

[123] Juenger, *supra* note 118, at 13.

[124] *Restatement (First) of Conflict of Laws* § 322 (1934).

[125] Story, *supra* note 112, at 11 (three divisions are described: personal, real and mixed).

[126] Story, *supra* note 112, at 12-13.

the fourth century B.C., they came to rely upon what one important author described as the Greeks' "private international law."[127] This Greek law, applicable to trading between politically independent city-states, was a kind of *lex mercatoria*, based upon commercial customs and practices developed in antiquity.[128] The Greeks thus employed the substantive law solution to the needs of international trades.

The Romans employed the same solution. In a manner not dissimilar to our American institution of diversity jurisdiction,[129] the Romans developed a separate tribunal for disputes involving non-Romans.[130] This institution of the *praetor peregrinus* applied a law of universal purport that Cicero called the "*ius gentium*."[131] The *ius gentium* was "more flexible and functional than the *ius civile* that governed relations between Roman citizens."[132] "From an ignoble appendage of the Jus Civile, the Jus Gentium came to be considered a great though as yet imperfectly developed model to which all law ought as far as possible conform."[133]

Conflicts in a form recognizable to us probably began as a discipline in Upper Italy in the twelfth century.[134] With the revival of Roman law at this time, law teachers called glossators began to teach Justinian's code.[135] Master Aldricus, usually credited with the invention of our subject,[136] thought that multistate problems should be solved by a reference to the "better and more useful"

---

[127] 2 Paul Vinogradoff, *Outlines of Historical Jurisprudence* 158 (1922).

[128] Juenger, *supra* note 118, at 6.

[129] *See* Patrick J. Borchers, *The Origins of Diversity Jurisdiction, the Rise of Legal Positivism, and a Brave New World for Erie and Klaxon*, 72 Tex. L. Rev. 79, 83 (1993)(comparing Roman institutions to diversity jurisdiction).

[130] Juenger, *supra* note 118, at 8.

[131] *Id.* at 9.

[132] *Id.* at 8.

[133] *Id.* at 9 (quoting H. Maine, *Ancient Law* 50 (F. Pollack ed. 1906)).

[134] *Id.* at 11.

[135] *Id.*

[136] Hessel E. Yntema, *The Comity Doctrine*, 65 Mich. L. Rev. 9, 12 (1966).

law.[137] But contemporaries also invented the unilateral and multilateral approaches that competed with Aldricus' substantive law approach. The unilateralists -- or statutists, because of their preoccupation with the wording and spacial purport of local statutes -- attempted to distinguish between "real" and "personal" laws.[138] The former were thought to be limited by the geography of the government enacting them; the second were thought to follow the government's subjects as they travelled, as a shell follows a turtle.[139]

The medieval multilateralists invented some modern-looking choice-of-law rules. Joseph Beale -- not coincidentally the reporter of the first Conflicts Restatement -- translated the work of the great Italian jurist Bartolus,[140] and ascribed to him some choice-of-law rules that bore a strong similarity to those that Beale restated. Beale, for instance, understood Bartolus to say that the validity of contracts is governed by the place of their making,[141] exactly the rule adopted in the First Restatement.[142] Even if there are reasons to doubt the perfection of Beale's translation, there can be no doubt that the multilateral approach was alive and well early on.

After the decline of Italian scholarship on the subject, the torch was passed to the French and then by the seventeenth century to the Dutch.[143] To Americans, the best known Dutch scholar was Ulrich Huber, who adopted the notions of sovereignty and comity to blend his peculiar form of multilateralism.[144] Although Huber is not regarded as a major figure in conflicts law by Europeans, his influence through Joseph Story in the United States proved to be profound.

---

137 Juenger, *supra* note 118, at 12.

138 Story, *supra* note 112, at 12-13.

139 Story, *supra* note 112, at 12-13.

140 Bartolus of Sassoferrato, *Bartolus on the Conflict of Laws* (Joseph Beale trans, (1914).

141 *Id.*

142 Restatement (First) of Conflict of Laws 322, 358 (1934).

143 Juenger, *supra* note 118, at 19-21.

144 *Id.* at 21.

Story, the greatest American conflicts scholar, set about in 1834 to do what had not been done before: create a successful and systematic American treatise on the subject.[145] Story's treatise has been criticized as lacking "theoretical consistency"[146] and for being "one of the least scientific and one of the least conclusive books."[147] It is true, of course, that Story's treatise treats the works of civilians and the common law as essentially interchangeable. But Story demonstrated great comparative acumen, and his methodology -- and his careful attention to his sources -- produced a work of far greater worth than most of what passes for conflicts scholarship these days.

Story's heavy reliance on civilian authors -- especially Huber -- is easily explained. As Story pointed out in the introduction to his book, conflicts "has never been systematically treated by the writers on the common law of England...."[148] Undoubtedly this was due to the fact that the subject had relatively little fascination for English courts. England early on took the view that its courts had no jurisdiction unless the dispute called for the application of English law. This was a product both of England's geographic situation as an island nation removed from Europe's "legal checkerboard,"[149] and its system of powerful central courts.[150] Of course this proved awkward for cases involving substantial foreign elements, but the English courts allowed litigants to dodge the requirement with absurdly fictional, but non-traversable, allegations that all elements of the case took place in England.[151] The fact that this persisted until a few decades before Story put pen to paper clearly accounts

[145] Story's effort was preceded by American lawyer Samuel Livermore, whose treatise was not widely read. Livermore, however, bequested his collection of conflicts works to the Harvard law library, "where Story could put it to good use." Juenger, *supra* note 117, at 29.

[146] 1 Albert Ehrenzweig, *Private International Law* 54 (1967).

[147] F. Harrison, *On Jurisprudence and the Conflict of Laws* 119 (1919).

[148] Story, *supra* note 112, at 9.

[149] Juenger, *supra* note 118, at 22.

[150] *Id.*

[151] *E.g.*, Ward's Case, 82 Eng. Rep. 245, 246 (K.B. 1625-1628)(allegation that Hamburg is located in London).

for the lack of analytical tools in the common law to handle complex multistate problems.

In terms of diversity of legal systems, the United States -- as Story pointed out -- had, even then, much more in common with the European continent than it did with England.[152] Thus, the better-developed civilian conflicts principles were far more suitable for transplantation to the United States, and Story proved to be a meticulous gardener. But none of this is to say that Story accepted civilian doctrine uncritically. He credited the civilian writers with "a much more comprehensive philosophy, if not with a more enlightened spirit."[153] Moreover, a good deal of the civilian writing did not appeal to Story, who was a pragmatist. "Their works," he wrote, ". . . abound with theoretical distinctions, which serve little purpose other than to provoke idle discussions, and with metaphysical subtilties [*sic*], (subtleties) which perplex, if they do not confound, the inquirer."[154]

Although Story's method was implicit, it is unfair to say that it was non-existent. Story sought to borrow the central tenets of conflicts from the civilian writers, particularly where they agreed with what common law doctrine there was. Story's method was to find the common ground, not because it necessarily represented the objective truth, but rather because synthesis represented the best hope for decisional harmony. And Story saw decisional harmony as the best hope for protecting expectation interests in cross-border transactions. An examination of Story's chapter on contracts and commercial transactions -- the source of our discussion here and much modern concern -- reveal the essence of Story's approach.

Story's work is usually placed in the multilateralist camp, and his chapter on contracts reflects this for the most part. Following the important civilian writers, including Huber, Story took the position that the *lex loci contractus* generally governed contractual relations.[155] Following a distinction that the first Conflicts

---

152 Story, *supra* note 112, at 9.

153 *Id.*, at 10.

154 *Id.*, at 10.

155 *Id.*, at 193-201.

Restatement would embrace exactly a century later,[156] Story thought this rule to have a dual character. The validity of a contract is determined by the law of the place of its making,[157] but matters of the performance of the contract are governed by the place of the performance.[158]

A close reading of Story's treatise, however, reveals a pragmatic spirit that has informed conflicts issues in international commercial transactions throughout history. Story believed the *lex loci contractus* rule to be essential to successful commercial intercourse. Because of its broad endorsement by civilian writers, Story argued that any nation "which should refuse to acknowledge the common principles, would soon find its whole commercial intercourse reduced to a state" that he described as "barbarous."[159]

Moreover, Story did not rest the workings of the international system entirely upon the edifice of the rule of *lex loci contractus*. Rather, he advocated several practical supplements to it. He argued, for instance, for a rule to be "universally adopted by all nations" that contracts involving "moral or political turpitude" ought not be enforced.[160] Story also thought that issues of contractual interpretation -- as opposed to enforcement and validity -- were controlled by "certain general rules ... recognised by all nations, which form the basis of all reasoning on the subject of contracts."[161] Story also apparently believed in the principle of party autonomy, that is, that parties ought be able to stipulate the law governing their contracts.[162] Story also believed in the fundamental nature of negotiable instruments; he was of the view

---

156 *Restatement (First) of Conflict of Laws* §§ 322, 358 (1934).

157 Story, *supra* note 112, at 201, 248.

158 *Id.*, at 233, 248.

159 *Id.*, at 202.

160 *Id.* at 204.

161 *Id.* at 225.

162 *Id.* at 232 (quoting with approval from an English case adopting the *lex loci contractus* "unless [the merchant] has taken care to stipulate for performance in some other country, or has in some other way excepted his particular contract from the laws of the country, where he is.").

that paper negotiable under the law of the place of the original transaction was negotiable everywhere.[163]

Story the Supreme Court justice was every bit attuned as Story the treatise writer to the need for pragmatism in the commercial transactions. The notion that commercial transactions were a subject of "general law" -- as opposed to individual state laws -- was well entrenched in the federal courts before Story assumed the bench.[164] But it was Story who penned the most famous exposition of this principle in *Swift v. Tyson*.[165] In *Swift*, Story refused to apply a backwater New York rule that discharge of an antecedent debt could not qualify as consideration to insulate a subsequent holder of a note from the defense of fraud in the underlying transaction. Instead, expressly relying on the need for national uniformity, Story applied the general rule that discharge of an antecedent debt is sufficient consideration.[166]

Not only was Story the most influential American conflicts writer, he truly was, as Wolff would later say, "the secret teacher of the world."[167] Almost contemporaneously with publication of Story's Commentaries came the most important modern civilian contribution to conflicts law. In 1849 Friedrich Carl von Savigny published volume 8 of his massive treatise entitled "System of Current Roman Law."[168] Savigny paid to tribute Story, and clearly relied upon his *Commentaries* largely because of the brilliant exposition of the civilian authorities.[169] In an important way, therefore, Savigny closed the circle of unification between the common law and civilian traditions. The most influential of common law conflicts writers relied heavily upon the civilians, and

---

[163] *Id.* at 285.

[164] Borchers, *supra* note 129, at 112-13.

[165] 41 U.S. (16 Pet.) 1 (1842).

[166] *Id.* at 18-19.

[167] Martin Wolff, *Internationales Privatrecht* 17 (1933) [translation supplied by the author].

[168] Juenger, *supra* note 118, at 34.

[169] *Id.* at 31-33.

the most influential of civilian writers relied in part on a common lawyer.

Savigny, like Story, took a primarily multilateralist approach. Every legal transaction, according to Savigny, has a "seat," and it is the local law of this seat that determines the legal consequences. Thus, unlike his immediate German predecessor -- Carl Georg von Wächter, who advocated the primacy of forum law and was unilateralist in his orientation[170] -- Savigny thought that legal relationships ought not vary with the court enforcing them.[171] On this fundamental point he agreed with Story, who argued that decisional consistency was essential for cross-border commercial transactions. On some of the details he disagreed with Story. Savigny, for instance, thought that the parties' domiciles were the most important connecting factor for contract choice of law.[172] As a multilateralist rule this is clearly inferior to Story's *lex loci contractus* rule on the twin grounds of decisional consistency and ease of application.[173] But just as Story redefined forever the terms of conflicts debate in the realm of the common law, Savigny still holds sway both on the continent and in some nations whose traditions are primarily those of the common law.[174]

III. The Substantive Law Tradition in Commercial Conflicts Law

Each of the three major traditions has thus enjoyed dominance in various legal systems and at various times. The substantive law tradition is the oldest and has been fashionable at least since the time of the dominance of the Greek empire. Unilateralism saw perhaps its first expression in the medieval personal law principle and has had powerful supporters such as Wächter, the German author, and French writers, such as Pillet.[175] Probably the two

---

170 Kurt Nadelmann, *Wächter's Essay on the Collision of Private Laws of Different States*, 13 Am. J. Comp. L. 414 (1963).

171 Juenger, *supra* note 118, at 36.

172 *Id.* at 37, n. 263.

173 *Id.* at 37, n. 263.

174 Brian Opeskin, *The Price of Forum Shopping: A Reply to Professor Juenger*, 16 Sydney L. Rev. 14, 14-16 (1994).

175 Patrick J. Borchers, *Professor Brilmayer and the Holy Grail*, 1991 Wisc. L. Rev. 465, 467 (reviewing Lea Brilmayer, *Conflict of Laws: Foundations and Future*

most famous conflicts writers, Story and Savigny, were primarily multilateralist in their origin.

Indeed, the current state of affairs in the United States is a microcosm of the world. Interest analysis as expounded by Brainerd Currie[176] is a form of unilateralism; in the apt phrase of a modern Dutch author it is "neo-statutist."[177] The First Conflicts *Restatement*[178]

(1934). -- still followed by about a dozen states[179] -- is rigidly multilateralist, including the *lex loci contractus* rule advocated by Story. Its successor, the Second *Restatement*,[180] is more flexible, but is a soft form of multilateralism nonetheless.[181] And several states follow the teachings of Professor Leflar, whose five-factor test calls for application of the "better rule of law"[182] and is thus substantive in its orientation.

Despite this undeniable diversity of conflicts theories, it is my thesis that the substantive law solution enjoys a position of special prominence -- both in antiquity and the present -- in commercial transactions. The *lex mercatoria* is usually defined as a "supranational" body of principles held substantially in common by states and nations and applicable to cross-border commercial transactions.[183] There has been a good deal of debate as to whether the *lex mercatoria* "exists" or not,[184] but in my view this asks and

---

Directions (1991).

176 Brainerd Currie, *Selected Essays on the Conflict of Laws* (1963).

177 Theodore M. De Boer, *Beyond Lex Loci: Methodology and Multistate Torts in American Case Law* 1-5 (1987).

178 *Restatement (First) of Conflict of Laws*

179 Patrick J. Borchers, *The Choice-of-Law Revolutions: An Empirical Study*, 49 Wash. & Lee L. Rev. 357, 370-72 (1992).

180 *Restatement (Second) of Conflict of Laws* (1971).

181 Borchers, *supra* note 179, at 362-63.

182 Robert A. Leflar, *Choice-Influencing Considerations in Conflicts Law*, 41 N.Y.U. L. Rev. 267, 282-304 (1966).

183 Cremades, *supra* note 110, at 318-19.

184 A. Kassis, *Théorie Général des Usages du Commerce* 271-578 (1984); F.A. Mann, *England Rejects "Delocalised" Contracts and Arbitration*, 33 Int'l & Comp. L.Q.

answers the wrong question. The *lex mercatoria* is simply the name most commonly given to the substantive law solution to cross-border commercial conflicts questions. It is perfectly possible to debate whether a substantive (as opposed to a multilateralist or unilateralist) solution is the best, and it is perfectly possible to debate the exact nature of the appropriate substantive law solution (just as it is possible to debate the utility of differing multilateralist solutions to conflicts problems). But asking whether it "exists" is akin to asking whether the number three "exists." The substantive law solution to commercial conflicts is, as history shows, a plausible one and thus it exists in the same sense that multilateralist and unilateralist solutions exist. The relevant debate is not "existence," it is the utility of the competing solutions.

The historical evidence preponderates in favor of the substantive law solution. First, as we have seen, the substantive law solution is the oldest of the three. The far-flung Greek and Roman empires were probably the first in times of recorded history to generate "conflicts" problems, and they did so primarily in the context of commercial transactions. It is striking, therefore, that both would employ a system of special courts to apply special substantive rules.

Second, the fact that we have the well-known term "*lex mercatoria*" is itself some evidence of the dominance of the substantive law solution in this context. As alluded to above, the English courts took the view that forum law applied to conflicts problems. But this did not blind them to the special nature of multistate problems. For international commercial transactions, the English courts followed what they termed a "*lex mercatoria*" which they derived in large part from the special rules applied by the Roman courts. Blackstone, for instance, asserted the cross-border commercial transactions were governed by a shared substantive law.[185] By the 17th century

193, 196-98 (1984). *Cf.* Daniel R. Coquillette, *Legal Ideology and Incorporation IV: The Nature of Civilian Influence of Modern Anglo-American Commercial Law*, 67 B.U. L. Rev. 877, 880 (1987). (Coquillette cites J.H. Baker to the effect that in Britain, the common law itself created a "law merchant" which had not existed before the eighteenth century.)

185 1 William Blackstone, *Commentaries* *273.

Lord Coke could assert that "the law merchant is part of the law of thisrealm."[186]

Third, the principle of party autonomy has enjoyed wide support through history in commercial transactions. "Party autonomy" is the phrase that describes the ability of parties to choose the substantive law governing their transaction, usually through a choice-of-law clause. The idea that parties can select the law in advance cuts against the grain of both unilateralist and multilateralist doctrine.[187] If legal relationships really have "seats" -- as Savigny posited -- or laws really have spatial reach -- as the unilateralists posit -- then the parties' preferences ought make no difference. Given this, the array of supporters that the principle has earned is truly astonishing. Story -- as noted above -- and Savigny[188] both endorsed it. The Second Conflicts *Restatement* approves of it[189] as does nearly every state court in the United States. Ancient cultures at least as far back as Ptolemaic Egypt employed some form of it.[190] No recent international convention on the subject of commercial transactions has failed to include some provision for it.[191] Indeed, despite the conceptual difficulties it causes for both multilateralism and unilateralism, few are on record as opposing the idea that parties ought be able, at least in most cases, to agree in advance on the law governing their transaction.[192]

While party autonomy is difficult to explain in unilateralist or multilateralist terminology, it is easy to explain in substantive terminology. The rule that parties can, within reasonable limits, stipulate to the governing law is really a rule of substantive contract

---

[186] Theodore F.T. Plucknett, *A Concise History of the Common Law* 663 (5th ed. 1956)(quoting Sir Edward Coke).

[187] Juenger, *supra* note 118, at 54.

[188] *Id.* at 54.

[189] *Restatement (Second) of Conflict of Laws* § 187 (1971).

[190] Juenger, *supra* note 118, at 7-8.

[191] Francis A. Gabor, *Stepchild of the New Lex Mercatoria: Private International Law From the United States Perspective*, 8 Nw. J. Int'l L. & Bus. 538, 541-565 (1988).

[192] Joseph Beale, the Reporter of the First Restatement, was one who opposed it as "theoretically indefensible." 2 Joseph Beale, *A Treatise on the Conflict of Laws* 1083 (1935).

law.[193] As it turns out, it is a rule endorsed by a large number of nations for both domestic and international dealings. But its widespread endorsement obviates the need for making a "choice" of governing law, and thus properly understood the principle of party autonomy is part of a substantive law solution to transnational commercial transactions.

One of the most famous cases ever to endorse party autonomy lends support to the notion that it is part of the *lex mercatoria*. In *The Bremen v. Zapata Offshore Co.*[194] the United States Supreme Court enforced a forum-selection clause in a contract between a German and United States company requiring that their dispute over a deep sea towing operation be litigated in an English court. Although one might have expected the Court to worry about theoretical niceties such as whether the clause "ousted" the federal courts of their admiralty jurisdiction, or whether the clause should be governed by domestic or foreign law, the Court wrote a magnificently cosmopolitan opinion.[195] Relying on "ancient concepts of freedom of contract," and noting the worldwide endorsement of the idea that parties ought be able to choose their forum and governing law in advance, the Supreme Court followed suit and enforced the clause.[196] Perhaps *Zapata* rests on principles of admiralty law (for it is, after all, a case founded on admiralty jurisdiction)[197] but it is probably more accurate to see it as resting on the *lex mercatoria* because of its appeal to universal standards.[198]

Turning to even more recent developments, a few ought make clear that the substantive law solution is alive and well in international commercial transactions. Many international agreements call for

---

193 Cremades, *supra* note 109, at 328 (referring to "freedom of contract" as the "cornerstone of a non-national new lex mercatoria").

194 407 U.S. 1 (1972).

195 Patrick J. Borchers, *Forum Selection Agreements in the Federal Courts After Carnival Cruise: A Proposal for Congressional Reform*, 67 Wash. L. Rev. 55, 63 (1992).

196 407 U.S. at 9-11.

197 Harold Maier, *The Three Faces of Zapata: Maritime Law, Federal Common Law, Federal Courts Law*, 6 Vand J. of Transnt'l L. 387 (1973).

198 Juenger, *supra* note 118, at 216.

dispute resolution in the form of arbitration. Arbitration clauses are a "specialized kind of forum-selection clause,"[199] and their popularity in modern times ought come as no surprise. In the United States, despite some early misgivings,[200] the Supreme Court has endorsed their use, even for disputes with public law components such as antitrust[201] and securities[202] cases. Ever since the New York Convention of 1958 now ratified by over 80 nations (including the United States in 1970), arbitration awards are easier to enforce than foreign judgments in many circumstances.[203] Often the parties to arbitrations do not stipulate to any governing law, and in others they stipulate to application of "general principles" or even "the *lex mercatoria*."[204] But no matter how the agreement reads, there is no denying that arbitrators often make use of commercial custom in the decisions.[205] Indeed, it is the rise of commercial arbitration that has caused several commentators to refer to it as the source of a "new *lex mercatoria*."[206] Even arbitrators on record as denying the "existence" of the *lex mercatoria* occasionally find themselves confronted by agreements that leave no choice but to employ substantive and comparative law solutions to transnational commercial disputes.

Another engine driving the substantive law solution to transnational commercial transactions is the broad reach and uniform nature of commercial law these days. The Uniform Commercial Code applies in 49 states, and parts of it apply in the

---

[199] Quijas v. Shearson/American Express, 490 U.S. 477, 483 (1989)(citing Scherk v. Alberto -Culver Co., 417 U.S. 506, 519 (1974).

[200] *E.g.*, Wilko v. Swan, 346 U.S. 427 (1953).

[201] Mitsubishi Motors Corp. v. Soler Chrysler-Plymouth, Inc., 473 U.S. 614 (1985).

[202] Quijas v. Shearson/American Express, 490 U.S. 477.

[203] *See, e.g.*, Parsons & Whittemore Overseas Co., Inc. v. Societe Generale de L'Industrie du Papier *(RAKTA)*, 508 F.2d 969 (2d Cir. 1971). *See generally* A.J. van den Berg, *The New York Arbitration Convention of 1958: Towards a Uniform Judicial Interpretation* (1981).

[204] Note, *General Principles of Law in International Commercial Arbitration*, 101 Harv. L. Rev. 1816, 1816 (1988).

[205] Cremades, *supra* note 110, at 336.

[206] *See generally Lex Mercatoria and Arbitration: A discussion of the New Law Merchant* (Thomas E. Carbonneau, ed., 1990).

lone holdout -- Louisiana.[207] The drafters of the UCC thought their job in part to "restate" the *lex mercatoria*,[208] and the Code's choice-of-law provision confirms this broad mission. The Code applies to all transactions that bear an "appropriate" relationship to the state, a standard designed to give it the broadest possible application.[209] The recently-ratified Vienna Sales Convention applies as the national law to transnational disputes involving over a dozen countries, including the United States.[210] The Vienna Sales Convention adopts many UCC concepts, and it seems likely that its adoption will spur reform of some UCC chapters.[211] This substantive interplay will doubtlessly further unify standards in commercial transactions.

Even for commercial transactions not covered by an international convention, there is now an authoritative statement of international commercial law standards. The "UNIDROIT" project has been involved as part of an international effort to restate shared standards of law between the participating nations. One of the most comprehensive is the nearly completed project to state principles of commercial law, and an extensive symposium from the participants in the drafting process appears in the *American Journal of Comparative Law*.[212] The UNIDROIT principles are available both to parties who wish to stipulate to their usage and in other circumstances in which an arbitrator or judge must employ the *lex mercatoria*.[213]

---

[207] Robert E. Scott & Douglas L. Leslie, *Contract Law and Theory* 91 (1990).

[208] Gabor, *supra* note 191, at 551.

[209] Juenger, *supra* note 118, at 116-17.

[210] Richard E. Spiedel, *Introduction to Symposium: Reflections on the International Unification of Sales Law*, 8 Nw. J. Int'l L. & Bus. 531, 532 n. 5 (1988).

[211] Mitchell Stocks, *Risk of Loss Under the Uniform Commercial Code and the United Nations Convention on Contracts for the International Sale of Goods: A Comparative Analysis and Proposal for Revision of UCC Sections 2-509 and 2-510*, 87 Nw. U. L. Rev. 1415 (1993).

[212] Symposium, *Contracts Law in a Changing World*, 40 Am. J. Comp. L. 541 (1991).

[213] *UNIDROIT*, *Principales for International Commercial Contracts*, 40 Am. J. Comp. L. 703, 704 (1992)(article 1.2)(consultative document, twelfth consolidated version as prepared by the Secretariat on the basis of drafts by the Working Group for the Preparation of Principles for International Commercial Contracts).

The UNIDROIT principles have had a substantial impact already. The Organization of American States -- of which the United States is, of course, a member -- is in negotiations over a convention governing transnational commercial transactions. The most recent draft Convention endorsed the principle of party autonomy, but employed a soft multilateralist rule -- that the governing law be that of the nation with the "closest link" to the transaction -- in the event that the parties fail to stipulate to the governing law. The recently-completed UNIDROIT principles -- as an authoritative substantive law solution -- caused the delegates to rethink the necessity for employing a multilateralist solution.[214]

This development is consistent with the recent O.A.S. trend of employing overtly substantive solutions in international agreement. For instance, the recent O.A.S. convention on matters relating to child support and other maintenance obligations requires that as between the law of the habitual residence of the maintenance debtor and creditor, the law most favorable to the maintenance creditor (support receiver) be employed.[215] This rule makes overt a substantive preference for favoring the generous over grudging when it comes to support law.

IV. A Look to the Future

Both history and present circumstances demonstrate that successful regulation transnational commerce depends on two factors. The first is predictability. Predictability is essential because it allows parties to assess in advance the risks they are taking in entering into the transaction. Predictability is also important because if controversies develop, parties can settle them more easily. If the legal standards are in doubt, parties will be tempted to engage the entire dispute resolution mechanism to attempt to persuade the judge or arbitrator that the rules most favorable to them ought apply. Such instability inevitably increases transactions costs.

The second factor is the availability of familiar legal standards. When sophisticated parties negotiate agreements, they do so

---

[214] Conversation with O.A.S delegate Friedrich K. Juenger, on April 25, 1994.

[215] Inter-American Convention on Support Obligations, 71 O.A.S.T.S., 29 I.L.M. 75 (1990)(article six).

against the background of a tentative understanding of the applicable law. If the parties' tentative understandings of the applicable law do not match each other the negotiations may encounter difficulty later on, raising the costs of doing business. Thus, a successful conflicts strategy must make some effort to match the applicable law with the parties' intuitions.

The only conflicts approach able to deliver on both counts is the substantive law approach. Multilateral rules, such as the *lex loci contractus*, can deliver predictability if rigidly applied. But by making the choice of law depend upon fortuitous connecting factors, such as the place of the acceptance of the contract, they run the risk of applying laws that are unfamiliar to the parties. In the worst case, an arbitrarily-selected law voids an agreement that both parties believed in good faith to be enforceable. Unilateralism, with its heavy bent towards forum law, does better at matching the intuitions of at least one of the parties, but it scores poorly on predictability. By making the choice depend upon forum choice, it renders impossible a prospective assessment of the applicable standards.

The substantive law approach, however, is predictable. The applicable standards depend neither on forum choice nor seemingly irrelevant criteria. The substantive law approach also does well on matching the parties' intuitions. By emphasizing the commonality of national standards, it avoids application of backwater, unfamiliar rules that lurk as dangerous traps for the unwary trader.[216]

Unlike its two competitors, the substantive law approach has the added benefit of contributing to the development of the substantive law. The UNIDROIT principles, and the masterful comparative analyses behind them,[217] are sure to lead to the improvement of domestic law throughout the world. The Vienna Sales Convention will surely lead to improvements in our own Uniform Commercial Code. The development of substantive standards of universal or

---

216 *Cf.* Swift v. Tyson, 41 U.S. (16 Pet.) 1 (1842)(application of New York rule would have invalidated transaction; application of *lex mercatoria* led to enforcement of the transaction).

217 *See* Symposium, *supra* note 212, at 617-702.

near-universal purport also improves the quality of judging. Both unilateralism and multilateralism raise the possibility of judges having to apply unfamiliar foreign rules, and thus run the attendant risk of misapplication or substantive standards. If one considers the job of conflicts theory as simply one of making a "choice" between competing domestic laws, the growth of domestic law will be stunted. The substantive law approach to conflicts in commercial transactions thus holds the key to the past and a torch for the future.

INTERNATIONAL HARMONIZATION OF PRIVATE LAW

Peter Winship
James Cleo Thompson Sr. Trustee Professor
Southern Methodist University School of Law

I. Introduction To The Problems Of Trading Across National Boundaries

[What follows is an excerpt from Peter Winship & John A. Spanogle, *Transnational Sales, Contracts: Course Materials* 1, 3-6 and 11 (Spring 1994)]

After that magic day when you have graduated, a second magic day when you have found an employer or "just the perfect spot" to hang out your shingle, and the third magic day when the bar examiners notify you that (of course!) you passed the bar with flying colors -- after all that, a potential client walks into your office, says that she is about to sell 500 electronic notepads to a buyer in France, and announces that she wants you to "set up" the transaction for her. What do you do? Read on. . . .

If your potential client had negotiated to sell 500 electronic notepads to a buyer in Missouri, she and the buyer are unlikely to have bargained hard, if at all, over what law governs the sales contract. Drawing on your knowledge of Article 2 of the Uniform Commercial Code you will realize that the risk of surprise or disadvantage is slight. Article 2 will almost always govern and, with limited exceptions, the parties' agreement will displace the Code's provisions, as will the usages of the electronic notepad trade. If you are asked to memorialize the transaction, you will discover that your study of contract law, the Uniform Commercial Code, and all those legal writing exercises in Law School now pay dividends.

When, however, your potential client wishes to sell the same notepads to a buyer in France, the risks of surprise and disadvantage are higher. U.C.C. Article 2, after all, is not the law outside the United States, no matter what your sales law instructor thought. Consider what happens when a dispute arises between the parties and the contract does not designate the law applicable to the contract. Because the parties did not choose the applicable law, the judge or arbitrator will have to do so. If the claim is brought before a French judge, he or she will use French choice-of-law rules -- and these rules may be quite different from the choice-of-law rules that a U.S. judge would apply if the claim were brought before a U.S. court.

When you analyze your client's claim you will therefore have to go through three steps. First, you will have to determine what forum will hear the claim. Only *after* the forum has been selected can you analyze the second step: whether U.S. law, French law, or some other country's law governs the parties' rights and obligations. You must then construe the applicable law to predict how the dispute will be resolved by the judge or arbitrator. All three steps of the analysis are costly to carry out and subject to a greater possibility of error than if the transaction were a domestic sale governed by the Uniform Commercial Code.

Are these problems resolved if you have the parties designate U.S. law as the applicable law? A moment's reflection suggests that the answer is a qualified "no". Although the risk of non-enforcement is slight, you still must consider whether all possible fora will enforce the choice-of-law clause. Even if a French court would enforce the clause, would you feel comfortable having to prove the content (translated into French) of U.S. law to that court? Finally, consider your own professional responsibility. If French law gives greater protection to the seller than U.S. law does, have you necessarily advised a client properly if you have the parties designate U.S. law as applicable? Aren't you obliged, in other words, to know enough about the possible alternatives (*e.g.*, U.S. law, French law) to advise a client on the best possible alternative? Given these considerations, of course, the practical problem is that the initial question assumes that you or the seller can persuade the French buyer to accept U.S. law as the applicable law. Remember that to the French buyer U.S. law and the Uniform Commercial Code will be unfamiliar and he will therefore probably prefer French law.

Your life, in other words, would be much simpler if U.C.C. Article 2 -- or some other uniform sales law -- were the law in both the United States and France. Put another way, the non-uniformity of national sales laws creates "transaction costs" for international trade.

There are several possible ways to reduce, if not eliminate, these transaction costs.

First, as just suggested, all the world's States might adopt a uniform sales law for transnational sales, or, more ambitiously, for both domestic and transnational sales.

Second, but more modestly, these same States might unify choice-of-law rules, thereby assuring parties that the same national sales law will govern no matter what forum considers the dispute.

Third, courts and arbitral tribunals might recognize and enforce a supranational "law merchant" (sometimes referred to as *lex mercatoria*) incorporating principles and rules of contract law tailored for international trade.

Finally, international traders themselves might develop standard form contracts or general conditions incorporated into their agreements.

These techniques, of course, are not incompatible with each other. International organizations concerned with elimination of these transaction costs, however, have tended to specialize in one or more of these techniques.

A growing body of draft conventions, uniform laws, model laws, and less formal international instruments draws upon one or more of these techniques to address transnational sales, payments, and financing. If you are familiar with articles 2, 3, 4, 4A, 5 and 9 of the Uniform Commercial Code you will find analogues to these articles in this body of "transnational" law. Although their comments are premature, some commentators already speak about "codification" of private international trade law.[218]

II. The Principal International Organizations Devoted To Harmonization Or Unification Of Private Law

For the past 150 years there have been numerous international attempts to unify or harmonize private law in different

[218] *See, e.g.*, Clive M. Schmitthoff, *The Codification of the Law of International Trade*, 1985 J. Bus. L. 34; *Symposium: The Codification of International Commercial Law: Toward a New Law Merchant*, 15 Brooklyn J. Int'l L. 1 (1989).

countries.[219] Projects for harmonization of business law are the most widely-known today, but there have also been numerous efforts in the fields of personal status, property, and judicial procedure and cooperation.

The closest we have to a survey of contemporary projects is the "Digest of Legal Activities of International Organizations and Other Institutions" published in loose-leaf form by the International Institute for the Unification of Private Law.[220] A quick perusal of that text reveals the wide variety of on-going projects and sponsors.

A similar impression comes from reading the 1966 U.N. Secretary-General on harmonization and unification of international trade law, *Progressive Development of the Law of International Trade*.[221] The report identifies the following public and private organizations as engaged in relevant projects:

A. Inter-governmental Organizations
   1. The International Institute for the Unification of Private Law (UNIDROIT)
   2. The Hague Conference on Private International Law
   3. The League of Nations
   4. The United Nations
      (a) The Convention on the Recognition and Enforcement of Foreign Arbitral Awards of 1958
      (b) Industrial property legislation
      (c) United Nations regional economic commissions
      (d) United Nations Conference on Trade and Development (UNCTAD)

---

[219] For a general survey of the history of the unification of law (and much more), see René David, *The International Unification of Private Law*, in 2 Int'l Encyc. Comp. L. ch. 5 (1971). *See also* Arthur Rosett, *Unification, Harmonization, Restatement, Codification, and Reform in International Commercial Law*, 40 Am. J. Comp. L. 683 (1992).

[220] International Institute for the Unification of Private Law (UNIDROIT), *Digest of Legal Activities of International Organizations and Other Institutions* (Dobbs Ferry, N.Y.: Oceana Publications, 10th ed. 1994).

[221] *Progressive Development of the Law of International Trade: Report of the Secretary-General*, U.N. GAOR, 21st Sess., Annex, Agenda Item 88, U.N. Doc. A/6396 and addenda (1966), *reprinted in* [1968-1970] 1 UNCITRAL Y.B. 18, U.N. Doc. A/CN.9/SER.A/1970.

(e) Centre for Industrial Development
5. The United Nations Specialized Agencies
(a) International Bank for Reconstruction and Development (IBRD)
(b) Inter-governmental Maritime Consultative Organization (IMCO)
(c) The International Civil Aviation Organization (ICAO)
6. United International Bureaux for the Protection of Intellectual Property (BIRPI)

B. Regional Inter-governmental Organizations and Groupings
1. The Council for Mutual Economic Assistance (CMEA)
2. The European Economic Community (EEC)
3. The European Free Trade Association (EFTA)
4. The Latin American Countries (OAS)
5. The Council of Europe
6. The Benelux Countries
7. The Nordic Council
8. The Organization of African Unity (OAU)
9. The Asian-African Legal Consultative Committee

C. Non-governmental Organizations
1. The International Chamber of Commerce (ICC)
2. The International Maritime Committee (IMC)
3. The International Association of Legal Science
4. The International Law Association (ILA)
5. The Institute of International Law

As a result of this 1966 report, the United States General Assembly created a Commission on International Trade Law (UNCITRAL) charged with, *inter alia* "[c]o-ordinating the work of orginizations active in this field and encouraging the work of co-operation amang them.[222]

Four inter-governmental institutions are of particular interest to the United States. One body -- the Hague Conference on Private

[222] G.A. Res. 2205, U.N.G.A.O.R., 21st Sess., Supp. No. 16 at 100; U.N. Doc. A16594 (1966).

International Law ("Hague Conference") -- celebrated its centenary in 1993. A second, the International Institute for the Unification of Private Law ("UNIDROIT") in Rome, was a gift by Mussolini to the League of Nations in 1926. More recently, in 1966 the U.N. General Assembly created the Commission on International Trade Law ("UNCITRAL"). While these three bodies are dedicated to global unification efforts, the fourth body -- the Organization of American States ("OAS") -- is a regional political grouping that convenes Specialized Conferences on Private International Law.

The United States participates actively in all four bodies. After considerable debate, the United States became a member of the Hague Conference and UNIDROIT in 1963 after receiving congressional approval. The United States has been elected a member of UNCITRAL since its inception. Because the United States has always been a member of the United Nations, Congress has not had specifically to approve participation in UNCITRAL. Likewise, as a member of the OAS, the United States has participated in the Specialized Conferences on Private International Law without the need for congressional action. Participation in the work of these bodies, of course, does not commit the United States to any particular text developed by these bodies.

Individuals from the United States also participate in the harmonization efforts of non-governmental organizations. The most influential of these bodies are the International Chamber of Commerce ("ICC") and the International Maritime Committee ("IMC" or "CMI", the latter being the initials of its French name, Comité maritime international).

While one should not overlook the activities of the non-governmental organizations, the following materials focus on the four inter-governmental bodies of particular interest to the United States.[223]

---

[223] *See generally* Rudolf Dolzer, *International Agencies for the Formulation of Transnational Economic Law*, in *The Transnational Law of International Commercial Transactions* 61-80 (Norbert Horn & Clive M. Schmitthoff eds. 1982).

A. The Hague Conference On Private International Law

The Hague Conference on Private International Law is -- despite its name a permanent inter-governmental body with its headquarters at The Hague in the Netherlands.[224] Its present status is determined by a "Statute" set out in an international treaty that came into force on July 15, 1955.[225]

The Hague Conference's purpose, as stated in Article 1 of its Statute, is "to work for the progressive unification of the rules of private international law." The phrase "private international law" approximates "conflict of laws" in Anglo-American usage. Thus, the Hague Conference concentrates on preparing uniform rules for determining which national law governs a particular transaction or issue. By tradition, these uniform rules are incorporated in multilateral treaties or conventions rather than model laws, although as from 1980 the Conference is willing to prepare model laws and adopt recommendations.

The Conference has been most successful in the areas of personal status, family obligations, and judicial procedure or cooperation. Although it has adopted several commercial law conventions, few of these have come into force.

The United States is a party to the Convention on the Service Abroad of Judicial and Extra-Judicial Documents in Civil or Commercial Matters,[226] Convention on the Taking of Evidence Abroad in Civil or Commercial Matters,[227] Convention Abolishing the Requirement of Legalization for Foreign Public

---

224 Hague Conference on Private International Law, 6 Scheveningseweg, 2517 KT The Hague, The Netherlands. (tel. 31-70-363-3303; fax 31-70-360-4867).

225 Statute of The Hague Conference on Private International Law, October 31, 1951, 15 U.S.T. 2228, 220 U.N.T.S. 121 (1955). The Statute entered into force for the United States on October 15, 1964.

226 Convention on the Service Abroad of Judicial and Extrajudicial Documents in Civil or Commercial Matters, November 15, 1965, 20 U.S.T. 361, 658 U.N.T.S. 163. The service convention entered into force for the United States on February 10, 1969.

227 Convention on the Taking of Evidence Abroad in Civil or Commercial Matters, March 18, 1970, 23 U.S.T. 2555, 847 U.N.T.S. 231. The evidence convention entered into force for the United States on October 7, 1972 and is codified at 28 U.S.C.A. § 1781 (West Supp. 1989).

Documents,[228] and Convention on the Civil Aspects of International Child Abduction.[229] In addition, the United States has signed but not yet ratified the Convention on the Law Applicable to Trusts and on their Recognition.[230]

As of March 1994 the Conference had 41 members.[231] When the United States became a member in 1964 there were 23 members, most from western Europe. In the last 30 years, membership has become more diverse. Australia and Canada are now members, as are six countries from Latin America (Argentina, Chile, Mexico, Suriname, Uruguay, and Venezuela). In more recent years, China and East European countries have also become members.

Financial support for the Conference comes from subventions provided by the government of the Netherlands and by agreed contributions from member States. This support finances the Conference's permanent bureau at The Hague. The secretariat at the permanent bureau consists of a Secretary-General, two Deputy Secretary-Generals, and supporting staff. The three principal officers must be nationals of different States. As of 1994, one of the Deputy Secretary-Generals is from the United States.

The history of the Hague Conference falls into two distinct periods. Prior to World War II, the Conference met six times in 1893, 1894,

---

[228] Convention Abolishing the Requirement of Legalization for Foreign Public Documents, October 5, 1961, 33 U.S.T. 883, T.I.A.S. No. 10072, 527 U.N.T.S. 189. The legalization convention entered into force for the United States on October 15, 1981. 28 U.S.C.A. App., Rules of Civil Procedure No. 44 (Supp.).

[229] Convention on the Civil Aspects of International Child Abduction, October 25, 1980. T.I.A.S. No. 11670, Hague Conference on Private International Law, *Recueil des Conventions* (hereinafter R.C.H.) 264, 1951-1988. The abduction convention entered into force for the United States on July 1, 1988.

[230] Convention on the Law Applicable to Trusts and on their Recognition, July 1, 1985, Hague Conference on Private International Law, *Recueil des conventions* 1951-1988.

[231] Members as of March 1, 1994 include: Argentina, Australia, Austria, Belgium, Canada, Chile, China, Cyprus, Czech Republic, Denmark, Egypt, Finland, Former Yugoslav Republic of Macedonia, France, Germany (F.R.G.), Greece, Hungary, Ireland, Israel, Italy, Japan, Latvia, Luxembourg, Mexico, Morocco, Netherlands, Norway, Poland, Portugal, Romania, Slovak Republic, Slovenia, Spain, Suriname, Sweden, Switzerland, Turkey, United Kingdom, U.S.A., Uruguay, and Venezuela. 83 Rev. crit. dr. internat. privé 195, 195 (1994).

1900, 1904, 1925, and 1928. The Netherlands government convened a seventh session in 1951 at which the delegates adopted the present Statute. Starting in 1956, the Conference has usually met every four years with several additional extraordinary sessions. The most recent meeting was rescheduled from October 1992 to May 1993 in honor of the Conference's centenary. The next meeting of the Conference is scheduled for October 1996.

At the time of the Conference's centenary in 1993, law reviews published a number of articles examining the work and influence of the Conference. In the United States, *Law and Contemporary Problems* will publish papers presented at a symposium that reviewed the Conference's work.

The Conference's working methods have been relatively consistent since 1951.[232] In the year before the quadrennial session, a Special Commission on General Affairs and Policy of the Conference meets to consider the future work of the Conference. The secretariat then prepares feasibility studies which are circulated to the member states. The Conference then adopts an agenda for future work as part of the Conference's Final Act of its regular session. For each topic on the agenda, the secretariat prepares a research paper and a questionnaire which it then circulates to member States for comments. A Special Commission, consisting of representatives of member states, will then meet to review this material and draft a text for submission to the next session of the Conference. At this session, one of the Commissions will review this draft and recommend a proposed text for adoption at a plenary meeting. If approved, the Conference incorporates the draft Convention in the Final Act of the session. The Conference publishes the acts and documents of its sessions, with a volume usually devoted to each draft convention adopted at a session.

At the May 1993 session, the Conference adopted[233] the following agenda of future work:

---

232 For a more detailed description of the Hague Conference's working methods, see *United Nations Legislative Series: Review of the Multilateral Treaty-Making Process* at 513-521, U.N. Doc. ST/LEG/SER.B/21, U.N. Sales No. E/F.83.V.8 (1985).

233 Hague Conference on Private International Law, *Final Act of the Seventeenth*

1. Decides to include in the Agenda of the Eighteenth Session the revision of the *Convention of 5 October 1961 concerning the powers of authorities and the law applicable in respect of the protection of minors*, and a possible extension of the new convention's scope to the protection of incapacitated adults.

2a. Decides to include in the Agenda for the work of the Conference the question of the recognition and enforcement of foreign judgments in civil and commercial matters;

b. Requests the Secretary General to convene as soon as is feasible a Special Commission charged with the following matters:

- studying further the problems involved in drafting a new convention, on the basis of a document prepared by the Permanent Bureau, taking into account the discussions of the Seventeenth Session,
- making proposals with respect to the work which might be undertaken,
- suggesting the timing of such work;

c. Leaves it to the Special Commission on General Affairs and Policy of the Conference to make recommendations to the Eighteenth Session on the further steps to be taken.

3. Decides to include also in the Agenda for the work programme of the Conference the question of the determination of the law applicable, and possibly questions arising from conflicts of jurisdiction, in respect of civil liability for environmental damage.

4. Decides to include or retain in the Agenda of the Conference, but without priority -

---

Session at Part B (1993), *reprinted in* 40 Neth. Int'l L. Rev. 292, 306-307 (1993).

a. jurisdiction, and recognition and enforcement of decisions in matters of succession upon death,

b. protection of privacy in connection with transfrontier data flows,

c. the law applicable to unmarried couples,

d. the law applicable to negotiable instruments,

e. the international legal problems raised by electronic data interchange,

f. the law applicable to bank guarantees,

g. the law applicable to unfair competition.

5. Requests the Secretary General to convene at appropriate times Special Commissions to study the operations of the following Conventions -

a. Hague Conventions on the law applicable to or on the recognition and enforcement of decisions relating to maintenance obligations, as well as the *New York Convention of 20 June 1956 on the Recovery Abroad of Maintenance*,

b. Hague Conventions on civil procedure and on international judicial and administrative co-operation.

The Conference's Permanent Bureau edits a bibliography relating to the work of the Conference which it publishes as part of the volume of miscellaneous matters for each session.[234] An annual report on the Conference appears in the second issue each year of The *Netherlands International Law Review*.[235] This issue lists the member

[234] For the most recent edition, see *Bibliography Relating to the Work of the Conference (1945-1991)*, in 1 Hague Conference on Private International Law, *Proceedings of the Sixteenth Session (3 to 20 October 1988): Miscellaneous Matters* 284-347 (1991).

[235] *See, e.g., Information concerning the Hague Conventions on Private International Law*, 40 Neth. Int'l L. Rev. 257 (1993).

states and reports on the present status of each of its conventions.[236]

B. International Institute For The Unification Of Private Law

The International Institute for the Unification of Private Law (UNIDROIT) is an inter-governmental body with its headquarters in Rome, Italy.[237] Originally established in 1926 and affiliated with the League of Nations, the Institute was reestablished after World War II as an independent organization. Its present status is determined by a "Charter."[238]

As of October 1993, the Institute had 56 members.[239] When the United States became a member in 1964 there were 40 members. Many of the same countries that have joined the Hague Conference in recent years have also joined the Institute. These members and the Italian government provide the financing for the Institute's operations.

The Institute's purpose, as stated in Article 1 of the Charter, is "to examine ways of harmonizing and co-ordinating the private law of States and groups of States, and to prepare gradually for the

---

236 Similar reports appear periodically in the *Revue critique de droit international privé*. *See, e.g.*, 83 Rev. crit. dr. internat. privé 195 (1994) (state of signatures and ratifications as of 1 March 1994).

237 International Institute for the Unification of Private Law, Palazzo Aldobrandini, Via Panisperna, 28, 1-00184 Rome, Italy (tel. 39-6-684-1372; fax 39-6-684-1394).

238 Statute of the International Institute for the Unification of Private Law, March 15, 1940, 15 U.S.T. 2494, The Statute has been amended several times. (See UKTS 78 (1977), Cmnd. 6946 (consolidated text with all amendments to 1977) and UKTS 93 (1991), Cmnd.1728 (1984 amendment)). It entered into force for the United States on March 13, 1964.

239 Members as of October 1, 1993 include: Argentina, Australia, Austria, Belgium, Bolivia, Brazil, Bulgaria, Canada, Chile, China, Colombia, Cuba, Czech Republic, Denmark, Egypt, Finland, France, Germany, Greece, Holy See, Hungary, India, Iran, Iraq, Ireland, Israel, Italy, Japan, Luxembourg, Malta, Mexico, Netherlands, Nicaragua, Nigeria, Norway, Pakistan, Paraguay, Poland, Portugal, Republic of Korea, Romania, Russian Federation, San Marino, Senegal, Slovakia, South Africa, Spain, Sweden, Switzerland, Tunisia, Turkey, United Kingdom, USA, Uruguay, Venezuela, and Yugoslavia. UNIDROIT, *News Bulletin* No. 93/94 at 1 (January/April 1993), No. 95/96 at 1 (July/October 1993).

adoption by the various States of uniform legislation in the field of private law." To carry out this objective, the Institute has prepared uniform texts of substantive law, many of which are set out in international instruments. Thus, unlike the Hague Conference, the Institute promotes unification or harmonization of law by seeking to have states adopt uniform substantive law.

Since 1926 the Institute has worked principally in the areas of sales law, credit law, transportation law, procedural law, and law relating to civil liability. The 1964 uniform sales laws were prepared under the auspices of the Institute, as were the 1973 uniform law on the form of an international will and the 1988 factoring and leasing conventions.

As important as these legal texts are the Institute's scholarly activities and publications. It has sponsored three "Congresses on Private Law" and five "Meetings of the Organisations concerned with the Unification of Law." Proceedings of these meetings have been published.[240]

Proceedings of the five meetings of organizations involved in unification or harmonization efforts appear in 1956 UNIDROIT Y.B., vol. 2 (1957) (Unification of Law); 1959 UNIDROIT Y.B. 48-509 (1960) (The Methods in the Unification of Law; The Differences in the Interpretation of Uniform Law); 1963 UNIDROIT Y.B. (1964) (The Differences in the Interpretation of Uniform Law; Relations Between Unification at a regional and at a Universal Level); 1967-1968 UNIDROIT Y.B., vol. 2, 33-323 (1969) (Unification and Harmonization of Law: The criteria governing the choice between the various methods); 1973-II Unif. L. Rev. 13-197 (Uniform Law as a Means of Technical Assistance to Developing Countries; Methods of Co-ordinating the Different International Organizations and Team-Work Among Them). In addition, the Institute edits the

---

240 The proceedings of the three congresses appear in UNIDROIT, *Actes du Congrès international de droit privé tenu à Rome en juillet 1950*, Unification of Law, 2 (1951); UNIDROIT, *New Directions in International Trade Law: Acts and Proceedings of the 2nd Congress on Private Law held by the International Institute for the Unification of Private Law, Rome, 9-15 September 1976 (1977)*; UNIDROIT, *International Uniform Law in Practice: Acts and Proceedings of the 3rd Congress on Private Law held by the International Institute for the Unification of Private Law*, Rome, 7-10 September 1987 (1988).

digest of legal activities of international bodies mentioned earlier,[241] and publishes the semi-annual *Revue de droit uniforme/Uniform Law Review* and a semi-annual *News Bulletin*. The *Uniform Law Review* includes digests of court decisions and arbitral awards construing "uniform" laws, while both the *Uniform Law Review* and the *News Bulletin* contain bibliographies.

Although U.S. legal experts have participated actively in the work of the Institute, the United States has not yet adopted any of the UNIDROIT texts. The State Department is, however, preparing to send to Congress draft legislation to implement the Convention Providing for a Uniform Law on the Form of an International Will, 1973, a treaty that received Senate advice and consent in 1991.[242]

Soon after the 1973 conference, the National Conference of Commissioners on Uniform State Laws referred the Wills Convention text to the Editorial Board for the Uniform Probate Code. The Editorial Board recommended that the National Conference adopt a uniform state law implementing the Convention and in 1977 the Conference adopted the Uniform International Wills Act. States may adopt the Act as a free-standing act or as an amendment (new Part 10) of Article 2 of the Uniform Probate Code. [243] In addition, the State Department plans to forward the Conventions on international factoring[244] and international financial leasing[245] to the Senate for advice and consent in the near future.[246]

---

[241] *See* note 219 *supra*.

[242] The United States sponsored the diplomatic conference at which this text was adopted and as a consequence the text is often cited as the "Washington" wills convention. The United States signed the convention on October 27, 1973. The Senate gave its advice and consent to ratification on August 2, 1991 subject to enactment of federal implementing legislation.

[243] 8 U.L.A. 178 (Master ed. 1983).

[244] UNIDROIT Convention on International Factoring, May 28, 1988, 27 I.L.M. 943 (1988).

[245] UNIDROIT Convention on International Financial Leasing, May 28, 1988, 27 I.L.M. 931 (1988).

[246] Remarks of Harold S. Burman at the 46th meeting of the Secretary of State's Advisory Committee on Private International Law (May 16, 1994) in Washington, D.C.

The Institute's working methods have evolved over time and vary with the subject matter.[247] Once the Governing Council decides what topics should be on the Institute's work program, the secretariat or a consultant will prepare a comparative law study of each topic. This study may be prepared after questionnaires are circulated to member governments and interested persons. On completion of the study, the Governing Council may convene a study group of private experts or a committee of governmental experts. If a study group is used, the Governing Council will usually submit its work to a committee of governmental experts.

On completion of the review by the committee of governmental experts, the Governing Council may choose to forward the draft text to another international body, such as UNCITRAL, or to arrange for the convoking of a diplomatic conference to adopt the text. A recent example of a text developed within UNIDROIT and forwarded to another body is the 1991 United Nations Convention on Liability of Operators of Transport Terminals.[248] After a decade of work on the topic, the Institute submitted its draft text to UNCITRAL for completion of the project. The factoring and leasing conventions are recent examples of texts submitted directly to an international conference.

At its June 1992 session, the Institute's Governing Council adopted[249] the following work program for the period, 1993-1995:

1. Principles for international commercial contracts
2. International protection of cultural property
3. International aspects of security interests in mobile equipment

[247] For further elaboration on UNIDROIT's working methods, see *United Nations Legislative Series, Review of the Multilateral Treaty-Making Process*, note 231 *supra*, at 478-482.

[248] United Nations Convention on the Liability of Operators of Transport Terminals, April 19, 1991, United Nations Conference on the Liability of Operators of Transport Terminals in International Trade, Official Records, at 101, U.N. Doc. A/Conf. 152/14 (1991); I.L.M. 1506 (1991).

[249] UNIDROIT, *Governing Council 71st session (Genoa, 22 to 24 June 1992): Report on the Session (prepared by the Secretariat)*, UNIDROIT 1992, C.D. (71) 18 at 3-4 & Appendix III (August 1992).

4. International franchising
5. Inspection agency contracts
6. Civil liability connected with the carrying out of dangerous activities
7. Legal issues connected with software
8. Program of legal assistance
9. Organization of an information system or data bank on uniform law
10. Organization of a congress or meeting on uniform law during the triennial period 1993-1995.

At its May 1994 meeting, the General Council approved the final text of the first of these items, the Principles for International Commercial Contracts.[250] This project (Study L) restates the general principles governing transnational commercial contracts much in the same way that the Restatement of Contracts does for domestic U.S. contracts. Although the text has been circulated among governments and international organizations for comment, the Institute will not present the text for formal adoption at an international diplomatic conference or by national legislation. The Principles will apply if parties to a contract agree that their contract will be governed by them. They may also be considered "general principles of contract law" or "lex mercatoria" by arbitrators or judges.

At a request of UNESCO, the Institute has also undertaken work on draft convention on stolen or illegally exported cultural objects (Study LXX). As presently drafted, the convention will provide private law rules governing the rights of owners and purchasers of cultural property that has been stolen or that has been exported illegally. It is hoped that the text will be attractive to art-importing countries that have not accepted the 1970 UNESCO Convention.[251] A committee of governmental

---

[250] UNIDROIT, *Principles for International Commercial Contracts* (forthcoming).

[251] Convention on the Means of Prohibiting and Preventing the Illicit Import, Export, and Transfer of Ownership of Cultural Property, November 14, 1970,

experts has been meeting since May 1991 to review a text prepared by an UNIDROIT study group. This committee had its fourth session in October 1993. As of March 1994, the UNIDROIT secretariat hoped that the Italian government would convoke a diplomatic conference to review the draft convention in early 1995.

Buoyed by the success of the 1988 Ottawa conference that adopted the factoring and leasing conventions, the Institute has begun work on draft rules governing the recognition of security interests in mobile equipment (Study LXXII). A study group has met several times, most recently in February 1994. It is not yet clear, however, what the scope of this project will be.

C. United Nations Commission On International Trade Law

The United Nations General Assembly created the United Nations Commission on International Trade Law (UNCITRAL) in 1966 for "the promotion of the progressive harmonization and unification of the law of international trade."[252]

Thus, like UNIDROIT and unlike the Hague Conference, the U.N. Commission prepares uniform substantive law texts rather than texts unifying the conflict of laws. The topics addressed by UNCITRAL are limited, however, to ones related to trade and its mandate is consequently more limited than that of UNIDROIT. At the same time, the Commission has been more eclectic in the methods used, adopting not only international conventions but also model laws, voluntary rules, and guidelines. This is consistent with the charge to the Commission to "prepar[e] or promot[e] the adoption of new international conventions, model laws and

---

823 U.N.T.S. 231, 10 I.L.M. 289 (1971).

[252] G.A. Res. 2205, U.N. GAOR, 21st Sess., Supp. No. 16 at 99, U.N. Doc. A/6316 (1966) as amended by G.A. Res. 3108, U.N. GAOR, 28th Sess., Supp. No. 30 at 145 para. 8, U.N. Doc. A/31/390 (1973) and G.A. Res. 31/99, U.N. GAOR 31st Sess., Supp. No. 34 at 182 para. 10(b), U.N. Doc.A/9408 (1976). The Commission is a "subsidiary organ" within the meaning of Article 22 of the United Nations Charter. Rules governing UNCITRAL's composition and work are set out in the cited General Assembly resolutions. For more detailed information about the origin and working methods of the U.N. Commission, see *United Nations Commission of International Trade Law*, U.N. Sales No. E.86.V.8 (1986; 2d ed. forthcoming). This volume also includes the texts adopted by the Commission.

uniform laws and promot[e] the codification and wider acceptance of international trade terms, provisions, customs and practices, in collaboration, where appropriate, with the organizations operating in this field."[253]

The Commission meets annually, usually for a three-week session. At these sessions, it reviews reports submitted by one or more of its working groups. Annual meetings of the Commission and meetings of its working groups alternate between Vienna and New York. The Commission's Secretariat is located in Vienna, Austria.[254]

The General Assembly elects the 36 members of the Commission for six-year terms. Members are selected to represent the different economic, social, and political viewpoints. The United States has been a member from the Commission's inception.

The Commission reports to the General Assembly through its Sixth Committee. The Commission also submits its annual report to the United Nations Conference on Trade and Development (UNCTAD) for comments. Documents generated by the Commission, relevant UNCTAD and Sixth Committee reports, and General Assembly resolutions are published in the UNCITRAL yearbook.

UNCITRAL's working methods are now well-established.[255] Having identified a topic it wishes to pursue, the Commission refers it to a working group. In recent years there have been three working groups. These working groups meet once or twice a year to prepare, with the help of the secretariat, a draft text. Although the working groups reports to the Commission after each working group meeting, the Commission will not usually intervene in the ongoing work. When a working group submits a final report with a draft text, the Commission reviews the text at an annual session. In recent years the Commission has devoted much of its annual

---

[253] G.A. Res. 2205, U.N. GAOR, 21st Sess., Supp. 16 at 99, para. 8(c), U.N. Doc.A/6316 (1966).

[254] UNCITRAL, Vienna International Centre, P.0. Box 500, Wagramer Strasse 5, A-1400 Vienna, Austria (tel. 43-1-21131-4060; fax 43-1-237485).

[255] *United Nations Commission on International Trade Law* 7-12, U.N. Sales No. E.86.V.8 (1986). A second edition of this volume is forthcoming.

session to the review of one text. The resulting text is incorporated in the Commission's report to the General Assembly together with a recommendation on the disposition of the text. In the case of draft UNCITRAL conventions, the General Assembly will usually convoke a diplomatic conference although in at least one recent instance the General Assembly itself adopted the Convention after thorough review by its Sixth Commission.[256] As for model laws and other texts, the General Assembly will usually adopt a resolution endorsing the text. The Commission publishes an annual report setting out the Status of these texts.[257] Current information about the status of UNCITRAL conventions is available from the Treaty Section of the U.N. Office of Legal Affairs.[258]

Its arbitration and sales law texts are the best known of the UNCITRAL texts. In the field of arbitration, the Commission has adopted the UNCITRAL Arbitration Rules[259] and the Model Law on International Commercial Arbitration.[260] Adoption of the 1980 U.N. Convention on Contracts for the International Sale of Goods[261] is also wide-spread. A Limitations Convention for claims arising from international sales contracts[262] supplements the 1980 convention.

---

256 The United Nations Convention on International Bills of Exchange and International Promissory Notes was promulgated by the General Assembly without reference to a diplomatic conference. *See* [1988] 19 UNCITRAL Y.B., Annexes I & II at 173 and 187, U.N. Doc. A/CN.9/SER.A/1988.

257 *See, e.g.*, United Nations Commission on International Trade Law, *Status of Conventions: Note by the Secretariat*, U.N. Doc. A/CN.9/381 (14 July 1993).

258 Treaty Section of the Office of Legal Affairs, United Nations, New York, N.Y. 10017 (tel. [212] 963-5047).

259 *Report of the United Nations Commission on International Trade Law on the Work of Its Ninth Session*, U.N. GAOR, 31st Sess., Supp. No. 17, at 34, U.N. Doc. A/31/17 (1976).

260 *Report of the United Nations Commission on International Trade Law on the work of its eighteenth session (June 3-21, 1985)*, U.N. GAOR, 40th Sess., Supp. No. 17, at Annex I, 81-93, U.N. Doc. A/40/17 (1985).

261 United Nations Convention on Contracts for the International Sale of Goods, Apr. 10, 1980, U.N. Doc. A/CONF.97/18 (1980) Annex I, reprinted in 19 I.L.M. 668 (1980).

262 Convention on the Limitation Period in the International Sale of Goods, June. 4, 1974, U.N. Doc. A/CONF.63/15, (1974), reprinted in 13 I.L.M. 952 (1974), and Protocol Amending the Convention on the Limitation Period in the

UNCITRAL has also been active in the areas of transportation and international payments. In the field of transportation, the U.N. Convention on the Carriage of Goods by Sea, 1978 (commonly known as the "Hamburg Rules")[263] recently came into force. The more recent U.N. Convention on the Liability of Operators of Transport Terminals in International Trade[264] is not yet in force. Adoption of UNCITRAL texts governing different aspects of international payments -- the U.N. Convention on International Bills of Exchange[265] and International Promissory Notes and the Model Law on International Credit Transfers has been slow.[266]

The State Department is considering whether to incorporate provisions in the North American Free Trade Agreement to bring the text of the Convention into force among Canada, Mexico, and the United States.[267] Efforts to approve the Model Law on International Credit Transfers-- have been slow.

The Commission's most recent work has focused on government procurement and aspects of arbitration. At its 1993 session the Commission adopted a Model Law on Procurement of Goods and Construction.[268] In the course of

---

International Sale of Goods, April 11, 1980, U.N. Doc. A/CONF.97/18, reprinted in 19 I.L.M. 696 (1980).

263 United Nations Convention on the Carriage of Goods by Sea, 1978, U.N. Doc. A/CONF.89/13, reprinted in 17 I.L.M. 608 (1978).

264 United Nations Convention on Liability of Operators of Transport Terminals, 1991, U.N. Doc. A/CONF.152/13, *reprinted in* 30 I.L.M. 1506 (1991).

265 United Nations Convention on International Bills of Exchange and International Promissory Notes, G.A. Res. 43/165 U.N. GAOR, 43rd Sess. Supp. 49 at 280, U.N. Doc. A/43/820 (1988), 19 UNCITRAL Y.B. 19.

266 UNCITRAL Model Law on International Credit Transfers, U.N. GAOR, 47th Sess., Supp. 17 at 48, U.N. Doc. A/47/17 (1993), reprinted in 32 I.L.M. 588 (1993). The Model Law is similar in scope and content to Article 4A of the Uniform Commercial Code.

267 Remarks of Harold S. Burman at the 46th meeting of the Secretary of State's Advisory Committee on Private International Law, May 16, 1994, in Washington, D.C.

268 UNCITRAL Model Law on Procurement of Goods and Construction, U.N. GAOR, 48th Sess., Supp. 17 at 67,U.N. Doc. A/48/17, (1993), reprinted in 33 I.L.M. 456 (1994). G.A. Res. 48/33, *U.N.* GAOR, 48th Sess., Supp. 49 at 330, U.N. Doc. A/48/613 (1193). *See also* United States Commission on International Trade Law, Guide to Enactment, of UNCITRAL Model Law on

debate on this Model Law it was agreed that there should also be model legal rules for procurement of services. The Commission adopted a draft text modifying the 1993 Model Law to provide for procurement of[2] services.[269] Work on procurement was entrusted to the Working Group on the New International Economic Order. At the 1994 session the Commission also considered Guidelines for Preparatory Conferences in Arbitral Proceedings.[270]

Working Groups continue work on electronic data interchange and international guarantees and stand-by letters of credit. Looking ahead, the Commission is also considering the feasibility of several other projects. These include cross-border insolvency and legal aspects of receivables financing. To explore how to proceed with possible insolvency issues, the Commission and INSOL, an organization of national associations interested in international insolvency, sponsored a colloquium in April 1994.

To encourage uniformity in the interpretation of the UNCITRAL texts, the Commission has established a case-reporting system under the acronym "CLOUT" (Case Law On Uncitral Texts). The Commission has invited states to appoint national correspondents charged with collecting relevant court opinions and arbitral awards and with preparing an abstract of these decisions. The Commission will then publish compilations of these abstracts and make copies of the full decisions available upon payment of a fee.[271] The U.S. national correspondents are Professor John O. Honnold (Univ. of Pennsylvania) and Professor Peter Winship (S.M.U.). As of October

---

Procurement of Goods and Construction, U.N. DocA/CN.9/393 (1993).

[269] For the draft text submitted to the Commission's 1994 session, see United Nations Commission on International Trade Law, *Report of the Working Group on the New International Economic Order on the Work of Its Seventeenth Session (New York, 14-25 March 1994), U.N. Doc. A/CN.9/392 (1994).*

[270] For the draft text submitted to the Commission's 1994 session, see United Nations Commission on International Trade Law, *Draft Guidelines for Preparatory Conferences in Arbitral Proceedings: Report of the Secretary-General,* U.N. Docs. A/CN.9/396 and A/CN.9/396/Add.1/(1994).

[271] For an explanation of CLOUT, see United Nations Commission on International Trade Law, Case Law on UNCITRAL Texts (CLOUT), *User Guide,* U.N. Doc. A/CN.9/SER.C/GUIDE/1 (19 May 1993).

1994, the Commission has published five compilations of abstracts.[272]

The United States is a party to the Sales Convention and the Limitations Convention. In addition, the United States has signed the Hamburg Rules, the International Bills of Exchange Convention, and the Terminal Operators Convention but has not yet ratified these treaties. Individual states (California, Connecticut, Oregon, and Texas) have enacted the Model Law on International Commercial Arbitration.

D. Organization Of American States

The Organization of American States was established in 1948 as a successor to the Pan American Union. Although known primarily for its political and public international law activities, the OAS has convoked specialized conferences on private international law.[273] There have been five such conferences (CIDIP-I through CIDIP-V), the most recent one in Mexico City in March 1994.

Although the term "private international law" is used, the texts adopted at these conferences reflect an eclectic methodology. Thus, some of the conventions incorporate substantive law rules as well as conflict of laws rules.

Unlike the three other inter-governmental bodies already described, there is no permanent secretariat devoted specifically to OAS harmonization efforts. The OAS General Secretariat, through the Bureau of Legal Affairs (formerly the Department of Legal Affairs), prepares technical and information documents to facilitate the work of the Conference. Scholarly review of particular topics is

---

[272] United Nations Commission on International Trade, *Case Law on UNCITRAL Texts (CLOUT)*, U.N. Doc. A/CN.9/SER.C/ABSTRACTS/1-5(1993-1994).

[273] Organization of American States, 17th Street and Constitution Ave., N.W., Washington, DC 20006 (tel. (202) 458-6046). All members of the OAS are invited to attend these specialized conferences. Membership in the OAS includes: Antigua & Barbuda, Argentina, The Bahamas, Barbados, Belize, Bolivia, Brazil, Canada, Chile, Colombia, Costa Rica, Cuba (participation suspended), Dominica, Dominican Republic, Ecuador, El Salvador, Grenada, Guatemala, Guyana, Haiti, Honduras, Jamaica, Mexico, Nicaragua, Panama, Paraguay, Peru, St. Christopher-Nevis, St. Lucia, St. Vincent and the Grenadines, Suriname, Trinidad and Tobago, United States, Uruguay, and Venezuela. 3 U.S. Department of State Dispatch 99 (1992).

left to the Inter-American Juridical Committee, a body of 11 jurists elected by the OAS General Assembly. Article 105 of the OAS Charter charges the committee "to promote the progressive development and the codification of international law; and to study juridical problems related to the integration of the developing countries of the Hemisphere and insofar as may appear desirable, the possibility of attaining uniformity in their legislation."[274] The committee may prepare and review drafts to be submitted to the specialized conferences, although the committee membership is composed principally of jurists with public international law interests.

Critics of the OAS process suggest preparatory work is inadequate. Although there has been a meeting of experts for each of the conventions submitted to the last two conferences, these meetings are *ad hoc* and relatively poorly funded. Recognizing the lack of resources, delegates to CIDIP-V adopted a resolution calling on the Secretary General to report on the allocation of resources to support these harmonization efforts.[275]

The topics covered by the CIDIP conventions include general principles of private international law,[276] family law,[277] commercial law,[278] procedural law and judicial cooperation.[279] At

---

274 Protocol of Amendment to the Charter of the Organization of American States, 1967, art. 105, 21 U.S.T. 607, 721 U.N.T.S. 324 (1967).

275 CIDIP-V/RES. 10 (94) (1994).

276 Inter-American Convention on General Rules of Private International Law, 54 O.A.S. T.S., 1979, 18 I.L.M. 1236 (1979); Inter-American Convention on Domicile of Natural Persons in Private International Law, 55 O.A.S. T.S., 1979, 18 I.L.M. 1234 (1979); Inter-American Convention on Personality and Capacity of Juridical Persons in Private International Law, 1984, 63 O.A.S. T.S., 24 I.L.M. 465 (1985).

277 Inter-American Convention on Conflict of Laws concerning the Adoption of Minors, 62 O.A.S. T.S., 1984, 24 I.L.M. 460 (1985); Inter-American Convention on the International Return of Children, 70 O.A.S. T.S., 1989, 29 I.L.M. 66 (1990); Inter-American Convention on Support Obligations, 1989, 71 O.A.S. T.S., 29 I.L.M. 75 (1990).

278 Inter-American Convention on Conflict of Laws concerning Bills of Exchange, Promissory Notes, and Invoices, 1975, 40 O.A.S. T.S., 14 I.L.M. 332 (1975); Inter-American Convention on Conflicts of Laws concerning Checks, 1979, 49 O.A.S. T.S., 18 I.L.M. 1220 (1979); Inter-American Convention on Conflicts of

the most recent specialized conference, CIDIP-V, the delegates approved a draft Inter-American Convention on international traffic in Minors, March 18, 1994, 33 I.L.M. 723 (1994).[280] and a draft Inter-American Convention on the law applicable to international contracts.[281] The conference also adopted a resolution[282] recommending that the following topics be included in the agenda of the next conference:

(a) Power of attorney and commercial representation.

(b) Conflict of laws on extracontractual liability; (limited to a specifically defined scope).

(c) Standardized commercial documentation for free trade.

(d) International bankruptcy.

Laws concerning Commercial Companies, 1979, 50 O.A.S. T.S., 18 I.L.M. 1222 (1979); and Inter-American Convention on Contracts for the International Carriage of Goods by Road, 1989, 29 I.L.M. 83 (1990).

279 Inter-American Convention on the Legal Regime of Powers of Attorney to be used Abroad, 45 O.A.S. T.S., 1975, 14 I.L.M. 325 (1975); Inter-American Convention on the Taking of Evidence Abroad, 1975, 44 O.A.S. T.S., 14 I.L.M. 328 (1975), and 1984 Protocol, 65 O.A.S. T.S., 24 I.L.M. 472 (1985); Inter-American Convention on International Commercial Arbitration, 1975, S. Treaty Doc. No. 12 97th Cong., 1st Sess., 42 O.A.S. T.S., 14 I.L.M. 336 (1975); Inter-American Convention on Letters Rogatory, 1975, S. Treaty Doc. No. 27, 98th Cong. 2d Sess., 43 O.A.S. T.S., 14 I.L.M. 339 (1975), and 1979 Additional Protocol, S. Treaty Doc. No. 27, 98th Cod Sess., 56 O.A.S. T.S., 18 I.L.M. 1238 (1979); Inter-American Convention on Extraterritorial Validity of Foreign Judgments and Arbitral Awards, 1979, 51 O.A.S. T.S., 18 I.L.M. 1224 (1979); Inter-American Convention on Execution of Preventive Measures, 1979, 52 O.A.S. T.S., 18 I.L.M. 1227 (1979); Inter-American Convention on Proof of and Information on Foreign Law, 1979, 53 O.A.S. T.S., 18 I.L.M. 1231 (1979); and Inter-American Convention on Jurisdiction in the International Sphere for the Extraterritorial Validity of Foreign Judgments, 1984, 64 O.A.S. T.S., 24 I.L.M. 468 (1985).

280 Inter-American Convention on International Traffic in Minors, March 18, 1994 33 I.L.M. 723 (1994).

281 Inter-American Convention on the Law Applicable to International Contracts, March 17, 1994, 33 I.L.M. 733 (1994).

282 CIDIP-V.RES.8 (94) (1994).

(e) Problems in private international law regarding private international loan contracts.

(f) Civil international liability for crossboundary pollution. Aspects of private international law.

(g) International protection of children in private international law: authority over children, custody, visitation rights, status.

(h) Uniformity and harmonization of secured transactions law.

The United States is a party to only two of the OAS private international law treaties: the arbitration convention,[283] and the Convention on Letters Rogatory.[284] Acting on the advice of the private sector, the State Department has shown interest in forwarding the evidence convention for advice and consent of the Senate.[285]

III. ILLUSTRATION OF HARMONIZATION AND UNIFICATION EFFORTS: TRANSNATIONAL SALES

The following excerpt turns from a study of the organizations engaged in international unification or harmonization efforts to a study of how these bodies have addressed unification efforts for a specific topic, the law of sale. Discussion of non-governmental means by which merchants develop uniform rules suggest the limits of formal unification efforts.

[also from Peter Winship & John A. Spanogle, *Transnational Sales Contracts: Course Materials* 6-10 (Spring 1994):[286]]

---

283 The Senate gave its advice and consent on October 6, 1986 but Congress did not enact implementing legislation until 1990. Pub. L. 101-369 (1990) (codified as 9 U.S.C. §§ 301-307).

284 The treaty came into force in the United States on August 27, 1988.

285 Lucinda A. Low, *Inter-American Convention on the Taking of Evidence Abroad*, 24 Int'l Law. 880 (1990).

286 Reproduced with the permission of the authors. These materials are not published: they may not be used without the permission of the authors.

A. UNIFORM SUBSTANTIVE SALES LAW

The International Institute for the Unification of Private Law (UNIDROIT) began work in 1929 on preparation of uniform substantive legal rules to govern international sales. Although the issue was hotly debated, the Institute decided for political reasons to limit the proposed unification to legal rules governing *international* sales rather than to sales law governing both national and international sales. A diplomatic conference meeting at The Hague in 1964 ultimately incorporated the Institute's work in two uniform sales laws appended to international conventions and usually known by the acronyms *ULIS* and *ULF*.[287] These uniform laws dealt respectively with the formation of international sales contracts and the substantive rights and obligations of parties to such contracts. The United Nations Commission on International Trade Law (UNCITRAL), in turn, redrafted these 1964 texts and proposed a 1978 draft incorporating the substance of the two earlier uniform laws. This UNCITRAL text was the basis of the U.N. Convention on Contracts for the International Sale of Goods adopted at a 1980 diplomatic conference meeting in Vienna.[288]

Regional efforts to unify sales law have also been successful. Early in the 20th century, for example, the Scandinavian countries agreed to adopt a uniform sales law. More recently, they have amended this uniform law to conform with the 1980 Sales Convention.[289] Prior to the events of 1989, Socialist States that were members of the Council for Mutual Economic Assistance had adopted "General Conditions of Delivery of Goods between Organizations of the Member Countries of the [CMEA]."[290]

---

[287] Convention Relating to a Uniform Law on the International Sale of Goods, 1964, 834 U.N.T.S. 107 (1972); Convention Relating to a Uniform Law on the Formation of Contracts for the International Sale of Goods, 1964, 834 U.N.T.S. 169 (1972). . . .).

[288] United Nations Convention on Contracts for the International Sale of Goods (A/CONF.97/18, Annex I), *reprinted in* United Nations Conference on Contracts for the International Sale of Goods, *Official Records* 178-90 (1981) (A/CONF.97/19).

[289] *See* Swedish Act of June 20, 1905, Relating to the Purchase and Exchange of Goods (Generally cited as The Sale of Goods Act) (English translation *printed in* UNIDROIT, 1961 *Unification of Law Yearbook* 203. . . .

[290] General Conditions of Delivery of Goods between Organizations of the

B. UNIFORM CHOICE-OF-LAW RULES.

The Hague Conference on Private International Law also began work in the late 1920s on a proposal to unify choice-of-law rules for international sales, a project that led to a 1955 convention[291] and the 1986 Convention on the Law Applicable to Contracts for the International Sale of Goods.[292] Although the former convention is in force it has had limited success; the latter convention is not yet in force. More successful has been the regional European Economic Communities Convention on the Law Applicable to Contractual Obligations, which came into force on January 1, 1991.[293]

C. RULES OF THE "LAW MERCHANT."

In the last 30 years legal writers in Europe have expressed great interest in the development of what they describe as a new "law merchant" or lex mercatoria. Relying especially on evidence in arbitral awards that arbitrators look to general principles of law for the resolution of contract disputes, these authors argue that there is now a body of supranational legal principles and rules that govern transnational contracts. Working against this background, UNIDROIT has worked on "Principles for International Commercial Contracts"[294] that, although not in the form of an

---

Member Countries of the Council for Mutual Economic Assistance, 1968 (English translation *printed in* 1 United Nations, *Register of Texts of Conventions and Other Instruments Concerning International Trade Law* 72 (1971)).

291 Convention on the Law Applicable to International Sales of Goods, 510 U.N.T.S. 147 (1964). (Although adopted in 1951 at the Seventh Session of the Hague Conference on Private International Law, the convention was first signed in 1955 and therefore bears that official date.)

292 Convention on the Law Applicable to Contracts for the International Sale of Goods, *in* Hague Conference on Private International Law, *Proceedings of the Extraordinary Session, 14 to 30 October 1985* at 691 (1987) and *reprinted in* 24 I.L.M. 1573 (1985). Adopted at the 1985 extraordinary session of the Hague Conference, the convention was signed in 1986 and therefore bears the later date.

293 Convention on the Law Applicable to Contractual Obligations, 1980, 23 *Official Journal of the European Communities* (L266) 1980. The convention came into force on April 1, 1991.

294 UNIDROIT, *Principles for International Commercial Contracts (Draft text and comments)* (Study L - Doc. 52) (May 1993).

international convention, might serve as the basis of a supranational "Restatement" of the *lex mercatoria*.

D. STANDARD CONTRACTS AND GENERAL CONDITIONS.

Several trades actively engaged in international sales have developed standard contracts which are then adopted in whole or in part by traders who enter into these sales. The Grain and Feed Trade Association, for example, have developed such standard contracts widely used in the sale abroad of North American grain.[295] Other trades have developed usages of trade that may not be codified or expressly incorporated in sales contracts although recognized by the parties.[296]

States need not have any role in the development and enforcement of these standard contracts other than making available their courts for the enforcement of contracts or arbitral awards. In the 1950s, however, the United Nations Economic Commission for Europe prepared widely-used standard form contracts and general conditions for particular types of sale or for particular industries.[297] After its creation in 1966, UNCITRAL also studied ways to encourage general conditions of sale and standard contracts.[298]

---

295 *See* "Contract for Canadian and United States of America Grain in Bulk No. 30 (for use in export from North America of grain in bulk)," *reprinted in* 1 Andreas F. Lowenfeld, *International Private Trade* at DS-30 (rev. 2d ed. 1988); A. Slabotzky, *Grain Contracts and Arbitration for Shipments from the United States and Canada* (1984).

296 For an interesting study of usages and standard terms in the international oil trade, see Leon E. Trakman, *The Law Merchant: The Evolution of Commercial Law*, ch. 4 (1983) (assessing interdependence between commercial practice and commercial law).

297 *See, e.g., General Conditions for the Supply of Plant and Machinery for Export* (574), *reprinted in* 1 Andreas F. Lowenfeld, note 294 *supra*, at DS-53 (rev. 2d ed. 1988); Peter Benjamin, *The ECE General Conditions of Sale and Standard Forms of Contract*, 1961 J. Bus. L. 113.

298 *See, e.g.,* United Nations Commission on International Trade Law, *General Conditions of Sale and Standard Contracts: Report of the Secretary General*, U.N. Doc. A/CN.9/78 (1973), *reprinted as* Report of the Secretary General: the feasibility of the developing general conditions of sale embracing a wide scope of commodities *in* IV UNCITRAL Y.B. 80 (1973).

IV. THE UNITED STATES AND INTERNATIONAL UNIFICATION PROJECTS

Until the 1960s the United States was reluctant to participate in private international law unification efforts. Questions of constitutional authority or propriety were said to inhibit action by the federal government. In the late 1950s and early 1960s, however, leaders of the bar urged Congress to authorize the United States to participate in the Hague Conference and UNIDROIT. A 1961 report of a special A.B.A. committee on international unification of private law was particularly influential.[299] The result of these efforts was that in 1963 Congress enacted legislation authorizing the United States to join these inter-governmental bodies.[300] The following year the United States formally became a member of the two bodies and sent a delegation to the conference at The Hague convoked to adopt uniform sales laws

The Legal Adviser's Office in the Department of State is the principal office in the federal government charged with organizing U.S. participation in international unification projects. This allocation of responsibility is not essential. In many other countries these efforts fall within the jurisdiction of the Ministry of Justice rather than the Ministry of Foreign Affairs. In the earlier part of the century, there was even consideration of authorizing individual states to participate in the international projects.[301]

Within the Legal Adviser's Office there is an office devoted specifically to private international law.[302] This office has not received consistent support within the State Department. Ambassador Richard Kearney, who began work on unification projects in 1964, resigned in July 1978 and the work of his office dispersed within the Legal Adviser's Office. At the end of 1979 he

---

299 1961 A.B.A. Rep. 219.

300 77 Stat. 775 (1963), codified as 22 U.S.C. § 269g (1988).

301 For discussion of some of these proposals for state action, see Peter Winship, *The National Conference of Commissioners on Uniform State Laws and the International Unification of Private Law*, 13 U. Pa. J. Int'l Bus. L. 227, 239-252 (1992).

302 Office of the Legal Adviser, L/PIL, Suite 203, South Building, 2430 E Street, N.W., Washington D.C. 20037-2800 (tel. (202)776-8420 fax (202) 776-8482).

was replaced by Peter H. Pfund, who was designated the assistant legal adviser for private international law. Mr. Pfund has continued in that position and, as of April 1994, has the assistance of one other full-time lawyer.

The office of private international law arranges for representation by U.S. delegates in the operations of the four international organizations described in Part II. The office prepares the position papers during the drafting process, represents the United States at diplomatic conferences, and shepherds resulting texts through the subsequent review by the administration and Congress. The lawyers in the office have periodically published reports on the work of the office.[303]

When carrying out these tasks, the office relies heavily on the private sector. The Secretary of State's Advisory Committee on Private International Law provides a formal vehicle for consultation. Established in 1964, the Advisory Committee's purpose is "to serve the Department in a solely advisory capacity with respect to significant issues of private international law arising or likely to arise in the work of international organizations of which the United States is a Member State or in the foreign relations of the United States."[304] Membership includes representatives from other executive bodies and nominees of eleven national legal organizations.[305]In the early years, the Advisory Committee met

---

[303] *See, e.g.*, Richard D. Kearney, *The United States and International Cooperation to Unify Private Law*, 5 Cornell Int'l L.J. 1 (1972; Richard D. Kearney, *Progress Report -- International Unification of Private Law*, 23 Rec. Ass'n Bar of the City of N.Y. 220 (1968); Peter H. Pfund, *Overview of the Codification Process*, 15 Brooklyn L. Rev. 7 (1989); Peter H. Pfund, Annual Report, *International Unification of Private Law: A Report on U.S. Participation – 1987-88*, 22 Int'l Law. 1157 (1988); Peter H. Pfund, Annual Report, *International Unification of Private Law: A Report on U.S. Participation -- 1985-86*, 20 Int'l Law. 623 (1986); Peter H. Pfund, *United States Participation in International Unification of Private Law*, 19 Int'l Law. 505 (1984). For a brief overview of the work of the State Department office, see Patricia B. Rogers, *Private International Law*, 23 Int'l Law. 207 (1989).

[304] Charter of the Secretary of State's Advisory Committee on Private International Law, art. I (November 20, 1992).

[305] As of November 1992, the following private organizations have been invited to nominate representatives: American Society of Comparative Law, American Bar Association, American Branch of the International Law Association, American Corporate Counsel Association, American Law

several times a year and had numerous study groups that met as appropriate. In recent years, full meetings have been at least one year apart and there have been numerous study group meetings. All meetings are open to the public and notices of the meetings are published in the *Federal Register*.

Institute, American Society of International Law, Association of American Law Schools, National Association of Attorneys General, National Conference of Commissioners on Uniform State Laws, the Conference of Chief Justices, and the Judicial Conference of the United States.

ORGANIZATIONS ACTIVE IN THE UNIFICATION OF PRIVATE LAW

Hague Conference on Private Law
International Institute for the Unification of Private Law (UNIDROIT)
United Nations Commission for International Trade Law (UNCITRAL)
Inter-American Specialized Conference on Private Law (CIDIP)

A Select Bibliography

by Kenneth Rudolf
Yale Law School Library

I. INTRODUCTION

Many organizations are active in efforts to advance the unification of private law. The following bibliography, however, emphasizes only four of those institutions—the Hague Conference on Private Law, the International Institute for the Unification of Private Law (UNIDROIT), the United Nations Commission for International Trade Law (UNCITRAL), and the Inter-American Specialized Conference on Private Law (CIDIP)—because they were the ones emphasized at the Seattle Institute on Transnational Legal Transactions by Professor Peter Winship, whose lecture this bibliography was intended to complement.

No attempt was made to provide a comprehensive bibliography. Rather, the goal has been to identify the most pertinent documents, including those tools which will lead the researcher to additional materials. Since three of the four organizations included here publish extensive bibliographies, it did not seem necessary to replicate those bibliographies. They are listed prominently, and the researcher should seek them out to find materials not included here.

Since the focus of this bibliography is on the institutions generally, not on the specific activities of the institutions, many works dealing with individual conventions have not been listed. Researchers can find more information on the institutions and their activities by searching periodical indexes, library catalogs, and bibliographic databases using the name of the organization as a (corporate) author and as a subject. In addition, the names of many conventions can be searched as subjects. For example, there is a vast body of literature dealing with the United Nations Convention on Contracts for the International Sale of Goods. Virtually none of that literature was included here, but the researcher who needs specific information on this convention can easily find material searching under the convention's name as a subject.

During the preparation of this bibliography, it soon became apparent that these organizations produce a large number of documents, drafts, studies, and other materials in the course of their work. In general, these individual documents have not been included in this bibliography, even though some libraries catalog them separately. Three of the organizations (all but CIDIP) publish compilations of official documents, and these compilations have been listed, along with indications of the kinds of documents they contain. The compilations facilitate access to these documents, but there often is, unfortunately, a significant gap between the time the original documents are issued and the time that the compilation is published. When a document is needed before it appears in a compilation, the best approach is to contact the organization directly and request a copy. (Professor Winship has included the necessary information in his paper.) See Chapter 7.]

At the institute in Seattle, this bibliography was presented with spoken comments and sample pages. The main points of the spoken comments, intended primarily to emphasize certain sources or to describe them more fully than the written annotations, have been included at the end of each section of the bibliography in a section labelled "Comments." The sample pages that were included in the Seattle document were intended to demonstrate the scope of material contained in some of the sources. Although those pages are not reproduced here, the "Comments" section also describes much of the material included in the sample pages. Items in the bibliographical sections that are mentioned in the "Comments" are marked with an asterisk (*).

II. HAGUE CONFERENCE ON PRIVATE INTERNATIONAL LAW

A. Official Publications

La Codification du droit international privé: Bulletin des Conférences de La Haye. La Haye: Belinfante Frères, 1907-9. Contains texts of conventions, information regarding adoption by member countries, and jurisprudence.

*Hague Conference on Private International Law. *Recueil des conventions = Collection of Conventions (1951-1988).* Stoneham, Mass.: Butterworth [distributor], [1989?]. Items 1-10 in French only; items 11-32 in French and English. For unofficial translations of items 2-12, see *The American Journal of Comparative Law* 1: 275-288 (1952); 5: 650-61 (1956); 9: 701-11 (1959). For an English version of the Statute of The Hague Conference on Private International Law, October 31, 1951 (item 1), see 15 U.S.T. 2228, 220 U.N.T.S. 121 (1955).

B. Conference Proceedings

Hague Conference on Private International Law. *Actes de la Conférence de La Haye chargée de réglementer diverses matières de droit international privé (12-27 septembre 1893).* La Haye: Imprimerie nationale, 1893.

Hague Conference on Private International Law. *Actes de la deuxième Conférence de La Haye chargée de réglementer diverses matières de droit international privé (25 juin-13 juillet 1894).* La Haye: Imprimerie nationale, 1894.

Hague Conference on Private International Law. *Actes de la troisième Conférence de La Haye pour le droit international privé (29 mai-18 juin 1900).* La Haye: Imprimerie nationale, 1900.

Hague Conference on Private International Law. *Documents relatifs à la troisième Conférence de La Haye pour droit international privé.* La Haye: Imprimerie nationale, 1900.

Hague Conference on Private International Law. *Actes de la quatrième Conférence de La Haye pour le droit international privé (16 mai-7 juin 1904).* La Haye: Van Langenhuysen Frères, 1904.

Hague Conference on Private International Law. *Documents relatifs à la quatrième Conférence de La Haye pour le droit international privé.* La Haye: Van Langenhuysen Frères, 1904.

Hague Conference on Private International Law. *Actes de la cinquième session tenue du 12 octobre au 7 novembre 1925.* La Haye: Imprimerie nationale, 1926.

Hague Conference on Private International Law. *Documents relatifs à la cinquième session tenue du 12 octobre au 7 novembre 1925.* La Haye: Imprimerie nationale, 1926.

Hague Conference on Private International Law. *Actes de la sixième session tenue du 5 au 28 janvier 1928.* La Haye: Imprimerie nationale, 1928.

Hague Conference on Private International Law. *Documents relatifs à la sixième session tenue du 5 au 28 janvier 1928.* La Haye: Imprimerie nationale, 1928.

*Hague Conference on Private International Law. *Actes* .... La Haye: Imprimerie nationale, 1951-1956.

*Hague Conference on Private International Law. *Documents* .... La Haye: Imprimerie nationale, 1951-1956.

*Hague Conference on Private International Law. *Actes et documents* .... La Haye: Bureau permanent de la Conférence, 1960-. For a complete list of official records beginning with the seventh session (1951), see "Publications of the Conference," in *Actes et documents de la seizième session = Proceedings of the Sixteenth Session* (The Hague: Bureau permanent de la Conférence, 1991), pp. 293-94.

*"Final Act of the Seventeenth Session of the Hague Conference on Private International Law, 29 May 1993." *Netherlands International Law Review* 40: 292-309 (1993).

C. Bibliography

Hague Conference on Private International Law. *Bibliographie relative aux travaux de la Conférence (1945-1985): mise à jour au 31 décembre 1985 = Bibliography Relating to the Work of the Conference (1945-1985): Up to Date as of 31 December 1985.* The Hague: Permanent Bureau of the Conference, [1985]. See also the cumulative bibliography published in the first volume of *Actes et documents* for each session. For the most recent, see *Actes et documents de la seizième session*, vol. 1 *Matières diverses = Miscellaneous Matters*, pp. 283-347.

D. Secondary Sources

Asser, T.-M.-C. "La codification du droit international privé: première conférence tenue a La Haye du 12 au 27 septembre 1893." *Revue de droit international et de législation comparée* 25: 521-48 (1893).

Asser, T.-M.-C. "La codification du droit international privé: deuxième conférence tenue a La Haye du 25 juin au 13 juillet 1894." *Revue de droit international et de législation comparée* 26: 349-77 (1894).

Flaischlen, Georges. "Le chapitre du divorce dans le protocole final de la Conférence pour la codification du droit international privé réunie en 1894 à La Haye." *Revue de droit international et de législation comparée* 27: 254-62 (1895).

Olivi, Louis. "Le projet néerlandais de programme pour la troisième conférence de droit international privé." *Revue de droit international et de législation comparée,* deuxième sèrie 2: 26-48, 135-150 (1900).

Asser, T.C.M. "La question du renvoi devant la troisième conférence de droit international privé." *Revue de droit international et de législation comparée,* deuxième sèrie 2: 316-19 (1900).

Buzzati, M.J.C. "Les projets de conventions de la Haye pour le droit international privé: étude critique." *Revue de droit international et de législation comparée,* deuxième sèrie 3: 269-99 (1901).

Asser, T.-M.-C. "Les projets de convention de la Haye pour le droit international privé." *Revue de droit international et de législation comparée,* deuxième sèrie 3: 437-447(1901).

Seresia, A. "La convention de La Haye du 14 novembre 1896 relative à la procédure civile." *Revue de droit international et de législation comparée,* deuxième sèrie 3: 569-93 (1901).

Kosters, J., and F. Bellemans. *Les Conventions de La Haye de 1902 et 1905 sur le droit international privé: Recueil de législation et de jurisprudence.* Harlem: H.D. Tjeenk Willink & Fils, 1921.

Nadelmann, Kurt H. "The United States and the Hague Conferences on Private International Law." *American Journal of Comparative Law* 1: 268-74 (1952).

Sumampouw, Mathilde. *Les Nouvelles Conventions de La Haye: Leur application par les juges nationaux.* Leyden: A.W. Sijthoff, 1976-84.

Droz, George A.L., and Adair Dyer. "The Hague Conference and the Main Issues of Private International Law for the Eighties." *Northwestern Journal of International Law and Business* 3: 155-210 (1981).

Hague Conference on Private International Law. *Practical Handbook on the Operation of the Hague Convention of 18 March 1970 on the Taking of Evidence Abroad in Civil or Commercial Matters.* Antwerpen: Maarten Kluwer, 1984--.

Reese, Willis L.M. "The Hague Conference on Private International Law: Some Observations." *International Lawyer* 19: 881-86 (1985).

Gabor, Francis A. "Emerging Unification of Conflict of Laws Rules Applicable to the International Sale of Goods: UNCITRAL and the New Hague Conference on Private International Law." *Northwestern Journal of International Law and Business* 7: 696-726 (1986).

Hague Conference on Private International Law. *Rapport sur les travaux de la Commission spécial d'avril 1989 sur le fonctionnement des Conventions de La Haye du 15 novembre 1965 relative à la signification et la notification à l'étranger des actes judiciaires et extrajudiciaires en matière civile ou commerciale et du 18 mars 1970 sour l'obtention des preuves à l'étranger en matière civile ou commerciale = Report on the Work of the Special Commission of April 1989 on the Operation of the Hague Conventions of 15 November 1965 on the Service Abroad of Judicial and Extrajudicial Documents in Civil or Commercial Matters and of 18 March 1970 on the Taking of Evidence Abroad in Civil or Commercial Matters.* The Hague: Permanent Bureau of the Conference, [1989].

Hague Conference on Private International Law. *Practical Handbook on the Operation of the Hague Convention of 15 November 1965 on the Service Abroad of Judicial and Extrajudicial Documents in Civil or Commercial Matters.* Second edition. Antwerpen: MAKLU Uitgevers, 1992.

Alley, Edwin R. "New Developments Under the Hague Evidence and Service Conventions: The 1989 Special Commission." *International Business Lawyer* 17: 380-382 (1989).

"Les travaux de la Conférence de La Haye de droit international privé: dans les coulisses de la session du centenaire." *Revue belge de droit international* 24: 385-503 (1992).

*"Information Concerning the Hague Convention on Private International Law: Situation as of 1 August 1993." *Netherlands International Law Review* 40: 257-91 (1992). Information on parties to the various Hague conventions. This listing appears annually in the *Netherlands International Law Review.*

T.M.C. Asser Instituut. *The Influence of the Hague Conference on Private International Law: Selected Essays to Celebrate the 100th Anniversary of the Hague Conference on Private International Law.* Dordrecht; London: Nijhoff, 1993. Also published at *Netherlands International Law Review* 40: issue 1 (1993).

Pfund, Peter H. "The Hague Conference Celebrates Its 100th Anniversary." *Texas International Law Journal* 28: 531-538 (1993).

Overbeck, Alfred E. von. "Les cent ans de la Conférence de La Haye de droit international privé." *Schweitzerisches Zeitschrift für europäisches Recht* 3: 137-152 (1993).

E. Comments

Texts of all the conventions adopted by the Hague Conference since 1951 are published in *Recueil des conventions = Collection of Conventions (1951-1988)*, a compact volume that has been updated after each session. It seems likely that another will appear in the near future incorporating the texts adopted at the 1993 session of the Conference. Until the new edition is available, the texts adopted in 1993 can be found in "Final Act of the Seventeenth Session of the Hague Conference on Private International Law," *Netherlands International Law Review* 40: 292-309 (1993).

The list of conventions is printed on the front and back covers of the *Collection of Conventions*. In the following list, where the title is given in French, only the French text is published; where the title is given (here) in English, French and English versions are published on facing pages.

I Statut de la Conférence de La Haye de Droit International Privé – Entré en vigueur le 15 juillet 1955

II Convention relative à la procédure civile (1954)

III Convention sur la loi applicable aux ventes à caractère international d'objets mobiliers corporels (1955)

IV Convention sur la loi applicable au transfert de la propriété en cas de vente à caractère international d'objets mobiliers corporels (1958)

V Convention sur la compétence du for contractuel en cas de vente à caractère international d'objets corporels (1958)

VI Convention pour régler les conflits entre la loi nationale et la loi du domicile (1955)

VII Convention concernant la reconnaissance de la personnalité juridique des sociétés, associations et fondations étrangères (1956)

VIII Convention sur la loi applicable aux obligations alimentaires envers les enfants (1956)

IX Convention concernant la reconnaissance et l'exécution des décisions en matière d'obligations alimentaires envers les enfants (1958)

X Convention concernant la compétence des autorités et la loi applicable en matière de protection des mineurs (1961)

XI Convention on the Conflict of Laws Relating to the Form of Testamentary Dispositions (1961)

XII Convention Abolishing the Requirement of Legalisation for Foreign Public Documents (1961)

XIII Convention on Jurisdiction, Applicable Law, and Recognition of Decrees Relating to Adoptions (1965)

XIV Convention on the Service Abroad of Judicial and Extrajudicial Documents in Civil or Commercial Matters (1965)

XV Convention on the Choice of Court (1965)

XVI Convention on the Recognition and Enforcement of Foreign Judgments in Civil and Commercial Matters (1971)

XVII Supplementary Protocol to the Hague Convention on the Recognition and Enforcement of Foreign Judgments in Civil and Commercial Matters (1971)

XVIII Convention on the Recognition of Divorces and Legal Separations (1970)

XIX Convention on the Law Applicable to Traffic Accidents (1971)

XX Convention on the Taking of Evidence Abroad in Civil or Commercial Matters (1970)

XXI Convention Concerning the International Administration of the Estates of Deceased Persons (1973)

XXII Convention on the Law Applicable to Products Liability (1973)

XXIII Convention on the Recognition and Enforcement of Decisions Relating to Maintenance Obligations (1973)

XXIV Convention on the Law Applicable to Maintenance Obligations (1973)

XXV Convention on the Law Applicable to Matrimonial Property Regimes (1978)

XXVI Convention on the Celebration and Recognition of the Validity of Marriages (1978)

XXVII Convention on the Law Applicable to Agency (1978)

XXVIII Convention on the Civil Aspects of International Child Abduction (1980)

XXIX Convention on International Access to Justice (1980)

XXX Convention on the Law Applicable to Trusts and on their Recognition (1985)

XXXI Convention on the Law Applicable to Contracts for the International Sale of Goods (1986)

XXXII Convention on the Law Applicable to Succession to the Estates of Deceased Persons

The "Notice" page near the front of the *Collection of Conventions* includes references to unofficial English versions of the texts published only in French. It also contains a useful table of references to specific volumes in the *Proceedings* where the travaux préparatoires (legislative history) for individual conventions can be found.

The *Collection of Conventions* does not give information about accessions or reservations to the conventions because such data is constantly changing. Current information on the status of the various conventions is published annually in the *Netherlands International Law Review.*

Official records of the Hague Conference can be found in the elegant *Actes et documents de la . . . session = Proceedings of the . . . Session.* (Before 1960 the proceedings and documents were published in separate series.) For each session the first volume contains general materials for the session, and subsequent volumes collect materials relating to specific conventions adopted at the session. For example, the first volume of *Proceedings* for the eleventh session includes:

- Summary of the proceedings and documents
- Delegates and observers to the session
- Secretariat for the session
- Verbal proceedings of the open, closing, and plenary sessions
- Rules of the session
- Final act of the session, including texts of conventions adopted, recommendations, and plan of work for the future session
- General documents, including a materials on subjects not related to texts adopted at the session
- Bibliography

The fourth volume of the *Proceedings* for the eleventh session contains the travaux préparatoires for the Convention on the Taking of Evidence Abroad. Among the contents are:

- List of documents

- Questionnaire and responses from governments
- Draft convention adopted by the Special Commission
- Report to accompany the draft convention
- Observations of governments on the draft convention
- Working documents for the convention
- Verbal proceedings of the Third Commission
- Draft convention submitted to the Conference
- Verbal proceedings of the plenary session where the text was debated
- Final text of the convention (from the Final Act)
- Report to accompany the final text
- Index to proceedings arranged by article of the convention
- Subject index to the proceedings

The bibliography included in the first volume of the *Proceedings* is an important source for finding further information about the Hague Conference and its work. The organization, by form and topic, makes it extremely useful.

A. Selection of articles and books on the Conference and the Hague Conventions in general

B. Publications of the Conference

C. Bibliography of the Conference's sessions (from the seventh session in 1951)

D. Recent books and articles on the Hague Conventions adopted before 1945

E. Books and articles on topics dealt with at the Conference's sessions (subdivided by general topics and specific conventions)

III. INTERNATIONAL INSTITUTE FOR THE UNIFICATION OF PRIVATE LAW (UNIDROIT)

A.Official Publications

*International Institute for the Unification of Private Law. *Proceedings and Papers = Actes et documents*. [Rome: International Institute for the Unification of Private Law, 1928- .] Annual compilation of official documents, reports, studies, etc. Latest received: 1992. Also available in microfilm from Oceana.

International Institute for the Unification of Private Law. *L'unification du droit: aperçu général des travaux pour l'unification du droit privé (projets et conventions) = Unification of Law: A General Survey of Work for the Unification of Private Law (Drafts and Conventions)*. Rome: Éditions Unidroit, 1948-71. Vol. 1 (1948) covers the years 1926-46; vol. 3 (1954) the years 1947-52; vol. 4 (1956) the years 1953-55. Annual volumes cover the years 1956-71. Continued by *Revue de droit uniforme = Uniform law review*. After 1958 the review of cases continued in *Jurisprudence du droit uniforme = Uniform law cases*. [Vol. 2 is *Actes du congrès international de droit privé tenu à Rome en juillet 1950*.]

International Institute for the Unification of Private Law. *Jurisprudence de droit uniforme = Uniform law cases*. Rome: Editions Unidroit, 1959-1971. Continues the review of cases included in *L'unification du de droit*; continued by *Revue de droit uniforme = Uniform law review*.)

*International Institute for the Unification of Private Law. *Revue de droit uniforme = Uniform law review*. 1973- . Semiannual. Most recently received 1991, issue 2. Continues *L'unification du droit* and *Jurisprudence de droit uniforme*.

*International Institute for the Unification of Private Law. *News Bulletin = Bulletin d'informations = Boletin de informacion*. 1969-. Quarterly (but recently published semiannually in double issues). Most recently received: No. 95-96 (July/October 1993). The *News Bulletin* is included in *Papers and Proceedings*.

B. Conference Proceedings

International Institute for the Unification of Private Law. *Actes du congrès international de droit privé tenu à Rome en juillet 1950.* Rome: Éditions Unidroit, 1951. (L'unification du droit, 2)

International Institute for the Unification of Private Law. *New Directions in International Trade Law: Acts and Proceedings of the 2nd Congress on Private Law Held by the International Institute for the Unification of Private Law UNIDROIT, Rome, 9-15 September 1976.* Dobbs Ferry, N.Y.: Oceana Publications, 1977.

International Institute for the Unification of Private Law. *International Uniform Law in Practice: Acts and Proceedings of the 3rd Congress on Private Law Held by the International Institute for the Unification of Private Law UNIDROIT, Rome, 7-10 September 1987.* Rome: Unidroit; Dobbs Ferry, N.Y.: Oceana Publications, 1988.

C. Diplomatic Conferences

Diplomatic Conference on a proposed Convention relatif to a Uniform Law on the Sale of Movable Goods. *Actes de la conférence convoquée par le gouvernement royal des Pays-Bas: sur un projet de convention relatif à une loi uniforme sur la vent d'objets mobiliers corporels.* Rome: Éditions Unidroit, 1952.

International Institute for the Unification of Private Law. *Diplomatic Conference for the Adoption of the Draft Unidroit Conventions on International Factoring and International Financial Leasing. Acts and Proceedings.* Rome: Unidroit, c1991-c1992.

Schwarze, Jürgen. *The Role of the European Court of Justice (ECJ) in the Interpretation of Uniform Law Among the Member States of the European Communities (EC): A Contribution to an International Congress of UNIDROIT on "Uniform Law in Practice" held in Rome, 7-10 September 1987.* Baden-Baden: Nomos, 1988.

D. Reference

Harvard Law School Library. *Index to Proceedings and Documents of the International Institute for the Unification of Private Law, 1928-1965.* Cambridge: Harvard Law School Library, 1967.

*International Institute for the Unification of Private Law. *Digest of Legal Activities of International Organizations and Other Institutions.*

Tenth edition. Paula Howarth, editor. London; New York: Oceana Publications, 1994. Subject index to unification activities of various organizations. Each entry gives the name of the organization, terms of reference, brief summary of the subject, and status of the work.

E. Bibliographies

Bibliographie en matière d'unification du droit = Bibliography on the unification of law. Rome : Éditions Unidroit, 1951.

Also see the bibliographies in *News Bulletin* (alphabetical) and *Uniform Law Review* (classified by subject).

F. Secondary Sources

Angiolini, Mario. *Legislazione e giurisprudenza sulle borse, sulla mediazione e sui titoli di credito in Italia.* Roma: Tipografia ditta F.lli Pallotta, 1933.

International Institute for the Unification of Private Law. *The Methods of the Unification of Law. General Report.* Rome: Editions Unidroit, 1956.

International Institute for the Unification of Private Law. *Tableau des matières juridiques faisant l'objet des programmes de travail des organisations s'occupant de l'unification du droit.* Rome, 1961.

International Institute for the Unification of Private Law. *Unidroit et l'unification du droit privé, 1928-1962.* Rome: Palais Aldobrandini, 1962.

Matteucci, Mario, and Riccardo Monaco. *UNIDROIT, 1926-1976.* Rome: International Institute for the Unification of Private Law, 1976.

G. Comments

Three important publications from Unidroit report on the work of the Institute—Proceedings and Papers, published annually; *Uniform Law Review*, published twice a year; and the *News Bulletin*, now also appearing twice a year. While only the *Proceedings and Papers* includes actual Unidroit documents, all three contain reports on the activities of the Institute, so it is possible to follow the work in progress using any one of the three. One should remember, however, that the *News Bulletin* appears first, while the *Proceedings and Papers* appears much later.

The *News Bulletin* appears in three editions—English, French, and Italian. Most material in *Uniform Law Review* appears in both English and French. Both items contain summaries of cases dealing with uniform law and a bibliography; however, in *Uniform Law Review* the bibliography is classified and the case summaries are indexed. Notice the similarity in organization between the two publications:

Table of Contents for *Uniform Law Review* (1991)

Part I: Activities concerning the unification of law

- The activity of the International Institute for the Unification of Private Law (from 1 January to 31 December 1990)
- Reflections on the harmonization of commercial law

Part II: Drafts and conventions

- Explanatory Report on the Convention of Civil Liability for Damage caused during the Carriage of Dangerous Goods by Road, Rail and Inland Navigation Vessels (CRTD)

Part III: Select Bibliography

Part IV: Uniform Law Cases

- Uniform Law Cases
- Case-law Index
- Case-law Summary

Table of Contents for *News Bulletin* (no. 95/96, July-October 1993)

I. Organisation of the Institute

II. Activity of the Institute

III. Uniform Law Bibliography

IV. Uniform Law Cases

Proceedings and Papers is a collection of mimeograph documents bound together at the end of the year. Each document is paginated separately in the volume, although there is a list of documents at the beginning. Because the work on individual topics often spans a number of years, one must look in successive volumes to follow the progress of any particular activity. The individual topics are organized as numbered "studies," and all the documents for any study are grouped together for that year. The documents for each study, however, are numbered sequentially through the life of that study. For example, one can trace the documents for a current study, the protection of cultural property (LXX), through several volumes of the *Proceedings and Papers*. Not only does this example illustrate how one must look through several volumes to follow a topic, but it also shows the type of documents one can expect to find associated with a project.

Proceedings and Papers (1986)

Governing Council, Report of the 65th Session, Item 6 "Adoption of the Work Programme for the triennium 1987 to 1989" (p. 21)—reports on the introduction of a study on the protection of cultural property commissioned by Unesco.

Text of the study on protection of cultural property (C.D. - Doc. 11)

***Proceedings and Papers* (1988),** List of documents (pp. 3-4)

Study LXX - The international protection of cultural property

Doc. 2 Outlines for a private law Convention on the International Protection of Culteral Property

Doc. 3 Preliminary draft Convention on the restitution of cultural property

Doc. 4 Second study requested from Unidroit by Unesco on the international protection of cultural property with particular reference to the rules of private law affectingthe transfer of title to cultural property and in the light of the comments received on the first study

Doc. 5 Extract from the report of the 67th session of the Governing Council (Rome, 14 to 17 June 1988)

Doc. 6 Good faith redefined, a practical solution (paper)

Doc. 7 Observations submitted by Ms Lyndel Prott

Proceedings and Papers **(1988),** List of documents (pp. 3-4)

Doc. 8 UNESCO Convention on the means of prohibiting and preventing the illicit import, export and transfer of ownership of cultural property (14 November 1970)

Doc. 9 Unidroit draft Convention providing a uniform law on the acquisition in good faith of corporeal movables (LUAB, 1974)

Doc. 10 Summary report on the first session of the Unidroit study group on the international protection of cultural property

Doc. 11 Preliminary draft Convention on the restitution and return of cultural objects

Doc. 12 Summary of the statement of Mr Pieter van Nuffel (observer and representative of the Commission of the European Communities) at the first session of the Unidroit study group

Doc. 13 Notes on the first session of the Unidroit study group

Doc. 14 Summary report on the second session of the Unidroit study group

Doc. 15 Preliminary draft Convention on the restitution and return of cultural objects

Doc. 16 Observations relating to the preliminary draft Convention on the restitution and return of cultural objects

Doc. 17 Communication from the Commission of the European Communities to the Council on the protection of national treasures possessing artistic, historic or archeological value: needs arising from the abolition of frontiers in 1992

Proceedings and Papers (1990), List of documents (p. 4)

Doc. 16 Add. 1– Observations relating to the preliminary draft Convention on the restitution and return of cultural objects

Doc. 16 Add. 2 – Observations relating to the preliminary draft Convention on the restitution and return of ultural objects

Doc. 18 Summary report on the third session of the Unidroit study group on the international protection of cultural property

Doc. 19 Preliminary draft Convention on stolen or illegally exported cultural objects approved by the Unidroit study group on the international protection of cultural property with Explanatory Report

Finally, it is instructive to look at the outline of the "Report on the Activity of the Institute, 1991," as recorded in *Proceedings and Papers* for 1992. Section II (Scientific Activity) and Section III (Implementation) give a thorough overview of the projects in which Unidroit has been involved.

Outline of the "Report on the Activity of the Institute, 1991" (published in *Proceedings and Papers,* 1992)

I. Administration and Organization

A. Presidency, Governing Council and PermanentCommittee, General Assembly and Finance Committee, Administrative Tribunal

B. Diplomatic conferences, study groups and committees of experts

C. Relations with Governments

D. Diplomatic conferences and meetings in the framework of other intergovernmental organizations

II. Scientific Activity

A. Work in progress

1. Principles for international commercial contracts
2. The hotelkeeper's contract
3. International protection of cultural property
4. The franchising contract
5. Relations between principals and agents in the international sale of goods
6. Security interests in mobile goods
7. Forwarding agency contracts
8. Quality and quantity control of goods
9. Civil liability connected with the carrying out of dangerous activities
10. Marketing of software

B. Unidroit drafts on which work is being pursued in other organizations

1. Liability of operators of transport terminals

C. Activities subsidiary to the unification of law

1. Programme of legal assistance
2. Organization of an information system or data bank on uniform law
3. Organization of a congress or meeting on uniform law during the triennial period 1993-1995
4. Acceptance and promotion of Unidroit Conventions
5. Interns

D. Publications

1. Uniform Law Review

2. Digest of Legal Activities of International Organizations and other Institutions

3. Acts and Proceedings of the diplomatic Conference for the adoption of the draft Unidroit Conventions on International Factoring and International Finance Leasing

4. News Bulletin

5. Other publications

E. Library

III. Implementation of Instruments Based on Work Continued Within Unidroit

A. Conventions drawn up by Unidroit and approved at diplomatic Conferences convened by member States of Unidroit

1. Convention relating to a Uniform Law on the Formation of Contracts for the International Sale of Goods (ULFIS)

2. Convention relating to a Uniform Law on the International Sale of Goods (ULIS)

3. International Convention on the Travel Contract (CCV)

4. Convention providing a Uniform Law on the Form of an International Will

5. Convention on Agency in the International Sale of Goods

6. Unidroit Convention on International Financial Leasing

7. Unidroit Convention on International Factoring

B. Unidroit drafts which have served as the basis for international instruments adopted under the auspices of other organizations and which have entered into force

1. Draft Convention on the Contract for the International Carriage of Goods by Road (CMR)

2. Draft International Convention for the Protection of Cultural Property in Case of War

3. Preliminary draft Convention for the Protection of Interpreting and Performing Artists, as well as of Manufacturers of Phonographic Records and other Phonograms and the preliminary draft Convention for the Protection of Radio Broadcasts

4. Draft Convention on the Recognition and Enforcement abroad of Maintenance Obligations

5. Draft uniform law on the hotelkeeper's liability for damage to or destruction or theft of his guests' property

6. Draft uniform rules on the compulsory insurance of motorists

7. Draft Convention on the reciprocal treatment of nationals as between member states of the Council of Europe

8. Draft Convention concerning rights in rem in boats in inland navigation

9. Draft Protocol on attachment and forced sale of inland navigation vessels

10. Convention relating to a Uniform Law on the Formation of Contracts for the International Sale of Goods (ULFIS) and Convention relating to a Uniform Law on the International Sale of Goods (ULIS)

C. Unidroit drafts that have served as the basis for instruments adopted under the auspices of other organizations and which have not yet entered into force

1. Draft Convention on the Contract for the International Carriage of Passengers and Luggage by Road (CVR)

2. Draft Convention relating to the Limitation of the Liability of Owners of Inland Navigation Vessels (CLN)

3. Draft Convention on the Contract for the International Carriage of Passengers and Luggage by Inland Waterways (CVN)

4. Preliminary draft model law on investment funds

5. Preliminary draft uniform law on arbitration in private law matters in international relations

6. Draft of a uniform law on the civil liability of motorists

7. Draft articles for a Convention on civil liability for damage caused during carriage of dangerous goods by road, rail and inland navigation vessels

8. Preliminary draft Convention on Operators of Transport Terminals

D. Draft Convention drawn up by Unidroit which has served as the basis for uniform rules published by the International Chamber of Commerce and as such applied on a voluntary basis

1. Draft Convention on Contracts for the Combined International Carriage of Goods

E. Instruments based on preliminary studies prepared by Unidroit

1. European Convention on Products Liability in regard to Personal Injury and Death of 27 January 1977

2. Resolution (78)3 on Penalty Clauses in Civil Law adopted by the Committee of Ministers of the Council of Europe on 20 January 1978

In addition to the documents dealing with its own work, Unidroit publishes one significant work for anyone seeking information on the broad spectrum of unification activities. The *Digest of Legal Activities of International Organizations and Other Institutions*, now in its tenth edition (1994), lists unification projects by over twenty organizations. The activities are arranged by subject matter and indicate the organization sponsoring the work, the current state of the work, and the kinds of documentation which are available.

IV. UNITED NATIONS COMMISSION ON INTERNATIONAL TRADE LAW (UNCITRAL)

A. Official Documents

Report of the United Nations Commission on International Trade Law on the Work of Its ____th Session. New York: United Nations, 1968-. Issued as a supplement to GAOR. Most recent: 26th session, 5-23 July 1993, GAOR, 48th Sess., Suppl. no. 17 (A/48/17). Also published in the *Yearbook*.

United Nations Commission on International Trade. *Summary Records of the ... Meetings*. New York: The Commission, 1968-. (A/CN.9/SR.--) Also published in the *Yearbook*.

*United Nations Commission on International Trade Law. *Yearbook*. New York: United Nations, 1971- . Includes "Report of the Commission on Its Annual Session; Comments and Action Thereon" (Part I), "Studies and Reports on Specific Subjects" (Part II); "Annexes" (Part III), including draft documents, summary records of meetings, check list of UNCITRAL documents, and bibliography. Most recently received: vol. 23 (1992).

B. Other UNCITRAL Publications

United Nations Commission on International Trade Law. *UNCITRAL Arbitration Rules*. New York: United Nations, 1977.

United Nations Commission on International Trade Law. *UNCITRAL Conciliation Rules*. New York: United Nations, 1981.

United Nations Commission on International Trade Law. *UNCITRAL : The United Nations Commission on International Trade Law*. New York: United Nations, 1986. Overview of the work and organization of UNCITRAL.

United Nations Commission on International Trade Law. *UNCITRAL Legal Guide on Electronic Funds Transfers*. New York: United Nations, 1987.

United Nations Commission on International Trade Law. *UNCITRAL Legal Guide on Drawing Up International Contracts for the Construction of Industrial Works*. New York: United Nations, 1988.

C. Bibliographies

Will, Michael R. *Internationale Bibliographie zum UN-Kaufrecht*. Saarbrücken: Europa-Institut der Universität des Saarlandes, 1987.

*Also see the annual "Bibliography of Recent Writings Related to the Work of UNCITRAL: Note by the Secretariat," published as a U.N. document and republished in the *Yearbook*. The document number of the most recent bibliography is A/CN.9/402

D. Secondary Sources

"Unification of International Trade Law: UNCITRAL's First Decade." *American Journal of Comparative Law* 27: 201-563 (1979).

"United Nations Convention on Contracts for the International Sale of Goods: Message from the President of the United States Transmitting the United Nations Convention on Contracts for the International Sale of Goods, Adopted by a United Nations Conference of Sixty-Two States on April 11, 1980." Washington, D.C.: U.S. G.P.O., 1983. (Treaty Doc. no. 98-9) (Y 1.1/4:98-9)

"International Sale of Goods: Hearing Before the Committee on Foreign Relations, United States Senate, Ninety-eighth Congress, Second Session on Treaty Doc. 98-9 . . . April 4, 1984." Washington, D.C.: U.S. G.P.O., 1984. (S. hrg. 98-837) (Y 4.F 76/2:S.hrg.98-837)

Kavass, Igor I., and Arno Liivak. *UNCITRAL Model Law of International Commercial Arbitration: A Documentary History*. Buffalo, N.Y.: W.S. Hein, 1985- .

Dore, Isaak I. *Arbitration and Conciliation under the UNCITRAL Rules: A Textual Analysis*. Dordrecht; Boston: Nijhoff, 1986.

Law Reform Commission of Hong Kong. *Report on the Adoption of the UNCITRAL Model Law of Arbitration (topic 17)*. Hong Kong : The Commission, [1987?]

Holtzmann, Howard M., and Joseph E. Neuhaus. *A Guide to the UNCITRAL Model Law on International Commercial Arbitration: Legislative History and Commentary*. Deventer; Boston: Kluwer Law and Taxation Publishers; The Hague: T.M.C. Asser Instituut, 1989.

Honnold, John. *Documentary History of the Uniform Law for International Sales: The Studies, Deliberations, and Decisions That Led to the 1980 United Nations Convention with Introductions and Explanations*. Deventer: Kluwer Law and Taxation Publishers, 1989.

Kritzer, Albert H. *Guide to Practical Applications of the United Nations Convention on Contracts for the International Sale of Goods*. Deventer; Boston: Kluwer Law and Taxation Publishers, 1989.

Broches, Aron. *Commentary on the UNCITRAL Model Law on International Commercial Arbitration*. Deventer; Boston: Kluwer Law and Taxation Publishers, 1990.

The Convention for the International Sale of Goods: A Handbook of Basic Materials. Edited by Daniel Barstow Magraw and Reed R. Kathrein. Second edition. Washington, D.C.: American Bar Association, Section of International Law and Practice, 1990.

Dore, Isaak I. *Theory and Practice of Multiparty Commercial Arbitration with Special Reference to the UNCITRAL Framework*. London; Boston: Graham & Trotman/M. Nijhoff, 1990.

Hof, Jacomijn J. van. *Commentary on the UNCITRAL Arbitration Rules: The Application by the Iran-U.S. Claims Tribunal*. Deventer; Boston: Kluwer Law and Taxation Publishers, 1991.

Honnold, John. *Uniform Law for International Sales Under the 1980 United Nations Convention*. Second edition. Deventer; Boston: Kluwer Law and Taxation Publishers, 1991.

Ackerman, Grant R. *U.N. Convention on Contracts for the International Sale of Goods: Annotated*. Boston: Warren Gorham & Lamont, 1992- .

Baker, Stewart Abercrombie, and Mark David Davis. *The UNCITRAL Arbitration Rules in Practice: The Experience of the Iran-United States Claims Tribunal*. Deventer; Boston : Kluwer Law and Taxation Publishers, 1992.

Enderlein, Fritz, and Dietrich Maskow. *International Sales Law: United Nations Convention on Contracts for the International Sale of Goods: Convention on the Limitation Period in the International Sale of Goods: Commentary*. New York: Oceana, 1992.

Dore, Isaak I. *The UNCITRAL Framework for Arbitration in Contemporary Perspective*. London; Boston: Graham & Trotman/M. Nijhoff, 1993.

Fisher, Geoff. "UNCITRAL Gives International Trade Law CLOUT." *Australian Business Law Review* 21: 362-367 (1993).

E. Comments

While UNCITRAL produces many documents, the most important publication is the *Yearbook*, which brings together all the pertinent documents of its activities into one place. Published in the *Yearbook* are various reports, including the report of the annual session to the General Assembly, studies on specific subjects, summary records of meetings, a bibliography, and a checklist of UNCITRAL documents. Each document in the *Yearbook* is identified by title and by U.N. document symbol.

The checklist of documents is arranged by U.N. document symbol and gives both the title and the location in the *Yearbook* when published there. A quick look through the list reveals that nearly all the documents on the checklist find their way into the *Yearbook*.

The bibliography appears as a separate document before it is reproduced in the *Yearbook*. Since the *Yearbook* runs several years behind, anyone doing serious work on UNCITRAL should attempt to get the bibliography as a separate document. The most recent bibliography (A/CN.9/402) was issued on 11 April 1994, while the most recent *Yearbook* covers 1991.

The report of the annual session of UNCITRAL, which also appears as a supplement to the Official Records of the General Assembly (usually as Supplement 17), contains a good overview of the work of UNCITRAL and the projects in which it is involved. It also contains a report on the status of UNCITRAL conventions. An outline of the report on the twenty-second session of UNCITRAL held in Vienna from 16 May to 2 June 1989 (A/44/17 and *Yearbook*, 1989) shows the scope of work of the commission.

Report of the United Nations Commission International Trade Law on the Work of Its Twenty-Second Session (*Yearbook*, 1989)

Introduction

I. Organization of the Session
    A. Opening

B. Membership and attendance
C. Election of officers
D. Agenda
E. Adoption of the report

II. Draft Convention on the Liability of Operators of TransportTerminals in International Trade
A. Introduction
B. General discussion on the draft Convention
C. Form of uniform rules
D. Title of the draft Convention
E. Discussion of individual articles of the draft Convention prepared by the Working Group on International Contract Practices
F. Consideration of draft final clauses prepared by the secretariat
G. Consideration of articles of the draft Convention submitted by the drafting group
H. Procedure for adopting the draft Convention as a convention
I. Decision of the Commission and recommendation to the General Assembly

III. Internal Payments

IV. New International Economic Order

V. Guarantees and Stand-by Letters of Credit

VI. International Countertrade

VII. Co-ordination of Work

VIII. Status of Conventions
A. Convention on the Limitation Period in the International Sale of Goods
B. Signatures, ratifications, accessions and approvals

IX. Training and Assistance

X. Relevant General Assembly Resolutions and Other Business
A. General Assembly resolutions on the work of the Commission
B. Future programme of work
C. Publications
D. Liability limits and units of account in international transport conventions
E. Date and place of the twenty-third session of the Commission

F. Sessions of the working groups

Annexes

I. Draft Convention on the Liability of Operators of Transport Terminals in International Trade

II. List of documents before the Commission at its twenty-second session

V. INTER-AMERICAN SPECIALIZED CONFERENCE ON PRIVATE INTERNATIONAL LAW (CIDIP)

A. Conference Proceedings

Inter-American Juridical Committee. *Draft Conventions and Other Documents on Topics 1 to 11 of the Draft Agenda for CIDIP*. Washington, D.C.: General Secretariat of the Organization of American States, [1974].

Conferencia Especializada Interamericana sobre Derecho Internacional Privado, Panamá, 14 a 30 de enero de 1975. *Acta final = Final act*. Washington, D.C.: Secretaría General de la Organización de los Estados Americanos, 1975. (OEA/Ser.C/VI.21.1)

Inter-American Specialized Conference on Private International Law. *Actas y documentos de la Conferencia Especializada Interamericana sobre Derecho Internacional Privado (CIDIP): Panamá, República de Panamá 14 a 30 de enero de 1975*. Washington, D.C.: Secretaría General de la Organizacion de los Estados Americanos, 1975. (OEA/Ser.K/XXI.1, CIDIP/64)

Segunda Conferencia Especializada Interamericana sobre Derecho Internacional Privado. *Proyecto de reglamento = Draft rules of procedure*. Washington, D.C.: Secretaría General de la Organización de los Estados Americanos, [1978].

Segunda Conferencia Especializada Interamericana sobre Derecho Internacional Privado. *Acta final = Final act*. Washington: Secretaría General de la Organización de los Estados Americanos, 1979. (OEA/Ser.C/VI.21.2)

Inter-American Specialized Conference on Private International Law. Actas *y Documentos segunda Conferencia Especializada Interamericana sobre Derecho Internacional Privado (CIDIP-II).*

Washington, D.C.: Secretaría Generale la Organizacíon de los Estados Americanos, 1980. (OEA/Ser.K/XXI.2, CIDIP-II/103)

Inter-American Judicial Committee. *Trabalhos da Comissão Jurídica Interamericana: Projetos de protocolo e de convenção e outros documentos some [i.e., sobre] temas do projeto de agenda da CIDIP-III*. Washington, D.C.: Subsecretaria de Assuntos Jurídicos, Secretaria Geral da Organização dos Estados Americanos, [1983].

Cuarta Conferencia Especializada Interamericana sobre Derecho Internacional Privado, CIDIP-IV. *Acta final = Final act*. Washington, D.C.: Secretaría General de la Organizacion de los Estados Americanos, 1990. (OEA/Ser.C/VI.21.4)

B. Secondary Sources

Rouvier, Juan María. *El derecho procesal civil internacional en las convenciones aprobadas por la Conferencia Especializada Latinoamericana sobre Derecho International Privado: CIDIP I y II, 1975-1979*. [S.l.: s.n., ca. 1980].

Herbert, Ronald. Del Congreso de Lima a la CIDIP III: El derecho internacional privado en América Latina (1878-1984). [Saarbrücken]: Europa-Institut der Universität des Saarlandes, 1984.

Parra-Aranguren, Gonzalo. *La tercera conferencia interamericana sobre derecho internacional privado: CIDIP III, La Paz 1984)*. Caracas: Universidad Catolica Andres Bello, [1984?].

Solari Barrandeguy, Marcelo. *Pactos procesales de la paz: análisis de los convenios aprobados en la tercera Conferencia Especializada Interamericana sobre Derecho Internacional Privado*. Montevideo: Fundación de Cultura Universitaria, 1986.

C. Comments

Documentation from the Organization of American States can be difficult to trace. Unlike the other organizations discussed in this bibliography, the OAS's Inter-American Specialized Conference on Private International Law (CIDIP) has not always published the proceedings of its sessions. Thus, many individual documents have found their ways into libraries through a variety of formal and informal sources and have been cataloged. The paucity of documents is the reason that Spanish and Portuguese titles figure prominently in this section of the bibliography. Since Professor Winship has been active in this organization, he has collected citations to the literature over a period of time.

Because it was impossible to locate a convenient list of all the conventions promulgated by CIDIP, the following list has been compiled along with citations to *International Legal Materials*, a source which is generally more readily available than the OAS Treaty Series or individual documents.

Conventions adopted at Panama City, 30 January 1975

- Inter-American Convention on Conflict of Laws Concerning Bills of Exchange, Promissory Notes, and Invoices, 14 I.L.M. 332 (1975).
- Inter-American Convention on Conflict of Laws Concerning Checks, 14 I.L.M. 334 (1975).
- Inter-American Convention on International Commercial Arbitration, 14 I.L.M. 336 (1975).
- Inter-American Convention on Letters Rogatory, 14 I.L.M. 339 (1975).
- Inter-American Convention on the Taking of Evidence Abroad, 14 I.L.M. 328 (1975).
- Inter-American Convention on the Legal Regime of Powers of Attorney to Be Used Abroad, 14 I.L.M. 325 (1975).

Conventions adopted at Montevideo, 23 April to 8 May 1979

- Inter-American Convention on Conflicts of Laws Concerning Checks, 18 I.L.M. 1220 (1979).
- Inter-American Convention on Conflicts of Laws Concerning Commercial Companies, 18 I.L.M. 1222 (1979).
- Inter-American Convention on Extraterritorial Validity of Foreign Judgments and Arbitral Awards, 18 I.L.M. 1224 (1979).
- Inter-American Convention on Execution of Preventive Measures, 18 I.L.M. 1227 (1979).
- Inter-American Convention on Proof of and Information on Foreign Law, 18 I.L.M. 1231 (1979).

- Inter-American Convention on General Rules of Private International Law, 18 I.L.M. 1236 (1979).
- Inter-American Convention on Domicile of Natural Persons in Private International Law, 18 I.L.M. 1234 (1979).
- Additional Protocol to the Inter-America Convention on Letters Rogatory, 18 I.L.M. 1238 (1979).

Conventions adopted at La Paz on 15 to 24 May 1984

- Inter-American Convention on Conflict of Laws Concerning the Adoption of Minors, 24 I.L.M. 460 (1985).
- Inter-American Convention on Personality and Capacity of Juridical Persons in Private International Law, 24 I.L.M. 465 (1985).
- Inter-American Convention on Jurisdiction in the International Sphere for the Extraterritorial Validity of Foreign Judgments, 24 I.L.M. 468 (1985).
- Additional Protocol to the Inter-American Convention on the Taking of Evidence Abroad, 24 I.L.M. 472 (1985).

Conventions adopted at Montevideo on 9 to 15 July 1989

- Inter-American Convention on the International Return of Children, 29 I.L.M. 66 (1990).
- Inter-American Convention on Support Obligations, 29 I.L.M. 75 (1990).
- Inter-American Convention on the Contracts for the International Carriage of Goods by Road, 29 I.L.M. 83 (1990).

Conventions adopted at Mexico City on 17 and 18 March 1994

- Inter-American Convention on International Traffic in Minors, 33 I.L.M. 723 (1994).
- Inter-American Convention on the Law Applicable to International Contracts, 33 I.L.M. 733 (1994).

INTERNATIONAL ESTATE PLANNING AND INTERNATIONAL FAMILY LAW

SELECTED SOURCES

Randall J. Snyder[306]
Law Librarian in the Office of the Legal Adviser
U.S. Department of State

I. Introduction

This bibliography was originally prepared to accompany a talk given at the American Association of Law Libraries 1994 Institute entitled "Transnational Legal Transactions", and has been edited for publication.

The intent of this bibliography, as originally prepared for the institute, was twofold: First, to providc a fairly brief list of easily obtainable articles and books about international family law; Second, to present sources of information that may not be well known, or readily available. This second category of material includes an electronic bulletin board, an automated fax system, and unusual publications of interest. The bibliography covers a few general sources of information on international family law, but focuses primarily on two areas: international child abduction and intercountry adoption. Most areas of international family law are fairly well established, but while researching the bibliography it was discovered that there was considerable work currently being done, in both the governmental and private sectors, on international child abduction and intercountry adoption. Thus, more information sources are currently available on these two "hot" topics.

The author hopes that the reader will find this information useful. It must be noted that some of the information sources discussed are subject to change; that is, Internet sources may dry up, where some

---

306 The opinions expressed herein are those of the author and not necessarily those of the U.S. Dept. of State.

other sources may evolve to an electronic format and ultimately be available on a database or via the Internet.

General Sources

The U.S. Dept. of State, Bureau of Consular Affairs, has created an automated fax system that provides information in many areas of interest to U.S. Citizens. Of particular interest for our purposes are International Adoption, International Child Abduction, and Visas for Family-Based Immigrants. Information may be obtained by dialing (202) 647-3000 from the receiver on a fax machine and then following the prompts. An index is available by dialing the above number, pressing the "star" key when instructed to do so, followed by the "pound" key, then pressing the start/connect button.

II. International Estate Planning

A. General

Bruch, Carol S. "The Hague Convention on the Law Applicable to Succession to the Estates of Deceased Persons: do quasi-community property and mandatory survivorship laws need protection?" 56 *L. & Contemp. Probs.* 309 (1993).

Finch, Edward R. Jr. "Some common mistakes in international estate planning (with form)." 4 *Prac. Tax Law.* 67 (1990).

Frankel, Lisa N. "Ratification of the Hague Conference on the law applicable to the estates of deceased persons: toward uniformity in United States estate planning." 12 *N.Y.L. Sch. J. Int'l & Comp. L.* 177 (1991).

Landy, Burton A. et al. "Transnational probate and estates: procedural strategy in light of Latin American law and practices." 19 *U. Miami Inter-Am. L. Rev.* 285 (1987/88).

Lawrence, Robert C. "International tax and estate planning." 17 *U. Miami Inter-Am. L. Rev.* 711 (1986). (book review).

Maracini, Michele A. and Donna E. Miller. "International estate planning and probate: a legal bibliography of selected sources." 19 *U. Miami Inter-Am. L. Rev.* 469 (1987-88).

Henner, M. (Murray). *A compendium of state statutes and international treaties in trust and estate law: a reference and referral guide for practicing attorneys,* Quorom Books (1985).

Stephenson, Charles G. *International estate planning.* M. Bender (1992).

B. Wills

Convention on the Law Applicable to Succession to the Estates of Deceased Persons. 28 I.L.M. 150 (1989).

Chase, Peter. "The uniform international will: the next step in the evolution of testamentary disposition." 6 *B. U. Int'l L.J.* 317 (1988).

Kaufman, Nina L. "'Old wine in new bottles': the Uniform International Will revisited." 11 *Probate L.J.* 29 (1992).

Kearney, Richard D. "The International Wills Convention." 18 *Int'l Law.* 613 (1984).

Quam, David. "The resurgence of the international will: a call for federal legislation." 26 *Vand. J. Transnat'l L.* 417 (1993).

Schoenblum, Jeffrey. "Choice of law and succession to wealth: a critical analysis of the ramifications of the Hague Convention on succession to decedents' estates." 32 *Va. J. Int'l L.* 83 (1991).

C. Trusts

Convention on the Law Applicable to Trusts and on Their Recognition. 23 *I.L.M.* 1389 (1984).

Gaillard, Emmanuel and Donald T. Trautman. "Trusts in non-trust countries: conflict of laws and the Hague convention on trusts." 35 *Am. J. Comp. L.* 307 (1987).

III. International Family Law

A. General

Danilov, Dan P. and Mark B. Nerheim. "Marriage, divorce, legal separation and the alien." 18 *Int'l Law.* 675 (1984).

Palsson, Lennart, "Marriage and divorce." *International Encyclopedia of Comparative Law,* Vol. III (Private International Law) Ch. 16. (Kurt Lipstein ed., 1978).

B. Marriage

Gleizer, Guillermo. "Regulating administrative discretion: immigration and marriage." 4 *Yale L. & Pol'y Rev.* 479 (1986).

Juenger, Friedrich K. "Marital property and the conflict of laws: a tale of two countries." 81 *Colum. L. Rev.* 1061 (1981).

Spiering, Kristi J. "Comment: Irrebuttable exile under the immigration marriage fraud amendments: a perspective from the eighth amendment and international human rights law." 58 *U. Cin. L. Rev.* 1397 (1990).

"Marriage and cohabitation in contemporary societies: areas of legal, social, and ethical change: an international and interdisciplinary study." 98 *L.Q. Rev.* 328 (1982) (book review).

C. Divorce

Beaumont, Paul R. "Conflicts of jurisdiction in divorce cases: forum non conveniens." 36 *Int'l & Comp. L.Q.* 116 (1987).

Hernanz, Francisca. "Recognition - exequatur - of foreign judgments, especially of U.S. divorce judgments in Spain." 38 *Am. J. Comp. L.* 567 (1990).

Nichols, John F. "Recognition and enforcement: American courts look at foreign decrees." 9 (no. 4) *Fam. Advoc.* 9 (1987).

Pilkington, M.P. "Transnational divorces under the Family Law Act 1986." 37 *Int'l & Comp. L.Q.* 131 (1988).

"Recent case: International Law - diplomatic immunity - American courts have jurisdiction over real property claims incident to divorce proceedings." 102 *Harv. L. Rev.* 1403 (1989).

D. Children

1. General

Blakesley, Christopher L. "Child custody - jurisdiction and procedure." 35 *Emory L.J.* 291 (1986).

Dyer, Adair. "Childhood's rights in private international law." 5 *Austl. J. Fam. L.* 103 (1991).

King, Michael. "Parental rights, child protection and the European Convention." 15 *Fam. L.* 150 (1985).

Skoler, Daniel L. "The U.N. children's convention: international triumph, national challenge." 15, no. 4 *Fam. Advoc.* 38 (1993).

Vinion, Lon. "When custody conflicts cross the border; a primer on international disputes over children." 15, no. 4 *Fam. Advoc.* 30 (1993).

(a) Misc. sources

Electronic discussion list on the U.N. Convention on the Rights of the Child. Subscribe to "Childri-" by sending to LISTSERV@NIC.SURFNET.N. or LISTSERV@HEARN.BITNET: subscribe childri- your name.

2. Adoption

Hague Convention on Protection of Children and Co-operation in Respect of Intercountry Adoption, 32 *I.L.M.* 1134 (1993). Includes an introductory note by Peter Pfund, Assistant Legal Adviser for Private International Law, U.S. Dept. of State, and head of the U.S. Delegation to the 17th Session of the Hague Conference.

Bell, Cynthia J. "Consent issues in inter-country adoption." 6, no. 3 *Childrens Legal Rts. J.* 2 (1985).

Bogard, Howard E. "Who are the orphans? Defining orphan status and the need for an international convention on intercountry adoption." 5 *Emory Int'l L. Rev.* 571 (1991).

Carlson, Richard R. "Transnational adoption of children." 23 *Tulsa L.J.* 317 (1988).

Davidson, Howard and Mallory King. "Our Peruvian adventure; what we learned about international adoptions." 15, no. 4 *Fam. Advoc.* 58 (1993).

Ellis, Jane T. "The law and procedure of international adoption: an overview." 7 *Suffolk Transnat'l L.J.* 361 (1983).

Horne-Roberts, Jennifer. "Intercountry adoption." 142 *New L.J.* 286 (1992).

Jonet, Ahilemah. "International baby selling for adoption, and the United Nations Convention on the Rights of the Child." 7 *N.Y.L. Sch. J. Hum. Rts.* 82 (1989).

Jonet, Ahilemah. "Legal measures to eliminate transnational trading of infants for adoption: an analysis of anti-infant trading statutes in the United States." 13 *Loy. L.A. Int'l & Comp. L.J.* 305 (1990).

Kennard, Holly C. "Curtailing the sale and trafficking of children: a discussion of the Hague Conference Convention in Respect of Intercountry Adoptions." 14 *U. Pa. J. Int'l Bus. L.* 623 (1994).

Nichols, Suzanne B. "Private adoptions overseas; when your client wants to adopt a foreign baby." 15, no.4 *Fam. Advoc.* 54 (1993).

Pfund, Peter. "Intercountry adoption: the 1993 Hague Convention - its purpose, implementation and promise." 28 *Fam. L.Q.* 53 (1994).

Rosenstock, Lucille. "The Hague Conference on Intercountry Adoption." 15 *Fam. Advoc.* 60 (1993).

Rytting, Paul D. "Immigration restraints on international adoption." 1986 *B.Y.U. L. Rev.* 809 (1986).

U.S. Dept. of State, *Circular* on "International Adoptions."

U.S. Dept. of Justice, Immigration and Naturalization Service, *The Immigration of Adopted and Prospective Adoptive Children*, 1990.

(a) Misc. sources

The Washington & Lee Univ. netlink contains materials on adoption. Telnet liberty.uc.wlu.edu, login: lawlib. Select "Adoption Law and Resources."

3. Abduction

Convention on the Civil Aspects of International Child Abduction, 19 *I.L.M.* 1501 (1980). Text of the Convention may also be found in the *Martindale-Hubbell* International Law Digest, which contains "Selected International Conventions."

Inter-American convention on the International Return of Children, 29 *I.L.M.* 63 (1990).

Agopian, Michael W. "International abduction of children; the United States experience." 11 *Int'l J. Comp. & Appl. Crim. Just.* 231 (1987).

American Bar Assoc. Center on Children and the Law in Cooperation with the Dept. of State, *North American Symposium of International Child Abduction: how to handle intentional child abduction cases*, Sept.30-Oct.1, 1993, A.B.A. (1993).

Anton, A.E. "The Hague Convention on International Child Abduction." 30 *Int'l & Comp. L.Q.* 537 (1981).

Blakesley, Christopher L. "Child custody - jurisdiction and procedure." 35 *Emory L.J.* 291 (1986).

Blynn, Esther L. "In re: international child abduction v. best interests of the child; comity should control." 18 *U. Miami Inter-Am. L. Rev.* 353 (1986).

Bodenheimer, Brigitte. "The international kidnapping of children: the United States approach." 11 *Fam. L.Q.* 83 (1977).

Bodzin, Martin J. "International parental child abduction: the need for recognition and enforcement of foreign custody decrees." 3 *Emory J. Int'l Disp. Resol.* 205 (1989).

Copertino, Monica M. "Hague Convention on the Civil Aspects of International Child Abduction: an analysis of its efficacy." 6 *Conn. J. Int'l L.* 715 (1991).

Crouch, Richard E. "International child-snatching." 9, no. 4 *Fam. Advoc.* 16 (1987).

Daigle, Dorothy C. "Due process rights of parents and children in international child abductions; an examination of the Hague Convention and its exceptions." 26 *Vand. J. Transnat'l L.* 865 (1993).

Dehart, Gloria F. "Getting support over there: jurisdiction, comity, adequate notice, garnishment; how the Hague Convention will bring order out of chaos." 9, no 4 *Fam. Advoc.* 34 (1987).

Dehart, Gloria F., ed. *International child abductions: a guide to applying the Hague Convention, with forms*. 2nd ed., A.B.A. (1993).

Dorosin, Mark. "You must go home again: Friedrich v. Friedrich [983 F2d 1396 (1993)], the Hague Convention and the International

Child Abduction Remedies, "Act. 18 *N.C. J. Int'l L. & Com. Reg.* 743 (1993).

Fabrizio, Elizabeth J. "Operation and enforcement of the Hague Convention on the Civil Aspects of International Child Abduction." 4 *Divorce Litig.* 82 (1992).

51 *Fed. Reg.* 10494 (1986), "Public Notice 957," contains the text and a Legal Analysis of the Hague International Child Abduction Convention.

Frank, Robin Jo. "American and international responses to international child abductions." 16 *N.Y.U. J. Int'l L. & Pol.* 415 (1984).

Greenhouse, Geoffrey. "International child abduction and the enforcement of foreign custody orders." 135 *New L.J.* 710 (1985).

Helzick, Cathy S. "Returning United States children abducted to foreign countries: the need to implement the Hague Convention on the Civil Aspects of International Child Abduction." 5 *B.U. Int'l L.J.* 119 (1987).

Hoff, Patricia M. "Rx for international parental kidnapping: the Hague Convention on the Civil Aspects of International Child Abduction." 8 *Childrens Legal Rts. J.* 13 (1987).

Kindall, Mark P. "United Kingdom Case Note: Treaties - Hague Convention on Child Abduction - wrongful removal - grave risk of harm to child." 83 *Am. J. Int'l L.* 586 (1989).

Leich, Marian N. "Hague Convention on the Civil Aspects of International Child Abduction." in *Contemporary Practice of the United States Relating to International Law,* 80 *Am. J. Int'l L.* 342 (1986).

McClean, David. "Return of internationally abducted children." 106 *L.Q. Rev.* 375 (1990).

McDonald, Elizabeth C. "More than mere child's play: international parental abduction of children." 6 *Dick. J. Int'l L.* 283 (1988).

Morgenstern, Barbara R. "The Hague Convention on the Civil Aspects of International Child Abduction: the need for ratification." 10 *N.C. J. Int'l L. & Com. Reg.* 463 (1985).

Oberdorfer, Daniel. "Comment: Larson v. Dunn: toward a reasoned response to parental kidnapping." 75 *Minn. L. Rev.* 1701 (1991).

Pfund, Peter H. "The Hague Convention on International Child Abduction, the International Child Abduction Remedies Act, and the need for availability of counsel for all petitioners." 24 *Fam. L.Q.* 35 (1990).

Rivers, Dana R. "The Hague international child abduction convention and the International Child Abduction Remedies Act: closing doors to the parent abductor." 2 *Transnat'l Law.* 589 (1989).

Rutherford, Julia R. "Removing the tactical advantages of international parental child abductions under the 1980 Hague Convention on the Civil Aspects of International Child Abductions." 8 Ariz. J. Int'l & Comp. L. 149 (1991).

Schwartz, Philip. "Getting a child back; how the State Department can help." 15, no. 4 *Fam. Advoc.* 42 (1993).

Schwerin, Barbara U. "The Hague Convention on International Child Abduction: a practical application." 10 *Loy. L.A. Int'l & Comp. L.J.* 163 (1988).

Shirman, Brenda J. "International treatment of child abduction and the 1980 Hague Convention." 15 *Suffolk Transnat'l L.J.* 188 (1991).

Starr, Lynn A. "United States implementation of the Hague Convention on the civil aspects of international child abduction." 24 *Stan. J. Int'l L.* 289 (1987).

Stranko, W.A. "International child abduction remedies." 1993 *Army Law.* 28 (1993).

U.S. Dept. of State, Bureau of Consular Affairs. *International Parental Child Abduction*." 1993.

Westbrook, Gayle R. "Law and treaty responses to international child abductions." 20 *Va. J. Int'l L.* 669 (1980).

"International child abduction and the Hague Convention: emerging practice and interpretation of the discretional exception. 25 *Tex. Int'l L.J.* 287 (1990).

(a) Misc. sources

HILTON HOUSE BBS is an electronic bulletin board system providing information on the Convention on the Civil Aspects of International Child Abduction. It may be reached at (408) 246-0387 (8 data bits, 1 stop bit, no parity, full duplex).

RESEARCH GUIDE TO THE MAIN SOURCES IN INTERNATIONAL INTELLECTUAL PROPERTY LAW

Jonathan Pratter
International and Foreign Law Librarian and Lecturer in Law
Tarlton Law Library of the University of Texas

I. Introduction

This research guide makes an attempt to provide references to the main sources, both primary and secondary, mostly in English, in a field that has come to be called international intellectual property law. The guide has no pretensions to great originality. Virtually all of the information it contains can be gathered elsewhere, although the compiler would like to think that it has not before now been brought together in one place. Nor does the guide make any claim to be comprehensive. Librarians know instinctively that attempts at all-inclusiveness are as futile as they are senseless. More to the point, the disclaimer made here has much to do with the nature of the subject it tries to cover.

"Intellectual property" is an umbrella term covering an array of sub-topics. The problem arises when trying to determine just what comes under the umbrella. W.I.P.O. views intellectual property as "compris[ing] two main branches: *industrial property*, chiefly in inventions, trademarks and industrial designs, and *copyright*, chiefly in literary, musical, artistic, photographic and audiovisual works." The Convention Establishing the World Intellectual Property Organization elaborates:

"Intellectual property shall include the rights relating to:

- literary, artistic and scientific works,
- performances of performing artists, phonograms, and broadcasts,
- inventions in all fields of human endeavor,
- scientific discoveries,
- industrial designs,

- trademarks, service marks, and commercial names and designations,
- protection against unfair competition,

and all other rights resulting from intellectual activity in the industrial, scientific, literary or artistic fields." (Art. 2(viii)).

Even this extended definition excludes rights in trade secrets and know-how. But after defining intellectual property rights, you would have to go on to consider transactions -- all the various kinds of plans and agreements that have intellectual property at their center: agreements between creators and exploiters, e.g., between authors and publishers or between inventors and manufacturers, licenses and franchises, etc. Other fields of activity and of regulation impinge so strongly on intellectual property that they would demand consideration: international trade with respect to parallel imports of trademarked goods, licensing and requirements related to transfer of technology in developing countries, competition (antitrust) law and the full range of potentially anti-competitive effects of intellectual property rights and transactions. Then, the practical and technical matters of patent and trademark searching would come into play. Clearly then, a research guide must limit itself to some workable idea of what it can usefully cover.

Taking a cue from the W.I.P.O. definition, this guide concentrates on what could be considered the classic topics of intellectual property: patent, copyright and trademark -- their protection beyond jurisdictional boundaries, i.e, internationally. Inevitably, much of the guide is taken up with an attempt to survey the main international agreements in these fields. True, this information can be extracted from several other sources, but the plain fact remains that a bibliographic document in this area simply can not ignore the significance of international agreements.

However, for reasons that would require a substantive course in intellectual property to elaborate, international protection depends significantly on the precise terms of domestic, i.e., national law. For one thing, national treatment is a leading principle of the main international agreements. Obviously, the idea of a workable guide required the omission of references to national law. The final caveat concerns patent and trademark information and searching --

with the exception of a few sources mentioned in the guide, this aspect of the subject had to be excluded. Perhaps a companion guide will deal with it in the future.

A glance at the main headings of the guide (Roman numerals) will show how it is organized. It begins with secondary sources for the now well-understood reason that research often better starts with secondary sources. Additional notes on the use of the guide appear *passim*, either at the beginning of a section or in footnotes.

Abbreviations Used in Citations to Primary Sources[307]

B.D.I.E.L. *Basic Documents on International Economic Law* (59)

Bevans Bevans, Charles I. *Treaties and Other International Agreements of the United States*, 1776-1949. Washington: U.S.G.P.O., 1968-76.

C.L.T.W. ***Copyright Laws and Treaties of the World*** (62)

C.N.R.L.T. ***Copyright and Neighboring Rights Laws and Treaties*** (61)

COM Commission (European Communities, now European Union)

C.T.S. ***Consolidated Treaty Series***

D.T.W. ***Designs and Utility Models Throughout the World*** (63)

E.I.P.R. ***European Intellectual Property Review*** (13)

E.T.S. ***European Treaty Series***

E.Y.B. ***European Yearbook***

I.L.M. ***International Legal Materials***

I.P.L.T. ***Industrial Property Laws and Treaties*** (65)

---

307 The numbers in parentheses refer to entries in the guide where fuller information will be found.

L.N.T.S. *League of Nations Treaty Series*

O.J. *Official Journal of the European Communities*

P.T.W. *Patents Throughout the World* (67)

Stat. *United States Statutes at Large*

T.I.A.S. *Treaties and Other International Acts Series* (U.S.)

T.S. *Treaty Series* (U.S.)

T.T.W. *Trademarks Throughout the World* (68)

U.K.T.S. *Treaty Series* (U.K.)

U.N.T.S. *United Nations Treaty Series*

U.S.T. *United States Treaties and Other International Agreements*

II. Periodicals -- All Fields

Obviously, not all of the journals listed here deal exclusively or even mainly with the international dimensions of intellectual property protection. Those that do (or with a significant international component) are given in bold type. The others are included because it is quite likely that they will not infrequently carry an article on point. Many of these journals are covered by the main legal periodical indexes.

1. *AIPLA Quarterly Journal*. Vol. 12, 1984-. New York: American Intellectual Property Law Association, 1984-. Quarterly. Focus on patent law. Continues *APLA Quarterly Journal*.

2. *Albany Law Journal of Science and Technology*. Vol. 1, 1991-. Albany, N.Y.: Students of Albany Law School of Union University, 1991-. Annual.

3. *Archiv für Urheber-, Film-, Funk- und Theaterrecht*. Bd. 1, 1928-. Berlin: Schweitzer Verlag, 1928-. Frequency varies.

4. Arts and Entertainment Law Review. No. 1, 1992-. North Ryde, NSW: Law Book Co., 1992-. Bimonthly. Focus on Australia.

5. *BNA's Patent, Trademark & Copyright Journal.* Washington, D.C.: Bureau of National Affairs. Weekly.

6. *Bulletin of Law, Science and Technology.* No. 1, 1976-. Quarterly. Chicago: American Bar Association, 1976-. Quarterly. Newsletter of the ABA Section of Science and Technology.

7. *Canadian Intellectual Property Review.* Vol. 1, 1984. Ottawa: Patent and Trademark Institute of Canada, 1984-. Three numbers a year. Focus on Canada.

8. Cardozo Arts & Entertainment Law Journal. Vol. 1, 1982-. New York: Cardozo School of Law, Yeshiva University, 1982-. Semiannual.

9. *China Patents & Trademarks.* Hong Kong: China Patent & Trademark Publications, 1985-. Quarterly. Focus on China.

10. *Columbia-VLA Journal of Law & the Arts.* Vol. 10, 1985-. New York: Columbia University School of Law and Volunteer Lawyers for the Arts, 1985-. Quarterly. Continues *Art & the Law.*

11. *Copyright.* Vol. 1, 1965-. Geneva: World Intellectual Property Organization, 1965-. Monthly. Since 1987 contains insert section of materials updating the collection *Copyright and Neighboring Rights Laws and Treaties.*

12. *Copyright Bulletin.* Vol. 1, 1967-. Paris: UNESCO, 1968-. Quarterly.

13. *EIPR -- European Intellectual Property Review.* Vol. 1, 1978-. Oxford: ESC Publishing, 1978-. Monthly. Focus on EC developments. Separately paginated news section covering many countries.

13a. *Entertainment and Media Law Reports.* Vol. 1, 1993-. Oxford: Sweet & Maxwell/ESC. Pub., 1993-. Bimonthly. Focus on UK.

14. *Entertainment Law Review.* Vol. 1, 1990-. Oxford: Sweet & Maxwell, 1990-. Bimonthly. Focus on UK.

15. Global Intellectual Property Series. New York: Practising Law Institute, 1991[?]-. More or less annual. Various sub-titles. Part of the Patents, Copyrights, Trademarks, and Literary Property Course

Handbook Series. Repetitive and generally undistinguished in the usual PLI format.[308]

16. *GRUR International.* 1980, Heft 1-. Weinheim: VCH Verlag, 1980-. Monthly. Full title: *Gewerblicher Rechtsschutz und Urheberrecht -- Internationaler Teil.*

17. *Harvard Journal of Law & Technology.* Vol. 1, 1988-. Cambridge: Harvard Law School, 1988-. Annual.

18. *Hastings Communications and Entertainment Law Journal (Comm/Ent).* Vol. 13, 1990-. San Francisco: University of California, Hastings College of the Law, 1990-. Quarterly. Continues Comm/Ent.

19. *High Technology Law Journal.* Vol. 1., 1986-. Berkeley: University of California, Boalt Hall School of Law, 1986-. Semiannual.

20. *IIC: International Review of Industrial Property and Copyright Law.* Vol. 1, 1970-. Weinheim: VCH Verlag, 1970-. Bimonthly. Edited by the Max Planck Institute for Foreign and International Patent, Copyright and Competition Law in Munich.

21. *Idea.* Vol. 8, 1964-. Washington, D.C.: Patent, Trademark, and Copyright Research Institute, George Washington University, 1964-. Quarterly.

22. *Industrial Property.* Vol. 1, 1962-. Geneva: World Intellectual Property Organization, 1962. Monthly. Chronicles activities of WIPO. Updates status of international agreements administered by WIPO in the field of industrial property. Contains insert section of materials updating the collection Industrial Property Laws and Treaties.

23. *Intellectual Property Journal.* Vol. 1, 1990-. North Ryde, N.S.W.: Law Book Co., 1990-. Quarterly. Focus on Australia.

---

308 [Ed. note] This comment is intended as an expression of opinion only, not as a statement of fact.

24. *Intellectual Property Law Review.* Vol. 10, 1978-. Deerfield, Ill.: Clark Boardman Callaghan, 1992-. Annual. Continues Patent Law Review.

24a. *International Media Law.* 1995[?]-. London: FT Law & Tax, 1995-. Monthly. Continuous title by same name formerly published by Oyez Longman.

25. *Journal of Intellectual Property Law.* Vol. 1, 1993-. Athens, Ga.: University of Georgia School of Law, 1993-. Semiannual.

26. *Journal of Law and Information Science.* Vol. 1, 1981-. Hobart, Tasmania: Faculty of Law, University of Tasmania, 1986-. Irregular. Covers intellectual property issues in relation to computers.

27. *The Journal of Proprietary Rights.* Vol. 1, 1988-. Englewood Cliffs, N.J: Prentice Hall Law & Business, 1988-. Monthly.

28. *Journal of the Copyright Society of the U.S.A.* Vol. 29, 1981-. New York: The Society, 1981-. Bimonthly. Continues *Bulletin of the Copyright Society of the U.S.A.*

29. *Journal of the Patent and Trademark Office Society.* Vol. 67, 1985-. Arlington, Va.: The Society, 1985-. Monthly. Continues *Journal of the Patent Office Society.*

30. *Jurimetrics.* Vol. 8, 1968-. Chicago American Bar Association, Section of Science and Technology, 1966-. Quarterly.

31 *Law/Technology.* Vol. 1, 1968-. Washington: World Association of Lawyers, 1981-. Quarterly.

31a. *Les Marques Internationales.* Vol. 1, 1893-. Geneva: W.I.P.O., 1893-. Monthly. Publishes trademarks registered with W.I.P.O.

32. *Österreichische Blatter für gewerblichen Rechtsschutz und Urheberrecht.* Jahrg. 1, 1952-. Vienna: "Die Industrie" Zeitschriftenverlag, 1952-.

33. *Revue du Droit de la Propriété Intellectuelle.* No. 37, 1991-. Paris, CEDAT, 1991-. Bimonthly. Focus on France. Formed by union of Revue du Droit de la Propriété Industrielle and *Cahiers du Droit d'Auteur.*

34. *Revue Internationale du Droit d'Auteur*. No. 1, 1953. Paris: Association Française pour la Diffusion du Droit d'Auteur National et International, 1953-. Quarterly.

35. *Rights: Copyright and Related Rights in the Service of Creativity*. Vol. 1, 1987-. Geneva: International Publishers Association, 1987-. Quarterly.

36. *Santa Clara Computer and High Technology Law Journal*. Vol. 1, 1985-. Santa Clara: Cal.: University of Santa Clara School of Law, 1985-. Semiannual.

37. *Software Law Journal*. Vol. 1, 1985-. Manhattan Beach, Cal.: Center for Computer/Law, 1985. Quarterly.

38. *Tolley's Computer Law and Practice*. Vol. 8, 1992-. Surrey, England: Tolley Publishing, 1992-. Bimonthly. Focus on UK and EC. *Continues Computer Law & Practice*.

39. *The Trademark Reporter*. Vol. 1, 1911-. New York: United States Trademark Association, 1911-. Bimonthly.

40. *Trademark World: the International Journal for Trademark Professionals*. No. 1, 1986-. London: Intellectual Property Publications, 1986-. Ten numbers a year.

41. *University of Baltimore Intellectual Property Law Journal*. Vol. 1, 1992-. Baltimore: University of Baltimore School of Law, 1992-. Semiannual.

42. *World Intellectual Property Report*. Vol. 1, 1987-. London: BNA International, 1987-. Monthly newsletter in typical BNA format. Not available online.

43. *World Patent Information*. Vol. 1, 1979-. McLean, Va.: Maxwell Online; Oxford: Pergamon Press, 1979-. Quarterly. "The international journal for patent documentation, classification and statistics." Published in cooperation with W.I.P.O. and the Commission of the EC.

44. ZUM -- *Zeitschrift für Urheber- und Medienrecht*. 1985-. Baden-Baden: Nomos Verlag, 1985-. Monthly. Focus on Germany and EC. Continues *Film und Recht*.

III. Books -- All Fields[309]

45. *The Berne Convention for the Protection of Literary and Artistic Works, from 1886 to 1986.* Geneva: International Bureau of Intellectual Property, 1986.

46. Bogsch, Arpad. *The Law of Copyright Under the Universal Convention.* 3d ed. Leyden: A.W. Sijthoff, 1968.

47. *Chartered Institute of Patent Agents. European Patents Handbook.* 2d ed. London: Longman; New York: Matthew Bender, 1988-.

48. *The First Twenty-five Years of the World Intellectual Property Organization, from 1967-1992.* Geneva: International Bureau of Intellectual Property, 1992. W.I.P.O. publication 881(E).

49. *Guide to the International Registration of Marks* [under the Madrid Arrangement]. Jan. 1989 ed., updated to October 1, 1992. Geneva, W.I.P.O., 1989-.

50. Kumar, Umesh. *An Introduction to the African Industrial Property System.* Roma (Lesotho): Umesh Kumar, 1993.

51. Ladas, Stephen P. *Patents, Trademarks, and Related Rights: National and International Protection.* Cambridge: Harvard University Press, 1975.

52. Lipszyc, Delia. *Derecho de Autor y Derechos Conexos.* Paris: UNESCO, 1993.

53. Nimmer, Melville B. and Geller, Paul E., eds. *International Copyright Law and Practice.* New York, Matthew Bender, 1988-.

54. Nordemann, Wilhelm, Vinck, Kai and Hertin, Paul W. *International Copyright and Neighboring Rights Law: Commentary, with Special Emphasis on the European Community.* Weinheim: VCH Verlag, 1990.

55. *PCT Applicant's Guide.* 1991 ed. Geneva: World Intellectual Property Organization, 1991. W.I.P.O. publication no. 432(E).

---

[309] Titles the compiler considers part of a core collection are given in bold type.

56. Ricketson, Sam. *The Berne Convention for the Protection of Literary and Artistic Works: 1886-1986*. Brentford, England: Kluwer, 1987.

57. Stewart, Stephen. *International Copyright and Neighbouring Rights*. 2d ed. London: Butterworths, 1989.

58. *WIPO Worldwide Symposium on the Impact of Digital Technology on Copyright and Neighboring Rights, Harvard University, Cambridge Massachusetts, United States of America, March 31 to April 2, 1993*. Geneva: World Intellectual Property Organization, 1993. WIPO publication no. 723(E).

IV. Selected Subject Headings by Type

Type I	Type II
Copyright--[Name of jurisdiction] Industrial property Intellectual property Patent laws and legislation Trademarks	Industrial property (International Law) Intellectual property (International Law) Patents (International Law) Trademarks (International Law)
Type III	**Type IV**
Copyright International	Conflict of laws--Industrial property Conflict of laws--Intellectual property Conflict of laws--Patents
Type V	**Type VI**
Copyright--Computer programs Copyright--Data bases Copyright--Semiconductors	Biotechnology--Patents Plant varieties-- Patents
Type VII	**Type VIII**
Competition, Unfair--[Jurisdiction] Compulsory licensing of patents Design protection Marks of origin Models (Patents) Patent licenses Service marks	Berne Convention for the Protection of Literary and Artistic Works (1886) Patent Co-operation Treaty (1970)

V. International Agreements -- Collections

59. *Basic Documents of International Economic Law.* Zamora, Stephen and Brand, Ronald A., gen. eds. Chicago: CCH, 1990. Volume 1, part four contains six of the main international agreements concerning intellectual property.

60. *Collection of the Texts of the U.P.O.V. Convention and other Important Documents Established by U.P.O.V.* Geneva: U.P.O.V., 1984.

61. *Copyright and Neighboring Rights Laws and Treaties.* Geneva: W.I.P.O., 1987-. W.I.P.O. publication 616(E). Updated with pages inserted in monthly issues of *Copyright.*

62. *Copyright Laws and Treaties of the World.* Paris: UNESCO; Washington: Bureau of National Affairs, 1956-.

63. *Designs and Utility Models Throughout the World.* Greene, Anne Marie. Deerfield, Ill.: Clark Boardman Callahan, 1991-.

64. *Digest of Intellectual Property Laws of the World.* Nelson, Lester, ed. Dobbs Ferry, N.Y.: Oceana, 1990.

65. *Industrial Property Laws and Treaties.* Geneva: W.I.P.O., 1978-. W.I.P.O. publication 609(E). Updated with pages inserted in monthly issues of *Industrial Property.*

66. *International Treaties on Intellectual Property.* Leaffer, Marshall A., ed. Washington: Bureau of National Affairs, 1990.

67. *Patents Throughout the World.* Jacobs, Alan J., ed. 4th ed. New York: Clark Boardman, 1989-.

68. *Trademarks Throughout the World.* 4th ed. Morowitz, Nancy H., ed. Deerfield, Ill.: Clark Boardman Callaghan, 1994[?]-.

69. *World Patent Law and Practice: Patent Statutes, Regulations and Treaties.* Sinnott, John P., comp. New York: Matthew Bender, 1974-.

VI. International Agreements – Patents

Some of the major intellectual property treaties,[310] including the Paris and Bern Conventions and the U.C.C. have been revised several times.

[310] Throughout the guide, the names of agreements to which the U.S. is a party

Moreover, not all states-party to an earlier version of a treaty have seen fit to accede to later revisions. This raises a tricky question of treaty law as to the relations among states-party to differing revisions of a particular agreement. For research purposes, it is necessary to be aware that more than one version of a particular international agreement has continuing relevance. Therefore, this guide gives the citations to all versions (i.e., revisions) of an agreement to which at least one state is still a party. For historical purposes, the citation to the original versions of the Paris and Berne Conventions is given.

70. Paris Convention for the Protection of Industrial Property, Paris, March 20, 1883, 161 C.T.S. 409, 25 Stat. 1372, T.S. 379, 1 Bevans 80.

70a. Paris Convention for the Protection of Industrial Property, revised at The Hague, November 6, 1925, 74 L.N.T.S 289.

70b. Paris Convention for the Protection of Industrial Property, revised at London, June 2, 1934, 192 L.N.T.S. 17, P.T.W. App. B1(b).

70c. Paris Convention for the Protection of Industrial Property, revised at Lisbon, October 31, 1958, 828 U.N.T.S. 107, 13 U.S.T. 1, T.I.A.S. 4931, P.T.W. App. B1(c).

70d. **Paris Convention for the Protection of Industrial Property,** revised at Stockholm, July 14, 1967, 828 U.N.T.S. 305, 21 U.S.T. 1583, T.I.A.S. 6923, P.T.W. App B1(d).

70aa. **Convention for the Protection of Inventions, Patents, Designs and Industrial Models,** Buenos Aires, August 20, 1910, 155 L.N.T.S. 179, 38 Stat. 1811, T.S. 595, 1 Bevans 767.

71. **International Convention for the Protection of New Varieties of Plants,** Paris, December 2, 1961, 815 U.N.T.S. 89 (original text), 33 U.S.T. 2703, T.I.A.S. 10199 (1978 revised text), I.P.L.T.-Multilateral Treaties, Text 1-004 (1978 revised text) [U.P.O.V. Convention].

---

are in bold type.

72. Convention on the Unification of Certain Points of Substantive Law on Patents for Invention, Strasbourg, November 27, 1963, 1249 U.N.T.S. 369, E.T.S. 47, 11 E.Y.B. 335, U.K.T.S. 70(1980).

73. Patent Cooperation Treaty, Washington, June 19, 1970, 1160 U.N.T.S. 231, 28 U.S.T. 7645, T.I.A.S. 8733 (original version), I.P.L.T.-Multilateral Treaties, Text 2-006 (1979 amendment & 1984 modification), P.T.W. App. B2(a) (with amendment & modification), W.I.P.O. Publication 274(E) (with amendment & modification). The 1993 Regulations under the Patent Cooperation Treaty are at I.P.L.T.-Multilateral Treaties, Text 2-007.

74. **Strasbourg Agreement Concerning the International Patent Classification**, Strasbourg, March 24, 1971, 1160 U.N.T.S. 484, 26 U.S.T. 1793, T.I.A.S. 8140, P.T.W. App. C1(a), W.I.P.O. Publication 275(E).

75. Convention on the Grant of European Patents, Munich, October 5, 1973, 13 I.L.M. 270 (1974), U.K.T.S. 20(1978), I.P.L.T.-Multilateral Treaties, Text. 2-008, P.T.W. App. B3(a) [European Patent Convention].

76. Agreement on the Creation of the African Regional Industrial Property Organization, Lusaka, December 9, 1976, I.P.L.T.-Multilateral Treaties, Text 1-002. This is an agreement between several nations of Anglophone Central and East Africa. The 1982 Protocol is at I.P.L.T.-Multilateral Treaties, Text 1-008; the 1984/86 Regulations are at I.P.L.T.-Multilateral Treaties, Text 1-010.

77. Agreement Relating to the Creation of an African Intellectual Property Organization, Bangui (Central African Republic), March 2, 1977, I.P.L.T.-Multilateral Treaties, Text 1-005 [Bangui Agreement]. This agreement includes several nations of Francophone West Africa. The Regulations under the Agreement are at I.P.L.T.-Multilateral Treaties, Text 1-006.

78. **Budapest Treaty on the International Recognition of the Deposit of Microorganisms for the Purposes of Patent Procedure,** Budapest, April, 28, 1977, 32 U.S.T. 1241, T.I.A.S. 9768, 17 I.L.M. 285, I.P.L.T.-Multilateral Treaties, Text 2-004, P.T.W. App. C4(a), W.I.P.O. Publication 277(E).

79. Treaty on the International Recording of Scientific Discoveries, Geneva, March 3, 1978, I.P.L.T.-Multilateral Treaties, Text 1-003.

80. Agreement Relating to Community Patents, Luxembourg, December 15, 1989, O.J. 1989 L401 (December 30, 1989).

81. Draft Treaty Supplementing the Paris Convention for the Protection of Industrial Property as far as Patents are Concerned, W.I.P.O. Doc. PLT/DC/3 (December 21, 1990) [Patent Law Treaty or Patent Harmonization Treaty]. The drafting process under W.I.P.O auspices is currently underway. The diplomatic conference set for 1993 at which the draft would have been considered and possibly adopted was postponed because of controversy surrounding some of its terms. For background, see generally, R. Carl Moy, "The History of the Patent Harmonization Treaty: Economic Self-Interest as an Influence," 26 J. Marshall L. Rev. 457 (1993).

82. Eurasian Patent Convention, Geneva, February 17, 1994, reprinted in 8 *World Intellectual Property Report* 210 (1994).

83. Final Act Embodying the Results of the Uruguay Round of Multilateral Trade Negotiations, Doc. No. MTN/FA (December 15, 1993), Marrakech, April 15, 1994, reprinted in part in 33 I.L.M. 1 (1994). Annex 1C is the Agreement on Trade-Related Aspects of Intellectual Property Rights, Doc. No. MTN/FA II-A1C, reprinted in 33 I.L.M. 81 (1994).

VII. Note on the World Intellectual Property Organization (W.I.P.O.)

In 1893 the secretariats of the Paris Union and the Berne Union were merged to form the *Bureaux internationaux réunis pour la protection de la propriété industrielle* (BIRPI). That is the genesis of W.I.P.O. which was created by multilateral treaty in 1967. (See the Convention Establishing the World Intellectual Property Organization, Stockholm, July 14, 1967, 828 U.N.T.S. 3, 21 U.S.T. 1749, T.I.A.S. 6932.) W.I.P.O. is an intergovernmental organization with its headquarters in Geneva. In 1974 W.I.P.O. became one of the 16 specialized agencies of the United Nations under Articles 57 and 63 of the UN Charter. (See General Assembly Resolution 3346 (XXIX) approving the annexed agreement between the UN and W.I.P.O., reprinted at 22 U.N.Y.B. 720 (1974)).

The structure of W.I.P.O. is a little complicated and it has to be distinguished from the structure of each of the Unions for which W.I.P.O. performs administrative functions. W.I.P.O. is composed of a General Assembly, a Conference, a Coordination Committee and an International Bureau (secretariat). The International Bureau has these main functions: Depositary of the international agreements administered by W.I.P.O.; registration of protected marks, designs, patents, etc., under several of the treaties administered by W.I.P.O.; maintenance and development of the classification schemes developed under the various classification agreements administered by W.I.P.O.; assembling and disseminating information in the field of intellectual property. Acting through the International Bureau, W.I.P.O. assigns a high priority to development cooperation, i.e., legal and technical assistance to developing countries in the field of intellectual property.

W.I.P.O. has an active publishing program, including treaty collections and the texts of individual treaties. A 54-page *Catalogue of Publications* (1995) is available and makes a useful reference resource.

For more information about W.I.P.O. consult: the entries for W.I.P.O. in the *Yearbook of International Organizations* and the *United Nations Yearbook*. See also: *World Intellectual Property Organization (WIPO): General Information*, W.I.P.O. Publication 400(E), and Joseph Ekedi-Samnik, *L'Organisation Mondiale de la Propréité Intellectuelle* (Brussels: Emile Bruylant, 1975).

VIII. Note on W.I.P.O. Documentation on CD-ROM

Recently, W.I.P.O. issued a set of compact discs called IP-LEX. It contains the texts of and information regarding international treaties and regional laws in the field of intellectual property. Thus, IP-LEX appears to be a CD-ROM version of the W.I.P.O. collections of texts noted above in entries 61 and 65, enhanced with CD-ROM search capabilities.

Other W.I.P.O. CD-ROM databases are:

- ROMARIN, a monthly series of all international registrations of figurative marks effected under the Madrid Agreement, as well as all appellations of origin registered under the Lisbon Agreement;
- IPC-CLASS, an edition of the International Patent Classification in several languages;

- ESPACE-WORLD, a collection of the full text of published international applications filed under the Patent Cooperation Treaty.

World Intellectual Property Organization 34, chemin des Colombettes CH-1211 Geneva 20 Switzerland tel. (41)(22)730-9111 fax (41)(22)733-5428	WIPO Liaison Office at New York 2 United Nations PlazaRoom 560 New York, NY 10017 tel. (212)963-6813 fax (212)963-4801

IX. International Agreements – Copyright

84. Convention Concerning the Creation of an International Union for the Protection of Literary and Artistic Works, Berne, September 9, 1886, 168 C.T.S. 185 (French only), C.L.T.W.-Multilateral Conventions, Item A-1 [Berne Convention].

84a. Additional Act Amending Articles II, III, V, VII, XII, and XX of the Convention of September 9, 1886, and Numbers 1 and 4 of the Final Protocol Annexed Thereto; Declaration Interpreting Certain Provisions of the Berne Convention of September 9, 1886 and the Additional Act Signed in Paris on May 4, 1896, Paris, May 4, 1896, 182 C.T.S. 441 (French only), C.L.T.W.-Multilateral Conventions, Item B-1 [Paris Additional Act and Interpretive Declaration].

84b. Revised Berne Convention for the Protection of Literary and Artistic Works, Berlin, November 13, 1908, 1 L.N.T.S. 218, 208 C.T.S. 28, C.L.T.W.-Multilateral Conventions, Item C-1 [Berlin Revision].

84c. Additional Protocol to the Revised Berne Convention of November 13, 1908, Berne, March 20, 1914, 1 L.N.T.S. 244, 214 C.T.S. 330, C.L.T.W.-Multilateral Conventions, Item D-1 [Berne Additional Protocol].

84d. International Convention for the Protection of Literary and Artistic Works, revised at Rome, June 28, 1928, 123 L.N.T.S. 233, C.L.T.W.-Multilateral Conventions, Item E-1 [Rome Revision].

84e. Berne Convention for the Protection of Literary and Artistic Works, revised at Brussels, June 26, 1948, 331 U.N.T.S. 217, C.L.T.W.-Multilateral Conventions, Item F-1 [Brussels Revision].

84f. Berne Convention for the Protection of Literary and Artistic Works, revised at Stockholm, July 14, 1967, 828 U.N.T.S., C.L.T.W.Multilateral-Conventions, Item G-1, WIPO Publication 283(E) [Stockholm Act].

84g. Berne Convention for the Protection of Literary and Artistic Works, revised at Paris, July 24, 1971, C.L.T.W.-Multilateral Conventions, Item H-1, 1 B.D.I.E.L. 711, S. Treaty Doc. No. 27, 99th Cong., 2d Sess. 37 (1986), WIPO Publication 287(E) [Paris Act].

85. Convention on Literary and Artistic Copyright, Mexico City, January 27, 1902, 35 Stat. 1934, T.S. 491, 1 Bevans 339. Still in force only as between El Salvador and the other states party.

86. Convention on Literary and Artistic Copyright, Buenos Aires, August 11, 1910, 38 Stat. 1785, T.S. 593, 1 Bevans 758.

86a. Other Pan-American Conventions: Montevideo 1889, Rio de Janeiro 1906, Caracas 1911, Havana 1928, Montevideo 1939, Washington 1946. These are collected in: Organization of American States, General Secretariat. *Copyright Protection in the Americas*. 4th ed. Dobbs Ferry, N.Y.: Oceana, 1979.

87. Universal Copyright Convention and Protocols, Geneva, September 6, 1952, 216 U.N.T.S. 133, 6 U.S.T. 2731, T.I.A.S. 3324, C.L.T.W.-Multilateral Conventions, Item 1.

87a. Universal Copyright Convention, as revised, and Protocols, Paris, July 24 1971, 25 U.S.T. 1341, T.I.A.S. 7868.

88. Multilateral Convention for the Avoidance of Double Taxation of Copyright Royalties and Additional Protocol, Madrid, December 13, 1979, *Copyright* 1980/1.

X. Note on Updating the Status of International Intellectual Property Agreements

A. In the January issue of the W.I.P.O. journal, *Industrial Property*, there is a section titled "Treaties (Status on January 1, 199_)." This section covers the W.I.P.O. Convention and 14 agreements administered by W.I.P.O., as well as a few regional agreements not administered by W.I.P.O. The tables in this section give a list of the states-party to each agreement, the date they became a party, and an indication of the "latest act" to which they are a party (where applicable).

B. In the January issue of the W.I.P.O. journal, *Copyright*, there is a section titled "Treaties (Status on January 1, 199_)." This section covers the W.I.P.O. Convention and seven agreements administered by W.I.P.O., as well as a few not administered by W.I.P.O., including the U.C.C. The tables cover the same information noted just above.

C. Part 2 (Multilateral Treaties) of *Treaties in Force*, the annual State Department publication, has subject headings for Copyright, Industrial Property, Intellectual Property, Patents and Phonograms. These track the status of about 17 multilateral agreements to which the U.S. is a party. The appendix at the back of *Treaties in Force* is titled International Copyright Relations of the United States. This is a table arranged alphabetically by country. It summarizes the state of copyright relations between the U.S. and each of the countries using a set of abbreviations to refer to relations arising under both multilateral and bilateral agreements. The appendix is also published separately as a circular of the Library of Congress Copyright Office (LC3.4/2:38).

D. *Multilateral Treaties Deposited with the Secretary-General,* the annual publication of the United Nations tracks the status of the Rome Convention (entry 89). Declarations and reservations made by states are reproduced in this book.

E. The one-volume treaty index, *Multilateral Treaties: Index and Current Status* by Bowman and Harris (London: Butterworths, 1986) is a very useful source. It must be used together with the Ninth Cumulative Supplement (1992).

XI. International Agreements – Neighboring Rights

89. International Convention for the Protection of Performers, Producers of Phonograms, and Broadcasting Organizations, Rome, October 26, 1961, 496 U.N.T.S. 43, W.I.P.O. Publication 328(E) [Rome Convention].

90. **Convention for the Protection of Producers of Phonograms against Unauthorized Duplication of their Phonograms,** Geneva, October 29, 1971, 866 U.N.T.S., 25 U.S.T. 309, T.I.A.S. 7808 [Phonogram Convention].

91. Vienna Agreement for the Protection of Typefaces and Protocol, Vienna, June 12, 1973, W.I.P.O. Publication 267(E).

92. Convention Relating to the Distribution of Programme-Carrying Signals Transmitted by Satellite, Brussels, May 21, 1974, 1144 U.N.T.S. 3, 13 I.L.M. 1444, W.I.P.O. Publication 289(E) [Satellites Convention].

93. Treaty on Intellectual Property in Respect of Integrated Circuits, Washington, May 26, 1989, 28 I.L.M. 1484, I.P.L.T.-Multilateral Treaties, Text 1-011, C.N.R.L.T.-Multilateral Treaties, Text No. 2-01, W.I.P.O. Publication 202(E).

94. Treaty on the International Registration of Audiovisual Works, Geneva, April 20, 1989, I.P.L.T.-Multilateral Treaties, Text 1-01, Copyright June 1989, C.N.R.L.T.-Multilateral Treaties, Text 1-01 [Film Register Treaty].

XII. International Agreements -- Trademarks

94a. **General Inter-American Convention for Trademark and Commercial Protection**, Washington, February 20, 1929, 124 L.N.T.S. 357, 46 Stat. 2907, T.S. 833, 2 Bevans 751.

95. Madrid Agreement for the Repression of False or Deceptive Indications of Source on Goods, revised at Lisbon, October 31, 1958, 828 U.N.T.S. 163, T.T.W. App. C-120, W.I.P.O. Publication 261(E) [Madrid Arrangement].

96. Madrid Agreement Concerning the International Registration of Marks, revised at Stockholm, July 14, 1967, 828 U.N.T.S. 389, I.P.L.T.-Multilateral Treaties, Text 3-004, T.T.W. App. C-81, W.I.P.O. Publication 204(E) [Madrid Arrangement]. Regulations of April 22, 1988 under the Madrid Agreement are at I.P.L.T.-Multilateral Treaties, Text 3-005 and W.I.P.O. Publication 204(E).

96a. Protocol Relating to the Madrid Agreement Concerning the International Registration of Marks, Madrid, June 28, 1989, I.P.L.T.-Multilateral Treaties, Text 3-007, 28 *Industrial Property* 254 (1989), W.I.P.O. Publication 204(E), 15 E.I.P.R. 420 (1993).

97. Lisbon Agreement for the Protection of Appellations of Origin and their International Registration, as revised at Stockholm, July 14, 1967, 828 U.N.T.S. 178, W.I.P.O. Publication 264(E),

98. Central American Agreement for the Protection of Industrial Property (Marks, Trade Names and Advertising Slogans or Signs), San Jos, June 1, 1968, IPLT-Multilateral Treaties, Text 1-001.

99. Vienna Agreement Establishing an International Classification of the Figurative Elements of Marks, Vienna, June 12, 1973, U.K.T.S. 38(1975), W.I.P.O. Publication 266(E).

100. Trademark Registration Treaty, Vienna, June 12, 1973, S. Exec. Doc. H, 94th Cong., 1st Sess. (1975), 12 I.L.M. 1029 (1973).

101. **Nice Agreement Concerning the International Classification of Goods and Services for the Purposes of the Registration of Marks,** as revised at Geneva, May 13, 1977, W.I.P.O. Publication 292(E), T.T.W. App. C-138, IPLT-Multilateral Treaties, Text 3-001 [Nice Agreement].

XIII. International Agreements -- Designs, Models and Utility Models

102. Hague Agreement Concerning the International Deposit of Industrial Designs, revised at London, June 2, 1934, 205 L.N.T.S. 179, D.T.W. App. A2(b), W.I.P.O. Publication 262(E).

103. Hague Agreement Concerning the International Deposit of Industrial Designs, revised at The Hague, November 28, 1960, D.T.W. App. A2, W.I.P.O. Publication 262(E). See also: Additional Act, Monaco, November 18, 1961, D.T.W. App. A2(d); Complementary Act, Stockholm, July 14, 1967, D.T.W. App. A2(e); Protocol, Geneva, August 29, 1975, IPLT-Multilateral Treaties, Text 4-001, D.T.W. App. A2(f).

104. Locarno Agreement Establishing an International Classification for Industrial Designs, Locarno, October 8, 1968, 23 U.S.T. 1353, T.I.A.S. 7420, 8 I.L.M. 1, D.T.W. App. A3(a).

XIV. Selected European Union Primary Sources

Patents & Industrial Designs

105. Council Regulation 1768/92 of June 18, 1992 Concerning the Creation of a Supplementary Protection Certificate for Medicinal Products, O.J. 1992 L182 (July 2, 1992).

106. Amended Proposal for a Council Regulation on Community Plant Variety Rights, COM(93)104, O.J. 1993 C113 (April 23, 1993).

107. Proposal for a Council Directive on the Legal Protection of Designs, COM(93)344, O.J. 1993 C345 (December 23, 1993).

108. Proposal for a European Parliament and Council Regulation on Community Design, COM(93)342, O.J. 1994 C29 (January 31, 1994).

Copyright & Neighboring Rights

109. Council Directive 87/54 of December 16, 1986 on the Legal Protection of Topographies of Semi-conductor Products, O.J. 1987 L24 (January 27, 1987).

110. Green Paper on Copyright and the Challenge of Technology -- Copyright Issues Requiring Immediate Action, COM(88)172.

111. Follow-up to the Green Paper – Working Programme of the Commission in the Field of Copyright and Neighbouring Rights, COM(90)584.

112. Council Directive 91/250 of May 14, 1991 on the Legal Protection of Computer Programs, O.J. 1991 L122 (May 17, 1991).

113. Council Directive 92/100 of November 19, 1992 on Rental Right and Lending Right and on Certain Rights Related to Copyright in the Field of Intellectual Property, O.J. 1992 L346 (November 27, 1992).

114. Amended Proposal for a Council Directive on the Legal Protection of Biotechnological Inventions, COM(92)589, O.J. 1993 C44 (February 16,1993).

115. Council Directive 93/83 of September 27, 1993 on the Coordination of Rules Concerning Copyright and Rights Related to Copyright Applicable to Satellite Broadcasting and Cable Retransmission, O.J. 1993 L248 (October 6, 1993).

116. Amended Proposal for a Council Directive on the Legal Protection of Databases, COM(93)464, O.J. 1993 C308 (November 15, 1993).

117. Council Directive 93/98 of October 29, 1993 Harmonizing the Term of Protection of Copyright and Certain Related Rights, O.J. 1993 L290 (November 24, 1993).

Trademarks

118. Council Regulation 3842/86 of December 1, 1986 Laying Down Measures to Prohibit the Release for Free Circulation of Counterfeit Goods, O.J. 1986 L357 (December 18, 1986).

119. Council Directive 89/104 of December 21, 1988 to Approximate the Laws of the Member States Relating to Trade Marks, O.J. 1989 L40 (February 11, 1989).

120. Proposal for a Council Regulation Laying Down Measures to Prohibit the Release for Free Circulation, Export or Transit of Counterfeit and Pirated Goods, COM(93)329, O.J. 1993 C238 (September 2, 1993).

121. Council Regulation 40/94 of December 20, 1993 on the Community Trademark, O.J. 1994 L11/1 (January 14, 1994).

INTERNATIONAL ENVIRONMENTAL LAWS AND REGULATIONS: WASTE DISPOSAL IN EUROPE

Rodney L. Brown, Jr.[311]
Morrison & Foerster

I. Introduction

The safe handling and disposal of waste is an issue of great importance throughout the European Community ("EC" or "Community"). Over the past several years, newspaper articles and television reports have decried the shipment of hazardous wastes from the European Community to former Eastern Bloc and developing countries, as well as the importation of such wastes into certain EC Member States for disposal. Public attention has also focused on the risks to human health and the environment posed by the wide variations in waste handling and disposal practices across the Community. As the EC moves toward realization of an internal market without trade barriers, these variations also raise the possibility of "dumping zones" in Member States with less stringent regulations.

The European Community is responding to these concerns by expanding its already well developed legislation concerning wastes. Limited control by the EC over Member States, however, makes the task of regulating wastes on a consistent Community-wide basis difficult.

Unlike in the United States, where the federal government has the authority to prescribe detailed hazardous waste requirements in all states through statutes such as the Resource Conservation and Recovery Act or "RCRA,"[312] the process is more complicated in the EC. Frequently, Community legislation represents a balancing of Member State interests brought about by a process involving the

[311] The author would like to thank Zane Gresham (San Francisco), Diana Romeu (Brussels), Beth Bragonier and Brad Gentry (London), and Ellen Deason and Alissa J. Stern (Washington, D.C.) for their contributions.

[312] 42 U.S.C. §§ 6901-6992k (1988).

European Commission, European Parliament and Council of Ministers. As such, much of the existing waste legislation gives individual Member States a wide degree of discretion in deciding how to meet Community goals and implement specific directives. As the EC continues the move toward a single market, there is fear that the abolition of internal borders will weaken waste management controls even further.

In the past few years, however, the EC has embarked upon a program to narrow the scope of Member State discretion in regulating wastes, to harmonize regulations throughout the Community, and to strengthen regulatory requirements. To meet these goals, the Community has developed a Waste Management Strategy. This strategy was described by the Commission in a 1989 paper and endorsed by the Council of Ministers in May 1990 and the European Parliament in February 1991. The strategy concentrates on: (i) reduction of waste by preventative action; (ii) re-use of waste if at all possible; and (iii) disposal of waste as near as possible to the site of production.

The Waste Management Strategy both offers benefits and imposes burdensome requirements. On the one hand, harmonized regulations stabilize the business environment and reduce the need to anticipate and deal with diverse legislative approaches in each Member State. On the other hand, the emphasis on recycling and the disposal of wastes at the closest facility can lead to the imposition of costly requirements on business.

At the same time the Community is intensifying its efforts to improve waste management through the Waste Management Strategy and related initiatives, many Member States are also intensifying their efforts. Spain's autonomous community of Catalonia, for example, in 1991 merged many of its hazardous waste regulations into a single law.[313] The Law gives regional governments the power to act in the absence of municipal government action. Unfortunately, as with Community level laws that can entangle businesses in Community-Member State disputes, this law can embroil facilities in disputes between municipal and regional governments.

---

[313] Ley 18 Marzo 1991 Num. 2/1991, R.A.L., 1991, 2322.

In addition to considering waste management policies within Member States, the transboundary shipment of wastes necessitates that the Commission also concern itself with the activities of the international community.

The Basel Convention,[314] the primary international treaty governing movements of hazardous wastes, has significantly affected the formulation of EC legislation. The Convention sets out requirements and prohibitions for the transport of hazardous waste between countries. The EC recently ratified the Convention,[315] after first passing its own regulation on the shipment of waste within, into and out of the European Community.[316] Many non-EC Member European countries have also ratified the Basel Convention, including Hungary, Finland, Romania, the former states of Czechoslovakia,[317] and Yugoslavia.

This paper describes the existing EC legislation on wastes and the various proposals to expand that legislation. Where appropriate, the paper will highlight some of the related initiatives of Member States and the international community.

---

314 United Nations Environment Programme, Conference of Plenipotentiaries on the Global Convention on the Control of Transboundary Movements of Hazardous Waste, Basel Convention on the Control of Transboundary Movements of Hazardous Wastes and their Disposal, U.N.Doc. UNEP/IG.80/3, 22 March 1989 *reprinted in* 28 I.L.M. 657. The Basel Convention entered into force on 5 May 1992. A month later, new hazardous waste strategies were developed at the Earth Summit Conference held in Rio de Janeiro. United Nations Conference on Environment and Development, *Report of the United Nations Conference on Environment and Development, 3-14 June 1992: Rio de Janeiro, Brazil,* Annex II "Agenda 21," 335-353, U.N. Doc. A/CONF.151/21/Rev. 1 (Vol I), U.N. Sales No. E.93.I.8 (Vol. I) (1993).

315 *Council Decision of 1 February 1993 on the conclusion, on behalf of the Community, of the Convention on the control of transboundary movements of hazardous wastes and their disposal (Basel Convention).* 93/98/EEC, 1993 O.J. (L39) 1.

316 *Council Regulation of 1 February 1993 on the Supervision and Control of Shipments of Waste Within, Into and Out of the European Community,* 93/259/EEC, 1993 O.J. (L30) 1.

317 Although neither the Czech Republic nor Slovakia has independently signed the Convention, both have agreed to be bound by its provisions.

II. EC/EU Legislation On Waste

A. Overview

Community efforts at regulating solid wastes, including hazardous wastes, resemble measures used in the United States. Since the mid-1970s, the goals of Community legislation have been to: (i) encourage the recycling or other re-use of waste materials; (ii) ensure the proper disposal of waste materials without harming human health or the environment; (iii) urge Member States to designate competent authorities to supervise waste disposal, including the licensing and inspection of disposal facilities and the development of waste disposal plans; and (iv) make the "polluter pay" for the costs of this regulatory system by imposing such costs on the producers/holders of the wastes.

Recently, both the U.S. and the EC have directed more of their efforts to reducing waste at its source. The current thinking is that it is more cost-effective to reduce the scale of the problem in the first place than it is to clean-up afterwards. Furthermore, following the U.S. lead, the EC, in addition to specifying procedures and standards to avoid pollution, is moving toward assessing liability for actual damage done from improper waste handling. In doing so, however, the EC is expressly trying not to recreate the problems of the U.S. Superfund program.

EC directives usually set out policies which rely on Member States for implementation, but leave the actual implementing mechanisms to individual Member States. Due to concerns regarding national sovereignty, the EC has been reluctant to infringe too far on Members' traditional regulatory authority, and Members, for the most part, have been unwilling to relinquish all of their power. In addition, the Community is facing the practical difficulty of getting Members with diverse viewpoints on environmental issues to agree on a single set of standards. Finally, there are different notions among the Member States about which types of regulations are likely to succeed in controlling wastes.

For purposes of clarity, the following analysis of the EC's regulatory measures is organized under the following headings: Definitions of "Waste" and "Disposal"; Producer Requirements; Transportation Requirements; Disposal Requirements; and Reduction and Recycling Requirements. It should be emphasized, however, that most of the legislation regarding waste is not structured in this manner and contains provisions applicable throughout the waste handling chain.

B. Definitions of "Waste" and "Disposal"

In any regulatory scheme on waste disposal, the key issues are: What is a "waste"? and What constitutes "disposal"? Many of the strengths and weaknesses of the regulatory framework rest on these definitions. For industry specifically, these definitions might mean the difference between transporting what one country considers industrial wastes and another considers hazardous wastes.

"Wastes" were first defined by the EC in the 1975 directive on waste management (the "Waste Directive") as: "any substance or object which the holder disposes of or is required to dispose of."[318] This directive was substantially amended in March 1991, however, to expand and give greater specificity to the definition of waste.[319] The amended directive encompasses all materials that are "discarded," in addition to the more traditional wastes. It includes: production residues; off-specification products; out-of-date products; spilled materials; products the use of which has been banned by law; products for which the holder has no further use; clean-up residues; and any other materials sent for disposal.

In addition, the Waste Directive defines "disposal" and "recovery." Both of these activities constitute "discarding" for purposes of the waste definition. Disposal includes operations which do not lead to the possibility of re-use, such as: landfill; other releases into the environment; biological or chemical treatment prior to discarding a material; incineration; and storage, blending, mixing or repackaging pending any such operations. Recovery includes operations which may lead to re-use, such as: use as a fuel to generate energy; solvent reclamation or regeneration; other

---

318 *Council Directive of 15 July 1975 on a framework for waste management,* 75/442/EEC, 1975 O.J. (L194) 39.

319 *Council Directive of 18 March 1991, amending Directive 75/442/EEC, on the revised framework for waste,* 91/156/EEC, O.J. (L78) 32.

recycling or reclamation activities; land-spreading for agricultural use; and storage of materials intended for any such operations.[320]

Several other directives define sub-categories of wastes which are subject to special requirements because of their hazardous properties. The most extensive of these directives is the 1978 directive on toxic and dangerous waste (the "Toxic Waste Directive").[321] This directive broadly defines "toxic and dangerous" waste as any waste which contains certain materials which are "of such a nature, in such quantities or in such concentrations as to constitute a risk to health or the environment."[322] An Annex lists 27 types of compounds which are denoted as "requiring priority consideration" as constituents in toxic or dangerous wastes. These include: various heavy metals; phenols; organohalogen compounds; pharmaceutical compounds; asbestos; metal finishing substances; and other similar materials. The directive does not, however, provide further guidance as to the circumstances in which any such materials might constitute a "risk to health or the environment."[323]

---

[320] To ensure coordination with the international community, the directive references OECD and Basel Convention definitions for waste, disposal and recovery.

[321] *Council Directive of 20 March 1978 on toxic and dangerous waste*, 78/319/EEC, 1978 O.J. (L84) 43.

[322] *Id.* at 44.

[323] Four other directives which identify certain potentially dangerous wastes for special treatment are: (i) *Council Directive of 1975 on the disposal of waste oils*, 75/439/EEC, 1975 O.J. (L194) 23; amended by *Council Directive of 22 December 1986 amending Directive 75/439/EEC on the disposal of waste oils*, 87/101/EEC, 1987 O.J. (L42) 43, which covers mineral-based oils which have become "unfit for the use for which they were originally intended;" (ii) the 1975 directive on the disposal of polychlorinated biphenyls and polychlorinated terphenyls *Council Directive of 6 April 1976 on the disposal of polychlorinated biphenyls and polychlorinated terphenyls*, 76/403/EEC, 1976 O.J. (L108) 41; (iii) the 1987 directive on the prevention and reduction of environmental pollution by asbestos *Council Directive of 19 March 1987 on the prevention and reduction of environmental pollution by asbestos*, 87/217/EEC, 1987 O.J. (L85) 40; and (iv) the 1978 directive on waste from the titanium dioxide industry *Council Directive of 20 February 1978 on waste from the titanium dioxide industry*, 78/176/EEC, 1978 O.J. (L54) 19; amended by *Council Directive of 3 December 1982 on procedures for the surveillance and monitoring of environments concerned by waste from the titanium dioxide industry*, 82/883/EEC, 1982 O.J. (L378) 1; *Council Directive of 24 January 1983 amending directive 78/176/EEC on waste from the titanium dioxide industry*, 83/29/EEC, 1983 O.J. (L32) 29; and *Council Directive 92/112/EEC of 15*

In December 1991, in order to clarify and expand the definition of hazardous waste, the Council adopted the Hazardous Waste Directive.[324] When it comes into force (originally scheduled for December 1993), the "Hazardous Waste Directive" will replace the Toxic Waste Directive. The Hazardous Waste Directive defines hazardous waste with reference to three annexes which categorize wastes according to their origin, constituents and concentration. The directive then requires the Commission, using these annexes, to develop lists of hazardous wastes.

The Commission is now struggling to prepare such lists in the form of the European Waste Catalogue ("EWC"). As currently drafted, the EWC includes four categories of wastes: "H" - wastes which are virtually always considered hazardous; "NH" - wastes which are virtually always considered non-hazardous; "H*" - wastes which are usually considered hazardous, but which may in some circumstances be non-hazardous because they do not exhibit any of the hazardous characteristics; and "NH*" - wastes which are usually considered non-hazardous, but which may have sufficiently hazardous characteristics to constitute hazardous wastes in particular circumstances. The European Waste Catalogue was originally scheduled for completion in the Summer of 1993, but it is now mired in controversy.

Some Member States are augmenting the Commission's efforts with even stronger regulations. Germany, for example, is considering redefining wastes from "residues which cannot be recycled" to "unavoidable residues which cannot be re-utilized as secondary materials."[325] The new definition aims to distinguish wastes from "economic goods," thereby promoting the reuse or recycling of used materials. This distinction will become increasingly important as the EC focuses more attention on recycling issues.

December 1992 on procedures for harmonizing the programmes for the reduction and eventual elimination of pollution caused by waste from the titanium dioxide industry, 92/112/EEC, 1992 O.J. (L409) 11.

324 *Council Directive of 12 December 1991 on hazardous waste,* 91/689/EEC, 1991 O.J. (L377) 20.

325 HAZNEWS, No. 54, September 1992.

C. Producer Requirements

The EC has historically imposed relatively few express requirements on waste producers with respect to their handling of wastes generated at their own facilities. In general, reliance has been placed on the broader health and safety provisions in the EC and Member State legislation to protect against problems at a producer's site. More recently, however, the EC has begun increasing waste producer responsibilities.

The amended Waste Directive codifies the "polluter pays" principle and requires that waste producers pay disposal costs. It also requires all waste producers that carry out disposal and recovery operations on site to obtain a permit from the Member State in which their facility operates (for non-hazardous waste this requirement can be waived if the Member State has in place rules governing these activities).

When the Hazardous Waste Directive comes into force, producers will be subject to even more stringent controls. The Hazardous Waste Directive requires producers to: conduct waste analyses to identify the types of waste being produced; keep extensive records concerning the waste they generate and make these records available to competent authorities upon request; ensure that waste is disposed of only by licensed collectors and disposal facilities; separate hazardous waste from other materials for disposal, recovery, collection or transport purposes. The directive also imposes stricter monitoring and inspection controls.

Furthermore, waste producers must comply with the more stringent waste transport requirements laid out in the new Waste Shipments Regulation. (This is discussed in detail in the next section).

In addition to focusing upon detailed regulatory requirements concerning the handling of hazardous waste by producers, the EC has been considering legislation concerning the liability of waste producers for damage caused by their wastes. One of these measures is an amended proposal for a directive which would impose strict, joint and several liability on those enterprises which produce, handle or dispose of hazardous wastes in such a way that injures people, damages property, or harms the environment (the

"Producer Liability Proposal")[326] The emphasis of the proposal is on establishing liability for actual damage caused, rather than for procedures violated.

It seems increasingly unlikely, however, that the EC will adopt the Producer Liability Proposal. The trend seems to be moving toward a combination of a mixed liability system and a publicly administered compensation scheme funded by contributions levied on waste producing or processing industries. This is the approach taken in the Commission's recent "Green Paper" or discussion document on civil liability.[327]

The Green Paper advocates a mixed system of strict and fault-based liability. Strict liability would be limited to environmental damage caused by future high risk activities, while fault-based liability would be applied for damages arising from activities in the past. In order to pay for clean-up measures where no producer can be found accountable, the Green Paper proposes to combine these liability mechanisms with publicly administered compensation systems. The compensation systems would be financed by taxing the industry sectors most closely linked to the probable origins of particular types of damage.

The Green Paper also dovetails with the provisions of the Council of Europe ("COE") Convention on Civil Liability which was also agreed to in June 1993.[328] The Convention provides for strict, joint and several liability for environmental damage caused by certain industrial or waste disposal facilities. Unlike the Producer Liability Proposal, however, the Convention, in some cases, will hold disposers accountable for wastes previously disposed of, but currently harming the environment. Under the Convention, the liability would run for a five year period starting from the time the claimant should know or should have known of the damage,

---

[326] *Amended proposal for a Council Directive on civil liability for damage caused by waste*, com(91) 219, 1991 O.J. (C192)6, amending *Proposal for a Council Directive on Civil Liability for damage caused by waste*, com(89) 282, 1989. (C251)3.

[327] *Commission Green Paper on Civil Liability*, COM(93)52, approved March 17, 1993.

[328] *Convention on Civil Liability for Damage Resulting from Activities Dangerous to the Environment*, opened for signature, June 21, 1993, Eur. Treaty Series, No. 150.

subject to an absolute deadline of thirty years. The Convention also requires that disposers have sufficient insurance to cover potential liability and eases the way for private citizens to take non-complying disposers to court.

Because the COE Convention has been drafted by experts from COE member Countries, it is seen to represent the best text that these countries can agree upon at this time. Thus, it is likely to become the legal instrument of preference for at least some of the COE members,[329] and the Commission. At the same time, important countries such as Germany, the Netherlands and the U.K. have stated that they do not plan to ratify the Convention.

D. Transportation Requirements

Inadequate disposal capacity in the EC has resulted in a high volume of transfrontier waste shipments. In response to the problems associated with such shipments, the EC recently adopted a comprehensive set of rules governing the transport of wastes shipments within, into and out of the European Community.[330] The goals of this regulation are to replace and extend existing EC legislation on movements of waste, and bring Community rules into line with the Basel Convention and the OECD Decision of March 1992 on waste shipments destined for recovery operations.[331]

Under the Basel Convention, countries are prohibited from exporting hazardous waste to or importing hazardous waste from non-signatory countries for disposal purposes. Members of the Convention which do export hazardous waste for disposal must obtain written consent from importing countries for each specific cargo of waste (although different bilateral agreements can be reached). They also must ensure that the waste will be managed in

---

329 The Council now comprises 27 member countries including all 12 EC Member States.

330 *See supra* note 316.

331 Organisation for Economic Co-Operation and Development Council Decision concerning the control of transfrontier movements of wastes destined for recovery operations, adopted March 30, 1992 C(92)39/FINAL.

an "environmentally sound manner" upon arrival in the importing country.

The OECD Decision of March 1992 establishes a three-tiered framework for regulating wastes shipped internationally for recovery or recycling. It identifies three categories of such wastes — green, amber and red — according to their hazardous characteristics (as defined in the Basel Convention), and sets requirements according to the degree of hazard posed. Shipments of green wastes, which have none of the hazardous characteristics set forth in the Basel Convention, are regulated like shipments of any other good. Shipments of amber and red wastes, on the other hand, are more strictly controlled.

To implement these international treaties the regulation prohibits Member States from exporting wastes for disposal to non-EC countries, with the exception of European Free Trade Association signatories to the Basel Convention. Members are permitted to trade wastes with non-OECD countries for recovery purposes, but only under limited circumstances. The regulation also requires prior notification and authorization, as well as extensive record keeping, for all waste transported between Member States for disposal, or for amber or red wastes transported for recovery. The regulation requires more extensive documentation even for shipments of green wastes.

Notification shall take the form of a consignment note to provide information on: the source and composition of the waste; the transport routes and insurance for the shipment; the measures to be taken to ensure safe transport; and evidence of a contract with a consignee disposal facility "who should possess adequate technical capability" to process the waste. For wastes shipped outside the EC, the consignment note must show evidence of an agreement with the importing country. A competent authority must acknowledge receipt of a draft consignment note for the shipment or object to the shipment within one month of receiving the draft consignment note. Authorities objecting to proposed shipments must base their objections on relevant environmental laws.

The purpose of the notification requirement is to ensure that whoever is receiving hazardous waste shipments actually wants to receive them. It is also to establish a full RCRA-type paper trail on the movement of wastes. Non-complying transporters would be forced to take wastes back to the country of origin.[332]

The regulation imposes further requirements based on the principles of "proximity" and "self-sufficiency." The regulation requires producers to send their wastes to the nearest treatment or disposal centers (assuming that acceptable facilities are available). The regulation also, encourages Member States and regions within Member States to become self-sufficient in their waste disposal practices. In one of the most important gestures toward national sovereignty to protect public health and the environment, the EC regulation gives Member States the broad authority to ban imports of wastes intended for disposal from other Member States (with the exception of imports from smaller Member States lacking the facilities to process their own wastes). To further encourage self-sufficiency, the regulation prohibits Members from exporting their wastes out of the Community if suitable disposal facilities are available within the EC.

Besides implementing many of the provisions of the Basel Convention and OECD Decision, the regulation advances the principles of the Lome IV Convention. The EC signed Lome IV, which prohibits the exports of toxic and hazardous wastes to certain African, Caribbean and Pacific States, in response to the furor over shipment of waste into developing countries.[333]

Other specific requirements applicable to the transport of hazardous waste are contained in the Hazardous Waste Directive. Under this directive, more people would be subject to transporter requirements. The directive expands the definition of transporters to include "waste brokers" or businesses which arrange for the disposal or the recovery of waste on behalf of others. Formerly, these waste brokers operated freely in the void left by other piecemeal regulations. On this issue, the British take an even firmer stand. Comparable British regulations would broaden liability to

---

332 Beginning on April 1, 1993, the British will go even further by requiring those non-complying transporters to compensate authorities for finding the transporters' transgressions (Environmental Protection Act 1990), ch. 43 (Eng.)

333 Fourth ACP-EEC Convention (Lomé IV), TS, 1989, 1991 O.J. (L229) 3, 29 I.L.M. 809 (1990).

include any foreigners who arrange for the transportation of wastes within, into, or out of Britain.[334]

Despite these restrictions, many citizens still fear that too many dangerous wastes will be buried in their backyards. Pre-empting objections from single market advocates who resist restrictions on any goods, including hazardous wastes, environmental groups are urging regulators to restrain the importation of wastes under "public health" rather than "trade restriction" reasons. In 1988, the European Court of Justice ruled that national environmental legislation can take precedence over European free trade legislation. Efforts by groups within Member States are forcing the Community to take a more systematic look at the issue.

While the EC is working through the free trade aspects of hazardous waste transport, a few Member States have already tried to meet citizen concerns. France, for example, temporarily barred the importation of household wastes after finding used syringes, blood pouches, and other hospital wastes mixed in with domestic garbage imports. Since France has low waste disposal costs, especially relative to countries like Germany, France was an appealing disposal site for many countries' garbage. The result of France's temporary measure was the piling up of garbage -- too expensive to be treated elsewhere -- on French borders, itself creating a substantial hazard.

A small region in Belgium took more drastic measures. The region tried to stop completely wastes coming across its borders. Certain industrial companies fought back, citing a 1984 EC directive which prohibits members from completely banning imports of dangerous wastes.[335] The Court of Justice acknowledged the directive, but

---

334 Department of Environment, Draft Registration of Waste Brokers Scheme.

335 Council Directive of 6 December 1984 on the supervision and control within the European Community of the transfrontier shipment of hazardous waste, 84/631/EEC, 1984 O.J. (L326) 31; amended by *Council Directive of 12 June 1986 amending Directive 84/631/EEC on the supervision and control within the European Community of the trasnfrontier shipment of hazardous waste*, 86/279/EEC, 1986 O.J. (L181) *Council Directive of 23 December 1991 standardizing and rationalizing reports on the implementation of certain Directives relating to the environment*, 91/692/EEC, 1991 O.J. (L377) 48; to be replaced by *Council Regulation (EEC) No. 259/93 of 1 February 1993 on the supervision and control of shipments of waste within, into and out of the European Community*, 93/259/EEC, O.J. (L30) 1.

held that Member States may ban a specific transfer of hazardous wastes if the region has a pressing environmental, health or safety concern. The Court, however, stopped short of allowing a region to ban completely waste imports.[336]

E. Disposal Requirements

In the past, EC legislation imposed relatively few detailed requirements on the operations of waste disposal facilities. Directives have historically relied on Member States to "take steps to ensure that wastes are disposed of without endangering human health or harming the environment."[337] Member State authorities have regulated the operating, siting and record keeping procedures of waste handling facilities through the issuance of permits.

The EC is now attempting to tighten disposal regulations at the Community level. In a move to harmonize disposal standards, the Commission has drafted several proposals which would impose specific requirements on particular types of disposal facilities.

One proposed directive would harmonize standards for all landfills.[338] The proposal is designed to limit waste disposal in landfills and shift the emphasis to reducing waste production and increasing recycling. As proposed, the landfill directive would impose strict licensing, monitoring and reporting requirements. It would also mandate construction and operating requirements, including permeability and location standards. Further, as proposed, the directive would ban the landfilling of liquid, infectious and other wastes that do not meet certain leachability tests. Liability provisions for damage resulting from landfill of waste are currently under consideration.

Another directive has been proposed to harmonize standards for waste incinerators.[339] The proposed directive would apply an integrated permitting approach to emissions of dangerous

---

[336] *Reimports of Waste: EC Commission v. Belgium*, 259/93, 1993 C.M.L.R. 365 (1992).

[337] *See Council Directive of 15 July 1975 supra* note 316 at 40..

[338] *Proposal for a Council Directive on the landfill of waste*, COM(91)102 final — SYN 335, 1991 O.J. (C190) 1.

[339] *Proposal for a Council Directive on the incineration of hazardous waste*, COM(92)9

substances in an effort to reduce air, soil, surface and groundwater pollution. As proposed, the directive would prescribe standards for construction and operation of all hazardous waste incinerators. It would also impose strict licensing, record keeping and monitoring requirements.

Increasing regulation of waste disposal facilities, along with tighter restrictions on the export of hazardous wastes, is forcing Community officials to consider either updating existing facilities to meet new standards or building new, state-of-the-art facilities. This puts the Community in a sort of "Catch 22" situation. The prohibitive cost of improving existing facilities to meet the new requirements, would likely lead to their closure, while building new facilities would be politically difficult given the limited amount of available land and strong opposition to new facilities by private citizens.

While the Community debates this issue, a few Member States are already coming to terms with the difficulties raised by these options. The legislation is primarily focused on cutting down waste at the source so as to discourage the need for additional disposal facilities. The Dutch, for example, are proposing to tax wastes headed for landfill storage by directly taxing landfill operators. France is similarly planning to levy a tax of 50 Francs on each ton of waste deposited in a dump site. These measures assume that the landfill operators will pass on the tax to waste producers. The intent is to make landfills expensive enough to make producing less economically attractive even considering the cost of updating machinery or production processes.

Spain is considering a front-end tax imposed on sources that produce hazardous waste rather than a waste end fine assessed for damages caused.[340] The tax, similar to the tax Superfund imposes on the chemical and petroleum industries,[341] would be assessed on hazardous waste producers on an industry-wide basis. The idea is to force companies to internalize the cost of producing hazardous

---

1992 O.J. (C130), 1.

340 *See* Ley 18 Marzo, 1991 *supra* note 313.

341 CERCLA § 111, 42 U.S.C. § 9611 (1988).

wastes. Typically, costs associated with hazardous waste production are one of a number of environmental externalities left out of manufacturers' cost calculations. The tax encourages companies to reduce their production of hazardous wastes to gain a competitive edge. Other economic incentives are expected at both the Member State and Community levels.

England and Wales, on the other hand, have implemented a regulation focused on setting standards and procedures for operation of storage facilities. This regulation tries to ensure the safe storage of hazardous wastes by designating the amount of hazardous wastes that may be stored at a site.[342] In granting a consent, the regional hazardous substance authority can impose conditions on how, where, and for how long the wastes may be stored. Similar legislation is being considered for Scotland.

The England and Wales regulation has already been subject to abuse, however. Some overly aggressive disposal operators have tried to evade the regulation by dividing their sites and claiming to be able to store the maximum allowable quantity at each cut up portion of a site. Regulators are trying to remedy this loophole by counting the adjacent sites of parents and subsidiaries, or companies and branches, as single sites. This remedy is already running into other problems involving land transfers.

F. Reduction and Recycling Requirements

1. Packaging

With packaging wastes, the EC is increasingly turning to reduction, re-use and recycling to get at the source of the problem. In the mid-1980s, the EC began to promote the re-use and recycling of particular waste materials. The first initiatives targeted beverage containers. The 1985 "Beverage Containers Directive"[343] required Member States to take steps to increase recycling and re-use by reducing the amount of waste beverage containers produced, increasing consumer awareness of the benefits of re-use and recycling, facilitating re-use, recycling or collection of renewable or

---

[342] The Planning (Hazardous Substances) Act of 1990, ch. 10 (Eng).

[343] *Council Directive of 27 June 1985 on containers of liquids for human consumption.* 85/339/EEC, 185 O.J. (L176), 18.

non-renewable containers, and informing consumers of new refillable and/or recyclable containers by means of a label or other marking on the container itself.

To improve packaging legislation, the Commission first considered proposing amendments to existing directives. For example, the Commission wanted to improve the Beverage Containers Directive by introducing obligatory recycling schemes in the Member States. However, it instead chose to undertake work on an even broader proposal for a directive on plastics waste.

Early drafts of the proposed plastics directive envisioned requiring plastics producers and users to manage waste recovery and recycling programs. The drafts set different recycling targets for plastics waste according to their sources: packaging and domestic waste; construction; automobiles; agriculture; commerce and distribution; and production and processing activities.

Even this proposal, however, seemed too narrow in scope. The Commission thus, proposed a directive which would impose even stricter recovery, recycling and disposal duties on Member States.[344] This proposed directive would obligate packaging waste producers and distributors to ensure that packaging is re-usable or recoverable, or it will be banned from the market. Re-use and recycling targets would be set at 90% and 60%, respectively, within 10 years of the directive's application. The draft directive would also impose limits on concentrations of heavy metals and dangerous substances in packaging materials. Industry generally supports the proposal because it permits the use of a wide range of packaging material and bases its targets, at least in part, on economic criteria.

Member countries are also looking to control packaging wastes. In Germany, a recent ordinance obligates manufactures and distributors to take back used packaging.[345] The ordinance exempts manufactures and distributors who use private collection and recycling systems — a new market opportunity in the environmental field — to collect and reuse packaging waste. The

---

344 *Proposal for a Council Directive on packaging and packaging waste,* COM (92) 278 final SYN 436, 1992 O.J. (C263) 1. (Intended to replace 85/339/EEC).

345 German ordinance on the Avoidance and Reduction of Packaging Waste.

ordinance now requires the collection of transport and wrap around packaging, as well as sales packaging.

France recently enacted a similar decree which aims to recover 75% of household packaging wastes by 1997.[346]

The Netherlands has set even higher goals, hoping to reduce packaging wastes to zero by the year 2000. By using private agreements or "covenants" between the Government and individual businesses, the Netherlands hopes to achieve greater compliance with private contracts than it would with more traditional regulations.

2. Use of Hazardous Materials

Europe has been increasingly proactive about limiting the use of dangerous substances. For example, a 1976 directive restricts the marketing and use of certain dangerous substances and preparations.[347] Subsequent amendments expand the restrictions of this framework directive to include benzene,[348] certain fire retardants,[349] PCBs and PCTs[350] and certain asbestos products.[351]

A new directive, which entered into force on October 18, 1992, addresses the marketing and disposal of batteries and accumulators containing certain concentrations of heavy metals.[352] This directive bars the sale of batteries containing more than the prescribed levels of mercury and urges Members to recover or dispose of spent batteries. Similar use restriction measures are expected to follow.

---

346 Decret No. 92-377 du [1]er avril 1992 , J.O. 5,003 (1992).

347 *Council Directive of 27 July 1976 on the framework for the approximation of the laws, regulations and administrative provisions of the Member States relating to restrictions on the marketing and use of certain dangerous substances and preparations*, 76/769/EEC, 1976 O.J. (L262) 201.

348 82/806/EEC, 1982 O.J. (L339) 55.

349 83/267/EEC, 1983 O.J. (L147) 9.

350 85/467/EEC, 1985 O.J. (L269) 56.

351 91/659/EEC, 1991 O.J. (L363) 36.

352 *Council Directive of 18 March 1991 on the harmonization of laws for the separate collection and disposal of batteries and accumulators containing certain dangerous substances*, 91/157/EEC, 1991 O.J. (L78) 38.

III. CONCLUSION

The EC's waste management regulations are rife with political difficulties, especially those regulations dealing with hazardous waste. Whereas the American federal government can choose to occupy a regulatory field or to take a less intrusive but still dominant lead, the EC has the difficulty of contending with an emerging community of independent countries not completely sure how they want to be regulated from a centralized institution. This makes handling hazardous waste problems even more difficult. When regulating disposal sites, for example, the EC has to keep in mind the high amount of wastes produced in some countries and the need to attract capital in others. When restricting the transit of hazardous wastes, EC regulators have to balance public concerns in industrial localities with infringing on the idea of a single market, the primary reason the Members joined together in the first place. When passing regulations and directives, the EC is restricted by the limited power the Community has over individual Members and the vulnerability of the still new Community structure. Despite these impediments, the EC has, and continues to make great strides toward an effective system of waste management, particularly for hazardous waste.

INTERNATIONAL TRADE AND THE ENVIRONMENT: A RESEARCH GUIDE

Margaret Aycock
Foreign and International Law Librarian
The O'Quinn Law Library
University of Houston

I. INTRODUCTION

All known life exists in a thin layer wrapped around the globe between the earth's molten core and the hostile cold environment of space. Although life extends from the oceans' deepest trenches to the highest mountain peaks, in proportion to the earth, it is no thicker than the shine on a billiard ball.[353]

From space the earth appears to be a water planet. Land comprises only 30% of the earth's surface. This figure is misleading, since a third of the land is arid or semi-arid, 11% is permanently under ice, and 10% is tundra. Most of the rest of the land is too poor, too thin, or too wet to be of value for agriculture. Only 11% of the land is good for farming, and almost all of this is already in use.[354]

Already more than 1 billion people, nearly a quarter of the earth's population live in absolute poverty and are unable to meet their basic needs for food, housing, and clothing.

The world's population is expected to double by the year 2100. Most of this population growth is taking place in developing countries which are the least able to cope with the consequences. By the turn of this century, 19 of the world's largest 25 cities will be in developing countries.[355] Transportation, communication, health, and sanitation systems are likely to break down as these megacities grow. Population growth fuels both the destruction of the environment and human destitution.

---

353 Geoffrey Lean, and Don Hinrichsen, , *WWF Atlas of the Environment* (Santa Barbara, CA: ABC - CLIO, 1994), 11.

354 Ibid.

355 Ibid., 21.

The economic trends in both the industrialized and developing countries are even more harmful than the population growth in numbers. The rich are getting richer and the poor are getting poorer. Both phenomena intensify the environmental crisis.

In the Third World, poverty is the most destructive agent against the environment. Governments are over-exploiting their natural resources in an attempt to pay off their foreign debt. Governments also encourage the planting of cash crops to earn much needed foreign exchange.

The poorest people in the Third World are forced to clear the tropical forests and degrade marginal soils to feed their families. If people cannot afford to buy food, landowners choose to grow cash crops on their land, such as cotton, coffee, tea, or sugar for export. Cash crops take up the best land and eliminate its use for food production. The landowners who grow the cash crops receive most of the Third World's agricultural credit, fertilizers, pesticides, and agricultural advice which are then not available for food production.

If more developing countries industrialized, they could earn more from their commodities by processing them and turning them into finished products. Developing countries have the advantage of plentiful raw materials and cheap labor, but they lack the most sophisticated science and technology, large markets and established business connections. Even with the latest GATT/WTO agreement, world markets are not free and are not easy to penetrate.

The rich industrialized countries contribute the most to pollution. The industrialized nations, with only a fifth of the world's population, emit two thirds of the gases that cause global warming and 85% of the CFC's which are destroying the earth's stratospheric ozone layer. They are responsible for almost all the damage caused by acid rain.

In May 1990, 300 of the world's top experts convened to take part in the United Nations Panel on Climate Change. Their report predicted that by the year 2020, the earth would average 1.3 degrees centigrade warmer than now, and that the temperature would reach 3 degrees centigrade warmer by the year 2070. A rise of 2 degrees would produce temperatures last seen 125,000 years ago, and 3 degrees would make the world hotter than it has been in the last 2 million years. With every degree centigrade rise, plant and tree species have to move about 56 miles (90 kilometers) toward the poles to survive.[356] Many species will not be able to spread fast enough.

Species are now becoming extinct at 25,000 times the natural rate, and the disappearances are increasing. By the year 2050 half of all the species alive today could be driven to extinction,[357] and most before their economic potential can be assessed or tapped. Pollution, overhunting, and overfishing play a part, but the most important factor is the loss of habitat due to farming, industrial uses, and deforestation for fuel.

It is predicted that developing countries will be the hardest hit by the climate change. Arid regions are expected to dry out further, and millions of people will be displaced by droughts and harvest failures as rainfall patterns change. In the past as conditions grew harsher, people could move to more congenial areas. On a crowded planet, divided by national frontiers and strict immigration laws, it will be harder to find anywhere for economic refugees to go.

Although the linkage between the environment and development was recognized as far back as the 1972 Stockholm Conference, little progress has been made toward the integration of environmental dimensions into trade and development policy.

In 1983, the United Nations established the World Commission on Environment and Development also known as the Brundtland Commission. It was this commission which first discussed environmental survival through sustainable development.

The Commission noted that rising poverty in poor countries and increasing pollution in rich ones are both unsustainable. Poverty and pollution are destroying the earth's life support systems leading to economic collapse. The Commission found that economic growth, if it is to continue has to be sustainable, meaning that it must meet the needs of the present without jeopardizing the future of coming generations.

---

356 Ibid., 93.

357 Ibid., 127.

In many ways, the United Nations Conference on Environment and Development held in Rio in June 1992 was all about money. Delegates debated how much the North should give the South, how to relieve world debt, and how to open markets to developing countries.

UNCED, also known as the Earth Summit, produced several documents: The Rio Declaration on Environment and Development containing 27 principles; Agenda 21 which is the plan of action for sustainable development for the 21st century and beyond; a non-legally binding statement containing the principles on management conservation and sustainable development of all types of forests; an institutional arrangement resulting in the formation of the Commission on Sustainable Development; and a funding mechanism.

While important, these international agreements are at best a blueprint which by themselves will not save species, protect the oceans, improve health or alleviate poverty. The true test of Rio will be the commitment of governments to follow through with their own national programs, by participating in international organizations, and through the enforcement of international environmental treaties.

There has been an evolution of thought from conservation in the 1940's and 1950's to ecology in the 1970's and now international trade and the environment. Another way to characterize this is to speak of first and second generation environmental problems. First generation environmental problems include the pollution of water, air, and the soil by industry or through activities associated with poverty and underdevelopment. Second generation environmental problems include acid rain, depletion of the stratospheric ozone, global warming, deforestation, desertification, biodiversity, international traffic in toxic wastes, and protection of the environment in times of armed conflicts.

These concerns and ideas are reflected in the international environmental law literature. There is a wealth of materials in many formats concerning the first generation environmental problems, but the second generation environmental problems are relatively new. Most of the literature concerning international trade and the environment is especially recent. One finds second generation issues primarily being discussed in journals and law review articles, and books on these topics are only now appearing.

Environmental lawyers must know the science behind the environmental predictions and understand the studies which support the environmental impact assessments. Consequently, they must consult scientific literature as well as review strictly legal primary and secondary sources. This sometimes raises difficult issues for a law librarian who must acquire materials to support an attorney's or faculty member's research, but who must—because of financial, space, or anticipated use constraints—draw a line between technical and scientific literature and that which is appropriate for a law library collection.

Another often difficult distinction is that between law and policy. Are the reports, books, articles, newletters, and speeches of the "Green parties" and environmental organizations too policy-oriented for a law library? How does one handle materials which are of current interest, but may not be of interest in five years' time?

The scope of environmental law literature, whether national or international, is also difficult to define. When do national environmental problems become transnational, and when do transnational environmental problems become global? What material belongs in foreign law collections in contrast to publications of only domestic law interest to legal practitioners and planners within a particular country?

Since there is no easy way to resolve these problems, the scope of the literature and hence, of this guide, cannot be easily defined. I have included in this bibliography, primary and secondary materials which I hope will be helpful both for research and for collection development. I have annotated the entries whenever possible.

II. GENERAL WORKS

Lang, Winfried. *Internationaler Umweltschutz: Völkerrecht und Aussenpolitik zwischen Ökonomie und Ökologie.* Vienna: Wirtschaftsverlag Dr. Anton Orac, 1989. 210 p. This provides a good overview of international environmental law. However, the economic issues are barely mentioned despite the title. The bibliography, found on pp. 187-189, is a good one.

Low, Patrick, ed. *International Trade and the Environment*. World Bank Discussion Papers, no. 159. Washington, D.C.: World Bank, 1992. x, 365 p.

Smith, Turner T., and Pascale Kromarek. *Understanding US and European Environmental Law: A Practitioner's Guide. International Environmental Law and Policy Series*. London: Graham & Trotman, 1989. xiv, 176 p. This book grew out of a conference held in Brussels on February 26-27, 1987 which was co-sponsored by the ABA Standing Committee on Environmental Law and the Institute for European Environmental Policy. The book focuses on the role played by law, lawyers and legal institutions in environmental regulation in Europe and in the United States. An appendix discusses the role of technical and economic analysis in environmental regulation.

Wathen, Thomas A. *A Guide to Trade and the Environment*. New York: Environmental Grantmakers Association, 1992. 97 p.

Zaelke, Durwood, Paul Orbuch, and Robert F. Housman. *Trade and the Environment: Law, Economics and Policy*. Washington, D.C.: Island Press, c1993. xv, 318 p. This book is a collection of 20 articles covering global and regional perspectives on trade and the environment. It was published under the auspices of the Center for International Environmental Law, Washington, D.C.

III. Reference Sources

A. Bibliographies

Bartels, Martin, et al. *Bibliography on Transnational Law of Natural Resources*. Studies in Transnational Law of Natural Resources, Vol. 3, published for the Institut für Ausländisches und Internationales Wirtschaftsrecht, Frankfurt am Main. Deventer: Kluwer, 1981. 227 p. This bibliography focuses on the mining of metals in developing countries. References are to publications in English, Spanish, French, and German. Part I (pp. 17-70) is a bibliographical essay with brief citations to publications. Part II (pp. 73-227) is an alphabetical bibliography giving full citations to the publications mentioned in Part I. Headings include "Fiscal Regime," "Forms of Agreement," "Industrial Relations," "Investor Consortia under the Antitrust Law," "Natural and Social Environment," and "Politics of Transnational Investment".

Dean, Judith M. *Trade and the Environment: A Survey of the Literature.* Policy Research Working Papers, WPS 966. Washington, D.C.: Office of the Vice President, Development Economics, World Bank, 1992. 27 p.

Field, Barry C., and Cleve E. Willis. *Environmental Economics: A Guide to Information Sources.* Man and the Environment Information Series, vol. 8. Detroit: Gale, 1979. xix, 243 p.

Grieves, Forest L. *International Law, Organization, and the Environment: A Bibliography and Research Guide.* The Institute of Government Research, International Studies, no. 4. Tucson: The University of Arizona Press, c1974. 131 p. This bibliography includes selected materials on law, policy, and science that relate to the general subject area of international law, international organization, and the environment. Although now somewhat dated, it remains an excellent guide to the literature. The book contains a 13 page list of environmental organizations and their addresses.

Marine Affairs Bibliography. 1- 1980- 3x year plus annual cumulation. This bibliography of books, articles, government documents and conference proceedings devotes a section to the preservation of the marine environment in each issue. It is edited by Christian Wiktor and Larry Wenger and is published by the University of Virginia Law Library.

Munro, Robert J. *International Environmental Law: A Bibliography.* Dobbs Ferry: Oceana, 1990. ii, 121 p. This extensive bibliography of law and non-law sources is divided into 15 main headings and 24 geographical and subject subheadings. Six pages provide references to books, articles, and documents specifically concerned with economics and the environment. The European Communities, multinational corporations, and the Organisation for Economic Cooperation and Development are among the subheadings.

Public International Law: A Current Bibliography of Books and Articles. 1- 1975-. This bibliography which is published twice a year by the Max Planck Institute in Heidelberg includes headings on environmental protection and the economy. Subheadings include raw materials, transfer of technology, and transborder cooperation.

Templeton, Virginia Evans, and Howard J. Taubenfeld. *World Environment Law Bibliography: Non-periodical Literature in Law and the*

Social Sciences Published Since 1970 in Various Languages with Selected Reviews and Annotations from Periodicals. Littleton, Colo.: Rothman, 1987. xxi, 480 p. The bibliography includes 2324 items in 15 subject headings. Section 4, Economics and the Environment, lists items 317-441. The bibliography also covers databases. There are personal name, key word, and non-English title indexes as well as a list of periodical abbreviations.

B. Dictionaries

Collin, Peter Hodgson. *Dictionary of Ecology and the Environment*. London: Collin Pub., 1988. 197 p. This dictionary provides British terminology and usage. There is a 1992 edition.

Robinson, Nicholas A. *Environmental Law Lexicon*. New York: Law Journal Seminars Press, 1992. 1 v. (looseleaf). This dictionary of environmental science terminology is prepared primarily for lawyers. It includes the most frequently encountered environmental, scientific, and technical words giving the prevailing American usage. References are made to U.S. regulations, statutes and cases. Most of the book contains definitions arranged alphabetically. About a fourth of the contents is a list of acronyms and abbreviations.

Stoloff, Neil. *Environmental Law Dictionary*. New York: Oceana, 1993. 166 p. This dictionary defines all the environmental law terms commonly used today. Acronyms for statutes and regulations, and agencies are also included.

Tilleman, William A. *Dictionary of Environmental Law and Science*. Toronto: Emond Montgomery, 1994. 250 p. This dictionary defines over 10,000 legal, scientific, and technical terms in common usage in Canadian environmental law practice.

C. Guides and Handbooks

Salter, John R. *European Environmental Law*. Dordrecht: Kluwer, 1994. 1100 p. (looseleaf). This is a succinct compilation of current European environmental community legislation and cases.

Weiss, Edith Brown, Daniel Barstow Magraw, and Paul C. Szasz. *International Environmental Law: Basic Instruments and References*. Ardsley-on-Hudson and Dobbs Ferry: Transnational Publishers, 1992- xxiii, 749 p.

D. Atlases

Lean, Geoffrey, Don Hinrichsen, and Adam Markham. *WWF Atlas of the Environment*. New York: Prentice Hall, 1990. 192 p. This fascinating atlas contains maps, charts, graphs and commentary on all aspects of the environment. The current state of the world's environment as well as projections of future developments are discussed. Among the topics covered are the urban revolution, the GNP and the debt squeeze, industrialization and development, the tropical timber trade, acid rain, urban air pollution, toxic and hazardous wastes, and wildlife trade. The atlas concludes with a 5 page bibliography.

E. Encyclopedias

Boes, Marc, ed. *International Encyclopaedia of Laws: Environmental Law*. Deventer and Boston: Kluwer, 1991- 2 v. (looseleaf). The encyclopedia is divided into sections covering international law, EC law and selected foreign countries' laws. An in depth analysis of each country's environmental legal system as well as a complete list of sources is provided.

Cunningham, William P., ed. *The Environmental Encyclopedia*. Detroit: Gale, 1994. 981 p. This encyclopedia contains approximately 3000 entries by over 100 contributors. The encyclopedia includes definitions, articles and biographical sketches in roughly equal proportions. References are listed for further reading.

The Environment Encyclopedia and Directory. London: Europa; distributed by Gale, 1994. 381 p. This encyclopedia is divided into five sections and contains twenty maps. It covers climate, population, deforestation and pollution. Its glossary provides brief definitions of 1000 terms. There is a directory of 3000 government and nongovernmental agencies listed by country. The encyclopedia includes a bibliography of over 1000 periodical titles and biographical sketches for 600 environmental leaders.

Tromans, Stephen, Malcolm Grant, and Albert Mumma. *Encyclopedia of Environmental Law*. London: Sweet & Maxwell, 1993. 3 v. (looseleaf). This encyclopedia includes treaties and conventions, EC legislation, U.K. statutes and subordinate legislation, and codes of practice.

IV. Primary Sources

A. Document Collections

Hohmann, Harald, ed. *Basic Documents of International Environmental Law.* International Environmental Law and Policy Series. London: Graham & Trotman, 1992. 1850 pp. in 3 v. Volume I: The Important Declarations, Volume II: The Important Agreements, Volume III: The Important Agreements (continued). This compilation containing 200 documents reproduces the most important environmental resolutions, guidelines, decisions, recommendations and drafts of international organizations (especially UNO/UNEP, ECE, OECD, Council of Europe, and the International Law Association, Institut de Droit International, and the International Law Commission). It also includes important environmental conventions and draft conventions. Official citations to the documents are provided. There is a list of acronyms.

Molitor, Michael R., ed. *International Environmental Law. Primary Materials.* Deventer: Kluwer Law and Taxation, 1991. Approximately 70 instruments are reproduced. Most of the documents are derived from U.S. sources.

United Nations. *Agenda 21, Rio Declaration, Forest Principles: Drafts.* New York: United Nations, 1992. 1 v. Sales No. E 92.I.16. This is a collection of major environmental agreements discussed at the Earth Summit (UNCED). Among the issues addressed in these documents are international cooperation to accelerate sustainable development in developing countries, combatting poverty, changing consumption patterns, demographic dynamics, and integrating the environment and development in decision-making.

Weiss, Edith Brown, Daniel Barstow Magraw, and Paul C. Szasz. *International Environmental Law: Basic Instruments and References.* Ardsley-on-Hudson and Dobbs Ferry: Transnational Publishers, 1992- xxiii, 749 p. This is a very handy reference source. It contains a comprehensive list of more than 870 international environmental agreements, resolutions, decisions, and guidelines, organized by subject. Multiple citations to documents are given. 85 treaties are reproduced in full text and are arranged by subject matter. The book concludes with an index of popular names.

B. Treaties and Treaty Collections

Multilateral treaties, agreements and guidelines have emerged to protect the marine environment, to prevent air and water pollution, to conserve flora and fauna, and to regulate trade in chemical and toxic substances. Recent international treaties concern the depletion of the ozone layer, the transboundary movement of hazardous wastes, climate change, and the loss of biological diversity.

1. Treaty Collections

Burhenne, W., ed. *International Environmental Law, Multilateral Treaties = Internationales Umweltrecht, Multilaterale Verträge*. Berlin: E. Schmidt, 1974- 6 v. (looseleaf). This set provides the German and English texts of multilateral treaties concerning the environment.

Rüster, B., B. Simma, and M. Block, eds. *International Protection of the Environment*. Treaties and Related Documents. Dobbs Ferry: Oceana, 1970- 30 v. Second Series. 6 volumes (looseleaf). This is the most complete collection of treaties and related documents on the international protection of the environment. Until 1979, almost all of the declarations pertaining to the environment were reprinted. After that date, only selected declarations have been reprinted.

Selected Multilateral Treaties in the Field of the Environment. Cambridge: Grotius, 1991. 2 v. Vol. I, 1933-79 by Kiss, Alexandre Charles, ed. ix, 525 p. Vol. II, 1979-1989 by Rummel-Bulska, Ivana, and Seth Osafo. xi, 527 p. This set is limited to multilateral treaties. Basic data such as membership, parties, and dates of entry into force are provided in separate sections for each treaty. Regrettably, official citations are not provided. Volume I was originally published as UNEP Reference Series No. 3. Special features in Volume II include a chronological index of treaties, a classification of treaties, and a subject index.

Tratados Internacionales sobre Medio Ambiente suscritos por España. Madrid: Ministerio de Obras Publicas, 1993. 461 p. This is a compilation of environmental treaties to which Spain is a party.

2. Individual Treaties

Kramer, Ludwig. *EC Treaty and Environmental Protection Law.* 2nd ed. London: Sweet and Maxwell, 1994. 1 v. As head of Legal Matters and Community Law in DGXI of the European Commission, the author examines the effect of the environmental articles of the EC treaty. He also covers the EC decision-making process, national laws, and financing and implementing Community legislation.

Rest, Alfred. *Convention on Compensation for Transfrontier Environmental Injuries: Draft with Explanatory Notes = Convention sur l'indemnisation des dommages transfrontières causés à l'environnement: projet de texte et exposé des motifs =Abkommen über den Schadenenersatz bei grenzüberschreitenden Umweltschäden: Entwurf mit ausführlicher Begrundung.* Beiträge zur Umweltgestaltung, Heft A53. Berlin: E. Schmidt Verlag, 1976. 276 p. This book is a commentary on the draft convention. The right to compensation and methods of securing a claim for compensation are discussed in separate chapters.

3. Selected Treaties and Other International Acts Regarding International Trade and the Environment

1940 Convention on Nature Protection and Wildlife Preservation in the Western Hemisphere, Washington, D.C., 12 October 1940, entered into force 1 May 1942; 56 Stat. 1354; TS 981; 3 Bevans 630; 161 UNTS 193.

1945 Charter of the United Nations, San Francisco, 26 June 1945, entered into force 24 October 1945; 145 UKTS 805.

1946 International Convention for the Regulation of Whaling, Washington, D.C., 2 December 1946, entered into force 10 November 1948; 161 UNTS 72.

1947 General Agreement on Tariffs and Trade, Geneva, 30 October 1947, not yet in force (in force provisionally since 1 January 1948 under the 1947 Protocol of Provisional Application); 55 UNTS 187.

1949 Convention for the Establishment of an Inter-American Tropical Tuna Commission, with exchange of notes of March 3, 1950. Signed at Washington May 31, 1949; entered into force March 3, 1950. 1 UST 230; TIAS 2044; 80 UNTS 3.

1949 FAO Agreement for the Establishment of a General Fisheries Council for the Mediterranean, Rome, 24 September 1949, entered into force 3 December 1963; 126 UNTS 237.

1951 FAO International Plant Protection Convention, Rome, 6 December 1951, entered into force 3 April 1952; 150 UNTS 67.

1952 International Convention for the High Seas Fisheries of the North Pacific Ocean, Tokyo, 9 May 1952; entered into force June 12, 1953; 4 UST 380; TIAS 2786; 205 UNTS 65.

1958 Treaty Establishing the European Economic Community, Rome, 25 March 1957, entered into force 1 January 1958; 298 UNTS 3.

1958 Convention on Fishing and Conservation of the Living Resources of the High Seas, Geneva, 29 April 1958, entered into force 20 March 1966; 17 UST 138; TIAS 5969; 559 UNTS 285.

1959 Antarctic Treaty, Washington, 1 December 1959, entered into force 23 June 1961; 402 UNTS 71

International Convention for the Conservation of Atlantic Tunas. Done at Rio de Janeiro May 14, 1966; entered into force March 21, 1969. 20 UST 2887; TIAS 6767; 673 UNTS 63

1968 African Convention on the Conservation of Nature and Natural Resources, Algiers, 15 September 1968, entered into force 9 October 1969 (or June 1969); deposited with the OAU.

1969 FAO Convention on the Conservation of the Living Resources of the Southeast Atlantic, Rome, 23 October 1969, entered into force 24 October 1971; 801 UNTS 101.

1972 Convention for the Prevention of Marine Pollution by Dumping from Ships and Aircraft, Oslo, 15 February 1972, entered into force 7 April 1974; UKTS 119 (1975), Cmnd 6228

1973 Convention on International Trade in Endangered Species of Wild Fauna and Flora, Washington, 3 March 1973, entered into force 1 July 1975; 27 UST 1087; TIAS 8249; 993 UNTS 243

1974 Convention on the Protection of the Marine Environment of the Baltic Sea Area, Helsinki, 22 March 1974, entered into force 3 May 1980; 13 ILM 546, 2 Rüster 683

1974 Convention for the Marine Pollution from Land-Based Sources, Paris, 4 June 1974, entered into force 6 May 1978; UKTS 64 (1978), Cmnd 7251, 2 Rüster 748

1976 Convention for the Protection of the Mediterranean, Sea against Pollution, and Protocols. Barcelona, 16 February 1976, entered into force 12 February 1978; 15 ILM 290, 19 Rüster 9497

1976 European Convention for the Protection of Animals Kept for Farming Purposes, Strasbourg, 10 March 1976, entered into force 10 September 1978; ETS 87, UKTS 70 (1979), Cmnd 7684

1978 Protocol Relating to the 1973 International Convention for the Prevention of Pollution from Ships, London, 17 February 1978, entered into force 2 October 1983; Senate Executive Doc. No. 96-1, Executive C; 17 ILM 546

1979 Convention on the Conservation of Migratory Species of Wild Animals, Bonn, 23 June 1979, entered into force 1 November 1983; Misc 11 (1980), Cmnd 7888, 19 ILM 15

1979 Convention on the Conservation of European Wildlife and Natural Habitats, Berne, 19 September 1979, entered into force 1 June 1982; ETS 104, UKTS 56 (1982), Cmnd 8738, 23 Rüster 40

1979 Convention on Long-Range Transboundary Air Pollution, Geneva, 13 November 1979, entered into force 16 March 1983; TIAS 10541

1980 Convention on the Conservation of Antarctic Marine Living Resources, Canberra, 20 May 1980, entered into force 7 April 1982; 33 UST 3476; TIAS 10240

1982 Convention for the Conservation of Salmon in the North Atlantic. Done at Reykjavik March 2, 1982; entered into force October 1, 1983; TIAS 10789

1982 Regional Convention for the Conservation of the Red Sea and Gulf of Aden Environment, Jeddah, 14 February 1982, entered into force 20 August 1985. Text supplied by UNEP.

1982 United Nations Convention on the Law of the Sea, Montego Bay, 10 December 1982, UN Doc. A/CONF.62/122

1983 International Tropical Timber Agreement, Geneva, 18 November 1983, entered into force 1 April 1985; UNCTAD Doc TD/TIMBER/11; Misc. 11(1984), Cmnd 9240

1984 Protocol to the 1979 Convention on Long-Range Transboundary Air Pollution on Long-Term Financing of the Co-operative Programme for Monitoring and Evaluation of the Long-Range Transmission of Air Pollutants in Europe, 28 September 1984, entered into force 28 January 1988; UN Doc. EB.AIR/AC.1/4, 27 ILM 701.

1985 Convention for the Protection of the Ozone Layer, Vienna, 25 March 1985, entered into force 22 September 1988; TIAS 11097

1985 Protocol on the Reduction of Sulphur Emissions or Their Transboundary Fluxes by at Least 30 per cent, Helsinki, 8 July 1985, entered into force 2 September 1987; UN Doc ECE/EB.AIR/12; 27 ILM 707

1986 Single European Act, 17 February 1986, entered into force 1 July 1987; EC Bull. 12 (1986), Cmnd 9758; UKTS 31 (1988), Cmnd. 372; 25 ILM 506

1987 Protocol on Substances that Deplete the Ozone Layer, Montreal, 16 September 1987, entered into force 1 January 1989; UKTS 19 (1990), Cm 977; 26 ILM 1550

1988 Protocol Concerning the Control of Emissions of Nitrogen Oxides or their Transboundary Fluxes, Sofia, 31 October 1988, entered into force 14 February 1991; UKTS 1 (1992), Cm 1787

1989 Convention for the Prohibition of Fishing with Long Driftnets in the South Pacific. Done at Wellington November 24, 1989; entered into force May 17, 1991; for the United States February 28, 1992; 29 ILM 1454

1989 Convention on the Control of Transboundary Movement of Hazardous Wastes and Their Disposal, Basel, 22 March 1989, entered into force 24 May 1992; UN Doc. UNEP/WG.190/4

1991 Convention on the Ban of Imports into Africa and the Control of Transboundary Movement and Management of Hazardous Wastes within Africa, Bamako, 29 January 1991; 30 ILM 775 and 31 ILM 164

1991 Convention on Environmental Impact Assessment in a Transbounday Context, Espoo, 25 February 1991, not in force; UN Doc.E/ECE/1250

1991 Protocol on Environmental Protection to the Antarctic Treaty, Madrid, 4 October 1991, not in force; 30 ILM 1461

1992 Treaty on European Union, Maastrict, 17 February 1992; 31 ILM 253

1992 Convention on the Protection and Use of Transboundary Watercourses and International Lakes, Helsinki, 17 March 1992, not in force; UN Doc. ENVWA/R.53

1992 UN/ECE Convention on the Transboundary Effects of Industrial Accidents, Helsinki, 17 March 1992, not in force; UN Doc. ENVWA/R.54

1992 Convention on the Protection of the Black Sea against Pollution Bucharest, 21 - 22 April 1992, 32 ILM 1110

1992 United Nations Framework Convention on Climate Change, New York, 9 May 1992; UN Doc. A/AC.237/18 (Part II) / Add.1

1992 Convention on Biological Diversity, Rio de Janeiro, 5 June 1992, not in force; UN Doc. UNEP/Bio.Div/N7-INC.5/4

1992 Convention for the Protection of the Marine Environment of the North-East Atlantic, Paris, 22 September 1992, not in force; 32 ILM 1072

1992 North American Free Trade Agreement, Washington, Ottawa and Mexico City, 8, 11, 14, 17 December 1992, entered into force January 1, 1994; 32 ILM 296

1993 North American Agreement on Environmental Cooperation, 32 ILM 1482

1993 Agreement concerning the Establishment of a Border Environment Cooperation Commission and a North American Development Bank, 32 ILM 1547

1994 Final Act of the Uruguary Round
United States Office of the U.S. Trade Representative. Final Act Embodying the Results of the Uruguay Round of Multilateral Trade Negotiations. Version of 15 December 1993. Washington, D.C.: Office

of the U.S. Trade Representative, Executive Office of the President, For Sale by the U.S. G.P.O., Supt. of Documents, 1994. 1 v. (various pagings) The text is also printed in 33 ILM 1

4. Non-binding Instruments

Declaration of the United Nations Conference on the Human Environment, Stockholm (1972); 11 ILM 1416

Nairobi Declaraton on the State of Worldwide Environment (1982), UNEP/GC.10/INF.5; 21 ILM 676

Agenda 21, Rio de Janeiro (1992) Reprinted in Robinson, Nicholas A., ed. *Agenda 21: Earth's Action Plan Annotated.* Dobbs Ferry: Oceana, 1994. 683 p.

Rio Declaration on Environment and Development, Rio de Janeiro (1992); 31 ILM 876.

Statement of Principles of Forests, Rio de Janeiro (1992); 31 ILM 882

C. References to Selected International Environmental Law Cases

Adede, A. O., ed. *International Environmental Law Digest: Instruments for International Responses to Problems of the Environment and Development*, 1972-1992. Amsterdam: Elsevier, 1993. This is a collection of landmark cases and commentary.

Geradin, Damien. "Free Trade and Environmental Protection in an Integrated Market: A Survey of the Case Law of the United States Supreme Court and the European Court of Justice," *Journal of Transnational Law & Policy* 2 (1993): 141-197. This article compares the powers of the federal government and the states to the powers of the European Community and its member states as regards environmental protection. The limitations of both the states and the member states are analyzed.

Kramer, Ludwig. *European Environmental Law Casebook.* London: Sweet & Maxwell, 1993. 1 v. Cases pertaining to the principles of environmental protection in Community Law and national law, sectors of Community environmental policy, and procedural aspects are reported.

Wade-Smith, Richard, ed. *Environmental Law Reports*. London: Sweet & Maxwell, 1992-quarterly. This publication reports all the important Europe and U.K. environmental law cases. The majority of the cases are from the European Court of Justice and the High Court.

Permanent Court of International Justice. *SS Lotus* (France v Turkey) 1927 PCIJ (Ser A) No 10.

International Court of Justice.

Corfu Channel Case, 1949 ICJ Reports 4
Reparations for Injuries Case, 1949 ICJ Reports 174
Nuclear Test Case (Australia v France), 1973 ICJ Reports 99
Fisheries Jurisdiction Case (New Zealand v France), 1974 ICJ Reports 457
Nuclear Test Case(New Zealand v France), 1974 ICJ Reports 457
Case Concerning Certain Phosphate Lands in Nauru (Nauru v Australia), 1992 ICJ Reports 240.

European Court of Justice.

Case 8/74, *Dassonville*, 1974 ECR 837.
Case 120/78, Rewe v Zentralverwaltung, 1979 ECR 649
Case 91/79, Commission v Italy, 1980 ECR 1099
Cases 30-41/81, Commission v Italy, 1981 ECR 3379
Case 96/81, Commission v Netherlands, 1982 ECR 1791,
Case 97/81, Commission v Netherlands, 1982 ECR 1819
Case 220/81, Robertson, 1982 ECR 2349
Case 261/81, Rau, 1982 ECR 3961
Case 240/83, Procureur de la République v Association de Défense des Bruleurs D'Huiles Usagées (Used Oils), 1985 ECR 531
Case 50/85, Schloh, 1 CMLR 450 (1987)
Case 134/86, Commission v Belgium, 1987 ECR 2415
Case 302/86, Commission v Denmark (Danish Bottles), 1988 ECR 4607
Case 182/89, Commission v France 1 YIEL 274 (1990).

GATT Panel Decisions.

Superfund Tax Case, Report of the Panel, GATT Doc BISD5/16T (16 June 1987).

Yellow-Fin Tuna Decision, (Mexico v US) GATT Doc DS21/R, (3 September 1991).

International Arbitrations.

Pacific Fur Seals (Great Britain v United States), 1.
Moore's International Arbitration Awards 755 (1893).
Trail Smelter (United States v Canada), 3 RIAA 1905 (1941).
Lac Lanoux Arbitration (France v Spain), 24 ILR 101 (1957).

D. Legislation

Commission of the European Communities. Directorate-General XI. *Environment, Nuclear Safety and Civil Protection. European Community Environment Legislation*. Luxembourg: Office for Official Publication of the European Communities, 1992. 7 v. Vol. 1 General Policy, Vol. 2 Air, Vol. 3 Chemicals, Industrial Risks and Biotechnology, Vol. 4 Nature, Vol. 5 Noise, Vol. 6 Waste, Vol. 7 Water. It covers EC member nations laws as well as EC regulations, directives, and decisions concerning the environment.

Legislacion ambiental general en América Latina y el Caribe. Mexico: UNEP, 1992. 467 p.

OECD Council Regulation on the Use of Economic Instruments in Environmental Policy, 41 BNA. International Environment Reporter 2451 (1991).

United States: *High Seas Driftnet Fisheries Enforcement Act*, 106 Stat. 4900, Public Law 102-582

United States: *International Dolphin Conservation Act of 1992*, 106 Stat. 3425, Public Law 102-523

V. Looseleafs, Periodicals, and Yearbooks

BNA. *International Environment Reporter*. 1- Jan. 10, 1978-.

Reference File Binder 1 includes multilateral treaties, bilateral agreements, and European Conventions and OECD regulations.
Binder 2 summarizes each of the Canadian provincial and territorial environmental laws and regulations.
Binder 3 is divided into EEC General, EEC Air, EEC Water, EEC Toxic Substances.
Binder 4 covers EEC Noise, EEC Waste, EEC Biotechnology, and summarizes the environmental laws and regulations of

Australia, Belgium, Canada, Denmark, Finland, France, Germany, Greece, Ireland, Italy, Japan, Luxembourg, Mexico, the Netherlands, New Zealand, Poland, Portugal, South Korea, Singapore, Spain, Sweden, Switzerland, Taiwan, United Kingdom, United States.

The Current Reports binder contains biweekly reports on current developments.

Global Environmental Law Annual. Vol. 1- 1993-. This review published in cooperation with the Global Law Association and Tilburg University in the Netherlands reprints new environmental statutes and regulations. Its articles cover legal developments in 25 countries.

International Journal of Environmentally Conscious Manufacturing. 1992-.

Journal of Environmental Policy and Law in Latin America and the Caribbean. 1994-.

Trade and the Environment: News and Views from the General Agreement on Tariffs and Trade. 1993-.

Yearbook of International Environmental Law. Vol. 1- 1990-. The yearbook contains articles, and sections on the year in review, a review of the literature, and documents. Each volume is accompanied by a diskette containing documents, conventions, and declarations.

VI. Conference Proceedings and Symposia

Centre international de droit comparé de l'environnement. Semenaire international (1984: Limoges). *Les dechets industriels et l'environnement en droit comparé et international.* Publications de la Faculté de droit et des sciences économiques de Limoges, no. 12. Limoges: Presses Universitaires de France, 1985. 284 p.

Informal Encounter on International Trade and the Environment (1991: Oslo, Norway). *Informal Encounter on International Trade and the Environment*, Oslo, Norway, 28 February-1 March 1991. Geneva: UNCTAD, 1991. 15 p.

International Confederation of Free Trade Unions World Congress (15th: 1992: Caracas, Venezuela). *Environment and Development: the*

Trade Union Agenda. Brussels: International Confederation of Free Trade Unions, 1992. 57 p.

International Symposium on Trade and the Environment (1993: Minneapolis, Minn.) *International Symposium on Trade and the Environment*. Saint Paul, Minn.: Minnesota State Bar Association, Continuing Legal Education, 1993. 1 v. (various pagings)

Symposium: Free Trade and the Environment in Latin America (1992: Loyola of Los Angeles School of Law). *Symposium, Free Trade and the Environment in Latin America*. Los Angeles: Loyola School of Law, 1992. 147 p.

VII. Books and Articles

A. International Environmental Law

Law provides the legitimate basis for action by States and the international community as a whole. Consequently, the international community usually responds to environmental problems through law. International environmental law might be defined as the juridical articulation of the world's responses to environmental threats from human activities.

International environmental law is a rapidly evolving and expanding branch of international law. Concepts such as common concern of mankind, global partnership, common but differentiated responsibilities, anticipatory and preventive mechanisms, and incentives to compliance are evolving and are important for the formulation of international environmental agreements.

International environmental law has idiosyncratic legal features such as formal participation of non-governmental organizations in the international environmental process; and heavy reliance on so-called "soft law" instruments. International environmental legal regimes are emerging in which the making and application of law involve simplified procedures or processes that are actually inconsistent with the formality of the actual international treaties and agreements.

Campiglio, Luigi, et al. *The Environment After Rio: International Law and Economics*. International Environmental Law and Policy Series. London: Graham & Trotman, 1994. xvi, 285 p.

The Current State of International Environmental Law in Latin America and the Caribbean. Mexico: UNEP, 1993. 104 p.

Derecho Internacional Ambiental Regional. Mexico: UNEP, 1993. 629 p.

Government Institutes, Inc. *International Environmental Law: Special Report*. 1992 ed. Rockville, Md.: Government Institutes, 1992. v, 396 p.

Most of the 25 chapters were selected from session papers from the Institute's International Environmental Law and Regulations Conference of authorities from the legal, government, and business communities. Others were written by staff at foreign embassies in Washington. Chapters cover the European Community Product Liability Directive, and importing and exporting hazardous wastes. Recent developments in environmental law in Eastern Europe, Italy, Greece, Portugal, Canada, Mexico, Australia, Japan, Hong Kong, Indonesia, Malaysia, Papua New Guinea, Philippines, Singapore, South Korea and Taiwan are surveyed.

Lang, W.; H. Neuhold; and K. Zemanek. *Environmental Protection and International Law*. International Environmental Law & Policy Series. London: Graham & Trotman, 1991. x, 244 p. This compilation of papers from a conference held in Vienna in October 1990 takes an interdisciplinary approach to international environmental law issues.

Nowak, Jolanta, ed. *Environmental Law: International and Comparative Aspects: A Symposium*. London: British Institute of International and Comparative Law; Dobbs Ferry: Oceana Publications, 1976. vi, 191 p. One chapter discusses the OECD approach to the solution of transfrontier pollution problems.

Sands, Philippe, ed. *Greening International Law. International Law and Sustainable Development*. London: Earthscan Publications Ltd., 1993. xxvi, 260 p. This is the first volume in the International Law and Sustainable Development series of the Foundation for International Environmental Law and Development and Earthscan. This book and subsequent volumes aim to address and define the major legal issues associated with sustainable development and to contribute to the progressive development of international law. It includes a bibliography, a list of acronyms, and lists of treaties and cases.

Schlickman, J. Andrew, and Thomas M. McMahon. *International Environmental Law and Regulation.* Salem, N.H.: Butterworth Legal Publishers, 1991. 2 v. (looseleaf). This book provides an overview of the legal systems and significant environmental laws and regulations from Australia, Canada, Czechoslovakia, France, Germany, Italy, Japan, Mexico, the Netherlands, Poland, Singapore, South Korea, the former USSR, U.K., U.S. and the EC. Chapters conclude with a list including citations to the primary environmental laws of each country.

B. International Trade

International law is increasingly concerned with economics in two respects: in resolving or preventing economic conflicts and in that international law norms may themselves be modified and reformed by economic action.

Various means exist of avoiding, containing, and resolving economic conflicts. Management agreements for a single commodity, harmonization arrangements for particular regions are examples. Other means which are more general and institutional in form include the GATT, the IMF, the IBRD, OECD, and the European Community.

1. Trade Barriers, Trade Controls, and Economic Incentives

Baldock, David, and Edward Keene. "Incorporating Environmental Considerations in Common Market Arrangements," *Environmental Law* 23 (1993): 575-605.

European Bank for Reconstruction and Development. *Investors' Environmental Guidelines: Bulgaria, Czech and Slovak Republics, Estonia, Hungary, Latvia, Lithuania, Poland, and Romania.* London: Graham & Trotman; The Hague: Nijhoff, 1994. 540 p. This book will provide investors with a comprehensive reference to environmental requirements in Central and Eastern Europe. Environmental liability, environmental audit requirements, environmental assessment requirements, land use planning, air, water and noise requirements, chemical storage, handling and response. Annexes include lists of key current legislation, proposed legislation, information on approval processes and relevant institutions.

St. Pierre, Antoine. *Impact of Environmental Measures on International Trade.* Report, no. 76-91-E. Ottawa: Conference Board of Canada, 1991. 10 p.

Tang, Dennis Te-Chung. *On the Feasibility of Economic Incentives in Taiwan's Environmental Regulations: Lessons from the American Experience.* Taipei: Academia Sinica Institute of American Culture, c1990. xxiv, 551 p. Environmental regulation using economic incentives in the U.S. and Taiwan is discussed. One chapter reviews EPA's emission trading policy.

2. Trade and Economic Policy and the Environment

Anderson, Kym, and Richard Blackhurst. *The Greening of World Trade Issues.* New York: Harvester Wheatsheaf, 1992. xviii, 276 p.

Charnovitz, Steve. "The Environment v. Trade Rules: Defogging the Debate," *Environmental Law* 23 (1993): 475-517

Environmental Policies and Industrial Competitiveness. Paris: Organisation for Economic Co-operation and Development, 1993. 177 p.

Esty, Daniel C. "Beyond Rio: Trade and the Environment," *Environmental Law* 23 (1993): 387-396

Jenkins, Alan R. "NAFTA: Is the Environmental Cost of Free Trade Too High?," *North Carolina Journal of International Law and Commercial Regulation* 19 (1993): 143-174. At issue is whether free trade is a boon to environmental quality or an ecological disaster. The author describes the legal structure and procedure of NAFTA and the potential impact of NAFTA on the environment is predicted.

Kirton, John, and Sarah Richardson, eds. *Trade, Environment, and Competitiveness: Sustaining Canada's Prosperity.* National Round Table Series on Sustainable Development, no. 7. Ottawa, Ont.: National Round Table on the Environment and the Economy, 1992. xiv, 394 p.

Low, Patrick, ed. *International Trade and the Environment.* World Bank Discussion Papers, no. 159. Washington, D.C.: The World Bank, 1992. x, 365 p. This World Bank Discussion Paper is organized around six thematic headings: trade and environmental policy links, the relationship of environmental quality to industrial location, competitiveness, economic growth and trade liberalization, the political economy of environmental policy making, and international cooperation in the environment. A 20-page bibliography can be found on pp. 345-365.

Muñoz, Heraldo, and Robin Rosenberg. *Difficult Liaison: Trade and the Environment in the Americas.* Miami: North-South Center, University of Miami, 1993. xi, 285 p.

Raul, Alan Charles, and Paul E. Hagan. "The Convergence of Trade and Environmental Law," *Natural Resources & Environment* 8 (no. 2 1993): 3-6. The authors describe the tension between environmental law which is concerned with imposing restrictions on the production of goods and trade law which is chiefly interested in achieving liberalization on the sale of goods. The conflict is examined under the GATT rules.

Srinivasan, T. N. *Environment, Economic Development, and International Trade: Some Issues.* Occasional Paper, no. 13. St. Paul, Minn.: Bureau of Economic Studies, Macalester College, 1993. 28 p.

Stevens, Candice. "Trade and the Environment: The OECD Guiding Principles Revisited," *Environmental Law* 23 (1993): 607-619.

U.S. National Advisory Council for Environmental Policy and Technology. Trade and Environment Committee. *The Greening of World Trade: A Report to EPA.* Washington, D.C.: The Committee: For sale by the U.S. G.P.O., Supt. of Docs., 1993. 240 p.

Wiemann, Jurgen. *Environmentally Oriented Trade Policy: A New Area of Conflict between North and South?* Berlin: German Development Institute, 1992. 31 p.

VIII. Specific Aspects

A. Agriculture

Ozuna, Teofilo, Jr., and Gary W. Williams. *The Environment and U.S.-Mexico Agricultural Trade.* TAMRC International Market Research Report, no. IM-3-93. College Station, Tex.: Texas Agricultural Market Research Center, Dept. of Agricultural Economics, Texas Agricultural Experiment Station, Texas Agricultural Extension Service, Texas A & M University, 1993. iii, 14 leaves.

Runge, Carlisle Ford. *Trade in Disservices: Environmental Regulation and Agricultural Trade Competitiveness*. University of Minnesota, Dept. of Agricultural and Applied Economics, Staff Paper, no. P89-23. St. Paul, Minn.: Dept. of Agricultural and Applied Economics, University of Minnesota, 1989. 23 p.

Williamson, Caroline T. *Agriculture, the Environment and Trade: Conflict or Cooperation?* Washington, D.C.: International Policy Council on Agriculture and Trade, 1993. xxix, 287 p.

B. Air Pollution and Acid Rain

Wetstone, Gregory S., and Armin Rosencranz. *Acid Rain in Europe and North America: National Responses to an International Problem*. Washington, D.C.: Environmental Law Institute, c1983. xvi, 244 p. This book was undertaken as a study for the German Marshall Fund of the United States. National laws and policies in the U.S., Canada, Sweden, Norway, the U.K., Germany, and Japan are surveyed. International laws and policies are treated in another chapter. Existing control technologies are described, and the role of industry and non-government environmental organization is examined.

C. Biodiversity

Bilderbeek, Simone, ed. *Biodiversity and International Law: the Effectiveness of International Environmental Law*. Amsterdam: IOS Press, 1992. 213 p. This book is a report of a consultation of 250 experts organized by the Netherlands Committee for the IUCN during 1990-1991. The Bretton Woods Institutions and UNCTAD are discussed briefly.

Tisdell, Clement Allan. *Conservation, Protected Areas and the Global Economic System: How Debt, Trade, Exchange Rates, Inflation and Macroeconomic Policy affect Biological Diversity*. Discussion Paper, no. 80. Brisbane: University of Queensland, Dept. of Economics, 1992. iii, 43 p.

D. Biology

McGuire, Michael T., and Manfred Rehbinder. *Biology, Culture, and Environmental Law*. Schriftenreihe zur Rechtssoziologie und Rechtstatsachenforschung, Band 73. Berlin: Duncker & Humblot, 1993. 268 p. The book contains the conference proceedings of the

Gruter Institute for Law and Behavioral Research held in Tauberbischofsheim in 1991. The Institute aims to develop and refine theoretical framewords for understanding relationships between biology, law, and economics. Topics discussed include economics and the environment, the case for tradable emission permits, environmental liability and insurance within the EC and in Germany.

E. Chemical Substances

Brickman, Ronald, Sheila Jasanoff, and Thomas Ilgen. *Controlling Chemicals: The Politics and Regulation in Europe and in the United States*. Ithaca and London: Cornell University Press, c1985. 344 p. This book provides a systematic comparison of the policies and politics of toxic chemical regulation in the U.S., U.K., France, and Germany. One chapter is devoted to the chemical industry and regulatory challenges and strategies.

Goldberg, Donald M. *Provisions of the Montreal Protocol affecting Trade*. Washington, D.C.: Center for International Environmental Law, 1992. 13 p.

Steiger, Heinhard. *Le droit de l'environnement et les substances chimique = Environmental Law and Chemical Substances = Umweltrecht und Chemikalien*. Second European Symposium on Environmental Law. Giessen 27 to 29 September 1979. Beiträge zur Umweltgestaltung Band A82. Berlin: Schmidt, 311 p. In English and French. The first session concerned the regulation and control of the production of chemical substances. The second concerned the use of chemicals, their transport, sale and storage. The third covered the responsibility for accidents caused by chemical manufacturing.

F. Endangered Species

Favre, David S. *International Trade in Endangered Species: a Guide to CITES*. Dordrecht: Nijhoff, 1989. xx, 415 p. This book is a commentary on the Convention on International Trade in Endangered Species of Wild Fauna and Flora (CITES). It explains acceptable international trade of endangered species, interprets the words of the treaty, reports on the treaty's implementation. The documentary appendix reprints selected resolutions adopted at the Conferences of the Parties and also includes forms.

G. Environmental Liability and Compensation

Countries are concerned about promoting a partnership in the implementation of international legal obligations by establishing accurate differentiation of the responsibilities and obligations of States and through ensuring the application of compliance mechanisms.

Compensation for Pollution Damage. Paris: Organization for Economic Co-operation and Development, 1981. 208 p. The OECD Council has stressed the need to establish practical procedures promoting the prompt and equitable compensation of persons affected by transfrontier pollution. This book considers the experiences of OECD member countries with compensation and examines some of the legal and economic problems associated with the establishment and administration of compensation systems.

Dunné, Jan M. van. *Transboundary Pollution and Liability: the Case of the River Rhine*. Proceedings of an International Conference held in Rotterdam, 19 October 1990. Rotterdam: Erasmus University Institute of Environmental Damages, c1991. x, 214 p. Among the issues discussed are industrial discharges into the Rhine, the effect of possessing a license on liability, and multiple causation and joint tortfeasors in pollution cases.

IBA Section on Business Law Committee F (International Environmental Law). *Enviromental Liability: 7th Residential Seminar on Environmental Law, 9-13 June 1990, Montreux, Switzerland*. Chairman, Thomas, Patricia. International Bar Association Series. London: Graham & Trotman, 1991. 399 p. The book's five parts cover commercial implications of global responsibility for the environment; global recognition of the relationship between the economic and environmental management; international and economic weapons; regional perspectives on the use of economic and political weapons and the role of international law; enforcement; environmental audit, insurance, indemnities.

Francioni, Francesco, and Tullio Scovazzi, eds. *International Responsibility for Environmental Harm*. London: Graham & Trotman, 1991. xv, 499 p. The last three parts pertain to international trade and industry. They cover the export of technologies and substances causing environmental harm, domestic and international law regimes, and notification and assistance with regard to environmental harm.

Giesberts, Ludger. "Environmental Liability for Industrial Installations in Germany," *International Business Lawyer* (January 1994): 14-19. Corporate liability under the German Environmental Liability Act (ELA) is outlined. General liability under provisions of the German Civil Code and other pertinent acts are also discussed. EC legal developments and the Council of Europe's Convention on Civil Liability for Damages resulting from activities dangerous to the environment are also surveyed.

Payne, Simon, ed. *Commercial Environmental Law & Liability*. London: Longman, 2 v. (looseleaf). This looseleaf covers environmental liability from an EC and UK perspective. Texts of applicable statutes and forms are included.

Rest, Alfred. *Internationaler Umweltschutz und Haftung: Verantworlichkeit von Staat und Einzelperson bei grenzüberschreitenden Umweltbeeinträchtigungen – International Protection of the Environment and Liability: The Legal Responsibility of States and Individuals in Cases of Transfrontier Pollution*. Berlin: E. Schmidt Verlag, 1978. 178 p. State responsibility is discussed in Part I. Part II treats the responsibility of individuals and juridical persons in civil law and public proceedings.

Transnational Environmental Liability and Insurance. Chairman, Ralph P. Kröner. International Bar Association Series. London: Graham & Trotman, 1993. xviii, 303 p. This book discusses no fault liability, multiple tortfeasor theories, serial claims, clean up measures, and transportation of hazardous materials.

H. Environmental Policy

Bothe, Michael. *Trends in Environmental Policy and Law = Tendances Actuelles de la Politique et du Droit de l'Environnement*. IUCN Environmental Policy and Law Paper, no. 15. Gland, Switzerland: International Union for Conservation of Nature and Natural Resources, 1980. xxi, 404 p. This book includes papers on cost apportionment principles in environmental protection, governmental financial incentives for the protection of the environment, and the environmental considerations of the redeployment of industries to developing countries.

Funt, James A. "The North American Free Trade Agreement and the Integrated Environmental Border Plan: Feasible Solutions to U.S.-Mexico Border Pollution?" *Temple Environmental Law & Technology Journal* 12 (1993): 77-101. The management of toxic maquiladora waste and the maquiladora environmental degradation is the focus of this article. U.S. economic costs due to maquiladora pollution are projected.

Gibbons, David T. "NAFTA vs. The Environment: The Court's Mandate to Require the Preparation of Environmental Impact Statements for Trade Agreements," *Hamline Journal of Public Law and Policy* 15 (1994): 101-122. This article discusses the 1993 District Court decision ordering the United States Trade Representative to prepare an Environmental Impact Statement on the North American Free Trade Agreement in light of NEPA and the Administrative Procedure Act.

Gunningham, Neil. *Pollution, Social Interest and the Law. Law in Society Series*. London: Martin Robertson, 1974. 96 p. One chapter is devoted to past and present industry response to the environment.

Housman, Robert F. "A Kantian Approach to Trade and the Environment," *Washington and Lee Law Review* 49 (1992): 1373-1388

Hurrell, Andrew, and Benedict Kingsbury, eds. *The International Politics of the Environment: Actors, Interests, and Institutions*. Oxford: Clarendon Press, 1992. xiv, 492 p. The role of the World Bank and the European Community and international environmental policy are examined.

Love, Wendy Leigh. "International Trade Agreements and Domestic Environmental Policy: The NAFTA Example," *North Carolina Journal of International Law and Commercial Regulation* 19 (1994): 353-369. The author discusses the *Public Citizen v. United States Trade Representative* case, 5 F.3d 549 (D.C. Cir. 1993). She describes how the ruling limits the international impact of the National Environmental Policy Act by refusing to apply its requirement of an environmental impact statement to the North American Free Trade Agreement.

Nowicki, Maciej. *Environment in Poland: Issues and Solutions*. Dordrecht: Kluwer Academic Press, 1993. 191 p. This book provides a summary of the state of the Polish environment. It proposes a strategy for the restructuring of Polish industry, the energy sector, transport system, and agriculture in order to restore the environment and to follow sustainable development.

Sagoff, Mark. *The Economy of the Earth: Philosophy, Law and the Environment*. Cambridge: Cambridge University Press, 1988., 271 p. The author believes that cost benefit analysis and the associated standard of of economic efficiency only compare the competing weight of arbitrary private wishes. He argues that moral principles should be involved in all modern social regulation and especially in the regulation of the environment.

Trade and Environment: Conflicts and Opportunities. Background Paper. Washington, D.C.: U.S. Congress, Office of Technology Assessment, 1992. viii, 109 p.

Vasquez, Xavier Carlos. "The North American Free Trade Agreement and Environmental Racism," *Harvard International Law Journal* 34 (1993): 357-359. This article explores the environmental concerns raised by expanded economic trade between the United States and Mexico under NAFTA. It summarizes NAFTA, examines the Maquiladora industry, and considers their effect on the environment and on the health of U.S. and Mexican citizens. Environmental racism is examined in a broader context, and the side agreements are viewed in light of their influence on environmental racism.

I. Environmental Regulation

Goldman, Patti A. "Resolving the Trade and Environment Debate: In Search of a Neutral Forum and Neutral Principles." *Washington and Lee Law Review* 49 (1992): 1279-1298.

Handler, Thomas, ed. *Regulating the European Environment*. London: Chancery, 1994. 176 p. This book covers environmental regulation in the European Community, and in Belgium, the Czech Republic, Egypt, U.K., France, Germany, Hungary, Italy, the Netherlands, Poland, the Commonwealth of Independent States, Spain, Sweden, and Switzerland.

J. The General Agreement on Tariffs and Trade (The GATT)

Arden-Clarke, Charles. *International Trade, GATT, and the Environment*. WWF International Position Paper. Gland, Switzerland: WWF International, 1992. 14 p.

Audley, John. *A Critique of the GATT Secretariat Report, Trade and the Environment*. Washington, D.C.: Sierra Club Center for Environmental Innovation, 1992. 15 p.

Baker, Betsy. "Protection, Not Protectionism: Multilateral Environmental Agreement and the GATT," *Vanderbilt Journal of Transnational Law* 26 (1993): 437-468. This article examines the compatibility of multilateral environmental agreements with the provisions of the General Agreement on Tariffs and Trade. Key provisions of the Basel Convention on the Control of Transboundary Movements of Hazardous Waste, the Montreal Protocol on Substances that Deplete the Ozone Layer, the United Nations Framework Convention on Climate Change and the GATT are reviewed. The conflict between unilateral environmental protection and free trade under the GATT is described.

Esty, Daniel C. *Greening the GATT: Trade, Enviroment, and the Future*. Washington, D.C.: Institute for International Economics, 1994. xvi, 319 p.

Greijn, Heinz. *GATT, Environment and Development*. ELCI Discussion Paper, no. 2. Nairobi: Environment Liaison Centre International, 1991. vi, 48 p.

Grimmett, Jeanne J. *Environmental Regulation and the GATT*. Washington, D.C.: Congressional Research Service, Library of Congress, 1991. 43 p.

Harris, Stuart. *International Trade, Ecologically Sustainable Development and the GATT*. Australian National University, Department of International Relations, Working Paper, no. 1991/1. Canberra: Australian National University, Dept. of International Relations, 1991. 23 p.

McDonald, Janet. "Greening the GATT: Harmonizing Free Trade and Environmental Protection in the New World Order," *Environmental Law* 23 (1993): 397-474.

Smith, Michael B. "GATT, Trade and the Environment," *Environmental Law* 23 (1993): 533-544.

Snape, Richard H. *The Environment, International Trade, and GATT*. Department of Economics Seminar Papers, no. 8/91. Clayton, Vic.: Monash University, Dept. of Economics, 1991. 42 p.

Thomas, Jeffrey S. *The Real and False Interactions between the GATT and Environmental Regulation: Does the GATT Need to Be Greener?* Vancouver, B.C.: Ladner Downs, 1993. 25 p.

Von Moltke, Konrad. "The Last Round : The General Agreement on Tariffs and Trade in Light of the Earth Summit," *Environmental Law* 23 (1993): 519-531.

K. Hazardous Waste

Handl, Günther, and Robert E. Lutz. *Transferring Hazardous Technologies and Substances: The International Legal Challenge*. International Environmental Law and Policy Series. London: Graham & Trotman, 1989. viii, 275 p. This book is an outgrowth of a panel organized for the American Society of International Law in April 1985. Responsibilities of importing and exporting States, technology transfer, transboundary trade, and codes of conduct are among the issues discussed.

Hilz, Christoph. *The International Toxic Waste Trade*. New York: Van Nostrand Reinhold, 1992. xvi, 203 p.

Kwiatkowska, Barbara, and Alfred H.A. Soons. *Transboundary Movements and Disposal of Hazardous Wastes in International Law: Basic Documents*. International Environmental Law and Policy Series. Dordrecht: Nijhoff, 1993. cxxv, 1386 p. Documents are arranged under global instruments, regional instruments, and non-governmental instruments/publications. This book includes a list of abbreviations, tables of treaties, and a chronological table of selected instruments and developments.

Louka, Elli. *Overcoming National Barriers to International Waste Trade: A New Perspective on the Transnational Movement of Hazardous and Radioactive Wastes*. Dordrecht: Nijhoff, 1994. 240 p. This book covers the developing national standards and liability rules in the EC and in the U.S.

Organization for Economic Co-operation and Development. *Transfrontier Movements of Hazardous Wastes: Legal and Institutional Aspects*. Paris: OECD, 1985. 304 p. This book contains conference papers from a Seminar on Legal and Institutional Aspects of Transfrontier Movements of Hazardous Waste held in Paris, 12-14th June 1984. The conference of 80 experts was intended to provide the background information necessary to implement the OECD Decision and Recommendation on Transfrontier Movement of Hazardous Waste adopted the 1st February 1984. It discusses financial means of control and insurance issues.

L. Less Developed Countries

Carrillo Prieto, Ignacio, and Raúl Nocedal, eds. *Legal Protection of the Environment in Developing Countries: Colloquium of the International Association of Legal Science* (Mexico, August 25-28th, 1974). Instituto de Investigaciones Jurídicas. Serie D. Cuadernos de derecho comparado, Núm. 12. Mexico: Universidad Autonóma de Mexico, 1976. 473 p. In English and French. The second session of this conference is the most relevant. It concerned national environmental regulations and their effects on foreign trade and investment abroad.

Witzsch, Günter. *Lesotho Environment and Environment Law*. Rome: Environmental Law Project, Faculty of Law, National University of Lesotho, 1992. xviii, 280 p. The book's 25 chapters cover environmental law, environmental concerns, and draft legislation. Separate chapters are devoted to industry, wastes, and dangerous substances.

M. Mining Law

International Bar Association. Section on Business Law. Committee on Environmental Law. *Mining and Environmental Law: Proceedings of the Seminar held at Washington, D.C., 4-8 April 1982*. London: International Bar Association, c1981. 970 p. in 2 v. Environmental regulation of mining in the U.S., U.K., Germany, Australia, New Zealand, Canada, the Netherlands, and Belgium are discussed.

N. Multinational Corporations

Baram, Michael S., and Daniel G. Partan. *Corporate Disclosure of Environmental Risks: U.S. and European Law*. Salem, N.H.: Butterworth Legal Publications, 1989. x, 359 p. This volume presents papers and panel discussions from the International Symposium on Multinational Corporations and Their New Responsibilities to Disclose and Communicate Risk Information, which was held at Boston University School of Law, March 24-25, 1988. The U.S., the European Communities, and several IGO's now impose duties on corporations to disclose information on the hazardous attributes of their activities and to improve methods for managing risks.

Fischer, Kurt, and Johan Schot, eds. *Environmental Strategies for Industry: International Perspectives on Research Needs and Policy Implications*. Washington, D.C.: Island Press, 1993. x, 389 p.

Leonard, H. Jeffrey. *Pollution and the Struggle for the World Product: Multinational Corporations, Environment, and International Comparative Advantage*. Cambridge: Cambridge University Press, 1988. xii, 254 p. Urbani, Eric, Conrad Rubin, and Monica Katzman, eds. Transnational Environmental Law and Its Impact on Corporate Behavior. Irvington: Transnational Juris Publications, 1994. 1 v. This book discusses market-based environmental regulation. It covers compliance, enforcement, and treaties.

O. North American Free Trade Agreement (NAFTA)

Anderson, Terry L., ed. *NAFTA and the Environment. Studies on the Economic Future of North America.* San Francisco: Pacific Research Institute for Public Policy, 1993. xii, 107 p.

Cooke, Gregg A., and Amanda Atkinson. *The Evolving Protection of State Laws and the Environment: NAFTA from a Texas Perspective.* Dan Morales, Texas Attorney General. U.S. Mexican Occasional Paper, no. 5. Austin: Lyndon B. Johnson School of Public Affairs, University of Texas at Austin, 1994. viii, 54 p. The five sections in this study cover the growing impact of international trade agreements on states, the position of NAFTA's interpretive documents in U.S. law, the consultative framework for communications with states in future international trade matters, dispute resolution, NAFTA environmental provisions and environmental organizations, and the impacts on state legislative processes. There are nine documentary appendices.

Greenwald, Joseph. *Trade and Environment in a North American Free Trade Agreement*. Occasional Papers in International Trade Law and Policy, no. 21. Ottawa: Centre for Trade Policy and Law, 1992. 21 p.

Grossman, Gene M., and Alan B. Krueger. *Environmental Impacts of a North American Free Trade Agreement*. Discussion Paper, no. 158. Princeton: Woodrow Wilson School, Princeton University, 40 p.

Hofgard, Kurt C. "Is This Land Really Our Land?: Impacts of Free Trade Agreements on U.S. Environmental Protection," *Environmental Law* 23 (1993): 635-681.

Lash, William H., III. *NAFTA and the Greening of International Trade Policy*. Contemporary Issues Series, no. 60. St. Louis, Mo.: Center for the Study of American Business, Washington University, 1993. 24 p.

Makuch, Zen, and Scott Sinclair. *The Environmental Implications of the NAFTA Environmental Side Agreement*. Toronto: Canadian Environmental Law Association, 53 p.

North American Agreement of Environmental Cooperation, North American Agreement on Labour Cooperation: Background Information. Ottawa: Government of Canada, 1993. 1 v. (various pagings)

Robins, Michael. "The North American Free Trade Agreement: The Integration of Free Trade and the Environment," *Temple International and Comparative Law Journal* 7 (1993): 123-147. The author surveys the history, motivations and benefits of NAFTA under international law and compares present U.S. and Mexican law. He makes recommendations for constructing future trade agreements in environmentally sensitive ways.

Schoenbaum, Thomas J. "The North American Free Trade Agreement (NAFTA): Good for Jobs, For the Environment, and For America," *Georgia Journal of International and Comparative Law* 23 (1993): 461-506. Ten pages of this article are devoted to environmental protection. The author outlines product standards, process standards, environmental measures and investment, and border pollution.

United States. President (1993- : Clinton). *North American Free Trade Agreement, Supplemental Agreements and Additional Documents: Message from the President of the United States transmitting North American Free Trade Agreement, Supplemental Agreements, and Additional Documents*. U.S. Congress. House Document 103-160. Washington, D.C.: U.S. G.P.O., Supt. of Docs., Congressional Sales Office, 1993. 311 p.

P. Natural Resources

At the moment, international natural resource issues focus on the the allocation, utilization, and management of very concrete phenomena. The onset of problems concerning the earth's natural resources is likely only to be detected by specialists who understand the highly technical issues involved. These specialists have little political or legal clout. Many of the issues have not yet been defined in legal terms and the legal literature is not comprehensive.

"Acquisition of Natural Resource Interests by the State," *Journal of Energy & Natural Resources Law* (December 1987 Supplement) 105 p. This publication is a result of a study by the Academic Advisory Group of the International Bar Association, Section on Energy and Natural Resources Law which examined legal positions of selected countries, identified common issues, and compared responses. Country reports for Australia, Canada, U.K., U.S., and Norway are included.

Arsanjani, Mahnoush H. *International Regulation of Internal Resources: A Study of Law and Policy.* Virginia Legal Studies. Charlottesville: University Press of Virginia, 1981. 523 p. Chapter III concerns "The Inclusive Enjoyment of Resources through Agreement". These agreements are called development agreements, concessions, international contracts, and investment agreements. The agreements distribute natural resources, human resources, industrial resources such as technology from one country to another, either in their basic or processed form. Chapter V discusses "Control of Pricing of Resources".

Dupuy, Réné-Jean, ed. *Le règlement des différends sur les nouvelles ressources naturelles = The settlement of disputes on the new natural resources.* Colloque, La Haye, 8-10 novembre 1982 = Workshop, The Hague, 8-10 November 1982. The Hague: Nijhoff, 1983. xxiii, 487 p. This workshop on natural resources takes an innovative approach. Sections are devoted to radio frequencies and information as a new natural resource. One author, Francesca Klaver, points out that developing countries experience a lack of information, and that other countries receive little information about the Third World or a false image of the less developed countries and asks whether information is a resource in society, even a key resource, and therefore in principle part of the Common Heritage of Mankind, or whether it should be considered a commodity and treated as such?

Fawcett, J.E.S., and Audrey Parry. *Law and international Resource Conflicts*. Oxford: Clarendon Press, 1981. xvi, 254 p. This study issued under the auspices of the Royal Institute of International Affairs identifies and describes the role of law in the prevention and resolution of international resource conflicts. Chapter III concerns the prevention and resolution of particular resource conflicts involving foreign investment or the commodity trade. There are references to U.N. documents, and there is a short bibliography.

Jeffery, Michael I., ed. *Resource Investigation Funding & Control: Proceedings of the Fifth Environment Law Seminar*. Victoria/Vancouver, March 1986. London: International Bar Association, 1989. 1278 p. in 3 v. This Canadian conference discussed environmental decision-making, intervenor-funding, regulation of the mining industry, marine and land-based resources, water quality, and biotechnology.

Utton, Albert E., and Ludwik A. Teclaff. *Transboundary Resources Law*. Westview Special Studies in Natural Resources and Energy Management. Boulder and London: Westview Press, 1987. viii, 321 p. The 12 chapters by different authors cover various aspects of transboundary resource law and policy. Topics covered include patterns of cooperation in international water law, shared resources in EEC legislation, the electromagnetic spectrum, an institutional arrangement for developing oil and gas in Mexico, etc.

Q. Pollution

1. Pollution Controls

Control of pollution is considered central to the protection of the environment.

Les aspects juridiques de l'environnement. Actes du colloque de la Section belge de l'Institut international de droit d'expression française. Namur, 25 et 26 octobre 1974. Travaux de la Faculté de Droit de Namur, no. 12. Namur: Presses Universitaires de Namur, 1975. 208 p. The majority of the papers which are all in French concern the civil and criminal responsability of polluters under Belgian law, French law, Swiss law, and Luxembourg law.

Downing, Paul B., and Hanf, Kenneth, ed. *International Comparisons in Implementing Pollution Laws.* Boston: Kluwer, Nijhoff, c1983. x, 341 p. Regulatory enforcement in the U.S., U.K., Italy, Germany, the Netherlands, and France is discussed.

General Agreement on Tariffs and Trade (Organization). *Industrial Pollution Control and International Trade.* GATT Studies in International Trade, no. 1. Geneva: General Agreement on Tariffs and Trade, 1971. 26 p. The following books are part of a series which discuss pollution control in each the the EC countries. They include sections on control over products, controls relating to industries and processes, and controls relating to particular pollutants. At present, financial controls are only infrequently used to control pollution within the member states of the European Communities. Principal pollution control legislation, agencies, and authorities are described for each country. Topics covered are air pollution, inland waters, coastal waters, seas, deposit of wastes on land, noise and vibration, nuclear energy, and products.

Colliard, Claude-Albert. *The Law and Practice Relating to Pollution Control in France.*2d ed. London: Graham & Trotman, 1982. xxiv, 190 p. 12 p.

Dell'Anno, P. *The Law and Practice Relating to Pollution Control in Italy.*2d ed. London: Graham & Trotman, 1982. xxvii, 342 p. Unnumbered.

Didier, J.M. and Associates. *The Law Relating to Pollution Control in Belgium and Luxembourg.*2d ed. London: Graham & Trotman, 1982. xxvii, 496 p. 88 p.

Graeff, J.J. de, and J. M. Polack. *The Law and Practice Relating to Pollution Control in the Netherlands.*2d ed. London: Graham & Trotman, 1982. xxi, 184 p. Unnumbered.

Jensen, C. Haagen. *The Law and Practice Relating to Pollution Control in Denmark.*2d ed. London: Graham & Trotman, 1982. xxvii, 208 p. Unnumbered.

McLoughlin, J. *The Law and Practice Relating to Pollution Control in the Member States of the European Communities: A Comparative Survey.*2d ed. London: Graham & Trotman, 1982. x, 546 p. 40 p.

Scannell, Yvonne. *The Law and Practice Relating to Pollution Control in Ireland*.2d ed. London: Graham & Trotman, 1982. xix, 223 p. Unnumbered.

Steiger, Heinhard, and Otto Kimminich. *The Law and Practice Relating to Pollution Control in the Federal Republic of Germany*. London: Graham & Trotman, 1976. xxxii, 420 p. Updating Supplement 1978. 12 p.

2. Transfrontier Pollution

Betlem, Gerrit. *Civil Liability for Transfrontier Pollution: Dutch Environmental Tort Law in International Cases in the Light of Community Law*. London: Graham & Trotman; The Hague: Martinus Nijhoff, 1993. 640 p. This book analyzes the Brussels Convention on Jurisdiction and Enforcement of Judgments as it applies to protection of the environment. Dutch environmental tort law is thoroughly covered.

Dunné, Jan M. van. *Transboundary Pollution and Liability: the Case of the River Rhine*. Proceedings of an International Conference held in Rotterdam, 19 October 1990. Rotterdam: Erasmus University Institute of Environmental Damages, c1991. x, 214 p.

Ercmann, S. *Transatlantic Colloquy on Cross-Border Relations: European and North American Perspectives = Transatlantisches Kolloquium über Nachbarschaftliche Beziehungen: Europäische und nordamerikanische Perspektiven*. Schweizer Studien zum internationalen Recht. Band 49. Zurich: Schulthess Polygraphischer Verlag, 1987. 343 p. This book contains the reports and conclusions of colloquy which focused on transboundary environmental protection problems. Among the issues discussed was the long-distance impact of nuclear plant accidents.

Godwin, Diana L. "The Basel Convention on Transboundary Movements of Hazardous Wastes: An Opportunity for Industrialized Nations to Clean Up Their Acts?" *Denver Journal of International Law and Policy* 22 (1993): 193-208. The article discusses the issue of toxic waste dumping in developing countries. It also discusses the ends and means of the Basel Convention and the system of regulation of transboundary movement of hazardous waste.

Hague Academy of International Law. Centre for Studies and Research in International Law and International Relations. *La pollution tranfrontière et le droit international = Transfrontier pollution and international law.* Dordrecht: Nijhoff, 1986. 133 p. In English and French. This book contains the Rules Relative to the Protection of the Environment against Transfrontier Pollution established by the French-speaking Section of the Hague Academy of International Law. It reports on the current research of the Centre for Studies and Research.

Lucas, Robert E. B., David Wheeler, and Hemamala Hettige. *Economic Development, Environmental Regulation, and the International Migration of Toxic Industrial Pollution, 1960-88.* Policy Research Working Papers, WPS 1062. Washington, D.C.: Office of the Vice President, Development Economics, World Bank, 1992. 20 p.

Rest, Alfred. *Internationaler Umweltschutz und Haftung: Verantwortlichkeit von Staat und Einzelperson bei grenzüberschreitenden Umweltbeeinträchtigungen = International Protection of the Environment and Liability: The Legal Responsibility of States and Individuals in Cases of Transfrontier Pollution.* Berlin: E. Schmidt Verlag, 1978. 178 p.

Rest, Alfred. *Die Wahl des günstigeren Rechts im grenzüberschreitenden Umweltschutz: Starkung des Individualrechtes = The More Favourable Law Principle in Transfrontier Environmental Law: A Means of Strengthening the Protection of the Individual?* Beiträge zur Umweltgestaltung, Band A68. Berlin: E. Schmidt Verlag, 1980. 87 p. This study completed under the auspices of OECD inquires into the concept of private protection in transboundary liability. It discusses the more favorable law principle as a combination of the place of action and place of injury. The laws of the Netherlands, France, Belgium, Great Britain, Germany, Austria, Switzerland, Italy, Sweden, U.S., Poland, the EC are compared. Four landmark European judicial decisions are discussed.

3. Insurance

Pfennigstorf, Werner. *Pollution Insurance: International Survey of Coverages and Exclusions.* International Environmental Law and Policy Series. London: Graham & Trotman; The Hague: Nijhoff, 1993. x,245 p. Policy clauses, endorsements and forms used in 20 countries are analyzed and compared. All major policy terms are compared. This book was written under the auspices of the International Association for Insurance Law (AIDA).

R. Sustainable Development

Development and environmental protection are closely linked. Whenever people experience extreme poverty, nature too, is bound to suffer. Environmental protection must therefore go hand-in-hand with sustainable development and population policy.

Arden-Clarke, Charles. *The General Agreement on Tariffs and Trade, Environmental Protection and Sustainable Development*. A WWF International Discussion Paper. Gland, Switzerland: World Wide Fund for World Wildlife Fund, 1991. 32 p.

Arden-Clarke, Charles. *South-North Terms of Trade, Environmental Protection and Sustainable Development*. A WWF International Discussion Paper. Gland, Switzerland: WWF, World Wide Fund for Nature, 1992. 12 p.

Arntzen, J., I. Hemmer, and O. Kuik, eds. *International Trade and Sustainable Development*. Amsterdam: VU University Press, 1992. 172 p.

Collard, David, David Pearce, and David Ulph, eds. *Economics, Growth, and Sustainable Environments: Essays in Memory of Richard Lecomber*. New York : St. Martin's Press, 1988. viii, 205 p.

Elwell, Christine. *The European Approach to Sustainable Development: How Green Is the EEC?* Occasional Papers in International Trade Law and Policy, no. 24. Ottawa: Centre for Trade Policy and Law, 1992. 12 p.

Environmental Protection and Sustainable Development: Legal Principles and Recommendations: adopted by the Experts Group on Environmental Law of the World Commission on Environment and Development. R.D. Munro, Chairman: L.G. Lammers, Rapporteur. June 1986. London: Graham & Trotman, 1987. xxi, 196 p.

The principle mandate of the Experts Group was to prepare legal principles which ought to be in place before the year 2000 to support environmental protection and sustainable development within and among all States. This book contains the draft principles and final report of the Experts Group. The annexes contain a list of international agreements and selected reference documents are reprinted.

Housman, Robert F., and Durwood J. Zaelke. "Making Trade and Environmental Policies Mutually Reinforcing: Forging Competitive Sustainability," *Environmental Law* 23 (1993): 545-573

Proposal for a Basic Law on Environmental Protection and the Promotion of Sustainable Development. Mexico: UNEP, 1993. 96 p.

Robinson, Nicholas, and Wolfgang Burhenne. *International Protection of the Environment: Conservation in Sustainable Development*. Dobbs Ferry: Oceana, 1994. 1 volume (looseleaf) (forthcoming). This is the first in a new series subtitled Conservation in Sustainable Development.

Runnalls, David, and Aaron Cosbey. *Trade and Sustainable Development: A Survey of the Issues and a New Research Agenda*. Winnipeg: International Institute for Sustainable Development, 1992. 130 p.

Schmidheiny, Stephan. *Changing Course: A Global Business Perspective on Development and the Environment*. Cambridge, Mass.: MIT Press, 1992. xxiii, 374 p.

Trade andSustainable Development: Principles. Winnipeg: International Institute for Sustainable Development, 1994. 32 p.

S. Tuna - Dolphin Dispute

Hurlock, Matthew Hunter. "The GATT, U.S. Law and the Environment: A Proposal to Amend the GATT in Light of the Tuna/Dolphin Decision," 92 *Columbia Law Review* 92 (1992): 2098-2161.

Kirgis, Frederic L., Jr. "Environment and Trade Measures after the Tuna/Dolphin Decision," *Washington and Lee Law Review* 49 (1992):1221-1226.

Skilton, Thomas E. "GATT and the Environment in Conflict : The Tuna-Dolphin Dispute and the Quest for an International Conservation Strategy," *Cornell International Law Journal* 26 (1993): 455-494.

Spracker, Stanley M., and David C. Lundsgaard. "Dolphins and Tuna: Renewed Attention on the Future of Free Trade and Protection of the Environment," *Columbia Journal of Environmental Law* 18 (1993): 385-418.

T. United Nations Conferences on the Environment

The 1972 Stockholm Confence on the Human Environment led to the emergence of important legal principles and concepts and also resulted in the establishment of the United Nations Environment Programme (UNEP). The adoption by the UNEP Governing Council in May 1982, of the Montevideo Programme for the Development and Periodic Review of Environmental Law has contributed to the negotiation of important international treaties. The United Nations Conference on Environment and Development held in Rio in June 1992 provided a crucial international forum for the discussion of critical environmental issues. Chapter 38 of Agenda 21 asks UNEP to take the leading role in international environmental law.

American Bar Association. Division for Public Services. Standing Committee on Environmental Law. *The Role of Law in the 1992 United Nations Conference on Environment and Development.Presentations and Papers,May and August,1991* Washington, D.C.: American Bar Association, c1992. 49 p. Chapters of particular interest concern international financing mechanisms and institutional responses; and intellectual property rights and technology.

Campiglio, Luigi, et al. *The Environment After Rio: International Law and Economics.* International Environmental Law and Policy Series. London: Graham & Trotman, 1994. xvi, 285 p.

In the aftermath of UNCED, the Istituto per l'Ambiente and the Fondazione Eni Enrico Mattei held a conference from the 11-13 February 1993 to indentify trends of international environmental policy and to work out priorities for the near future. This book of conference papers explores the political, economic, and legal implications of the environmental themes discussed at Rio. The book is organized as follows: Part One: The Rio Conference between Policy and Law; Part Two: The Declarations and the Conventions Adopted in Rio; Part Three: Prospects for the Future in Light of Agenda 21 and of the Evolving Principles of

International Environmental Law; Part Four: Environment: Development and Interdependence.

Robinson, Nicholas A., ed. *Agenda 21: Earth's Action Plan.* Dobbs Ferry: Oceana, 1993. 1 v. This reprints the final version and includes commentary on tracing preparatory committee discussions and compares the language of earlier drafts.

Robinson, Nicholas A., ed. *Agenda 21 and the UNCED Proceedings.* Published in cooperation with the International Union for the Conservation of Nature and Natural Resources (IUCN) Dobbs Ferry: Oceana, 1992. 6 v. This reprints the final version of Agenda 21, background papers, treaties and other documents.

Roht-Arriaza, Naomi. *UNCED Undermined: Why Free Trade Won't Save the Planet: Report Prepared by Greenpeace International.* Greenpeace UNCED Reports. Washington, D.C.: Greenpeace International, 1992. iii, 16 p.

Spector, Bertram, Gunnar Sjostedt, and I. William Zartman, eds. *Negotiating International Regimes: Lessons Learned from the UN Conference on Environment and Development.* London: Graham & Trotman; The Hague: Nijhoff, 1994. 288 p. This is a collection of 15 papers and 3 documentary appendices. Perhaps the most relevant study for this bibliography is the paper, "The Search for Flexibility for Financial Issues at UNCED: an Analysis of Preference Adjustment" by B.I. Spector.

U. Wildlife

Grosse, W. Jack. *The Protection and Management of Our Natural Resources, Wildlife and Habitat.* Dobbs Ferry: Oceana, 1992. vii, 353 p. This provides an excellent survey of U.S. policy of natural resources and wildlife. The last chapter devotes 30 pages to U.S. international commitments under the more important international environmental treaties. The Atlantic fisheries and whaling are among the topics discussed.

Lyster, Simon. *International Wildlife Law: An Analysis of International Treaties Concerned with the Conservation of Wildlife.* Cambridge: Grotius, 1985. xxiii, 470 p. This book presents a comprehensive analysis of international wildlife law. It describes 27 treaties in detail, and many others briefly. Part I is a brief description of basic principles of international law and how they relate to wildlife treaties. Part II examines treaties designed to protect either a single species or a group of species by restricting the killing or trading of animals rather than protecting their habitat. Part III examines four regional nature conservation treaties affecting the Americas, Africa, Europe and Antarctica. Part IV covers the big four wildlife treaties. These cover wetlands, habitats of outstanding universal value, international trade in wildlife and migratory species. Fisheries treaties are excluded. Citations to official sources are provided in the footnotes.

STATE OF THE ART ADR:
MULTI-STEP DISPUTE RESOLUTION

George W. Coombe, Jr.
Graham & James

I. Introduction

Today, the complexity of commercial transactions, whether domestic or international, often reflect a willingness of the parties to create and sustain a comprehensive business relationship, over an extended period of time, in the expectation of mutual economic benefit. These contemporary endeavors are far more complex than those traditional undertakings, essentially simple and discrete, identified with an earlier world unaffected by dramatic technological change and the proliferation of free trade. Expectations of the parties to such commercial transactions must, of necessity, include the probability that disputes will arise in direct relationship to the complexity and duration of their several mutual undertakings. Accordingly, senior corporate executives have become more demanding and sophisticated in their expectations pertaining to the management of legal support services and the containment of corporate legal expense, both domestic and international. A brief description of those expectations provides a convenient point of departure for consideration of new approaches in the settlement of disputes.

II. Client Expectations

Client sensitivities to litigation exposure and the need for active client participation in early understanding of that exposure have become increasingly evident. Corporate executives now assume an aggressive role in the review and appraisal of major litigation and in the charting of a critical path to an efficacious resolution of the underlying controversy. Briefly put, management's objective is to create a preventive law/legal compliance environment to reduce legal risk and contain legal expense, particularly litigation expense. An important component of that environment is management understanding of dispute resolution alternatives ("ADR").

It is a reasonable assumption that, if properly informed, most individuals and most business entities would rather resolve their disputes in a timely and decent manner than be preoccupied with an interminable formal legal process. Business-related controversies rarely involve matters of principle or morality. Generally, the sole question is one of money, and corporate officers can manage that problem. Accordingly, many U.S. corporations, whether conducting domestic or international business, and regardless of size, have created a preventive law/legal compliance environment. In that regard, the corporate commitment begins with the chief executive, extends from that officer to all senior executives, including the general counsel, and on to every line manager. Often that commitment is manifested by a public statement of a corporate "pledge" to use ADR. The described environment relies heavily, in many corporations, upon the instruction of line officers in dispute resolution techniques with particular emphasis upon negotiation strategies to minimize future disputes. The ability of those officers to resolve business disputes, without the assistance of counsel, remains critical to the success of any such instructional effort. Finally, corporations are re-examining transactional documentation and attendant policies and procedures to assure a consistent and viable position in the address of any dispute involving their business activities.

III. The Relationship of the Parties

Accordingly, the basic objective throughout is to encourage amicable resolutions of those business disputes and, thereby, a continuation and strengthening of the underlying business relationship involved. Attainment of that basic objective will be enhanced through careful attention, during the negotiation of the underlying agreement, to the resolution of anticipated future disputes between the parties. Those engaged in such negotiations should consider the implications (or realities) of the litigation alternative (particularly, transnational litigation); determine the dispute resolution alternative most responsive to client priorities; and take advantage of the comparative good feeling and cooperation existing at this time when the parties manifest a strong desire to negotiate an agreement and continue a long-lived relationship. Again, it is important, at the onset of their negotiations, for the parties to focus their attention upon the probability that future disputes will arise between them, disputes derived from the language of the underlying agreement and its application. Thereby, the drafting process itself will reflect the growing determination of client executives to manage and control the dispute resolution process as they would manage and control any other aspect of the business relationship governed by the underlying agreement. Before focusing upon that drafting process, however, it will prove helpful to consider, briefly, the realities underlying traditional commercial litigation.

IV. The Litigation "Alternative"

Traditionally, in the absence of any dispute resolution clause, the only "alternative" when a dispute arose during the application of a business transaction was litigation. Domestic litigation presents any client with formidable risks familiar to counsel. The exposure to legal expense and delay; the ultimate "all or nothing" decision; the attendant publicity; and the damaging effect upon business relationships need no elaboration here. Transnational litigation presents two additional concerns: will the forum chosen accept jurisdiction; and will the client be able to make effective use of the judgment or decree that emerges from the litigation. Some uncertainty can be removed if the parties agreed upon resolution of any controversy by a designated national court. However, questions remain regarding the extent to which such "exclusivity" provisions, choice of forum and choice of law, will be honored. The scope of party autonomy in that regard may be constrained by the law of the forum or by that of another country under choice of law principles. Accordingly, it is not surprising that counsel and client often conclude that an arbitration clause can accomplish all of the objectives of the choice of forum provision while avoiding many of the inevitable transnational litigation burdens.

V. Commercial Arbitration

The relative attractiveness of commercial arbitration is a reflection of the shortcomings of litigation. The process, if properly applied, permits a maximum of party autonomy, minimal intrusion by courts, and, with regard to international arbitration, recognition and enforcement of the arbitral award pursuant to the New York Convention.[358] Thus, arbitration presents several advantages:

---

[358] *United Nations Convention on the Recognition and Enforcement of Foreign Arbitral Awards*, June 10, 1958, 21 U.S.T. 2517, 330 U.N.T.S. 3.

party choice of arbitrators (selection of desired expertise); priority over litigation; limited appeal from arbitral awards; confidentiality; party convenience; procedural informality; and enforcement of the arbitral award as a judgment.

Nevertheless, commercial arbitration frequently fails to live up to its billing as a "speedy and economical" substitute for litigation, especially in large or complex transnational disputes. In short, while commercial arbitration is superior to litigation, it often is characterized as a dispute resolution technique accompanied by high costs; procedural uncertainties depending upon the arbitral forum; absence of party involvement; uncertainty in application of regulatory law by foreign arbitrators; and lack of uniformity in the enforcement of awards against foreign nationals. Regardless of the care with which an arbitration agreement has been structured, problems of formality and procedure persist. Thus, getting to arbitration may prove a major hurdle. Resort to judicial process may be necessary to address various preliminary issues. These issues include the enforceability of the arbitration provision; the arbitration of the dispute; compliance with preconditions to arbitration; waiver of the right to arbitrate; and problems relating to multi-party disputes.

Once arbitration begins, the informality of the process may produce frustrations for those accustomed to traditional civil process. The absence of pre-hearing discovery and detailed pleadings may mean that a party comes to the hearings without a complete understanding of the character of the opposition's case, let alone knowledge of what documents are to be relied upon or what witnesses are to be called. Further, the failure to define disputed issues at the pre-hearing stage may have a dramatic impact on the presentation of evidence and the final resolution of the dispute. Difficulties may also arise when arbitrators are required to deal with procedural issues not specifically addressed by the arbitration rules. However, many in the business community believe that the most significant problems with modern arbitration do not relate to formal inadequacies but rather the increasing formalization of the process brought about by the legal profession. And, finally, serious problems may be encountered in the drafting of an arbitral award and its subsequent enforceability.

Accordingly, stimulated by a growing recognition of the counter-productive features of formal adjudicatory procedures such as litigation and arbitration, many within the legal profession have begun to concentrate on a search for better ways to resolve legal disputes. The principal objectives which have motivated the search for alternative procedures is a mirror image of the list of problems identified as inherent in the conventional procedures: i.e., the desire for management participation; the need to resolve the dispute without terminating the underlying business relationship or destroying the mutual confidence upon which it is based; the need to focus the attention of the parties upon the main issues in the dispute and to minimize the diversions of time and energy to procedural and other ancillary issues; and the encouragement of free dialogue.

VI. Negotiation Alternatives Precedent to Arbitration

In light of the foregoing considerations, one can take advantage of the non-binding negotiation procedures hereinafter discussed as alternatives for addressing complex disputes. Those procedures can be structured within the framework of arbitral proceedings. Indeed, the arbitral framework affords the parties great flexibility which will permit them to define the scope and mechanics of the proceeding so as to accomplish the main objectives of the alternative procedures and still lead to a final adjudication in the event that a negotiated settlement is not reached.

Any such framework must be carefully designed or the alternative procedures may undermine the effectiveness of the arbitration agreement if arbitration eventually is required. On the other hand, incorporation of the alternative procedures into a properly-structured arbitration agreement may offer the best means of avoiding some of the problems and complications arising out of differences in national laws and judicial proceedings. The incorporation into an arbitration agreement of provisions for the use of alternative procedures may be of substantial assistance in ensuring that the alternative procedures will work as intended and will not produce unanticipated results. This consequence flows both from the latitude afforded the parties in construing arbitral procedures and, with regard to international arbitration, from the international protection against judicial intervention provided by the New York Convention.

For example, it is possible to design arbitration agreements under which the demand for arbitration automatically would trigger preliminary non-binding procedures prior to the appointment of arbitrators. If properly structured, such provisions would not only insulate those procedures from judicial interference but also enable the party invoking the alternative procedures to obtain the assistance of the court in compelling a recalcitrant opponent to go forward with those procedures as an integral part of the arbitration. At present, use of the arbitral framework offers the most promising approach for the application of alternative non-binding, negotiation procedures to transnational business disputes. It will now prove helpful to address two questions: How should the process involved in drafting an appropriate dispute resolution clause for the underlying agreement proceed; and how should the clause be structured to assure compatibility with the described business objectives pertaining to dispute resolutions?

VII. Drafting the Dispute Resolution Clause

An important condition precedent to any successful drafting effort is careful client preparation to assure realistic consideration of the nature of potential future disputes arising under the underlying agreement or its application. Accordingly, both parties must approach the drafting process with motivation appropriate to assure an intention to satisfy the procedures prescribed in the event of a future dispute. The success of any ultimate negotiation will reflect the integrity of the parties in their mutual effort to create a viable dispute resolution process. The drafting effort also should address the inclusion of procedural formalities to assure party understanding of the merits of any future dispute and the need for timely address of that dispute by appropriate management representatives. Indeed, the negotiating process should confirm the existence of an internal corporate preventive law/legal compliance environment, including management understanding of dispute resolution alternatives, to reduce legal risk and contain legal expense. This environment should include management instruction in dispute resolution techniques, with emphasis upon negotiation strategies to minimize future disputes and to resolve them, whenever possible, without the involvement of counsel.

Any clause ultimately negotiated should prescribe fairly explicit procedures and create a framework within which to particularize provisions unique to the parties and their relationship. One example, suggested here, is a multi-step approach establishing an informal, tiered procedure for ironing out disputes before they threaten to ruin the ongoing business activity.

VIII. A Suggested Dispute Resolution Procedure

Most bona fide disagreements or disputes between reputable companies, and in particular disputes between companies in different countries, are best regarded as business problems to be resolved promptly through business-oriented negotiations. If such negotiations become deadlocked, a non-binding, non-adjudicative resolution should be attempted before resorting to an ultimate binding resolution, commercial arbitration.

Consideration should be given to the following three successive stages of dispute resolution:

A. *Negotiation.* A provision requiring negotiations between executives with decision-making authority, who are at a higher level than the personnel involved in the dispute.

B. *Non-Binding Resolutions.* A provision requiring some form of non-binding dispute resolution, such as mediation or minitrial.

C. *Binding Resolution.* A "backstop" final adjudication device, binding arbitration.

It is important the approach suggested reflect the management policy of both parties to the underlying agreement. Accordingly, it is advisable not to defer the subject of dispute resolution until the end of the contract negotiations. The other side may need time to reflect on the proposal, particularly if it has not previously employed multi-step clauses. Traditionally, dispute resolution clauses, when used at all, provided simply for arbitration of future disputes and were regarded as "boilerplate." Yet even a single dispute allowed to get out of hand can sour a business relationship. When two parties enter into an important or long term relationship, business executives should discuss how they intend to manage the relationship, including how they will deal with disputes. The type of multi-step clauses suggested should not be viewed as "boilerplate" but should represent the expression of both managements' resolve to assure the success of the venture by treating potential disputes as business problems and by providing a process to address them effectively and expeditiously. Management support for the multi-step approach is vital.

Suggested clauses for insertion in the underlying agreement follow, together with commentary.

A. The Negotiation Clause:

Negotiations Between Executives

> The parties shall attempt in good faith to resolve any dispute arising out of or relating to this agreement promptly by negotiations between executives who have authority to settle the controversy. Any party may give the other party written notice of any dispute not resolved in the normal course of business. Within 20 days after delivery of said notice, executives of both parties shall meet at a mutually acceptable time and place, and thereafter as often as they reasonably deem necessary, to exchange relevant information and to attempt to resolve the dispute. If the matter has not been resolved within 60 days of the disputing party's notice, or if the parties fail to meet within 20 days, either party may initiate mediation (or a minitrial) of the controversy or claim as provided hereinafter.
>
> If a negotiator intends to be accompanied at a meeting by an attorney, the other negotiator shall be given at least three working days' notice of such intention and may also be accompanied by an attorney. All negotiations pursuant to this clause are confidential and shall be treated as compromise and settlement negotiations for purposes of the United States Federal Rules of Evidence and State Rules of Evidence."

Commentary

Negotiation is the time-honored initial step in attempting to resolve disputes. However, because the particular representatives of the parties who are directly involved in the dispute are often so close to the dispute, it can be difficult for them to reach agreement. Therefore it often is useful to have a specific contract provision that requires, in the event of an impasse between the initial negotiating parties, the establishment of a structure for rational discussion, within which negotiations are more likely to continue to productive result. It is therefore suggested that the dispute be referred to the next level of management within each organization, so that managers who are not directly involved in the dispute can attempt, perhaps with greater objectivity, to resolve the dispute and that negotiations take place within specific time frames.

All deadlines specified in these sample clauses are of necessity arbitrary. The parties should feel free when drafting the underlying agreement to agree on deadlines more appropriate to their relationship. Moreover, deadlines can be extended by mutual agreement; this is likely to happen if, when a deadline approaches, satisfactory progress has been made but more time is needed.

Maintaining the confidentiality of information disclosed and positions taken in the course of dispute-settlement negotiations is a common concern. A negotiation clause should attempt to provide contractual assurance of confidentiality.

B. Non-Binding Resolution Clause

Mediation (or Minitrial)

> If the dispute has not been resolved by negotiation as provided herein, the parties shall endeavor to settle the dispute by (mediation) (minitrial). The neutral third party will be selected from the _______________ Panel of Neutrals. If the parties encounter difficulty in agreeing on a neutral, they will seek the assistance of ____________ in the selection process."

Commentary

Mediation or minitrial? Essentially mediation involves the introduction of a neutral third party who helps each party rationally evaluate its own claims and risks in relation to those of the opposing party, and who may in addition provide insights into the dispute which assist in a negotiated resolution. Mediation is a conciliatory procedure. Hopefully, the mediator will help the parties develop creative, business-oriented options for settlement.

A minitrial is a negotiating procedure generally, not always, assisted by a neutral third party whereby the dispute is presented in abbreviated "trial" form to senior officials of the disputing parties, who, after seeing the strengths and weaknesses of each side carefully and openly presented, attempt to reach a negotiated resolution. The neutral commonly explains to the negotiators how the case "played" to him and may evolve into a facilitator or mediator of the settlement negotiations. The minitrial is more structured than a mediation, and generally demands greater preparation from each side. It is particularly applicable to major disputes in which business decision makers find it worthwhile to maintain a strong personal involvement.

Alternative Clause

Mediation (or Minitrial) with Designated Neutral

If the dispute has not been resolved by negotiation as provided herein, the parties shall endeavor to settle the dispute by (mediation) (minitrial). The parties have selected ________ as the (mediator) (neutral advisor) in any such dispute, and he has agreed to serve in that capacity and to be available on reasonable notice. In the event ____________ is or becomes unwilling or unable to serve, the parties have selected ____________ as the alternative (mediator) (neutral advisor). In the event that neither ____________ nor ______________ is willing or able to serve, the parties, assuming they cannot agree on a neutral, will seek assistance of ______________ in the selection process."

Commentary

It is often easier to agree upon a designated neutral before any dispute actually arises. The neutral can be available for swift assistance if his selection and terms of retention already have been established. Moreover, if the neutral is known and respected by both sides, the mere possibility of his intervention may of itself be an inducement to a negotiated settlement. Given the importance of the neutral to both parties, it may be desirable to specify an alternate in the event that the first choice is unavailable or unwilling, for some reason, to serve. Only in the event that neither neutral was available would the parties face the task of agreeing on a neutral with a dispute between the parties pending.

C. Binding Dispute Resolution Clause.

Arbitration

Any dispute arising out of or relating to this Agreement or the breach, termination or validity thereof, which has not been resolved by non-binding means as provided herein within 60 days (90-120 days if the minitrial procedure was chosen) of the initiation of such procedure, shall be finally settled by arbitration conducted expeditiously in accordance with the ____________ Rules.

The place of arbitration shall be ________________.

The appointing authority shall be ________________.

The governing law of this Agreement shall be the substantive law of ______________________.

The arbitral tribunal shall be composed of three arbitrators, one to be appointed by each party, and the two arbitrators so appointed, shall, within ___________ days, appoint a third arbitrator, (who shall be chosen from a country other than those of which the parties are nationals, who shall be fluent in the language of the arbitration), who shall act as chairman of the tribunal.

The language of the arbitration shall be ________________.

Commentary

The arbitration clause proposal is self-executing, i.e., it incorporates by reference the rules of an arbitral institution thereby assuring resolution of all procedural problems pursuant to those rules. The arbitral institution or center chosen also will provide the administrative services and logistical support usually required by the parties and the arbitrators. The clause also recognizes the fact the parties to a transnational dispute may represent different nationalities. The right of the parties to appoint arbitrators of their own choosing and, in turn, to involve those party-appointed arbitrators in the choice of the third arbitrator, enhances party confidence in the integrity of the arbitral process and its outcome.

The geographical location of the arbitration is important as the national law of the situs or "seat" of the arbitration becomes the external legal reference for the procedural governance of the arbitration. Accordingly, whatever location is chosen, the parties should understand the local law application of any mandated procedural rules and their interaction with the rules adopted by the parties. Finally, it is most important the national state where an international arbitration proceeding is held has adopted the N.Y. Convention, to assure recognition and enforcement of any arbitral award.

APPENDIX:

DISPUTE RESOLUTION CLAUSE

1. Negotiation Between Executives

The parties shall attempt in good faith to resolve any dispute arising out of or relating to this Agreement promptly by negotiation between executives who have authority to settle the controversy. Any party may give the other party written notice of any dispute not resolved in the normal course of business. Within twenty (20) days after delivery of said notice, executives of both parties shall meet at a mutually acceptable time and place, and thereafter as often as they reasonably deem necessary, to exchange relevant information and to attempt to resolve the dispute. If the matter has not been resolved within sixty (60) days of the disputing party's notice, or if the parties fail to meet within 20 days, either party may initiate mediation (or a minitrial) of the controversy or claim as provided hereinafter.

If a negotiator intends to be accompanied at a meeting by an attorney, the other negotiator shall be given at least three (3) working days' notice of such intention and may also be accompanied by an attorney. All negotiations pursuant to this clause are confidential and shall be treated as compromise and settlement negotiations for purposes of the United States Federal Rules of Evidence and State Rules of Evidence.

2. Mediation (or Minitrial)

If the dispute has not been resolved by negotiation as provided herein, the parties shall endeavor to settle the dispute by (mediation) (minitrial). The neutral third party will be selected from the ____________ Panel of Neutrals. If the parties encounter difficulty in agreeing on a neutral, they will seek the assistance of __________ in the selection process.

[2. Mediation (or Minitrial) With Designated Neutral]

If the dispute has not been resolved by negotiation as provided herein, the parties shall endeavor to settle the dispute by (mediation) (minitrial). The parties have selected ___________ as (mediator) (neutral advisor) in any such dispute, and he has agreed to serve in that capacity and to be available on reasonable notice. In the event _________ is or becomes unwilling or unable to serve, the parties have selected __________ as the alternative (mediator) (neutral advisor). In the event that neither ___________ nor _________ is willing or able to serve, the parties, assuming they cannot agree on a neutral, will seek the assistance of ___________ in the selection process.]

In any mediation, evidence of anything said or of any admission made in the course of the mediation is not admissible in evidence, and disclosure of any such evidence shall not be compelled in any civil action in which, pursuant to law, testimony can be compelled to be given.

Unless the document otherwise provides, no document prepared for the purpose of or in the course of, or pursuant to, the mediation, or copy thereof, is admissible in evidence, and disclosure of any such document shall not be compelled in any civil action in which, pursuant to law, testimony can be compelled to be given.

3. Arbitration

Any dispute arising out of or relating to this Agreement or the breach, termination or validity thereof, which has not been resolved by non-binding means as provided herein within 60 days [90-120 days if the minitrial procedure was chosen] of the initiation of such procedure, shall be finally settled by arbitration conducted expeditiously in accordance with the ___________ Rules.

The place of arbitration shall be ______________.

The appointing authority shall be ______________.

The governing law of this Agreement shall be the substantive law of ______________.

The arbitral tribunal shall be composed of three (3) arbitrators, one to be appointed by each party, and the two arbitrators so appointed shall within ______ days, appoint a third arbitrator, who shall be chosen from a country other than those of which the parties are nationals, who shall be fluent in the language of the arbitration, and who shall act as chairman of the tribunal.

The language of the arbitration shall be ___________.

FINDING INFORMATION ABOUT INTERNATIONAL COMMERCIAL ARBITRATION[359]

Amber Lee Smith
Foreign and International Law Librarian
Los Angeles County Law Library

International commercial arbitration is used increasingly as a means of dispute resolution. Between 1979 and 1990, the International Chamber of Commerce alone received 3500 cases, as many as it had received between 1923 and 1978, the first 55 years of its history.[360] The result is an increase in the demand for information about all aspects of international commercial arbitration and publication of more sources for this information. But as librarians know, the mere proliferation of sources does not necessarily make finding specific information easier. Indeed, sometimes one can have too many sources and not enough useful information. The purpose of this chapter is to suggest sources which may be useful in answering questions about specific aspects of international commercial arbitration.

I. Research Strategies

It may be simplistic, but it is nonetheless true that research strategy for international commercial arbitration is determined by the sources available. For a librarian in a small collection, this frequently means consulting whatever sources are available in that collection and then knowing what sources are available in other collections. In larger collections research will be more efficient if the appropriate specialized source can be identified. Toward this end it is important to determine the type of information needed to answer the question and to elicit as much information as possible from the patron. Information about which arbitral institution is

---

[359] Some of the ideas in this chapter first appeared in briefer form in Amber Lee Smith, *Finding Texts of International Commercial Arbitral Awards*, 4 Cal. Int'l Prac., Spring-Summer 1993, at 81.

[360] Brower, Charles N., *Introduction*, International Arbitration in the 21st Century: Towards "Judicialization" and Uniformity? ix (Twelfth Sokol Colloquium, 1992), citing Bond, *The International Arbitrator from the Perspective of the ICC International Court of Arbitration*, 12 Nw. J. Int'l L. & Bus, 3, n. 5 (1991).

involved is especially useful. Many of the sources deal only with specific institutions and the rules of the institution determine whether, how, and where the text of an award is published. The subject of the arbitration and the date are helpful both as indexing points and as means of identifying particular arbitrations. The names of the parties are less important for most arbitrations because they tend to be deleted from the publication. Information about the country or countries involved is often more helpful.

In the bibliography which appears as the appendix to this chapter, there are numerous treatises and periodicals listed which give general information about international commercial arbitration. The introductory chapters in Rubino-Sammartano's *International Arbitration Law* and in Redfern and Hunter's *Law and Practice of International Commercial Arbitration* are particularly useful in this regard. However, most of the questions directed to law librarians require the use of specialized sources. Questions tend to fall into five categories: 1) the texts of national arbitration legislation; 2) the texts of treaties on international arbitration; 3) the rules of arbitral tribunals; 4) the texts of arbitral awards; and 5) court decisions on arbitral awards.

II. The Texts of National Arbitration Legislation

The text of arbitration legislation for a particular country will, of course, appear somewhere in that country's statutes. In most civil law jurisdictions arbitration is found in articles in the commercial code and/or in the code of civil procedure. The difficulty is finding the citation to the appropriate statute and, in many cases, finding a translation of the statute. The first source to consult is Reynolds and Flores, *Foreign Law: Current Sources of Codes and Legislation in Jurisdictions of the World*. In this source the subject heading is "Arbitration, domestic and international (civil)", and the references are to specific statutes and to sources for reprints and translations of those statutes. There are also references to arbitration treaties to which the country is a party. Many of the references to reprints and translations are to two sources: *World Arbitration Reporter* and *International Handbook on Commercial Arbitration*. *World Arbitration Reporter* covers more countries and includes countries of the Caribbean and South America, and a few countries of Africa and Asia. *World Arbitration Reporter* and *International Handbook of Commercial Arbitration* have similar, but not identical coverage of Europe. Legislation for some countries is reprinted in the *New York*

Convention section of Oceana's *International Commercial Arbitration.* All of these are looseleaf services so their contents are updated periodically, but the researcher is advised to check the dates carefully because translations of new legislation do not appear immediately. Arbitration legislation for a number of Asian countries was included in *Doyle's Dispute Resolution Practice,* but that looseleaf ceased publication in 1992, and is beginning to be out of date. Compilations of translated texts of laws for different countries or regions should also be consulted.

New arbitration legislation presents additional challenges. The first is being aware that new legislation has been enacted. This information tends to be easier to find for countries in Europe and Latin America. One source about new legislation in European countries is the Digests and National Lists of legislation found in *European Current Law Year Book* and its supplement *European Current Law Monthly Digest.* This publication includes English language summaries of "significant" legislation and citations to the official text of legislation enacted. For Latin America, Spain, Portugal and the Portuguese-speaking countries of Africa, information about recent legislation can be found in the *World Law Index,* available online through RLIN. This database indexes legislation in the official gazettes of the countries covered and gives English language abstracts of new laws with citations to the official gazette. The *Bulletin of Legal Developments* includes English-language summaries of new legislation for many countries on a selective basis.

The text of new legislation appears in the official gazette and other legislative sources of the country. But if a translation is wanted, new legislation is difficult to find. The major looseleaf sources for translated texts of arbitration legislation tend to be updated only annually. Recent legislation which is deemed significant by the editors may appear in translation in *International Legal Materials* and selected statutes from European countries are translated in *Commercial Laws of Europe.* However, the translation process takes time, so delays of several months between the enactment of new legislation and the appearance of its translation should be expected. Translations occasionally appear in practice journals, so it is advisable to check periodical indexes and the contents of recent issues of journals which cover particular geographic regions or subjects. If these sources are unavailing and a summary is not sufficient, the patron may need to have a translation made from the vernacular text.

III. International Arbitration Treaties

Treaties dealing with international arbitration fall into three categories: the major multilateral treaties on arbitration and the enforcement of arbitral awards, a few bilateral treaties dealing directly with arbitration, and numerous bilateral commercial and investment treaties which include provisions on arbitration. The texts of the major multilateral treaties are generally available and they are reproduced in many of the sources listed in the bibliography. *News and Notes from the Institute for Transnational Arbitration* includes as a regular feature a table of adherence to transnational arbitration treaties. Bilateral treaties on arbitration can be more difficult to locate, if the United States is not a party. Bilateral investment treaties, which often refer the parties to ICSID [International Centre for the Settlement of Investment Disputes] arbitration, are indexed in *Bilateral Investment Treaties, 1959-1991*, a joint publication of the United Nations Centre on Transnational Corporations and the International Chamber of Commerce. The texts can usually be found in the treaty volumes of *Investment Laws of the World*. General commercial treaties, known as treaties of "friendship, commerce, and navigation", and other bilateral arbitration treaties may be found in the *World Treaty Index* and in the treaty collections of the countries which are parties. Recent treaties may be found in the treaty compilations or official gazettes of the parties, but there is no general index of these treaties, and not all of the treaty compilations have individual indexes.

Commentaries and court decisions concerning the major multilateral treaties can be found in all of the treatises on international commercial arbitration and in many articles. The standard periodical indexes should be consulted, as well as the indexes for selected multilateral and bilateral treaties in the *Yearbook Commercial Arbitration* which are cumulated in the *Yearbook Key*. Treaties to which the United States is a party can be "shepardized" in *Shepard's United States Citations*.

There are private agreements between arbitral institutions, sometimes referred to as inter-association arbitration agreements. These are not treaties, but they may form the basis for arbitration between private parties in different countries. Many of these have been concluded by the American Arbitration Association. Because these are not treaties, the texts may be difficult to find. The American Arbitration Association reprints all of its private agreements in *The International Arbitration Kit: A Compilation of Basic and Frequently Requested Documents*.

IV. The Rules of Arbitral Tribunals

The rules of international arbitral institutions are reproduced in *World Arbitration Reporter, International Handbook of Commercial Arbitration*, and Oceana's *International Commercial Arbitration*. Rules are also be found in other regional and individual country sources listed in the bibliography. New rules may appear in *International Legal Materials* and in *Yearbook Commercial Arbitration*. If the rules of a particular institution are not in one of the looseleaf services, they may be in a pamphlet published by that institution. This is a case where the trial and error approach to reference is called for, and searches in RLIN and OCLC for the institutional author may produce an answer.

V. The Texts of Arbitral Awards

The texts of arbitral awards are the items most often sought by researchers in international commercial arbitration and they are also the items least likely to be available. The publication of arbitral awards is very limited and for good reasons: arbitrations are historically confidential and they have no precedential value. Isaak Dore explains this phenomenon as follows:

> The general nature of the arbitral and conciliation process is such that, in contrast to judicial proceedings, they can be conducted discreetly, privately, and confidentially. Because each of the former two processes proceeds only on a case-by-case basis, *there is no need to develop a body of case law to guide future arbitrators or conciliators. There is no need to publish the decisions and settlements reached*, as is the case with court decisions under both the common law and civil law systems. It is also possible that the avoidance of publicity may be the decisive consideration in choosing arbitration or conciliation. Private proceedings can protect the good name or image of the parties, while companies can rest assured that the privacy of the

> proceedings will preserve trade secrets and/or other proprietary information.[361]

But balanced against these considerations of privacy is the desire of practitioners and scholars to develop a kind of *lex mercatoria* of international commercial arbitration. This development involves understanding how arbitration works in particular kinds of disputes and how the rules of various arbitral tribunals are customarily applied. Awards that are deemed "public"- because they have been brought into court to be enforced or to be attacked- are traditionally published. The publication of other awards is determined by the rules of the arbitral institution. The desire for *lex mercatoria* for arbitration has led to rules which allow for publication of at least the legal rule of the award.

Most institutional rules continue to emphasize the confidential nature of awards, but take different approaches to publication. The UNCITRAL [United Nations Commission on International Trade Law] Rules provide that "[t]he award may be made public only with the consent of both parties." Others allow publication in some form if the names of the parties and other identifying facts are removed. The Iran-United States Claims Tribunal operates under the UNCITRAL rules, but the rule on publication was modified to provide that "all the awards . . . be made available to the public." However, the tribunal may, on the request of a party, "make public only portions . . . from which the identity of the parties, other identifying facts and trade or military secrets have been deleted." The ICSID Rule does not allow publication of the complete award without the consent of the parties, but allows for the publication of excerpts of the legal rules applied by the Tribunal. Parties who choose to arbitrate with the Society of Maritime Arbitrators do so with the understanding that the arbitration will be published.

This liberalization of publication policy has less effect in practice than in theory. Generally an arbitral award which can be published under the rules of one of the major arbitral institutions will appear in several locations, and be indexed, but an award from a less well-known institution, albeit publishable, will appear only in a

---

[361] Dore, Isaak I. *Arbitration and Conciliation under the UNCITRAL Rules: A Textual Analysis* 5 (1986) (emphasis added).

proprietary publication and probably will not be indexed. Finding the texts of arbitral awards is often a matter of trial and error.

The greatest variety of arbitral awards is found in *Yearbook Commercial Arbitration*. It publishes excerpts of arbitral awards from ICSID, ICC [International Chamber of Commerce], the European Union, maritime arbitrations and awards from arbitral institutions in various countries, and *ad hoc* arbitrations. The awards are published without the names of parties or other identifying data unless the award has been published in full in another source or is a matter of public record. Access is through a cumulative index known as the *Yearbook Key*, and through the annual indexes in each volume.

Extracts of decisions of the International Court of Arbitration of the International Chamber of Commerce have been published in the *ICC International Court of Arbitration Bulletin* since 1990. Selected awards of the court for the period 1974 - 1990 are published in the two volume *Collection of ICC Arbitral Awards*. These are awards which have appeared previously in *Yearbook Commercial Arbitration*, *Journal du Droit International (Clunet)*, or *International Construction Law Review*. The advantage to using the compilation is that it is well-indexed, and the Chronological Index includes references to commentary on specific awards.

Iran-United States Claims Tribunal Reports is the complete collection of published awards for that tribunal, but some of the awards have also appeared in other sources. *Arbitration Materials* has published awards of the Iran-United States Claims Tribunal and awards of the Society of Maritime Arbitrators. This publication is also one of the sources for the texts of *ad hoc* arbitrations. *International Legal Materials* may publish the texts of arbitral awards which have been made public, and is sometimes a source for *ad hoc* arbitrations. It has annual and ten year indexes. *Lloyd's Arbitration Reports* includes the texts of awards for ICSID, ICC, and the Society of Maritime Arbitrators. Another source available in some collections is Mealy's *International Arbitration Report*, a looseleaf which appears monthly and reportedly contains the texts of court and arbitral panel decisions.

For library patrons who can use foreign language sources, the following sources are be helpful. *Revue de l'arbitrage; Bulletin du Comité français de l'arbitrage* publishes the texts of French, international, and *ad hoc* arbitrations, and has annual and five year indexes. *Journal du Droit International (Clunet)* publishes excerpts of ICSID and ICC awards. It has an annual index and is also indexed in *Index to Foreign Legal Periodicals.* Awards from Italy and Germany may appear in *Rivista dell'arbitrato,* which continues *Rassegna dell'arbitrato,* and *Jahrbuch fur die Praxis der Schiedsgerichtsbarkeit,* respectively.

Occasionally the texts of awards, or fairly detailed summaries of awards, appear in other law journals. This is more often the case if the award has been the subject of court proceedings. The standard periodical indexes would not indicate the presence of these awards. There are also summaries of awards in bulletins from arbitral institutions.

VI. Court Decisions Concerning Arbitral Awards

Court decisions concerning particular arbitral awards or the various international agreements on arbitration are, of course, published in the reporter series of the court rendering the decision. However, since these decisions come from many different courts, it is convenient to use general indexes and to have references to sources in translation. *International Commercial Arbitration and the Courts* is a digest which includes court decisions arranged by country under each topic, covering material through 1988. *Yearbook Commercial Arbitration* publishes excerpts from court decisions on arbitration in general and court decisions which relate specifically to UNCITRAL, the New York Convention, and the Washington Convention. There are cumulative lists of these decisions in the *Yearbook Key.* Full texts of court decisions in English also appear in *International Legal Materials, Lloyd's Arbitration Reports,* and *Arbitration Materials.*

VII. Conclusion

As is the case with all bibliographic essays and bibliographies, this material will be out of date almost as soon as it is published. Some of the sources described will remain useful, but others will be supplanted by better sources. There will be new editions and coverage will be expanded by supplementation. The practices regarding the use and publication of arbitral awards may change as well. The researcher is advised to regard these materials only as a starting point and to keep abreast of developments.

APPENDIX

SOURCES OF PRACTICE, RULES, AND TEXTS OF AWARDS

Introduction

The focus of this bibliography is on material which relates to the settlement of international commercial disputes by means of arbitration. Sources which deal primarily with dispute resolution between states have been omitted, but material on the Iran-United States Claims Tribunal is included because it gives insight into the practical application of the UNCITRAL rules. Materials for specific countries are limited to those which include international as well as domestic arbitration considerations.

I. In General

A. Books

The arbitral process and the independence of arbitrators = La procedure arbitrale et l'independance des arbitres. Publication no. 472. Paris: ICC, 1991. viii, 144 p. In English and French. Covers AAA, ICSID and ICC. Includes bibliographical references.

Bellet, P. et al. *Multi-party arbitration: views from international arbitration specialists*. Publication no. 480/1. Paris: ICC, 1991. 257 p. In English and French. Includes bibliographical references.

Essays on international commercial arbitration. Petar Šarevi ed. Boston: Graham & Trotman, 1989. ix, 247 p.

Evidence in international arbitration proceedings. Peter V. Eijsvoogel, ed. London: Graham & Trotman/Martinus Nijhoff for Association Internationale des Jeunes Avocats, 1994. xvi, 309 p. Part I consists of General Reports on evidence in common and civil law systems and taking and defending U.S.-style depositions. Part II consists of National Reports for 21 countries: Austria, Belgium, Brazil, Denmark, England and Wales, Finland, France, Germany, Ireland, Italy, Luxembourg, Mexico, Netherlands, Peru, Scotland, Spain, Sweden, Switzerland, Tunisia, United States, and Uruguay.

Gebrehana, Teklewold. *Arbitration: an element of international law.* Stockholm: Almqvist Y Wiksell International, 1984. 161 p.

Includes appendices with translation of national arbitration legislation for Saudi Arabia, France and the USSR. Indexed.

Grigera Naón, Horacio A. *Choice-of-law problems in international commercial arbitration.* Tübingen: Mohr (Paul Siebeck), 1992. xii, 337 p. Bibliographical references.

ICC International Court of Arbitration. *Conservatory and provisional measures in international arbitration.* Publication no. 519. Paris: ICC Publishing, 1993. 128 p. Series of addresses which deal generally with the powers of arbitrators, the experiences of institutions--AAA, ICSID, ICC--and the role of the courts.

The immunity of arbitrators. Julian D.M. Lew, ed. London: Lloyd's of London Press, 1990. xix, 139 p. Examines immunity for arbitrators in thirteen jurisdictions: Argentina, Australia, Austria, England, France, Germany, Japan, Netherlands, Norway, Spain, Sweden, Sweden, United States, and Switzerland; and under the rules of three arbitral institutions: AAA, ICSID, and the Grain and Feed Trade Association. Index.

International Arbitration Congress (11th: 1993: Bahrain). *International arbitration in a changing world: conference, Bahrain, 14-16 February, 1993.* Albert Jan van den Berg, ed. Boston: ICCA Congress series no. 6. Kluwer Law and Taxation Publishers, 1994. ix, 289 p. International Commercial Arbitration Conference (1st: 1985: Quebec).

Proceedings of the 1st international commercial arbitration conference. Nabil Antaki and Alain Prujiner, eds. Montreal: Wilson & Lafleur, 1986. 471 p. In French and English. Primarily commentary on UNCITRAL which was newly adopted at the time of the conference. Includes a table comparing specific provisions of UNCITRAL with the Uniform Arbitration Act and the Federal Arbitration Act.

International Council for Commercial Arbitration. Xth International Arbitration Congress, Stockholm, 28-31 May 1990. *1. Preventing delay and disruption of arbitration; 2. Effective proceedings in construction cases.* Albert Jan van den Berg, ed. Boston: ICCA Congress series no. 5. Kluwer Law and Taxation Publishers, 1991. xi, 614 p.

Lex Mercatoria and arbitration: a discussion of the new law merchant. Thomas E. Carbonneau, ed. Dobbs Ferry, NY: Transnational Juris Publications, 1990. xxi, 227 p. Discussion of the developing jurisprudence of arbitration. Index.

Lookofsky, Joseph M. *Transnational litigation and commercial arbitration: a comparative analysis of American, European, and international law.* Ardsley-on-Hudson, NY: Transnational Juris Publications, 1992. ix, 782 p. Text/casebook on litigation and arbitration with chapters on extraterritorial jurisdiction, applicable law in contract and tort, service of process, evidence, and recognition and enforcement of judgments, as well as international commercial arbitration. Extensive appendices include texts of conventions on various aspects of transnational litigation, the UNCITRAL model law, and the New York Convention on enforcement of arbitral awards.

Oehmke, Thomas H. *International arbitration.* Rochester, NY: Lawyers Cooperative Pub., 1990. xxvi, 1012 p. Practitioner's handbook on arbitration. Introduces a variety of arbitral institutions but focuses on AAA. Reproduces AAA forms with directions for their use. Extensive appendices include the texts of international arbitration laws

Practicing Law Institute

Both the Corporate law and practice course handbook series and the Commercial law and practice course handbook series have titles on international commercial arbitration. These sometimes include the texts of arbitration statutes and rules, and often include sample forms. The following are examples:

> *International arbitration between private parties and governments.* Gerald Aksen and Robert B. von Mehren, chrs. Corporate law and practice course handbook series, no. 399. New York: Practising Law Institute, 1982. 478 p.
>
> *International commercial arbitration: recent developments.* Emmanuel Gaillard and Robert B. von Mehren, chrs. Commercial law and practice course handbook series, no. 476-477. New York: Practising Law Institute, 1988. 2 v.

Redfern, Alan, Martin Hunter, and Murray Smith. *Law and practice of international commercial arbitration.* 2nd ed. London:

Sweet & Maxwell, 1991. lvii, 838 p. A complete discussion of the processes of international arbitration. The extensive appendices include the texts of many rules of arbitration, national arbitration statutes for England, France, the Netherlands, and the United States, and arbitration treaties. Detailed table of contents, tables of arbitral awards, statutes, and court decisions, index, and bibliographical references.

Resolving disputes: an international guide to commercial arbitration procedures. (Special supplement to the September issue of *International Financial Law Review*). London: Euromoney Publications, 1991. 83 p. Overview of the international arbitration laws of China, France, Hong Kong, Ireland, Italy, Netherlands, Nigeria, Saudi Arabia, Sweden, Switzerland, United Kingdom, and the United States with citations to the text of the law.

Rubino-Sammartano, Mauro. *International arbitration law.* Boston: Kluwer Law and Taxation Publishers, 1990. xii, 537 p. Textbook with bibliographical references and index.

Samuel, Adam. *Jurisdictional problems in international commercial arbitration: a study of Belgian, Dutch, English, French, Swedish, Swiss, U.S., and West German law.* (Publications of the Swiss Institute of Comparative Law, no. 11). Zurich: Schulthess, 1989. 333 p. Includes bibliographical references.

Schwebel, Stephen M. *International arbitration: Three salient problems.* Cambridge: Grotius, 1987. xviii, 303 p. Discussion of the severability of the arbitration agreement, denial of justice through governmental negation of arbitration, and the authority of truncated international arbitral tribunals. Includes bibliographical references and index.

Sokol Colloquium (6th: 1982: University of Virginia). *Resolving transnational disputes through international arbitration.* Thomas E. Carbonneau, ed. Charlottesville: University of Virginia Press, 1984. x, 301 p. Part III covers arbitration in a transnational commercial setting, dealing with the problems of court intervention, and comparing arbitration and litigation. Includes bibliographical references and index.

Sokol Colloquium (12th: 1992: Charlottesville, VA). *International arbitration in the 21st century: towards "judicialization" and uniformity?* Richard B. Lillich and Charles N. Brower, eds. Irvington, NY: Transnational Publishers, 1994. Indexed.

Toope, Stephen J. *Mixed international arbitration: studies inarbitration between states and private persons.* Cambridge: Grotius Publications, 1990. xxxi, 404 p. Examines the principal examples of institutional mixed arbitration: ICC commercial arbitration, ICSID arbitration, and the Iran-United States Claims Tribunal. Table of Cases includes decisions of international tribunals and decisions of national courts. Index.

B. Periodicals

The American review of international arbitration. Vol. 1-; April 1990-. Ardsley-on-Hudson, NY: Transnational Juris Publications. Quarterly. Includes articles and case notes, list of recent books and articles on international arbitration. Annual Table of Contents.

Arbitration International. Vol. 1-; April 1985-. London: Chartered Institute of Arbitrators. Quarterly. Articles about international arbitration and book reviews.

Dispute resolution journal. Vol. 1-6; 1937-1942. n.s., Vol 1-; 1946-. New York: American Arbitration Association. Continues *Arbitration journal.* Includes reviews of recent court decisions on commercial arbitration.

Arbitration materials. Vol. 1-; March 1989-. Geneva: Werner. Quarterly. Includes court decisions, reports, arbitral rules, and texts of awards.

Forum USA. Vol. 4-; 1987-. New York: World Arbitration Institute. Newsletter of the World Arbitration Institute, continues Forum New York/World Arbitration Institute. Vol. 1-3, 1984-1986.

ICC International Court of Arbitration Bulletin. Vol. 1-; June 1990-. Paris: ICC International Court of Arbitration. Includes articles on arbitration and extracts of recent awards with names of parties and details removed. Special supplement issues focus on particular regions or topics.

International Center for the Settlement of Investment Disputes. *Annual report.* Washington: ICSID, 1966-67.

Journal of international arbitration. Vol. 1-; April 1984-. Geneva: D. Thompson and J. Werner. Quarterly. Includes index.

News and notes from the Institute for Transnational Arbitration. Vol. 1-; July 1986-. Houston: The Institute. Includes as a continuing feature a table of adherences to international arbitration treaties.

News from ICSID. Vol. 1-; 1984-. Washington, D.C.: International Centre for Settlement of Investment Disputes. Includes occasional brief articles. Continues Newsletter (International Centre for Settlement of Investment Disputes).

Revue de l'arbitrage; bulletin du comité français de l'arbitrage. Vol. 1-; 1955-. Paris: Sirey. Includes articles, rules, and texts of French, international and *ad hoc* arbitrations, primarily ICC. Indexes every 5 years.

II. Collections of Rules and Statutes

Doyle's dispute resolution practice. David Doyle and James P. Doyle, eds. North Hyde, New South Wales: CCH International, 1990-1992. 2 v. looseleaf. Includes background, statutory material, and rules of arbitral institutions for Australia, Canada, China, Hong Kong, India, Japan, Korea, Malaysia, Taiwan, Thailand, as well as international conventions and court decisions relating to alternative dispute resolution. CEASED PUBLICATION on October 30, 1992, so material is beginning to be dated.

International and commercial arbitration. Clive M. Schmithoff, ed. Dobbs Ferry, New York: Oceana Publications, 1974-. 12 v. looseleaf. Includes discussion of international conventions, arbitral institutions, and arbitration in such areas as shipping and commodities. Particular volumes are devoted to the New York Convention, ICC arbitration, Soviet commercial and maritime arbitration, and arbitration in Asia and the Pacific. Includes the texts of arbitral rules and arbitration statutes for approximately 30 countries. Supplementation is erratic so the researcher should check the date of each pamphlet.

International arbitration kit: a compilation of basic and frequently requested documents. Laura Ferris Brown, ed. 4th ed. New York: American Arbitration Association, 1993. v, 395 p. Particularly useful because it includes the texts of 44 agreements concluded between the American Arbitration Association and other arbitral institutions, as well as the texts of various conventions, the rules and procedures of AAA, UNCITRAL, ICC, London Court of International Arbitration, and ICSID, and a checklist of foreign national arbitration laws.

International Council for Commercial Arbitration. *International Handbook on Commercial Arbitration.* Pieter Sanders, ed. Boston: Kluwer Law and Taxation Pub., 1984. 3 v. looseleaf. Includes national reports on arbitration with annexes of legislation for 44 countries, several regional organizations, and UNCITRAL. These materials are updated in the annual volumes of *Yearbook, Commercial arbitration.*

Parker School of Foreign and Comparative Law, Columbia University. *World arbitration reporter.* Hans Smit and Vratislav Pechota, eds. 4 v. in 6 bks. looseleaf. Major compilation of international arbitration conventions, arbitration statutes of many countries, and rules of international and domestic arbitral bodies.

III. Sources of Award Texts

As a general rule the awards of arbitration proceedings are not published, but there are certain exceptions. Parties who elect to arbitrate with the Society of Maritime Arbitrators do so with the knowledge that the arbitration will be published. Other awards are sometimes published with the consent of the parties. The sources listed below publish arbitral awards from various arbitral bodies. Some of the sources publish these awards routinely, others only occasionally. It is as difficult to say where an award will be published as it is to say which awards will be published.

Arbitration materials. Vol. 1-; March 1989-. Geneva: Werner. Quarterly. Publishes the texts of arbitral awards for the Iran-United States Claims Tribunal and Society of Maritime Arbitrators.

Collection of ICC arbitral awards. (ICC Publication nos. 433, 514) Boston: Kluwer Law and Taxation Publishers, 1990-1994. 2 v. In English and French. Selected cases decided by the International Court of Arbitration, which have appeared previously in *Yearbook Commercial arbitration, Journal du Droit International (Clunet),* or *The International Construction Law Review.* Identifying references to parties have been removed. Volume I covers 1974-1985, and Volume II covers 1986-1990. Analytical Table in Volume II covers both volumes. Chronological Indexes include references to commentary on specific awards. Table of Cross-References. Indexed.

ICC International Court of Arbitration bulletin. Vol. 1-; June 1990-. Paris: ICC International Court of Arbitration. Publishes extracts from arbitral awards with the names of the parties and other identifying details removed.

ICSID Reports. R. Rayfuse, ed. Vol. 1-; 1993-. Cambridge: England: Grotius Publications. A new series which reprints the texts of awards and decisions relating to ICSID proceedings. Awards are in English and in full text if available. First volume covers 1972-1981. Also includes the text of the basic documents of the ICSID in their successive versions. Indexed.

International Legal Materials. Vol. 1-; August 1962-. Washington, D.C.: American Society of International Law. Publishes texts of arbitral awards from a variety of sources.

Iran-United States Claims Tribunal Reports. Vol. 1-; 1983-. Cambridge: Grotius Publications, Ltd. Series includes all decisions awards, interim awards, interlocutory awards, and refusal cases, and selected procedural orders and awards on agreed terms. Other procedural documents are included from time to time. Each volume includes Consolidated Index and Table of Cases for the series.

Lloyd's Arbitration Reports. London: Lloyd's of London Press, 1988-. Texts of awards from ICSID, ICC, and the Society of Maritime Arbitrators, and decisions of national courts regarding arbitral awards. Annual indexes and tables. *Revue de l'arbitrage; bulletin du comité français de l'arbitrage.* 1955-. Paris: Sirey. Publishes texts of French, international, and *ad hoc* arbitrations.

Rivista dell'arbitrato. Anno 1, no. 1-; 1991-. Milano: Guiffré. Publication of the Associazione italiana per l'arbitrato. Continues *Rassegna dell'arbitrato.*

Yearbook, commercial arbitration. Vol. 1-; 1976-. Deventer, Netherlands: Kluwer. Publishes excerpts of the texts of arbitral awards from many different tribunals, as well as court decisions on arbitration and on the various arbitration conventions. The awards are published without the names of the parties or other identifying data unless the award has been published in full in another source or has been the subject of a subsequent court action so that the names of the parties are a matter of public record. The cumulative index, known as the *Yearbook Key,* and the subsequent annual indexes provide the greatest access to these award texts.

IV. Court Decisions

International commercial arbitration and the courts. Dobbs Ferry, NY: Transnational Juris Publications, 1990. v, 460 p. Court decisions relating to arbitration appear in their respective reporter series and are reproduced in several of the periodicals listed above. This source serves as a digest to court decisions and legislation relating to judicial control and assistance in arbitration and to enforcement of arbitral awards. It is arranged by subject and each heading includes international conventions, national legislation and court decisions arranged by country, and a bibliography. Includes materials through 1988. Alphabetical Table of Cases and Table of Legislation by country.

V. Arbitral Institutions and Arbitrators

A. In General

Davidson, Paul. J. and Ludwik Kos-Rabcewicz-Zubkowski. *Commercial arbitration institutions: an international directory and guide.* 2nd ed. New York: Oceana, 1992. 262 p. Directory prepared in conjunction with the International Federation of Commercial Arbitration Institutions. Checklists of laws, conventions, and arbitral institutions for 57 countries, as well as several international and regional institutions. Some entries in French.

Parker School of Foreign and Comparative Law, Columbia University. *Guide to international arbitration and arbitrators.* 2d ed. Dobbs Ferry, NY: Transnational Juris Publications, 1992. 2 vol. In five parts: International Rules and Institutions, National Institutions and Rules, Code of Ethics for International Arbitrators, 1958 New York convention on the Recognition and Enforcement of Foreign Arbitral Awards, and International Arbitrators. The last consists of an alphabetical list of arbitrators, followed by lists by nationality, areas of specialization, and languages.

Survey of international arbitration sites. 3d ed. J. Stewart McClendon, ed. New York: American Arbitration Association, 1993. 141 p. Summarizes the arbitration statutes and institutional rules available in 16 countries, as well as other considerations for an attorney who is selecting a possible site for arbitration.

B. Specific Institutions

1. American Arbitration Association (AAA)

American Arbitration Association. Office of the General Counsel: *Arbitration & the Law: AAA General Counsel's annual report.* 1982-. Published: Irvington-on-Hudson, NY: Transnational Juris, 1993-.

2. Inter-American Commercial Arbitration Commission

Rules of procedure of the Inter-American Commercial Arbitration Commission. S.I.: American Arbitration Association, 1982. 23 p.

3. International Bar Association

International Bar Association. Section on Business Law. *Arbitration: the IBA rules of evidence: supplementary rules of evidence for use in international arbitration.* London: International Bar Association, 1986. 8 p.

4. International Center for Settlement of Investment Disputes (ICSID)

Additional facility for the administration of conciliation, arbitration and fact-finding proceedings. ICSID/11. Washington: The Centre, 1978. 69 p.

ICSID basic documents. ICSID/15. Washington. D.C.: ICSID, 1985. 107 p. Includes the text of the Convention on the Settlement of Investment Disputes between States and Nations of Other States, and the various rules and regulations pertaining to arbitration and conciliation under the ICSID convention.

5. International Chamber of Commerce (ICC)

Craig, W. Laurence, William W. Park and Jan Paulsson. *International Chamber of Commerce arbitration.* 2d ed. New York: Oceana Publications, 1990. 2 v. looseleaf.

Guide on multi-party arbitration under the rules of the ICC Court of Arbitration. Publication no. 404. Paris: ICC Pub., 1982. 8, 8p.

Guide to ICC arbitration. Publication no. 448. Paris: ICC, 1994. 112 p.

ICC arbitration: the international solution to international business disputes. Publication no. 301. Paris: ICC, 1977. 50 p.

ICC pre-arbitral referee procedure. Publication no. 482. Paris: ICC Publ, 1990. 24 p.

ICC rules of conciliation and arbitration: new conciliation rules and amended arbitration rules in force as from January 1, 1988. Publication no. 447. Paris: ICC Publishing S.A., 1987. 43 p.

International arbitration: 60 years of ICC arbitration: a look at the future. Publication no. 412. Paris: ICC, 1984. 421 p.

Introduction to ICC rules on international contracts. Paris: ICC Services S.A.R.L., 1981. 49 p.

Taking of evidence in the arbitral proceedings. (Dossiers of the Institute of International Business Law and Practice, no. 8/1989). Publication no. 440/8. Paris: ICC, 1990. 168 p.

6. International Council for Commercial Arbitration (ICCA)

International Council for Commercial Arbitration Interim Congress (1984: Lausanne, Switzerland). *Recueil de travaux suisses sur l'arbitrage international = Schweizer Beiträge zur internationalen Schiedsgerichtsbarkeit = Swiss essays on international arbitration*. Claude Reymond and Eugéne Bucher, eds. Zürich: Schulthess, 1984.

English, French, German and Italian. Bibliographical references.

7. Iran-United States Claims Tribunal

Baker, Stewart Abercrombie and Mark David Davis. *The UNCITRAL arbitration rules in practice: the experience of the Iran-United States Claims Tribunal*. Boston: Kluwer Law and Taxation, 1992. xvi, 314 p. Index.

Caron, David D. *The Iran-United States Claims Tribunal and the international arbitral process*. Leiden: [s.n.], 1990. 326 p. Summary in Dutch.

Hof, Jacomijn J. van. *Commentary on the UNCITRAL arbitration rules: the application by the Iran-U.S. Claims Tribunal*. Boston: Kluwer Law and Taxation Publishers, 1991. xiv, 361 p. Bibliographical references. Index.

Rahmatullah Khan. *The Iran-United States Claims Tribunal: controversies, cases, and contribution.* Boston: Nijhoff, 1990. xv, 343 p. Bibliographical references.

Sokol Colloquium (7th: 1983: University of Virginia). *The Iran-United States Claims Tribunal, 1981-1983.* Richard B. Lillich, ed. Charlottesville: University Press of Virginia, 1984. vii, 175 p.

8. UNCITRAL

Dore, Isaak I. *Arbitration and conciliation under the UNCITRAL rules: a textual analysis.* Boston: Nijhoff, 1986. ix, 246 p.

__________. *Theory and practice of multiparty commercial arbitration with special reference to the UNCITRAL framework.* Boston: Graham & Trotman/Nijhoff, 1990. viii, 201 p. Includes index.

__________. *The UNCITRAL framework for arbitration in contemporary perspective.* London: Graham & Trotman/Martinus Nijhoff, 1993. ix, 222 p. Compares the UNCITRAL Rules with the rules of the ICC and the London Court of International Arbitration, discusses the application of the UNCITRAL rules in the Iran-United States Claims Tribunal, and gives an overview of the UNCITRAL model law on international commercial arbitration. Indexed.

Holtzmann, Howard M, and Joseph E. Neuhaus. *A guide to the UNCITRAL Model Law on International Commercial Arbitration: legislative history and commentary.* Boston: Kluwer Law and Taxation Publishers, 1989. ix, 1307 p. Includes index.

UNCITRAL model law of international commercial arbitration: a documentary history. Igor I. Kavass and Arno Liivak, comps. Buffalo: W.S. Hein Co., 1985-. 2 v. looseleaf. Includes index.

UNCITRAL's project for a model law on international commercial arbitration. Pieter Sanders, ed. (ICCA congress series, no. 2). Boston: Kluwer Law and Taxation Publishers, 1984. viii, 267 p.

United Nations Commission on International Trade Law. *UNCITRAL conciliation rules.* New York: United Nations, 1981. 20 p.

9. New York Convention

Berg, Albert Jan van den. *The New York Arbitration Convention of 1958: towards a uniform judicial interpretation.* Boston: Kluwer Law and Taxation, 1981. xv, 466 p. Text in English, French, and Spanish. Bibliography. Index.

New York Convention. Giorgio Gaja, comp. and ed. Dobbs Ferry, NY: Oceana Publications, 1978-. 4 v. looseleaf.

Includes the text of the convention in English, French, Russian and Spanish with lists of contracting states and their reservations. Also includes texts of preparatory works, national legislation, and national judicial decisions. Table of cases and indexes.

VI. International Commercial Arbitration in Specific Countries, Regions, and Contexts

A. Countries

1. Australia

Pryles, Michael Charles and Kazuo Iwasaki. *Dispute resolution in Australia-Japan transactions.* Sydney: Law Book Co., 1983. xxix, 185 p. Includes bibliographical references and index.

2. Austria

Melis, Werner. *A guide to commercial arbitration in Austria.* 2nd ed. Vienna: Federal Economic Chamber, 1983. 45 p. Includes extracts of Austrian legislation in English translation and forms.

3. Belgium

Storme, Marcel and Bernadette Demeulenaere. *International commercial arbitration in Belgium: a handbook.* Boston: Kluwer Law and Taxation Publishers, 1989. xvii, 306 p. Includes bibliographical references, index, and forms.

4. Canada

British Columbia International Commercial Arbitration Centre. *International commercial arbitration: the Canadian advantage.* Vancouver: British Columbia International Arbitration Centre, [1989].

Casey, J. Brian. *International and domestic commercial arbitration manual.* Scarborough, Ontario: Carswell, 1993-. Looseleaf. Text discusses all aspects of international and domestic commercial arbitration in Canada. Appendices include international and domestic statutes and rules of commercial arbitration for Alberta, British Columbia, and Vancouver, as well as the federal acts and rules of various international arbitral bodies.

Commercial arbitration: advanced practice: materials prepared for a continuing Legal Education seminar held in Vancouver, B.C. on April 4, 1989. Bonita J. Thompson, course coordinator. Vancouver, B.C.: Continuing Legal Education Society of British Columbia, 1989.

UNCITRAL arbitration model in Canada: Canadian international commercial arbitration legislation. Robert K. Paterson and Bonita J. Thompson, eds. Toronto: Carswell, 1987. xii, 253 p. Covers international commercial arbitration in the Pacific Rim and the British Columbia international commercial arbitration act. Appendices include a table of Canadian arbitration legislation, the British Columbia Foreign Arbitral Awards Act, and the British Columbia International Commercial Arbitration Centre Rules, and comparisons with various aspects of UNCITRAL. Bibliographical references.

5. Chile

Eyzaguirre Echeverría, Rafael. *El arbitraje comercial en la legislación chilena y su regulación internacional.* Santiago: Editorial Juridica de Chile, [1981]. 591 p. Bibliography and related documents.

6. Colombia

Monroy Cabra, Marco Gerardo. *Arbitraje comercial.* Bogotá: Editorial Temis, Libreria, 1982. xii, 156 p. Bibliographical references.

7. France

Boisséson, Matthieu de. *Le droit français de l'arbitrage: interne et international.* Paris: GLN Joly, 1990. vii, 1131 p. Bibliographical references. Index.

Delvolve, Jean-Louis. *Arbitration in France: 'the French law of national and international arbitration.* Trilingual ed. Boston: Kluwer Law and Taxation Publishers, 1982. x, 165 p. In English, French, and German.

8. Germany

Glossner, Ottoarndt, Jens Bredow, and Michael Bühler. *Das Schiedsgericht in der Praxis.* 3d ed, rev. and enl. Heidelberg: Verlag Recht und Wirstschaft, 1990. 317 p. Bibliographical references. Index.

Schiedsgerichtsbarkeit im deutsch-amerikanischen Wirtschaftsverkehr = Arbitration in US-German business relations. Karl-Heinz Böckstiegel, ed. Köln: Heymann, 1985. vi, 287 p. Papers of a conference sponsored by the German Institute of Arbitration held in Frankfurt May 7, 1984. Includes texts of German and United States statutes, and the rules of AAA, the German Arbitration Committee, and ICC. All papers and materials in German and English.

9. Hong Kong

Bateson, David. *Commercial arbitration in Hong Kong.* Hong Kong: Longman,, 1989. 124 p. Includes material on the Hong Kong International Arbitration Centre.

Law Reform Commission of Hong Kong. *Report on the adoption of the UNCITRAL model law of arbitration (topic 17).* Hong Kong: The Commission, 1987. v, 121 p.

10. Italy

Bernardini, Piero and Andrea Giardina. *Codice dell'arbitrato.* Milano: Guiffre, 1990. xiii, 952 p. Includes documents in Italian, English, French, German, Portuguese and Spanish.

Bernini, Giorgio. *L'arbitrato: diritto interno, convenzioni internazionali.* Bologna: CLUEB, 1993. 720 p.

11. Jamaica

Stoppi, M.J. *Commercial arbitration in Jamaica.* Kingston, Jamaica: Heinemann Publishers, 1991. xviii, 107 p. Extensive appendices include the Arbitration (Foreign Awards) Act, comparisons of international arbitration rules, and forms.

12. Netherlands

Berg, A.J. van den, R. van Delden, and H.J. Snijders. *Netherlands arbitration law.* B. Ruijsenaars, trans. Boston: Kluwer Law and Taxation Publishers, 1993. xviii, 310 p. Treatise which explains the operation of the Netherlands Arbitration Act. Appendices include translations of the Netherlands Arbitration Act of 1986, the Rules of the Netherlands Arbitration Institute (NAI), the Statutes of the Court of Arbitration for the Building Industry in the Netherlands, and the Rules of Arbitration for NOFOTA (Netherlands Oils, Fats and Oilseeds Trade Association). Indexed.

Schultsz, Jan C.and Buruma, S.L. *Legislation in the Netherlands and international arbitration.* Deventer: Kluwer, 1986. iv, 100 p. In English and Dutch. Includes bibliography.

13. Norway

Thomsen, Hans Bjorn. *International business arbitration in Norway: with an unofficial translation of the Norwegian civil procedure act of 13th August 1915, no. 6, chapter 32 on arbitration.* Oslo: Norges Eksportrad, 1977. [2] leaves, 55 p. Includes texts of "Rules for the ICC Court of Arbitration" and "Rules in the Court of Arbitration of the Oslo Bourse."

14. Russia

Hobér, Kaj. *Enforcing foreign arbitral awards against Russian entities.* Irvington, NY: Transnational Juris Publications, 1993.

15. Scotland

Davidson, Fraser. *International commercial arbitration: Scotland and the UNCITRAL model law.* Edinburgh: W. Green/ Sweet & Maxwell, 1991. xviii, 266 p. Bibliographical references. Index.

16. Spain

Arbitration in Spain. Bernardo M. Cremades, ed. London: Butterworths, 1991. xiv, 167 p. Includes an English translation of the Spanish Arbitration Act, Law 36/1988. Index and Table of Legislation.

Chillón Medina, José María and José Fernando Merino Merchán. *Tratado de arbitraje privado interno e internacional.* 2d ed. Madrid: Editorial Civitas, 1991. 1379 p. Bibliographical references.

Legislación sobre arbitraje interno e internacional. José Carlos Fernández Rozas, ed. Madrid: Civitas, 1990. 242 p. Index.

Ramos Méndez, Francisco. *Arbitraje y proceso internacional.* Barcelona: Bosch, 1987. 280 p. Bibliographical references.

17. Switzerland

Bucher, Andreas and Pierre-Yves Tschanz. *International arbitration in Switzerland.* Basle: Helbing & Lichtenhahn, 1988. 230 p.

Lalive, Pierre, Jean-François Poudret, and Claude Reymond. *Le droit de l'arbitrage interne et international en Suisse.* Lausanne: Editions Payot, 1989. 508 p. Annotated edition of the Concordat on arbitration of March 27, 1969 and the portions of the Federal Law of December 18, 1987, on private international law relating to international arbitration. Text of the laws in English, French, German, and Italian; commentary in French. Bibliographical references.

Repertoire de droit international privé suisse: présentation systématique et synthétique du droit commun et conventionnel, de la jurisprudence et des sources doctrinales principales. Bernard Dutoit et al. Berne: Stämpfli, 1982-. 3 v. looseleaf. Bibliography.

18. United States

Born, Gary. *International commercial arbitration in the United States: commentary and materials.* Boston: Kluwer Law and Taxation Publishers, 1994. xliv, 1041 p. Casebook on all aspects of international commercial arbitration. Appendices include texts of conventions, rules of various arbitral institutions, and statutes. Indexed.

19. Vietnam

Foreign investment laws of Vietnam. Vietnam: State Committee for Co-operation and Investment. Melbourne, Australia: Phillips Fox, 1993-3. Looseleaf. Section XII Arbitration includes the translated text of the Ordinance on Economic Arbitration and the Statutes of the Vietnam International Arbitration Centre.

B. Regions

1. Asia

International Arbitration Congress (9th: 1988: Tokyo, Japan). *Arbitration in settlement of international commercial disputes involving the Far East and arbitration in combined transportation*. Pieter Sanders, ed. (ICCA congress series, no. 4). Boston: Kluwer Law and Taxation Publishers, 1989. x, 427 p.

2. Latin America

Centro de Arbitraje y Conciliación Mercantiles. *Panorama y perspectivas de la legislación iberoamericana sobre arbitraje comercial.* Santafé de Bogotá, Colombia: Camara de Comercio de Bogotá, 1993. 396 p. Not seen by bibliographer.

American Bar Association Section of International Law and Practice *Commercial and labor arbitration in Central America.* Alejandro M. Garro, ed. Ardsley-on-Hudson, NY: Transnational Juris Publications, 1991. v. 514 p. Translation of *Arbitraje comercial y laboral en América Central.* Proceedings of the American Bar Association conferences on commercial and labor arbitration in 1987 and 1988. Covers Costa Rica, El Salvador, Guatemala, Honduras, and Nicaragua, and includes presentations on the use of arbitration in Cuba, Argentina, and Spain.

3. Middle East

Saleh, Samir. *Commercial arbitration in the Arab Middle East: a study in shari'a and statute law.* London: Graham & Trotman, 1984. xxvi, 489, 4 p. Includes discussion of the arbitration laws of Lebanon, Jordan, Iraq, Egypt, Libya, Kuwait, Bahrain, Saudi Arabia, Qatar, United Arab Emirates, Oman, and North Yemen, and the Inter-Arab Convention on the Enforcement of Judgments and Awards. Dates of legislation should be checked against other sources as some of the laws have changed.

C. Contexts

1. Commodities

Johnson, Derek Kirby. *International commodity arbitration.* London: Lloyd's of London Press, 1991. xxviii, 321 p. Describes the organization and arbitration procedures of the London Trade

Associations. Appendices include the rules and addresses of 7 London Trade Associations, and related statutory material. Index.

2. Contracts

Bartels, Martin. *Contractual adaptation and conflict resolution: based on venture contracts for mining projects in developing countries.* James E. Silva, trans. (Studies in transnational law of natural resources, v. 8). Boston: Kluwer, 1985. 187 p. Bibliographical references.

Fox, William F. *International commercial agreements: a functional primer on drafting, negotiating, and resolving disputes.* Boston: Kluwer Law and Taxation Publishers, 1988. xiii, 394 p. Bibliography. Index.

Green, Allen B. and David A. Churchill. *Resolving international contract disputes: course manual.* Washington, D.C.: Federal Publications, 1989. Course material assembled for lawyers working with defense and aerospace contracts. Practical coverage of the arbitral process with extensive appendices for UNCITRAL, ICC, AAA, and NATO, and a sample mini-trial agreement.

Hague Academy of International Law, Centre for Studies and Research in International Law and International Relations. *L'arbitrage transnational et les contrats d'Etat: 1987 = Transnational arbitration and state contracts: 1987.* Boston: Nijhoff, 1988. [14] p. English and French.

Hunter, Martin et al. *The Freshfields guide to arbitration and ADR: clauses in international contracts.* Boston: Kluwer Law and Taxation Publishers, 1993. xii, 110 p. Brief guide to including dispute resolution clauses in contracts. Primary focus is on drafting arbitration clauses, but other considerations are discussed. Appendices include the recommended arbitration clauses of 10 major arbitral institutions, model clauses for *ad hoc* arbitration, conciliation, and mediation, and the addresses of the institutions and organizations referred to in the text.

Paasivirta, Esa. *Participation of states in international contracts and arbitral settlement of disputes.* Helsinki: Finnish Lawyers' Pub. co., 1990. xxiii, 357 p. Bibliographical references.

Peter, Wolfgang. *Arbitration and renegotiation of international investment agreements: a study with particular reference to means of conflict avoidance under natural resources investment agreements.* Boston: Nijhoff, 1986. xxiii, 297 p. Bibliography. Index.

Slabotzky, Albert. *Grain contracts and arbitration: for shipments from the United States and Canada.* London: Lloyd's of London Press, 1984. x, 109 p. Bibliography. Index.

3. GATT / WTO

Pescatore, Pierre, William J. Davey, and Andreas F. Lowenfeld. *Handbook of GATT dispute settlement.* Ardsley-on-Hudson, NY: Transnational Juris Publications, 1991-. 1 v. looseleaf. Includes bibliographical references and indexes.

4. Intellectual Property

Arbitration and transfer of patents, know how, trademarks and similar rights for promoting international industrial cooperation = Arbitrage et transfert de brevets, savoir-faire, marques de fabrique et de commerce et autres droits de nature a promouvoir la cooperation industrielle internationale: interim meeting, Vienna, Sept. 29 - Oct. 1, 1976. [s.l.]: International Council for Commercial Arbitration, [1977]. 112 p. English, French and German. Bibliographical references.

5. International Trade Regulation

Institute of International Business Law and Practice. *Competition and arbitration law.* Publication no. 480/3. Paris: International Chamber of Commerce, 1993. 351 p. Collection of signed articles in French and English.

6. Maritime

Hague-Zagreb Colloquium (3rd: 1978: Opatija, Yugoslavia). *Hague-Zagreb essays 3: carriage of goods by sea, maritime collisions, maritime oil pollution, commercial arbitration: Hague-Zagreb Colloquium on the Law of International Trade, session 1978, Opatija.* C.C.A. Voskuil and J.A. Wade, eds. The Hague: T.M.C. Asser Institute, Sijthoff & Noordhoff, 1980. xi, 329 p. Includes bibliographical references.

International Chamber of Commerce. *International maritime arbitration organization: ICC-CMI rules = Organization internationale d'arbitrage maritime: réglement CCI-CMI/ International Chamber of Commerce, Comité Maritime Internationale.* Paris: ICC Services, 1979.

23 p. Text of International maritime arbitration rules in English, French, and German.

International commercial and maritime arbitration. F.D. Rose, ed. London: Sweet & Maxwell, 1988. 118 p. Includes appendix of Lloyd's Standard Form of Salvage Agreement. Index.

7. Patents

Arbitration and transfers of patents, know how, trademarks and similar rights for promoting international industrial cooperation, interim meeting, Vienna, Sept, 29 - Oct. 1, 1976. [s.l.]: International Council for Commercial Arbitration, 1977. 112 p. In English, French, and German. Includes bibliographical references.

8. State Enterprises

Bockstiegel, Karl Heinz. *Arbitration and state enterprises: a survey on the national and international state of law and practice.* Deventer: Kluwer Law and Taxation Publishers, 1984. vi, 113p. Bibliography.